Finanzwirtschaft, Banken und Bankmanagement I Finance, Banks and Bank Management

Reihe herausgegeben von

Axel Wieandt, Königstein, Hessen, Deutschland

Sebastian C. Moenninghoff, Vallendar, Deutschland

Die Reihe präsentiert Forschungsbeiträge aus den Bereichen Finanzwirtschaft, Banken und Bankmanagement, die sich durch hohe wissenschaftliche Qualität und Praxisbezug auszeichnen. Sie richtet sich an Akademiker und Praktiker.

The series presents research from the fields of finance, banking and bank management, which are characterized by high scientific quality and practical relevance. It is aimed at academics and practitioners.

More information about this series at http://www.springer.com/series/16023

Tom Filip Lesche

Too-Big-to-Fail in Banking

Impact of G-SIB Designation and Regulation on Relative Equity Valuations

Springer Gabler

Tom Filip Lesche
Faculty of Management and Economics
Witten/Herdecke University
Witten, Germany

ISSN 2524-6429 ISSN 2524-6437 (electronic)
Finanzwirtschaft, Banken und Bankmanagement I Finance, Banks and Bank Management
ISBN 978-3-658-34181-7 ISBN 978-3-658-34182-4 (eBook)
https://doi.org/10.1007/978-3-658-34182-4

Responsible Editor: Anna Pietras
This Springer Gabler imprint is published by the registered company Springer Fachmedien Wiesbaden GmbH part of Springer Nature.
The registered company address is: Abraham-Lincoln-Str. 46, 65189 Wiesbaden, Germany

Foreword

Tom Lesche's thesis is dedicated to the perennial challenge that too-big-to-fail (TBTF) in banking poses to the financial, economic and political stability of national and global economies – a field of research that has received significant and increasing attention by both academics and regulators since the financial crisis of 2007-2009. This crisis made too-big-to-fail implicit guarantees explicit as governments in the US and Europe came to the rescue of banking systems with extensive guarantees, comprehensive bad-bank schemes and asset purchase programs, as well as significant recapitalizations of banks in trouble. In response to the crisis and under pressure from taxpayers and voters, politicians declared their intentions to abolish TBTF in banking. Since then, the competent regulatory bodies have developed and the respective legislative bodies have enacted specific regulation targeted at systemically relevant banks and other financial institutions.

The thesis consists of two significant contributions to the research on TBTF and the regulation of systemically relevant banks:

- A comprehensive summary of the relevant literature on TBTF in banking and the regulatory response in the US and Europe in Part I;
- An empirical analysis of the relative equity valuation of globally-systemically important banks (G-SIBs) with the help of a two-way fixed-effect regression analysis in Part II.

The conclusions of the empirical analysis in Part II are clear and compelling:

- The relative equity valuation of G-SIBs in the aftermath of the 2007–2009 financial crisis is characterized by a significant discount in the order of magnitude of 0.5x–1.0x price/tangible common equity (P/TCE).
- The relative equity valuation discount has grown over time as the G20 and the Financial Stability Board have explicitly designated certain banks G-SIBs and developed and implemented specific regulation for these banks.

- The empirical findings obviously raise the question to what extent the G-SIB discount provides an incentive to reduce size and complexity potentially leading to a G-SIB break-up.

The overall conclusions of Tom Lesche's work for bank-management and regulators/policy-makers are clear but not uncontroversial, namely to

- pay more attention to the valuation signal from equity markets – which are clearly reacting to the new TBTF regulation -, and, therefore,
- consider breaking up TBTF banks to reduce the equity valuation discount and increase overall financial stability.

It has been a great privilege to supervise Tom Lesche's thesis. I am looking forward to having many more fruitful exchanges and discussions with him as he continues to pursue his career as a fintech venture capitalist.

Königstein i. Ts.
October 2020

Axel Wieandt

Abstract

This dissertation consists of two parts:
Part I Too-big-to-fail in banking review is a comprehensive summary of the latest academic research on the important topic of too-big-to-fail (TBTF) in banking and explains TBTF from various perspectives. First, we explore how evolving systemic risk in the financial system shaped banking history. Then we trace the role of distortions from implicit government guarantees (IGGs) and identify moral hazards among creditors, shareholders, and bank management. Finally, we review the range of regulatory measures proposed to counter TBTF, most notably the globally accepted regulation of global-systemically important banks (G-SIBs) and its main tool of capital surcharges.

Part II Quantifying the shareholder value of too-big-to-fail in banking is an empirical analysis of quarterly observations from more than 750 global banks between Q2 2008 and Q3 2015. The main finding is that G-SIBs are confronted with a substantial relative valuation discount compared to non-G-SIBs. From the end of 2011 until the end of 2015, a stable discount of 0.6x–0.8x price-to-tangible common equity (P/TCE) is statistically highly significant. The results suggest that the *G-SIB designation effect*, which positively impacts G-SIBs' share prices because of funding benefits from IGGs, is dominated by the *regulatory G-SIB burden effect*, which negatively impacts G-SIBs' share prices because of lower profitability due to capital surcharges and other regulatory requirements placed on G-SIBs. The findings re-open the debate about whether breaking up G-SIBs would unlock shareholder value and whether G-SIBs are regulated efficiently.

Contents

Part II Quantifying the Shareholder Value of Too-Big-to-Fail in Banking

Abbreviations

APT	Arbitrage pricing theory
BCBS	Basel Committee on Banking Supervision
BIS	Bank for International Settlements
BRRD	Bank Recovery and Resolution Directive
BV/P	Book-to-market value
BVS	Book value per share
CAPM	Capital asset pricing model
CET1	Common equity tier 1
CoCos	Contingent capital or contingent convertible securities
CPP	Capital Purchase Program
CRD IV	Capital Requirements Directive IV
CRPS	Center for Research in Security Prices
CRR	Capital Requirements Regulation
D-SIB	Domestic-systemically important bank
DDM	Dividend discount model
DFA	Dodd-Frank Wall Street Reform and Consumer Protection Act
DGSD	Deposit Guarantee Schemes Directive
EaD	Exposure at default
EBA	European Banking Authority
EC	European Commission
EESA	Emergency Economic Stabilization Act
EGG	Explicit government guarantees
EL	Expected loss
EPS	Earnings per share
ESRB	European Systemic Risk Board
EU	European Union
EVA	Economic value added
FDIA	Federal Deposit Insurance Act
FDIC	Federal Deposit Insurance Corporation
FDICIA	FDIC Improvement Act

Fed	Federal Reserve System
FSB	Financial Stability Board
FSF	Financial Stability Forum
FSLIC	Federal Savings and Loan Insurance Corporation
FSOC	Financial Stability Oversight Council
G-10	Group of 10 countries
G-SIB	Global-systemically important bank
G-SIFI	Global-systemically important financial institution
GAAP	Generally Accepted Accounting Principles
GDP	Gross domestic product
GFC	Global financial crisis
ICAAP	Internal Capital Adequacy Assessment Process
IFRS	International Financial Reporting Standards
IGG	Implicit government guarantee
ITS	Implementing technical standards
LCR	Liquidity coverage ratio
LGD	Loss given default
LOLR	Lender of last resort
LSDV	Method of least squares dummy variables
LTCM	Long-Term Capital Management
M&A	Mergers and acquisitions
MarketCap	Market capitalisation
n	Number of shares
NA	Not available
NIM	Net interest margin
NSFR	Net stable funding ratio
NTA	Net tangible assets
O-SII	Other-systemically important institution
OCC	Office of the Comptroller of the Currency
OLA	Orderly Liquidation Authority
OLS	Method of ordinary least squares
OTC	Over-the-counter
P/BV	Price-to-book value ratio
P/E	Price-to-earnings ratio
P/TCE	Price-to-tangible common equity ratio
PD	Probability of default
PPS	Price per share
RFC	Reconstruction Finance Corporation
RIM	Residual income model
RoA	Return on assets
RoE	Return on equity
RTC	Resolution Trust Corporation

RTS	Regulatory technical standards
RWA	Risk-weighted assets
S&L	Savings & loan
SIFI	Systemically-important financial institution
SME	Small and medium-sized enterprise
SPV	Special purpose vehicle
SRB	Single Resolution Board
SREP	Supervisory Review and Evaluation Process
SRF	Single Resolution Fund
SRM	Single Resolution Mechanism
SSM	Single Supervisory Mechanism
TARP	Troubled Asset Relief Program
TBTF	Too-big-to-fail
TBV	Tangible book value
TCE	Tangible common equity
TLAC	Total loss absorbency capital
US	United States
USA	United States of America

List of Figures

List of Tables

Introduction and Overview 1

1.1 General Context and Current Developments

Banks Without Liability

Everyone knows that banks are special. Banks channel surplus funds from people or institutions without productive investment opportunities to those with such opportunities. This task is crucial for the growth of the real economy, and banks are well suited to providing this service to the public. In return, they enjoy special treatment. It requires responsible bank management to fully understand the importance of this public duty. The inherent risks that need to be managed responsibly stem mainly from debtor default (credit risk) and bank runs (liquidity risk). When poorly managed, these risks can trigger or worsen an economic crisis.

Under normal circumstances, responsibility and liability go hand in hand. However, this has grown less and less the case for banks over the past centuries. In the aftermath of several banking crises, bank stakeholders used their bargaining position to gradually shift their liability and risk to taxpayers, while keeping the profits for themselves. Special bankruptcy proceedings, public deposit insurance, and lender of last resort are just a few examples of bank shareholders' impressive negotiation achievements. Nowadays, to bolster financial stability, depositors are insured against any loss, other creditors rarely face write-offs, and the owners' liability is limited to their paid-in capital, if that.[1] Meanwhile,

[1]One might argue that the latter is the case for any type of firm. However, only banks achieve high leverage (the ration between assets or debt to equity) with the help of insured creditors and cheap funding. This might suspend the Modigliani–Miller theorem that the overall cost of capital stays the same regardless of leverage (Modigliani and Miller (1958)). In contrast, non-banks cannot achieve high leverage economically.

T. F. Lesche, *Too-Big-to-Fail in Banking*, Finanzwirtschaft, Banken und Bankmanagement I Finance, Banks and Bank Management, https://doi.org/10.1007/978-3-658-34182-4_1

asymmetric shareholder payoff schedules have incentivised the rise in the volatility of banks' assets. In combination with the privilege of claiming tax deductions for debt finance costs, prompted banks to leverage up their capital structure with debt. This fragile construct has enabled high growth of the overall economy for many decades, largely at the cost of the public and primarily to the benefit of shorter-term investors and bank management.[2]

The short-term and perverse support for no-liability bank stakeholders, including bank management, paved the way for some banks to turn themselves gradually, over decades, into mega-banks, which are irreplaceable in the medium term. Any reasonable government that cares about the real economy will safeguard these banks by guaranteeing their liabilities, and sometimes even protecting their equity. This is good for bank stakeholders, but bad for the public. Ultimately, the public always shoulders the burden of re-establishing a safer and sounder financial system. Taxpayers used to pay only hidden and implicit costs for various safety features, such as deposit insurance. These days they also pay explicitly for mega-banks that have grown beyond the size of the social optimum by bailing-out systemically important institutions. This is not beneficial but highly costly for the public.

Too-Big-to-Fail as Banking Pollution

The 'too-big-to-fail' (TBTF) doctrine was mentioned for the first time in the early 1960s.[3] However, it was not until 1984 that the term was first used by a government official, when it emerged in the context of the bailout of Continental Illinois National Bank and Trust Company, one of the largest banks at the time. Since the global financial crisis (GFC) of 2007–2009, most sceptics are convinced that this de facto governmental policy increased the severity of the crisis. Moreover, most policymakers are now aware that the costs associated with TBTF could outweigh the benefits. Since the end of 2011, every year the Financial Stability Board (FSB) officially designates 28 to 30 large banks as global systemically important banks (G-SIBs). For the sake of simplicity, in this dissertation we refer to all banks officially deemed or perceived as too-big-to-fail or included in the annual list of G-SIBs as 'G-SIBs'. The public bailouts of G-SIBs brought to light the massive direct costs for taxpayers and propelled the topic from academic discourse to the news headlines. The bailouts exposed the fact that large banks had accumulated large-scale systemic risk over the years due to implicit government guarantees (IGGs).

Such (expected) government interventions suspend general market forces driven by risk and return. As with many insurance contracts, they create moral hazard problems, such as, with regard to TBTF: (i) bank creditors inadequately monitoring their borrowing; (ii) banks taking excessive risk; and (iii) banks shareholders attracted to the better

[2]Cf. Haldane (2012).

[3]By Friedman and Schwartz (1963).

risk-return profile of G-SIBs. Increased risk leads to overproduction, more volatility, and higher probability of bank failure. In conjunction with increased systemic importance, this then leads to higher probability and greater severity of financial crises, economic cyclicality, and associated output losses. Most empirically analysed in this context are the funding differences of G-SIBs that stem from the creditors' moral hazard caused by IGGs. They presently range up to sizable benefits of hundreds of billions of US$ per annum[4], which are indirectly paid by the public. Hence, the indirect costs of TBTF seem to be much higher than the direct costs. Ultimately, the GFC showed that shifting liabilities from G-SIBs to governments can overburden the governments, as was the case in Iceland, and consequently destabilise the whole financial system.

In summary, the systemic risk externality of G-SIBs is a market failure and a source of economic inefficiency that ultimately leads to undesirable costs for taxpayers. It can be called 'banking pollution'[5] in the logic of environmental economics.

Regulation of Too-Big-to-Fail

'The invisible hand is powerful but not omnipotent'.[6] Scholars have provided many arguments for abolishing TBTF, such as to reduce the financial burden on future generations or to impose market discipline on banks.[7] Putting aside radical abolishment, how can this 'banking pollution' be regulated and measured? In the aftermath of the GFC, this topic has drawn enormous academic attention from economists, regulators, and central bankers. 'Next to monetary and fiscal policy, the promotion of safety and soundness of financial intermediaries has become the third major pillar of public policy'.[8] The European Banking Union, the Dodd-Frank Act in the USA, and Basel III are just a few examples of policy designed to regulate mega-banks. Most notably, the G20 countries founded the Financial Stability Board (FSB) in 2009 to coordinate global financial regulation with regard to G-SIBs. As mentioned above, every year the FSB designates 28 to 30 large banks as G-SIBs. These banks must meet a variety of additional regulatory obligations, of which the most important are significantly higher requirements with regard to common equity tier 1 capital (CET1), total loss-absorbing capacity (TLAC), and resolvability. As a result, the largest global banks must raise more than € 1 trillion by 2022 in equity and special debt.[9]

However, more drastic approaches seem to be off the table, such as the suggestion Bernie Sanders made during his 2016 presidential campaign that any bank deemed

[4] International Monetary Fund (IMF) (April 2014).

[5] A. G. Haldane (30 March 2010).

[6] Mankiw (2015).

[7] Moosa (2010, 332).

[8] Deli and Hasan (2017, 217).

[9] Hale, Binham, and Noonan (9 November 2015).

TBTF should be broken up[10]. Ten years after the onset of the GFC, the global economy has reached new heights and TBTF is no longer the centre of public attention. Some senior representatives of the banking industry call TBTF 'essentially solved'. Governments around the globe show 'regulatory fatigue'[11] or pledge to reverse the heavy regulation of large banks, most notably in the US. On 8 June 2017, the US House passed the Financial CHOICE Act, which will revoke many of the provisions of the Dodd–Frank Act, if enacted. Furthermore, the Basel Committee has put new banking policy initiatives on hold until 2019.

Bank Stock and Valuation Trends

During the GFC, the entire stock market fell substantially (see Fig. 1.1). Given their leveraged dependency on the real economy and high exposure to subprime mortgage securities, bank stocks suffered even more than broad indices, such as the Dow Jones Industrial Index and the Euro Stoxx, and recovered more slowly.

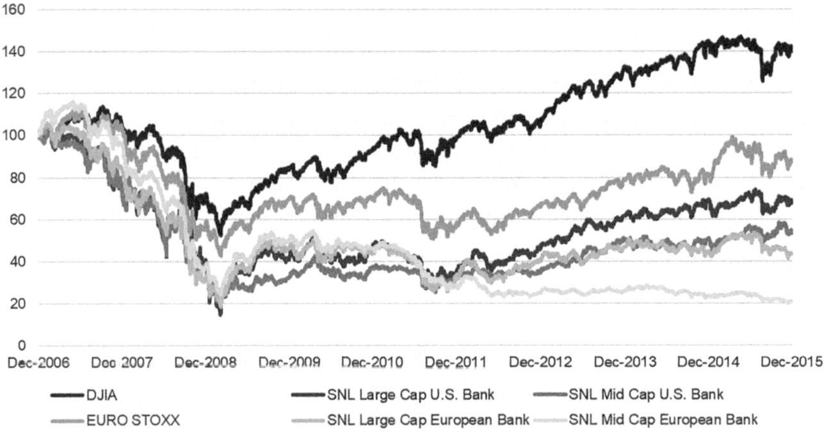

Fig. 1.1 Share price development 2006–2015

The development of bank valuations, according to the most common ratio of price-to-book value (P/BV), (see Fig. 1.2) is even weaker, since valuations have never returned to pre-GFC levels. The banking sector has undergone a structural change often referred to as 'the new normal' of the banking industry, with many factors potentially contributing to it. First, return expectations (RoE) have diminished due to higher capital requirements,

[10]Cf. Jopson, Weaver, and McLannahan (8 April 2016).
[11]Binham (25 April 2017).

the dilution of capital requirement increases, the low-interest environment as a fiscal reaction to the economic downturn, and higher general regulatory costs. Second, despite increased capital buffers, the capital costs of investors (*CoE*) have increased, mirroring the increased liability of shareholders and the higher uncertainty of bank profitability and regulation. Third, growth expectations (*g*) have shrunk because banks are more committed to de-leveraging their balance sheet and to disposing of non-core activities.

Structural changes seem most prevalent among the largest banks. Their valuations are still more depressed than those of their smaller counterparts, although large banks' share prices have outperformed those of the latter. In this context, a series of share-price event studies have shown that individual events connected to the TBTF doctrine have impacted large bank stocks.

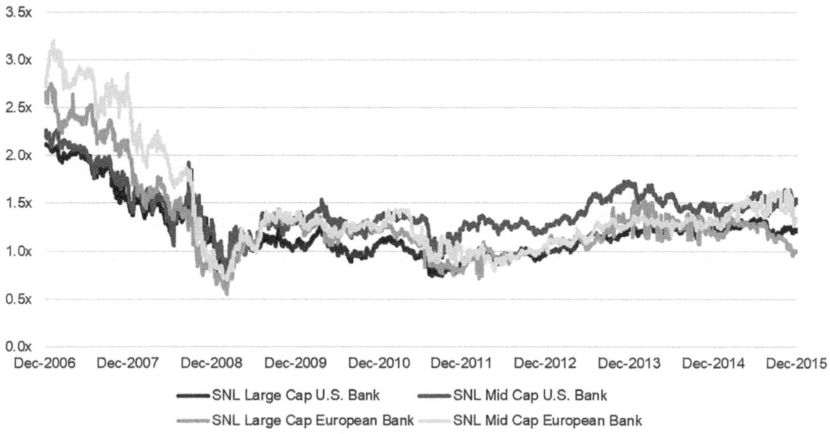

Fig. 1.2 Valuation (*P*/*BV*) development 2006–2015

1.2 Research Objective and Methodology

Part I—Too-Big-to-Fail in Banking Review

In the aftermath of the GFC, significant empirical and theoretical academic research has been dedicated to TBTF. Hundreds of studies of many facets of TBTF have been published and more than a dozen PhD monographs have explored subareas of TBTF.[12]

[12]Kleinow (2016, 3–10) presents a comprehensive overview of thirteen PhD monographs on TBTF. Their research focus can be categorised into (i) development of systemic risk measures, (ii) international financial contagion, (iii) identification of systemically important banks, and (iv) regulation of systemically important banks.

Several leading academics have published books 'telling the TBTF story' to the public at large.[13] Nonetheless, a minority in the academic community still doubts the relevance of TBTF and its impact on financial crises, and most financial experts believe that recent regulatory efforts have solved the problem of TBTF.

Part I of this dissertation has three main objectives. First, it fills a gap in academic literature on TBTF by combining wide scope with recent academic findings in niche areas. Second, it combines insights from various studies to demonstrate that the costs of TBTF outweigh its benefits. Third, it reveals how G-SIBs could internalise all costs of IGGs that lead to a social optimum.

Hence, the overall research question is:

Should TBTF in banking be abolished? And if so, how?

This interpretive literature review and qualitative study explains TBTF from various perspectives. First, how has evolving systemic risk in the financial system shaped the history of the banking landscape? Second, how do distortions resulting from IGGs reveal moral hazards among creditors, shareholders, and bank management? Third, what regulatory measures have been proposed to limit TBTF? Finally, what normative conclusion can be drawn to end the TBTF doctrine?

Part II—Quantifying the Shareholder Value of Too-Big-to-Fail in Banking

One subarea of TBTF that has received little theoretical or empirical attention is the impact of TBTF on equity (holders). Research on the impact of TBTF on debt (holders) and specifically on how the monitoring behaviour of bank creditors changes because of IGGs and is reflected in the pricing of bank debt instruments illustrate that bank creditor moral hazard is associated with substantial funding benefits for banks. The impact of TBTF on equity (holders), in contrast, appears to be much less straight-forward and more difficult to measure.

Several share-price event studies have been undertaken that demonstrate that individual events connected to the TBTF doctrine have impacted large bank stocks. One study[14] shows that banks, such as the Continental Illinois National Bank and Trust Company in 1984, are affected by positive abnormal share-price reactions. Later studies[15] assigned further events connected to TBTF to positive and negative abnormal share-price reactions. Most recently, several authors[16] link regulatory events with the share price of newly designated G-SIBs. However, these studies remain short on how all the positive and negative factors together affect the share prices of G-SIBs overall. In other words,

[13]Most notable is the popular but in part outdated book by Stern and Feldman (2009b).

[14]O'Hara and Shaw (1990).

[15]E.g. Angbazo and Saunders (1996).

[16]E.g. Moenninghoff, Ongena, and Wieandt (2015).

how is the valuation of G-SIBs distorted? Simply analysing long-term share prices does not provide sufficient evidence because share prices are affected by many factors, such as expected bank profitability. Both regulators and shareholders would benefit by better understanding positive and negative factors shaping the valuation of G-SIBs. Regulators could interpret a potential valuation premium of G-SIBs as a measure of elevated systemic risk in the financial system, but also as a measure of the financial robustness of G-SIBs, and vice versa. A valuation discount could also incentivise a bank break-up from a shareholder's perspective. Our fundamental research question is thus:

What drives the valuation of stocks of G-SIBs compared to stocks of other banks over time?

The present empirical study applies the ratio of price-to-tangible common equity (P/TCE) to capture the valuation of banks, a refined version of P/BV. The G-SIBs are thereby defined as G-SIBs designated by the FSB. To control for exogenous factors, other than the TBTF attribute, a variety of input factors have been deduced from profitability (*RoE*), risk (*CoE*), and growth (*g*). The sample comprises quarterly observations of more than 750 global banks for the period of Q2 2008 until Q3 2015, which is unprecedented in this field. This long and continuous period spans from the time before the establishment of the FSB (17 November 2008) to before the first publication of the list of other-systemically important institutions (O-SIIs) in the EU by the EBA on 26 April 2016. This period spans several relevant designation and regulation events for G-SIBs. To identify entity- and time-fixed effects (i.e. valuation developments of a subset of banks per quarter), a two-way fixed-fixed regression model is applied.

1.3 Dissertation Structure

The following provides an abstract of each part and chapter in order of the agenda. The dissertation starts with two introductory chapters.

Chapter 1 introduces TBTF generally, formulates the two core research questions, and defines the structure of the overall dissertation. It summarises the general context and latest developments of TBTF in banking, including bank stock and valuation trends since the GFC, identifies relevant gaps in TBTF research, and formulates the research questions and approaches.

Chapter 2 discusses TBTF and the research questions in closer detail. It lays out the fundamental concepts within banking necessary to understand the various aspects of TBTF. The chapter first defines the term 'bank' and explains how basic bank accounting works. Then it summarises basic banking economics to illustrate the importance of banks for the economy. Next it lays out a causal chain from banking risk to bank-runs, panic and economy-wide crisis. Subsequently, the chapter introduces measures originally taken to prevent crises which now seem to foster TBTF due to increased risk-taking: deposit insurance and weak failure-resolution policy. The chapter concludes by showing how bank and creditor moral hazard lead to heavy bank regulation.

Part I—Too-Big-to-Fail in Banking Review

The second part of this dissertation aggregates available academic research into TBTF in banking, ranging from TBTF history to TBTF policy recommendations for the future.

Chapter 3 introduces and defines the term 'TBTF' and evaluates systemic risk as the source of TBTF. It traces the history of TBTF and relevant major events to understand how TBTF has evolved over time.

Chapter 4 assesses the causal chain of TBTF from a theoretical perspective. It evaluates banks' incentives to become TBTF and illuminates the function of explicit government guarantees (EGGs), also known as bailouts, for G-SIBs. Subsequently, the chapter analyses how IGGs to G-SIBs foster moral hazard among creditors, banks, and even shareholders.

Chapter 5 analyses the welfare perspective of the TBTF doctrine as a negative externality and a major source of market failure and inefficiency in banking. This chapter conducts a cost-benefit analysis relevant to efforts to regulate TBTF.

Chapter 6 summarises bank-level policy recommendations for G-SIBs by academics and policymakers in reaction to the GFC, categorized chronologically into crisis prevention, crisis management, and crisis resolution recommendations.

Chapter 7 discusses the main TBTF policy initiatives since the GFC, namely the European Banking Union, the Dodd-Frank-Act in the USA, and Basel III, as well as the FSB regulation, which is the only global initiative specifically targeting TBTF.

Chapter 8 concludes Pt. I of the dissertation. After summarising each chapter, the chapter provides an outlook on future developments of the TBTF doctrine and its regulation, calling for fundamental reform.

Part II—Quantifying the Shareholder Value of Too-Big-to-Fail in Banking

This part presents the empirical analysis of the dissertation, which measures the relative equity valuation differences of G-SIBs. This part is structured like a standard research paper.

Chapter 9 summarises the literature closely related to how TBTF impacts stock prices and market equity, focusing on results and methodology. The chapter also reviews the literature on the applied bank valuation and regression model.

Chapter 10 develops hypotheses about the research question and the applied methodology.

Chapter 11 introduces the data and the empirical model used, explaining and deducing each input variable for the regression analysis. Subsequently, the chapter shows how and from where the data was extracted and outlines sample characteristics. Finally, evidence is provided that the study meets all formal requirements of a robust regression analysis.

Chapter 12 explains the results for each regressor and with regard to the G-SIB dummy and its development. The chapter draws conclusions from the empirical results and suggests avenues of future research.

Chapter 13 concludes Pt. II of the dissertation. It summarises the key findings and implications and deduces recommendations for bank management and policymakers.

2 A Primer for Economics of Banking

This chapter provides a general foundation for the following chapters about the too-big-to-fail (TBTF) problem in banking, defining relevant banking terms necessary for general understanding.

This overview of the fundamental principles of banking microeconomics draws on modern banking literature. Problems arises from transaction costs and information asymmetries are key to explaining the financial system. Theories of the new institutional economics—including transaction cost theory[1], principal-agent theory[2] and property rights theory[3]—are applicable in this context.

The chapter begins by illustrating the benefits of using banks to facilitate capital allocation in the economy as part of an overall financial system (see Sect. 2.1). Section 2.2 defines the term 'bank' and describes basic accounting concepts essential for understanding the empirical part of this study. It then discusses bank runs, which are a major threat to banks because they lead to significant bank bankruptcy costs (see Sect. 2.3). Section 2.4 explains the concepts of deposit insurance and lender of last resort (LOLR). Both instruments have been established to handle bank runs and their consequences, but also cause moral hazards (see Sect. 2.5). Section 2.6 describes a chain of events that begins with bank runs, is followed by banking crises and ultimately concludes in financial crisis. While the preceding sections illustrate the need for bank regulation, Sect. 2.7 provides an overview of the respective regulatory instruments.

[1]Coase (1937) and Williamson (1979).

[2]Jensen and Meckling (1976) and Eisenhardt (1989).

[3]Demsetz (1967) and Grossman and Hart (1986).

T. F. Lesche, *Too-Big-to-Fail in Banking*, Finanzwirtschaft, Banken und Bankmanagement I Finance, Banks and Bank Management, https://doi.org/10.1007/978-3-658-34182-4_2

2.1 Financial System

A well-functioning financial system is important to facilitating the growth and efficiency of the entire economy.[4] In such a financial system, surplus funds are channelled by financial intermediaries and financial markets from market participants who lack productive investment opportunities to market participants who have such opportunities. The first group of market participants, known as lenders or savers, are mainly households and firms. The latter group, known as borrowers or spenders, are primarily firms, governments, and households. Financial markets are run by service providers. Financial intermediaries can be banks or non-banks, such as mutual funds, private pension funds, and insurance companies. Financial intermediaries or financial markets are principally regulated entities.[5] Figure 2.1 illustrates the flow of funds in the financial system described above.

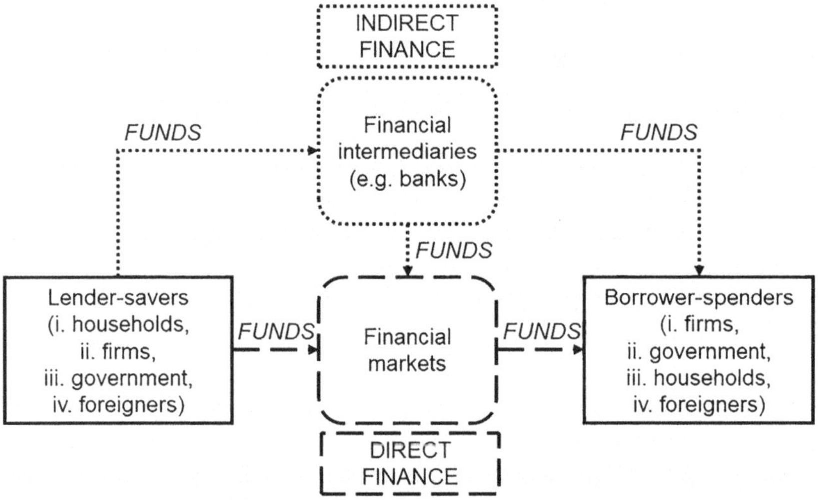

Fig. 2.1 Flows of Funds Through the Financial System. (Source: Mishkin (2004))

Financial intermediaries and financial markets are alike in that they provide specialised services that generate significantly greater economies of scale and scope than bilateral contracts between lenders and borrowers.[6]

They perform three main functions:[7]

---

[4]Cf. Bernanke (1983), Calomiris, James, and Stock (1986, 488), Freixas and Rochet (2008, 7), Friedman and Schwartz (1963), and Gilbert and Kochin (1989, 333) for western world, and Mishkin (1996) for the emerging markets.

[5]Shadow banking system is the term used for non-bank financial institutions that provide traditional banking services.

[6]Cf. Mishkin (1996, 2), Mishkin (2004, 375–76), and de Haan, Oosterloo, and Schoenmaker (2015, 3).

[7]Cf. de Haan, Oosterloo, and Schoenmaker (2015, 3).

1. Minimizing transaction costs by facilitating trading: A financial system facilitates the transfer of the property rights of financial streams with legal certainty between lenders and borrowers. Financial markets standardize financial contracts. Financial intermediaries convert lendings and borrowings on their balance sheets. When considering laws, rules, customs and norms, a financial system appears to be incomplete and full of friction, in particular due to indivisibilities and non-convexities in transaction technologies. Financial intermediaries exist alongside financial markets because they are well suited for minimising the costs associated with such imperfections and economic friction.[8]
2. Facilitating liquidity and risk-sharing: A financial system provides a broad range of lending and borrowing opportunities. It enables lenders and borrowers to diversify and share risks. Moreover, a financial system also reduces the risk of illiquidity, which could ultimately negatively affect consumption or investment needs. Without a financial system, all lenders would be locked into illiquid long-term borrowing.[9] Financial markets provide liquidity by amassing enough buyers and sellers for standardised financial contracts. Financial intermediaries always hold a fraction of liquid assets on their balance sheet in order to respond to liquidity needs.[10]
3. Minimizing costs associated with information asymmetries: A crucial impediment to the efficient functioning of a financial system is asymmetric information. An information asymmetry can occur *ex-ante* and *ex-post* closing a financial contract. *Ex-ante* information asymmetry arises because borrowers generally know more about their investment projects than lenders.[11] This leads to the typical risk of adverse selection and market failure.[12] Screening of borrowers is the preeminent measure taken to reduce this risk. *Ex-post* information asymmetry arises for two reasons, both of which lead to the risk of moral hazard. First, it is not certain how the borrower will actually spend the borrowed funds. Controlling borrowers is the preeminent measure taken to reveal covert intentions. Second, only borrowers can observe the development of the investment projects. Monitoring borrowers is the preeminent measure taken to illuminate covert actions and hidden information. Financial markets and financial intermediaries economise on all of the respective information-acquisition costs that stem from screening, controlling, and monitoring.[13]

Financial Markets vs. Banks vs. Non-Bank Financial Intermediaries

Three key questions about financial markets and financial intermediaries are (i) which are more effective, (ii) which lead to more innovation, and (iii) which result in greater economic growth and stability.[14]

[8]According to Freixas and Rochet (2008, 16, 18).

[9]de Haan, Oosterloo, and Schoenmaker (2015, 11).

[10]According to Freixas and Rochet (2008, 20–24).

[11]de Haan, Oosterloo, and Schoenmaker (2015, 9).

[12]This situation is similar to the textbook example of the market of lemons (Akerlof (1970)).

[13]Cf. Mishkin (1996, 2) and Freixas and Rochet (2008, 17, 30).

[14]The market-based system is predominant in the Anglo-American countries, while the bank-based system is in countries like Germany of Japan.

Financial markets and financial intermediaries differ especially in terms of the financial system function that deals with information asymmetries. Financial markets are best equipped to reduce costs arising from *ex-ante* information asymmetries, and financial intermediaries are best in solving *ex-post* information asymmetries.[15] In the controlling and monitoring function of financial markets, a so-called free-rider problem may emerge. If market participants who do not pay for information can use the information other participants have paid for, insufficient acquisition of information results. Consequently, financial markets are more 'hands-off'[16]: i.e., they are less likely to act to reduce incentives for committing moral hazards *ex-post*.

Hence, non-public controlling and monitoring is an essential advantage of financial intermediaries. Of banks and non-bank intermediaries, banks have a greater incentive to act as delegated controllers and monitors. Banks have substantial 'skin in the game': that is, monetary risk expressed by the proportional equity invested in every loan they grant. This 'first-loss piece' acts as a very effective natural incentive.[17,18]

Overall, academic research offers different judgements of how funds are optimally channelled in a financial system. Some researchers[19] conclude, from the information-asymmetry perspective, that financial intermediaries are best in an emerging financial system while financial markets are best in a developed financial system.[20] Other researchers argue that financial markets and financial intermediaries should be seen as complements rather than substitutes.[21]

2.2 Introduction to Banks

The Definition of *Bank*

A bank is a financial institution whose main operation is to grant longer-term loans funded principally by demand deposits by the public.[22]

15Boot and Thakor (1997).

16Chakrabort and Ray (2006).

17Cf. Diamond (1984).

18Cf. the five economic motivations for risk management in banks according to Dermine (2014, 269–70): (i) managerial self-interest, (ii) non-linearity of taxes, (iii) cost of financial distress, (iv) capital market imperfections, and (v) funding with short-term deposits.

19E.g. Boot and Thakor (1997).

20Cf. empirical research conducted by Tadesse (2002).

21Cf. Degryse, Kim, and Ongena (2009, 9), Mishkin (1996, 4–5), Levine (2002), de Haan, Oosterloo, and Schoenmaker (2015, 19), and Allen, Carletti, and Gu (2015, 39).

22Similar to Freixas and Rochet (2008, 1).

This simple definition has several important implications:

1. By lending money to others, banks are always taking a risk in order to get a return. Such activities are also called 'on-balance-sheet activities', which imply that the default risk remains until the loan is paid back.
2. Banks finance just a fraction of the loans with their own money, which is also referred to as equity. This inherent leverage leads to more volatile returns and limited loss absorbency, which is the first reason why banks tend to be fragile.
3. Banks finance the majority of longer-term loans through demand deposits. This inherent mismatch of maturities leads to the risk of illiquidity, comprising the second reason banks tend to be fragile.
4. The public might want to ensure that their deposits are invested in a trustworthy fashion. Hence, such activities and the use of the term *bank* in the firm name are normally subject to a banking license granted from a national regulator.

The term *bank* is used throughout this dissertation instead of other more ambiguous terms such as *financial institution*, *financial intermediary*, *company*, or *firm*. Lenders or savers in the financial system are depositors or creditors to banks, while spenders are debtors to banks.

Bank Services

Banks are a vital part of an economy because they have important relationships with borrowers and lenders. Banks establish these relationships over time through the exchange of unique information and therefore have the ability to monitor loan progress efficiently. Banks perform crucial functions for the economy (see Sect. 2.1) by providing services to their customers. These services can be classified into four main categories: (i) offering access to a payment system, (ii) transforming assets, (iii) managing risk, and (iv) processing information and monitoring borrowers.[23] In addition, there are services that involve the interaction of banks with financial markets, such as underwriting securities.[24]

Bank Accounting

Like other kinds of companies, banks are subject to accounting standards: namely, the Generally Accepted Accounting Principles in the US (US GAAP) and the International Financial Reporting Standards (IFRS), which are used in most countries in the world.[25]

---

[23]According to Freixas and Rochet (2008, 2–7).

[24]Cf. Allen, Carletti, and Gu (2015, 42).

[25]The principle differences between the two standards are the treatment of derivatives (US GAAP uses net figures; IFRS uses gross or notional amount) and the scope of consolidation (US GAAP allows certain assets to remain off-balance sheet; IFRS generally brings such assets onto the balance sheet) (Huertas (2014, 26)).

Although banks are treated like any other service provider, large differences arise from their main operations and financing structure. Their assets, for instance, comprise mostly legal titles, such as loan agreements and securities, with a completely different risk structure than tangible assets. While the funding is expedient for non-banks to expand their operations, the financing structure for banks is an active part of the business.

Structure of a Bank's Financial Statement

Consequently, the structure of the financial statements of banks is quite different from that of non-banks. Banks are, however, quite homogeneous in their accounting standards across the globe. The fundamental structure of the financial statements can be generalized as follows:[26]

Loans and securities are interest-earning assets. All assets are shown on the right-hand side of a balance sheet and are listed by their liquidity in descending order. These are funded by liabilities and equity, which is shown on the left-hand side of a balance sheet, and are listed by their liquidity in descending order as well. Deposits and borrowings are interest-bearing liabilities.[27] Figure 2.2 illustrates a simplified bank balance sheet that includes all essential items.

Assets

- Cash and cash equivalents
- Loans (net)
  - Interbank loans (gross)
  - Customer loans (gross)
  - Loan-loss allowances
- Securities
  - Trading book
  - Investment purposes
- Fixed assets
- Intangibles
  - Goodwill
  - Identifiable intangibles
- Other assets

Liabilities & equity

- Deposits
  - Non-interest bearing deposits
  - Customer deposits
- Borrowings
  - Bank borrowings
  - Senior debt
  - Subordinated debt
- Other liabilities
- Equity
  - Common shares
  - Retained earnings

Fig. 2.2 Simplified Bank Balance Sheet

[26]KPMG (June 2011)) provides a comprehensive guide to the structure of banks' financial statements in accordance with IFRS.

[27]In general there are three rules of thumb for banks' funding strategy: First, banks want to diversify their funding sources in order to avoid the risk of a potential drying-up of one source. Second, banks seek to finance themself primarily through retail deposits as those tend to be cheapest and relatively sticky. This means that bank deposits contribute to bank earnings by reducing the funding costs below market rate. Third, banks prefer to match the maturities of their lendings with their funding maturities before using derivatives.

Interest income and interest expenses are the top-line revenues and costs recorded in the income statement, as a bank conducts primarily loan-lending funded by deposits. This statement, also referred to as a profit-and-loss statement (P&L), is illustrated in simplified form in Fig. 2.3 including all essential items and their explanations. It shows that banks often also conduct so-called 'off-balance sheet activities': i.e., banking services that do not involve credit risks that result in fees, trading or other commission income.

+	Interest income (II)	• Interest earned on interest-earning assets
−	Interest expense (IE)	• Interest cost on interest-bearing liabilities
=	Net interest income (NII)	
+	Non-interest income (NonII)	• Fees and commission income from cross-selling services, insurance products sold, credit cards etc. • Trading income • Investment income
−	Non-interest expense (NonIE)	• Fees and commission expenses, etc.
=	Operating income (OpI)	
−	Operating expenses (Opex)	• Compensation / benefits, administrative expenses, occupancy / equipment, marketing expense, amortization of intangibles, technology and communication, etc.
−	Loan-loss provisions (LLP)	• Account for credit losses banks expect to incur on loans. LLP are accrued non-cash expenses, which are added to banks' reserves
=	Profit before tax (PBT)	
−	Taxes (t)	• Corporate income taxes
=	Net income (NI)	

Fig. 2.3 Simplified Bank Income Statement

Bank Valuation

Valuation of banks differs from normal corporate valuation.[28] When valuing non-banks, the value of the operations (which is also called the enterprise value) is generally calculated first, and the liabilities are deducted subsequently to derive the equity value. In contrast, valuation methods that derive the equity value directly are best suited for banks,[29] mainly for the following two reasons:

1. Capital and provisioning requirements: The banking industry is heavily regulated (see Sect. 2.7). To anticipate loan defaults and other risks, banks are obliged to retain significant amounts of their profits in the form of loan-loss reserves and other provisions for expected losses, and in the form of capital for unexpected losses. This means that not the earnings but the capacity to pay dividends to shareholders is the best approximation of real profits and should be used for valuation considerations.[30]
2. Capital structure: Banks aim not only to create value on the asset-side of the balance sheet as industrial corporations do, but also to create value on the liability side, e.g. by collecting low-cost deposits. Hence, bank debt is akin to raw materials. A bank heavily manages its diverse sources of funding, of which equity represents only a small fraction. This means that discounting dividends directly with the cost of equity works best for banks[31].

As consequence and because many of the banks' assets are traded on exchanges, banks' financial accounting is presented differently. On the balance sheet, assets are frequently recorded mark-to-market by fair value. Hence, banks' book value gives a fairly good and current view of their equity value from an accountant's perspective. Since not only regulatory requirements but also interest income and expenses are part of the current operations, only earnings (or dividends) are a suitable measure from a bank's income statement.

Table 2.1 shows the common valuation methods for banks used by professionals and scholars alike.[32] These methods are generally useful for both insiders and outsiders, i.e., for those who only have access to publicly available information. All of these methods derive the equity value directly and are meant for genuine banks that conduct primarily on-balance-sheet business, i.e. that generate most operating income through interest

[28]Countless articles and books have been published on valuation of non-banks, whereas less literature is available on the peculiarities of bank valuation that show the different methods and issues (cf. Adams and Rudolf ((24 November 2006)). Notable are Damodaran (2012) and Dermine (2014). Gross (2006) gives an overview of the developments made in bank valuation.

[29]Cf. Calomiris and Nissim (2007).

[30]In contrast, corporate valuation uses free cash flows attributable to debt and equity holders.

[31]Instead of discounting the entirety of free cash flows with the weighted average cost of capital (WACC) used in corporate valuation.

[32]Cf. Frost (2004), Dermine (2014), Damodaran (2012), and Koller, Goedhart, and Wessels (2015).

income from interest-bearing liabilities. Valuation methods are divided into market-oriented methods, which derive relative valuations based on other traded banks, and firm-specific methods, which derive absolute valuations based on the present value of a bank's future dividends.[33] Stand-alone and strategic (M&A) valuations are differentiated with regard to the purpose of the valuation.

Table 2.1 Bank Valuation Methods

	Market-oriented methods	Firm-specific methods
Stand-alone valuation		
	• Multiples based on trading comparables (P/E and P/BV) • Regression analysis (P/E and P/BV)	• Gordon growth model • Dividend discount model (DDM) • Economic value added (EVA) • Fundamental valuation model
Strategic (M&A) valuation		
	• Multiples based on precedent transactions (P/E and P/BV)	• Dividend discount model (DDM) incl. synergies and restructuring costs

The resulting equity value can be further broken down into liquidation value and franchise value.[34] The liquidation value represents the difference between the current value of the assets and the current value of the liabilities that is attributable to the shareholders. It would accrue if the bank were closed and liquidated at market price. On the other hand, the franchise value represents the value that is generated through the ownership of a banking license, also called charter value, and through client relationships. It is generated by the bank's ability to grant loans above and to generate deposits below the general market rate.

Banking Risks

Banks business activities are complex and deeply dependent on externalities which they cannot control, such as the development of the global economy. From a financial point of view, banks evaluate risks by comparing the cost of funding with equity to the cost or loss of revenue induced by a change of positions needed to reduce risk.[35]

---

[33]Market-based valuation and its value drivers are explained in detail in Sect. 9.3.

[34]Dermine (2014).

[35]Dermine (2014, 271).

In the common legal forms for banks, shareholders are only liable to the extent of paid-in capital. This asymmetric payoff schedule of shareholders generates the incentives to enhance the value of the equity option by rising in the volatility of the bank's assets.[36] In other words, volatility increases the upside return without affecting the downside risk. And because 'banks seek to maximise shareholder value, they will seek bigger and riskier bets'.[37] Risks a bank faces can be aggregated into six categories:[38]

1. Credit risk: the risk of the inability of a borrower to serve interest or principal payments on a loan on time.
2. Market risk: the risk of loss of revenue resulting from adverse changes in interest rates, foreign exchange rates, and the prices of securities or commodities.
3. Regulatory risk: the risk of losses arising from an unexpected change in regulations as well as in tax regime.
4. Strategic risk: the risk that a new entrant, firm, or product will change the competition.
5. Liquidity risk: the risk of a shortage of cash triggered by sudden withdrawals of short-term deposits, unexpected drawdowns on loan commitments, or margin calls on trading transactions.
6. Operational risk: each risk other than the ones already mentioned; Risks associated with inadequate or failed internal processes, reputation, people, systems, or external events.

Illiquidity of Assets and Liquidity of Liabilities

The liquidity risk is especially relevant for banks as they hold just a fraction of their assets in cash or other liquid assets in case of liquidity needs of their depositors. The main part of their assets consists of illiquid loans. Transformation constitutes the key service of banks, which frequently leads to an asset-liability mismatch with shorter maturity terms of liabilities. Short-term funding comes from the deposits of retail and corporate clients as well as from the interbank market. The herding behaviour of these creditors consequently leads to excessive withdrawals or market dry-up, which pose major liquidity risks for banks.[39]

[36]Haldane (2012). Cf. Merton (1973).

[37]Haldane (2012).

[38]According to Dermine (2014, 266–69).

[39]Cf. Diamond and Dybvig (1983).

2.3 Bank Run, Bank Panics, Systemic Risk and Bankruptcy

Bank Run

A bank run is triggered by what creditors subjectively perceive as a threat of bank insolvency. By monitoring borrowers ex-post and ex-ante granting loans, banks mitigate adverse selection and the threats of moral hazards (see Sect. 2.1). Granting loans, however, results in a further asymmetric information problem because lenders lack information about the loan quality and are reluctant to deposit money with banks.[40] Hence, bank runs are based on beliefs about the behaviour of other creditors, which means that they are a non-rational market behaviour.[41] Seeing that banks operate based on so-called sequential service constraint, creditors are strongly incentivised to withdraw their money before other creditors. This is also referred to as the first mover advantage,[42] and institutional creditors often act before retail depositors do.[43] Due to the inherent fragility of banks, they are frequently subject to runs.

During a run, a bank experiences heavy withdrawals by their depositors while access to the interbank market is impeded. Liquidity reserves are diminished and banks may be forced to undertake costly fire sales, i.e. urgent sell-offs of assets far below their fair value to meet the liquidity demands of their depositors. A run can last either until all liquidity is depleted and the bank is practically insolvent or until fire-sale losses have exhausted all equity, leading to bank bankruptcy.[44]

In conclusion, bank runs contribute greatly to the general instability of banks. This is the reason why banks themselves, as well as bank regulators, try to implement measures against such events. The most effective prevention is deposit insurance (see Sect. 2.4).

Bank Panic

A bank panic is when large-scale bank runs take place at many banks simultaneously. Under such circumstances, depositors might not even transfer their money to a bank that they perceive to be more solvent, but rather withdraw all funds in cash. This happens when creditors lose their confidence in the entire banking system and withdraw all of their money from banks.[45]

---

[40]Cf. Mishkin (2004, 513–14).

[41]Monopolkommission (9 July 2014).

[42]See Diamond and Rajan (2000), Diamond and Dybvig (1983) and Christiansen (2001, 117).

[43]See Duffie (2010).

[44]Oliveira, Schiozer, and Barros (2015, 191) present evidence that G-SIBs benefit during times of bank runs by receiving additional deposit inflows from other banks.

[45]Cf. Bougheas (1999, 131), Brown, Trautmann, and Vlahu (2012, 1), Chari and Jagannathan (1988, 749), Freixas and Rochet (2008, 217), Freixas (2010, 380) and Temzelides (1997, 3).

Systemic Risk

The term 'systemic risk' refers to the risk of collapse of one individual market participant that negatively affects the financial system at large.[46] It is the opposite of idiosyncratic risk which can be completely eradicated by holding the market portfolio.[47]

There are two ways an institution can exert systemic risk on the financial system:[48]

1. Systemic Risk Contribution: An individual shock can function as a trigger initially only affecting one or a few market participants or a particular region or sector that is relatively small from a global perspective. The default or distress of this financial market participant can leapfrog through interlinkages (see Sect. 3.3) to the rest of the financial sector.[49] A large shock that could potentially develop from the micro to the macro level is also referred to as financial contagion or the spill-over effect; its bottom-up development is illustrated in Fig. 2.4. The extent to which the financial system at large is subsequently affected depends on the system risk contribution of the respective market participant.
   Contagion may occur through four different nonexclusive channels to the other banks:[50] (i) change in expectations of investors, (ii) large-value payment systems, (iii) over-the-counter (OTC) operations (mainly derivatives), and (iv) interbank markets. This means that the main mechanism is the effect of aggregated liquidity shocks.[51]
2. Systemic Sensitivity: A macroeconomic event, such as a natural disaster or a change in bank rates, may trigger a large shock (see Sect. 2.6). Figure 2.5 depicts how this top-down shock evolves from the macro to the micro level. This is less influenced by shock transmission from one market participant to the other, and more by how shock-sensitive the market participants are.

---

[46]De Bandt and Hartmann (2000). For an overview of the evolution of the term 'systemic risk' see Kleinow (2016, 21).

[47]A. G. Haldane (30 March 2010).

[48]Cf. Freixas and Rochet (2008, 235) and Allen, Carletti, and Gu (2015, 35–38).

[49]Cf. Diamond and Dybvig (1983).

[50]According to Freixas and Rochet (2008, 235–36).

[51]The underlying assumption is the presence of incomplete markets with regard to the provision of liquidity. Consequently, market participants need to preserve liquidity and be ready to buy assets if other market participants are willing to sell. In equilibrium, the provider of liquidity must be compensated for bearing the opportunity cost of holding liquidity. Hence, on average, across all states, they need to make sufficient profit. This, in turn, implies large volatility in the asset prices (cf. Allen, Carletti, and Gu (2015, 36)).

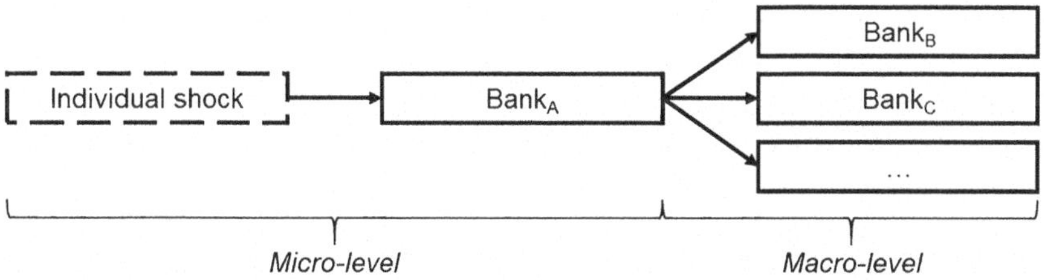

Fig. 2.4 Bottom-Up Shock or Systemic Risk Contribution. (Source: Kleinow (2016))

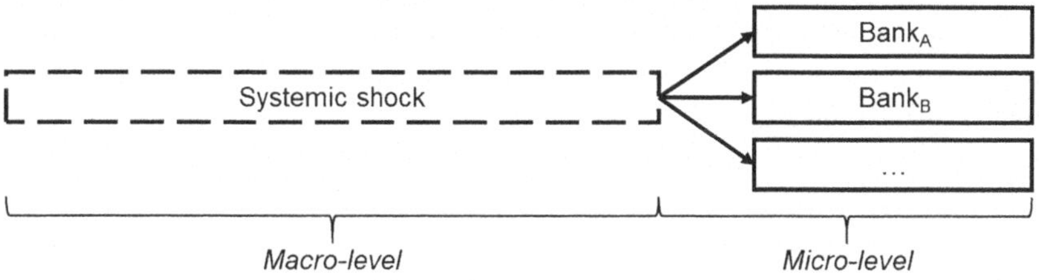

Fig. 2.5 Top-Down Shock or Systemic Sensitivity. (Source: Kleinow (2016))

There are three main explanations for why the banking sector generally tend to be more vulnerable to systemic risks than other sectors:[52]

1. The structure of the banks' balance sheets
2. The complex network of exposures among financial institutions
3. The intertemporal character of financial contracts and related credibility problems.

Bank Bankruptcy Costs

Standard bankruptcy codes allow for both, (i) firm liquidation and (ii) continued operation for a reorganization of a firm under supervision and in accordance with its debt holders.[53] These two procedures, however, appear not to work efficiently for banks. The problem with firm liquidation (i) are the assets, which are normally difficult to sell swiftly following a bank run in order to satisfy the creditors. Either asset prices have plummeted or assets are not easily sellable. The problem of continued operation (ii) are the liabilities, which are difficult to roll over during distress since uninsured depositors will use any opportunity to move their funds to safer banks.[54]

[52]According to De Bandt and Hartmann (2000, 6). Cf. Hellwig (1998).

[53]Both types, for instance, are regulated in Chapters 7 and 11 respectively of Title 11 of the U. S. Bankruptcy Code.

[54]Cf. Moyer and Lamy (1992) and French et al. (2010a, 13–14).

A textbook economic downturn is associated with a recovery process of ridding the market of unproductive banks. Bank runs and panics, however, cause real economic damage and social cost because productive banks are affected as well. This is why bank exits are governed by the regulator and not by market forces.[55] When a bank goes bankrupt, all of its stakeholders are directly affected. Management, equity holders, creditors, account holders, and counterparties 'bear losses in differing degrees depending on the legal priority of their claims'.[56] Indirectly, borrowers and the entire economy is affected due to the fact that the banking sector is temporarily prevented from delivering the critical banking functions (see Sect. 2.1) as efficiently as before.[57] Hence, the timing and the scope of the intervention by the regulator is crucial for overall health of the financial system. The direct and indirect costs of the bankruptcy depend on the orderliness of the liquidation process. These factors help explain why a disorderly termination of a bank's operations destroy value:[58]

1. The banks' franchise value depends on valuable knowledge about its counterparties (such as borrowers and trading partners), accumulated credit relationships, and specialized employees, all of which are not quickly transferable from one bank to another. Borrowers need to rebuild trustful relationships with creditors over time to regain access to crucial loans.[59]
2. Hasty fire sales of illiquid assets may not only reduce prices further, but also spread problems to other holdings of these assets.[60]
3. A disorderly liquidation increases the general uncertainty about the impact of failure on its competitors, counterparties, and claim holders. Such impact can precipitate or intensify a financial crisis.[61]

2.4 Bank Run Prevention and Management

Banks and bank regulators are strongly inclined to avoid bankruptcy, due to its substantial costs (see Sect. 2.3). Two major measures against bankruptcy have emerged early in banking history (see Sect. 3.4.2): the deposit insurance and the lender of last resort. Both measures were initially established as a result of the safeguarding ambitions of the banking sector itself. Nowadays, financial regulators mandate these measures (see Sect. 2.7).

---

[55] Brown and Dinç (2011, 1378).

[56] Labonte (30 June 2015, 5).

[57] Cf. Diamond and Dybvig (1983, 401), Moyer and Lamy (1992) and Freixas (2010, 380).

[58] In accordance with French et al. (2010a, 13–14).

[59] Slovin, Sushka, and Polonchek (1993).

[60] Shleifer and Vishny (1992) and Shleifer and Vishny (2010).

[61] Bernanke (1983).

Prevention: Deposit Insurance

Bank runs can be prevented through appropriate deposit contracts or by establishing deposit insurance. Deposit insurance can be viewed as a put option with a strike price equal to the promised redemption value.[62] It has the following advantages for banks, depositors, and society at large:

- For banks: (a) It has strong signalling effects with regard to limited reasons for withdrawing excessive amounts of money at once, and (b) it provides so-called 'sticky funds' which reduce uncertainty with regard to funding in particular.
- For depositors: (a) The freedom to withdraw money at all times, also referred to as 'safe haven', and (b) it provides fair and equitable treatment to depositors—eliminating the first-mover advantage.[63]
- For society: (a) It promotes economic efficiency by reducing the probability of dangerous contagious effects, and (b) it preserves the welfare of private savers with low asset diversification, which in turn incentivises individuals to privately save money for their retirement.[64]

In conclusion, deposit insurance is widely considered to be the most effective way to deal with bank runs. This is why deposit insurance is often either mandatory by law, or the government provides guarantees for the deposits directly, or both in complementary form.[65]

Management: the Lender of Last Resort

If a bank run or other excessive cash withdrawals are already taking place and a bank is unable to raise liquidity from the interbank market,[66] a crisis has already broken out. At this stage, an institution called lender of last resort (LOLR) temporarily protects banks

---

[62]Merton (1977).

[63]Cf. Diamond and Dybvig (1983) and Samartin (2003, 977).

[64]Cf. U.S. Congressional Budget Office (January 1992).

[65]Mandatory federal deposit insurance was first implemented in the US in 1933 (see Sect. 3.4.2), and it spread to 7 countries in the following 30 years, 12 countries in 1974, 71 in 1999, and to close to 90 in the beginning of the 2000s. Nowadays it is the norm in most parts of the worlds, in particular since the global financial crisis of 2007–2009 (see Demirgüç-Kunt, Kane, and Laeven (2014, 1) and Mishkin (2006, 989)). Even coverage increased after the crisis. Examples are the FDIC in the US, which insures deposits of up to US$ 250,000, and the 'Einlagensicherungsfonds' in Germany, which insures deposits of up to 20 percent of the banks' regulatory book equity per customer, i.e. quasi unlimited. Coverage on average 'is significantly higher in countries where poorly capitalized banks dominate the market and in countries where depositors are poorly educated' (Laeven (2004, 201)). An overview of the global deposit insurance schemes is provided by Demirgüç-Kunt, Kane, and Laeven (2014).

[66]Cf. Goodhart and Huang (2005).

from illiquidity. Central banks often function as LOLR and accept illiquid securities or loans as collateral for liquidity support. This liquidity insurance is intended to act as a safety net mitigating the risk of bankruptcies and the costs and disruptions related to it (see Sect. 2.3). Two types can be distinguished: LOLR as monetary policy action, when lending to all banks in response to a systemic event, and LOLR as emergency assistance, when lending to individual banks in response to a problem at the bank level.[67] The latter type has two main challenges: First, the LOLR needs to take into the account the trade-off between being too generous, thereby encouraging banks to go for more liquidity risk, and being too strict, thereby putting at risk the confidence in the banking system.[68] Second, the LOLR needs to distinguish in a timely manner between profitable banks that are threatened by insolvency, on the one hand, and unprofitable banks that are doomed to be actually bankrupt, on the other.[69] The support of unprofitable banks could promote the emergence of the so-called 'zombie banks'.[70] Finally, enabling inefficient banks to continue operating incentivises them to compete aggressively for business with efficiently run banks.[71]

2.5 Creditor and Bank Moral Hazard

Both the depositor insurance as well as the LOLR can be understood as insurances against illiquidity to stabilise banks. As is the case with every insurance contract, both insurances create further potential moral hazards,[72] especially for insurance arrangements with premiums that are not based on individual risks. Both measures are traditionally more or less fixed and unrelated to the assets of banks.

Creditor Moral Hazard (Decreased Monitoring)

In the first instance, depositors or agents are not as strongly incentivised to properly monitor the activities of a bank, its risk-taking, and liquidity reserves. They deem their deposits to be safe due to the deposit guarantee, and the fact that their funds can always be withdrawn, due to the LOLR. Consequently, the deposit insurance, as the creditor moral hazard, 'does not work well in countries with poor law and order, because it displaces private monitoring activity with poor-quality government monitoring of bank

[67]De Bandt and Hartmann (2000, 17)

[68]Cordella and Yeyati (2003, 300).

[69]Cf. Naqvi (2015). This potential weakness of the LOLR was first noted in the seminal work by Bagehot (1873).

[70]Kane (1987) invented this term in connection with the capital forbearance of the Federal Savings and Loan Insurance Corporation (FSLIC) during the savings and loan (S&L) crisis (see Sect 3.4.4).

[71]Cf. Freixas et al. (2000).

[72]De Bandt and Hartmann (2000, 17).

risk-taking'.[73] Because of the largely fixed deposit insurance premiums, banks with a weaker credit rating are willing to offer higher deposit rates. It is documented that retail and institutional depositors tend to play a deposit insurance arbitrage by moving the maximum amount that is covered to the weakest bank with the highest deposit rate.[74]

Bank Moral Hazard (Increased Risk-Taking)

There is a general bank or debtor moral hazard problem since the depositors lack information about the quality of the banks' assets (see Sect. 2.3). Due to the deposit insurance, this moral hazard increases further and banks tend to increase the riskiness of their assets for several reasons:[75]

1. Monitoring by the depositors is limited (see above).
2. In case of bank default, the deposit insurance offers a put option at par for the depositors. In turn, the depositors accept a lower deposit rate than without such protection.[76] The bank receives only limited price signalling from its depositors to limit the riskiness of its investments. Hence, the interest that is offered is virtually unrelated to the risk.
3. Deposit insurance premiums do not increase proportionally with risk-taking, i.e. the risk is shared among all banks that pay into the insurance scheme.
4. In case of a threat of failure, a bank can anticipate that the deposit insurance or government will cover the accumulated losses in order to avoid more losses or contagion effects from bankruptcy.

With regard to increased risk-taking, the insured banks appear to be not as well capitalised and less liquid than other banks.[77] Insurance incentivises banks to shift their asset portfolio to riskier loans, such as higher-risk real estate lending and off-balance sheet activities, and it also has the contradictory effect of biasing the subsidy towards loans that post systemic risk to the banking system.[78] The same holds for the LOLR, which acts as a double bottom.[79] Excessive bank liquidity encourages bank managers to act too aggressively by underpricing risk.[80] Before providing liquidity, the LOLR will consider

[73]Laeven (2002, 730).

[74]Cf. Wittkowski ((9 March 2016). Cf. Garcia (1999), Kane (1986, 175), Demirgüç-Kunt, Kane, and Laeven (2008, 435), and Gropp and Vesala (2004, 571) for discussions on the optimal design of deposit insurance to minimise creditor moral hazard.

[75]Cf. Christiansen (2001, 115–16) and Mishkin (2006, 989).

[76]Kaufman (2015, 4).

[77]Wheelock and Wilson (2012, 67–68).

[78]Penati and Protopapadakis (1988, 107) and Moyer and Lamy (1992).

[79]Sennholz (1992, 428).

[80]Acharya and Naqvi (2012).

the contagion and bankruptcy cost in the event of bank failure. These costs generally increase with bank size. Hence, establishing LOLR tends to protect large banks with bad fundamentals rather than small banks with good fundamentals. Moreover, it is an incentive for banks to grow sufficiently large to merit LOLR support (see Sect. 5.1).

Increased Instability

The deposit insurance and the LOLR have been established with the purpose of increasing the stability of the banking market. While both of which certainly at least partially fulfil their purpose,[81] they in fact also contribute to the instability because decreased creditor monitoring and increased bank risk-taking amplify potential investment losses of banks and ultimately lead to more bank failures.[82]

The destabilising effect may, however, only be exerted in the years leading up to a financial crisis. During a crisis, 'bank risk is lower and systemic stability is greater in countries with deposit insurance'.[83] In summary, the destabilising effect of deposit insurance during the period prior to the crisis appears to outweighs the stabilizing effect during turbulent times.

2.6 Financial and Economic Crises

Crises are the result of complex relationships among various and changing impact factors, which are almost impossible to foresee or to manage. This chapter attempts to extrapolate the main factors impacting financial and economic crises.

Banking Crisis or Financial Crisis

Financial crises include banking crises, sovereign debt crises, or currency crises.[84] The focus here is on banking crises, which 'are often also labeled financial crises in the

[81]Cf. Tucker (27–28 May 2009) with regard to the financial crisis of 2007–2009 and Sect. 3.4.2 to earlier historical experiences.

[82]Cf. Tasca, Mavrodiev, and Schweitzer (2014, 43) and Wheelock and Kumbhakar (1995, 186). O'Driscoll, Jr. (1988, 1) and Demirgüç-Kunt and Detragiache (2002) prove that deposit insurance can cause bank failure, and they conclude that it can ultimately trigger an entire banking crisis. It is worth mentioning, however, that technically inefficient banks are more likely to fail than the technically efficient ones (Wheelock and Wilson (1995, 689)). Demirgüç-Kunt and Detragiache (2002) found that the probability of banking crises correlates in particular with deregulated deposit interest rates and weak institutional monitoring. The study also showed that the adverse impact of deposit insurance is stronger on bank stability (i) the more extensive the coverage, (ii) in cases where the scheme is funded, and (iii) in in cases where it is operated by the government rather than the private sector.

[83]Anginer, Demirgüç-Kunt, and Zhu (2014b, 312).

[84]Willett and Wihlborg (2013) provide an analysis on these three types.

narrower sense'.[85] In the last centuries, banking crises have followed similar patterns, while government responses and thus the magnitude of the crises themselves have varied. Figure 2.6 presents a simplified illustration of the classical sequence of events leading to a financial crisis.[86]

1. There are three main foundations or macroeconomic shocks that worsen the adverse selection and moral hazards in financial markets. All of which can be the consequence of more deep-rooted causes, such as excessive monetary expansion or perverse incentive structures:[87]
   a. Increase in interest rates: This ultimately leads to a decline in lending. The credit rationing theory explains this as follows: if interest rates increase, 'there is a higher probability that lenders will lend to bad credit risks because good credit risks are less likely to want to borrow'. 'Because of the resulting increase in adverse selection, lenders will want to make fewer loans'.[88]
   b. Increase in uncertainty: This could occur due to the failure of a G-SIB or due to political turmoil. 'The increase in uncertainty therefore makes information in the financial markets even more asymmetric and makes the adverse selection problem worse'[89] which ultimately also reduces lending activity.
   c. Bursts of asset bubbles and stock market decline: This leads to the deterioration of balance sheets of firms. They make lenders less willing to lend because the deteriorating assets also act as collateral to banks. 'When the value of collateral declines, it provides less protection to lenders', and, as a result, the 'losses from loans are likely to be more severe'.[90] In addition, the asset value decline increases moral hazard incentives for borrowers to undertake risky projects because their prospective losses are higher in states of urgency.
2. Each of the above shocks results in the drop of the market prices of assets, which makes it less attractive for lenders to lend. Bankruptcies of the leveraged banks follow. The resulting failure of the payments mechanism and the inability to create credit induce a 'decline in investment and aggregate economic activity'[91].[92]

[85] Willett and Wihlborg (2013).

[86] Following Mishkin (1996, 26). See also Mishkin (1996, 18–27), Mishkin (2006, 988–89), and Shachmurove (2011, 225).

[87] Willett and Wihlborg (2013, 311).

[88] Mishkin (1996, 19).

[89] Mishkin (1996, 19).

[90] Mishkin (1996, 20).

[91] Mishkin (1996, 25).

[92] Cf. Feldstein (1991, 2).

3. As a consequence of a bank panic (see Sect. 2.3), a significant part of the banking sector becomes insolvent.[93] Both causes are deeply connected to each other.[94] Traditionally, two theories are used to explain the origins of a bank panic. It may, however, be difficult to clearly and de facto distinguish their origin. Both theories differ only in one element of the illustration and they result in the same bank panic:
   - One theory addresses changes originating in fundamental causes, as described above. The crises are seen as an intrinsic part of the natural business cycle.[95] They are triggered by periods of macroeconomic instability and problems affecting entire regions or industries. Hence, the problems in the banking sector do not stem from depositors, but from creditors and deterioration in asset quality. The banking sector amplifies the crisis as credit is expanded in the upswing and reduced in the downswing; this phenomenon is known as the credit crunch. A bank panic is 'a response of depositors to the arrival of some negative news regarding economic circumstances'[96]. 'Because of the worsening business conditions and uncertainty about their bank's health, depositors now begin to withdraw their funds from banks because they worry that the banks become insolvent'[97].[98]
   - The second theory traces the origins of bank panic to depositors themselves. In this case, a bank panic occurs spontaneously, with no connection to the real economy and the above described foundations. It is a random event stemming from 'mob psychology' or 'mass hysteria.'[99]
4. Due to a bank panic, the number of banks declines leading to a further increase of interest rates and a decrease in financial intermediation by banks. The financial system is increasingly unable to direct funds to the most productive investment opportunities. This is essentially the definition of a financial crisis.[100]
5. Again, 'the increase in adverse selection and moral hazard problems then lead to a decline in investment and aggregate economic activity'.[101]

[93]de Haan, Oosterloo, and Schoenmaker (2015, 39).

[94]Cf. de Haan, Oosterloo, and Schoenmaker (2015, 47–48).

[95]Allen and Gale (1998).

[96]de Haan, Oosterloo, and Schoenmaker (2015, 48).

[97]Mishkin (1996, 26).

[98]Cf. Jacklin and Bhattacharya (1988), Ramirez and Shively (2012, 433), and Allen and Gale (2004).

[99]Cf. Kindleberger and Aliber (2005) and Allen, Carletti, and Gu (2015).

[100]By Mishkin (1996, 17)

[101]Mishkin (1996, 27).

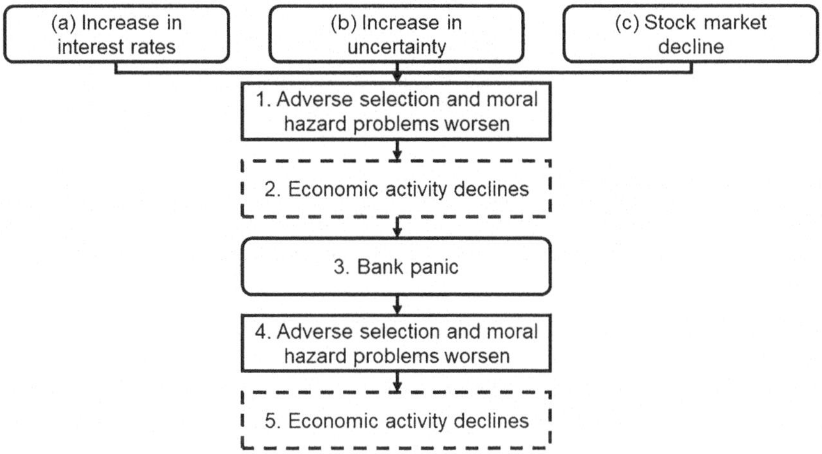

Fig. 2.6 The Sequence of Events in Financial Crises. (Source: Based on Mishkin (1996, 26))

The onset of a crisis can be facilitated by non-rational market behaviour, such as trend-led and pro-cyclical herding of market participants, or catastrophe blindness and a disposition to risk shifting, but also by accounting standards, such as the direct reflection of fair value losses.[102]

Economic Crisis or Recession

The financial crisis ultimately leads to an economic downturn because the banking sector is unable to perform its crucial functions (see Sect. 2.1) to the entire economy. Technically an economic crisis or recession is present when the GDP growth is negative for two or more quarters. History has shown that recessions in real economy are almost always associated with failures in the banking market, as we can observe from the examples of the Great Depression and the global financial crisis of 2007–2009 (see Sect. 3.4). Hence, most economist believe that economic growth is dependent on a sound financial market.

2.7 Banking Regulation

A well-functioning economy and financial system require particular government actions due to a variety of externalities. Such general regulations comprise competition policy, which 'seeks to protect consumers against exploitation of market power' or to protect property by enforcing contractual rights.[103] This section focuses only on regulation

[102]Monopolkommission (9 July 2014, 536). Laeven and Valencia (2013a, 234) develop a catalogue of quantitative criteria for determining when a banking crisis has erupted.

[103]de Haan, Oosterloo, and Schoenmaker (2015, 443).

distinctive to the soundness of banks. Generally, there are two different views on this kind of banking regulation: One group sees banking crises as unavoidable events, whereby regulation is meant to reduce the negative impacts, and the other group sees banking crises as avoidable events, when consistent and orderly regulation is in place.[104]

Difficulties of Bank Regulation

There are several arguments for proponents of deregulation to leave banking to the free-market forces since banking regulation is complex for the following reasons:

1. Regulatory arbitrage: Banks have strong incentives to find loopholes in the existing regulations.
2. Changing environment: The characteristics of the financial landscape and of each banking crisis are continuously changing and impossible to foresee. Thus, regulations apply to a 'moving target'.[105] Nevertheless, potential sources of disruption are mainly anticipated based on past experiences.
3. Pendulum hypothesis: New regulation causes further unintended consequences due to the integration into a complex adaptive systems. The pendulum hypothesis effects that a change in one regulatory subarea may require changes in other ones to avoid inconsistences of the regulatory system and future instabilities.[106]
4. Time-inconsistency: The short-term interests of policymakers in response to political pressure for votes result in a short-term perspective on the impacts of regulation.[107]

Reasons for Bank Regulation

To summarise this chapter thus far, on the one hand, banks play a very important role for the entire economy by performing crucial functions for the financial system (see Sect. 2.1). On the other hand, however,[108]

1. Banks are fragile because of the inherent leverage and maturity mismatch of their balance sheets (see Sect. 2.2);
2. Banks face many risks induced from internal and external sources (see Sect. 2.2);
3. Banks tend to take too many risks due to deposit insurance and resolution policies (see Sect. 2.4);
4. Banks are indiscriminately confronted with runs (see Sect. 2.3), which can trigger banking crises, that can consequently cause severe damage to the economy (see Sect. 2.6).

[104]Freixas (2010, 376).
[105]Mishkin (2004, 525).
[106]Bordo (2003, 158).
[107]Mishkin (2004, 526).
[108]Cf. de Haan, Oosterloo, and Schoenmaker (2015, 443).

In general, public regulation of banks is justified and seen as imperative by these market failures, which always stem from market power, externalities, or asymmetric information distribution.[109] Regulation aims to overcome or at least reduce these market inefficiencies. That is why banks are among the most regulated firms and most dependent on public authorities.

Additionally, the banking system as a whole can be considered a public good. Management and shareholders primarily calibrate risk management and protect the solvency of their own bank in order to maximize profits. They do not, however, take into account the adverse effects on the entire public in their considerations, that is, specifically to systemic risk.[110]

Types of Bank Regulation

The most common forms of bank regulation can be clustered into the following categories:[111]

1. Entry (chartering), branching, network, and merger restrictions,
2. Deposit insurance (see Sect. 2.4),
3. Interest rate ceilings for loans and deposits,
4. Asset restrictions (including reserve requirements),
5. Capital requirements,
6. Risk management requirements,
7. Disclosure requirements,
8. Regulatory monitoring and supervision (including prompt corrective action and bank examinations), and
9. Bankruptcy proceedings and resolution policy.

---

[109] Freixas and Rochet (2008, 306).

[110] Feldstein (1991, 15).

[111] Cf. Dewatripont and Tirole (1994), Mishkin (1996), and Freixas and Rochet (2008, 305).

Part I

Too-Big-to-Fail in Banking Review

Introduction to Too-Big-to-Fail in Banking

3

This chapter provides am introductory overview of TBTF in banking. First, TBTF will be defined and its implications examined (see Sect. 3.1). Second, the origin and development of the term TBTF will be traced (see Sect. 3.2). Third, the underlying attribute of TBTF, systemic importance, will be explained (see Sect. 3.3), not only by introducing the definition of the term 'systemic importance', but also the catalysts and measurement methods. The last section of this chapter (see Sect. 3.4) provides a chronology of the main events that contributed to the evolution of TBTF, including events dating back more than a century.

3.1 The Definition of 'TBTF'

A bank is considered to be TBTF when a government believes that it must safeguard the country's financial system and economic activity from a significant disruption caused by the adverse effect of possible default of the bank by guaranteeing the repayment of that bank's uninsured liabilities.[1]

This simple definition has several relevant implications for the presentation of arguments in the dissertation:

[1]This broadly corresponds with the definition of systemic importance by the Financial Stability Board (FSB) (2 September 2013, 2) ("The 'too-big-to-fail' (TBTF) problem arises when the threatened failure of a SIFI leaves public authorities with no option but to bail it out using public funds to avoid financial instability and economic damage.' and Bernanke (2 September 2010) ('A too-big-to-fail firm is one whose size, complexity, interconnectedness, and critical functions are such that, should the firm go unexpectedly into liquidation, the rest of the financial system and the economy would face severe adverse consequences.").

T. F. Lesche, *Too-Big-to-Fail in Banking*, Finanzwirtschaft, Banken und Bankmanagement I Finance, Banks and Bank Management, https://doi.org/10.1007/978-3-658-34182-4_3

1. TBTF designation: The government designates a bank as TBTF either ex-ante in an official statement or ex-post by granting government guarantees; the latter process is also called a public bailout. As long as there is no official government action, a bank can only be perceived as TBTF by the market.
2. The government's primary objective: The genuine objective of a bailout (see Sect. 4.1.1) is to safeguard the country's economic growth and stability, which is considered to be greatly dependent on a well-functioning financial system (see Sect. 2.1 and Sect. 2.6). The government of the country where the bank has its primary operations (and most commonly also its headquarters) decides on whether a bank will be bailed out.
3. The government's secondary objective: TBTF is not a term coined to address the failure of a single bank, but the potential of one bank to disrupt the entire financial system. This potential is known as systemic importance (see Sect. 3.3). Factors such as size, complexity or systemic interconnectedness of a bank are considered relevant in assessing the bank's systemic importance. Hence, the secondary objectives of a bailout are: (i) minimizing the risk of financial contagion (see Sect. 2.3), which implies that many financial market participants would severely suffer from the defaulting bank liabilities and (ii) re-establishing the stability of the distressed bank and the entire financial sector.
4. The forms of government bailout: A government bails out a bank by at least guaranteeing the repayment of the banks' uninsured liabilities (see Sect. 4.1.3). Equity instruments will not be necessarily guaranteed as it is expected that the holders are better prepared for bearing substantial losses. Equity holders may benefit in the second instance by either (i) directly receiving compensation payments as part of the government's takeover of the bank or (ii) indirectly avoiding bankruptcy due to government bailout.
5. The breach of free market principles: Government intervention on a selective basis in a free market economy results by definition in distortion of market forces and incentives. The TBTF doctrine incentivises banks to grow beyond the size of the social optimum and to become designated as TBTF (see Sect. 4.2.4). Creditors are less incentivised to monitor the risk of a safe G-SIB, and, in turn, the lack of market feedback leads to increased bank's risk taking (see Sect. 2.5).
6. The public subsidy of G-SIBs: A TBTF perception or designation will always incur costs for the public. An implicit government guarantee results in indirect public subsidies, e.g. in form of lower funding costs. An explicit government guarantee results in explicit public subsidies, e.g. in form of costs for open-bank assistance.
7. Time inconsistency of the decision: When the government bails out a bank or designates a bank as TBTF, it aims to prevent the entire economy from negative externalities. This implies that the respective government is led by the assumption that bankruptcy costs, including the costs of a financial crisis, would exceed the bailout costs, including the costs for social costs due to disincentives. Such a conclusion, however, is extremely difficult to foresee and to measure ex-ante and even ex-post (see Chap. 5).

3.2 The Term 'TBTF'

The term 'TBTF' is generally associated with banks and it is used solely in relation to banks throughout the dissertation. There are, however, also a few examples of industrial companies that have been labelled TBTF.[2] The term is closely connected to the bail-out of Continental Illinois National Bank and Trust Company in 1984 (see Sect. 3.4.3), although it was already used in media in 1975.[3] Many academics regard the Continental Illinois case also as first occurrence of TBTF. However, the foundations for TBTF were laid out much earlier and they include the key regulatory reforms of the modern banking sector (see Sect. 3.4).[4]

TBTF is a rare phenomenon in the history of banking; prior to 2007, TBTF was known only among banking experts. Many famous economists believed that the TBTF issue is of minor relevance[5] and some went as far as to deny its existence altogether. Thereupon the term 'TBTF doctrine' is often used to clearly designate that TBTF is based on economical beliefs. The massive public bank bailouts during the financial crisis of 2007–2009 removed the remaining uncertainty around the existence of TBTF and it utterly debunked the sceptics.[6] TBTF has increasingly received attention since then, not only in the academic and regulatory world, but also among the general public. This is hardly surprising if we consider the fact that bailouts noticeably affect the entire economy. Subsequently, TBTF received its own regulatory policies (see Chap. 7).

The term 'TBTF' as such can be misleading seeing that the size of the bank is not de facto relevant for a bank rescue, but rather the bank's systemic importance to negatively disrupt the financial system (see Sect. 2.3). Many terms similar to TBTF appear in literature, which simply highlight slightly different reasons for a bailout and differing implications for the stakeholders. For all that, all of the terms are versions of the same basic definition introduced above.[7] The banks are referred to with a variety of words

---

[2]Cf. Leathers and Raines (2004, 4) and Sprague (1988, 4).

[3]Cobbs (27 January 1975).

[4]Cf. Stern and Feldman (2009a, 14–16).

[5]E.g. Mishkin (2006).

[6]Schweikhard and Tsesmelidakis (1 November 2012, 1).

[7]Terms used in academic literature include, but are not limited to: too-complex-to-fail, too-big-to-liquidate, too-big-to-regulate, too-systemic-to-fail, too-connected-to-fail, too-political-to-fail, too-big-to-unwind, too-big-to-discipline-adequately, too-big-to-manage (Brewer III and Klingenhagen (2010, 59)), too big to unwind, too big to liquidate, too important to fail, too complex to fail, too interconnected to fail, too big to prosecute or jail (Kaufman (2014, 215)), too-big-to-liquidate, too-big to-impose-losses on important stakeholders (Kaufman (2000, 19)), too-politically-important-to-fail (Mishkin (2006, 992)), too politically connected to fail, too big to survive, so big that it has to fail, too big to succeed, too big to fail is too big, too big to save, too big for their boots (Moosa (2010, 320)), too big to fail and unwind, and too big to discipline adequately (Kane (2000, 673)).

such as LCFI ('large and complex financial institution') or SIFI ('systemically important financial institution'). For the sake of simplicity, the commonly used terms 'TBTF' and 'G-SIB' will be used throughout this dissertation.

3.3 Systemic Importance

Definition

Systemic importance, also called systematic relevance, relates to both sides of systemic risk (see Sect. 2.3):[8] *(i) the risk contribution from financial contagion, and (ii) the risk sensitivity to macroeconomical shocks. Systemic importance is thus defined as the potential of an institution to disrupt the whole financial system by either or both of the risks.*[9]

The term systemic importance entered economic jargon long after the term TBTF. It was introduced when it became obvious that systemic importance and not bank size determined TBTF around 1993 when systemic importance was introduced as requirement for bailouts by the FDIC (see Sect. 3.4.4) and it was rediscovered after the Lehman Brothers collapse in 2008 (see Sect. 3.4.5). Since then, extensive research has addressed this topic and systemic importance is widely acknowledged as the underlying source of financial stability.[10]

Market participants that can become systemically important include both providers of financial markets and financial intermediaries (see Sect. 2.1). Banks are the market participants with the biggest systemic impact on the financial system, followed by insurance companies.[11]

Systemic importance can be considered with regard to domestic or global financial systems. National governments and their financial regulators are primarily interested matters and entities of national interest. However, due to global financial linkages among banks, domestic and international systemic importance increasingly overlaps,

---

[8]Cf. De Bandt and Hartmann (2000).

[9]Cf. Alessandri, Masciantonio, and Zaghini (2015, 5), De Bandt and Hartmann (2000, 6), and Mishkin (2006, 989).

[10]De Bandt and Hartmann (2000, 8). The fact that various governmental institutions had been established exclusively to monitor systematic risk is symptomatic of the attention that the term has received. The European Systemic Risk Board (ESRB) was established in 2010 to oversee the financial system of the European Union (EU) and to prevent and mitigate systemic risk (see Sect. 7.1). The FSB was established in 2009 at the request of G20 for implementing global measures with the aim of reducing systemic risk (see Sect. 7.4). The Financial Stability Oversight Council (FSOC) in the USA was established in 2010 as part of the Dodd–Frank Wall Street Reform and Consumer Protection Act (see Sect. 7.2).

[11]Billio et al. (2012) and Engle, Jondeau, and Rockinger (2015).

particularly in the context of large economic areas like the EU.[12] In response to this increasingly international context, a unique global collaboration among supervisors, the Financial Stability Board (FSB), was formed to mitigate risks stemming from the systemic importance of banks (see Sect. 7.4).

Catalysts

There is neither consensus regarding the concept of systemic importance nor a conclusive definition of it. In fact, the factors determining systemic importance may be unique to each crisis.[13] Nevertheless, it is broadly accepted that certain catalysts influence the systemic risk contribution of banks, namely linkages in the financial system, the impact on the financial system, standard bank risks, and complexity. Both in theory and in practice, these categories may frequently overlap and be interdependent.[14] The more distinctive a certain criterion is, the greater the systemic risk it exerts on the financial system:[15]

- Interconnectedness in the financial system: Contagion in the financial system originates from significant price movements or defaults of exchanged assets.[16] The more linkages or interconnections there are between market participants, the higher the contagion risk. The more closely one financial participant is connected to others, the weaker the incentive to cut off an inefficient participant. However, there is also a trade-off between linkages (diversification) and systemic risk. Linkages initially help banks to diversify their asset portfolios, to improve risk sharing in the financial system, and to be less exposed to idiosyncratic risk. The connections make the financial system more resilient towards liquidity needs in normal financial times. The following stylized types of linkages can be identified:[17]
  - Direct balance sheet linkages: Banks have direct balance sheet linkages with each other through interbank deposits or through the exchange of bank securities. The maturities are generally short-term. Seeing that banks are well-informed market participants, there is a risk of a complete halt in interbank lending.
  - Indirect balance sheet linkages: Banks have indirect linkages between their balance sheets when they hold the same or similar assets undergoing the same price movements.[18] When banks hold roughly comparable portfolios[19], markets can dry

[12]Cf. Alessandri, Masciantonio, and Zaghini (2015, 6).

[13]Weiß, Bostandzic, and Neumann (2014, 92).

[14]Cf. Monopolkommission (9 July 2014).

[15]De Bandt and Hartmann (2000, 6) present a comprehensive literature review encompassing both the theoretical models and empirical evidence on the concept of systemic risk.

[16]Cf. Cifuentes, Ferrucci, and Shin (2005).

[17]Cf. Allen and Gale (2000).

[18]Tasca, Mavrodiev, and Schweitzer (2014, 43).

[19]De Vries (2005).

up entirely in a downward spiral if many banks attempt to dispose of their assets simultaneously[20]. Asset liquidation can cause large volatility because the original shocks are greatly amplified and potentially transmitted across different classes of assets.[21] This problem is increased through the accounting use of fair-value, where trading assets are recorded mark-to-market on balance sheets. Banks then need to recognise their unrealised losses, which induce cyclical behaviour and selling off troubled assets, directly through their P&L.[22]

  - Direct linkages with capital markets: In addition to bilateral funding, banks refinance themselves through debt and equity capital markets. Moreover, banks invest in securities as part of their liquidity strategy or for trading purposes. Capital market participants are better informed and quicker in making their decisions than traditional retail depositors. The maturities are also shorter, in fact, often overnight. These phenomena in tandem lead to the risk of institutional bank runs.[23]
  - Indirect linkages with capital markets: Banks use financial innovations, such as securitisations, to transfer credit risk onto other capital market participants with the aim of diversifying their risk. In addition, banks can act as providers of capital market platforms and they can support capital markets by helping corporates to issue securities (underwriting) or take care of the sufficient liquidity in the financial market (market making). Moreover, banks act as direct counterparties through financial derivatives they issue to their clients.
  - Cross-border linkages: Cross-border linkages do not, in fact, comprise an additional category as balance sheet linkages and capital markets linkages are not bound by national borders in the globalised world. This term is, however, often used to differentiate resolvability when operations are subject to different legal and regulatory jurisdictions, and to demonstrate the difference between domestic and global systemic importance.
- Impact on the financial system: The sub-criteria introduced below describe the potential of a bank to trigger financial contagion should the above linkages exist.[24]
  - Size: Bank size in terms of total assets and off-balance sheet exposure represents, on the one hand, the amount of funds that can be in circulation through the

[20]Brunnermeier and Pedersen (2009) and de Haan, Oosterloo, and Schoenmaker (2015, 47).

[21]Kyle and Xiong (2001) and Allen and Gale (2004). Cf. Allen, Carletti, and Gu (2015, 35–38). Lagunoff and Schreft (2001) identify two types of related contagion: 'One occurs gradually as losses spread, breaking more links. The other type occurs instantaneously when forward-looking agents preemptively shift to safer portfolios to avoid future losses from contagion.'

[22]Acharya (2009) finds that banks have a systemic risk-shifting incentive to increase asset correlation in their portfolios, thereby increasing economy-wide aggregate risk, in order to increase the chance of bailout (of all banks).

[23]Cf. Stern and Feldman (2009b, 70).

[24]Laeven, Ratnovski, and Tong (2016) and Rose and Wieladek (2012, 2038).

financial system linkages. On the other hand, it represents the default potential of a bank for its creditors.[25]

  - Substitutability and concentration: The higher the concentration in the financial system, the less quickly and easily a bank can be replaced. As banks frequently perform essential activities and operate important financial infrastructure, such as payment systems, failure disproportionately impacts the ability of market participants to channel their funds efficiently.[26]
- Standard bank risks: The set of these criteria refer to the standard bank risk (see Sect. 2.2) and to the degree of sensitivity to macroeconomic shocks (see Sect. 2.6).
- Complexity: The higher the complexity, the more difficult it is to resolve a bank in the event of bankruptcy.[27] What follows is that the longer it takes to resolve a bank, the higher the economic damage (see Sect. 2.3). The complexity of a bank can refer to the business, structural, or operational complexity. Examples are ramified legal entities, complex derivative portfolios, and legal arrangement with various bank stakeholders.

Section 3.4.5 below describes how the above criteria developed in the run-up to the financial crisis of 2007–2009.

Measurement

Measuring and identifying G-SIBs is a prerequisite for any regulatory effort, such as penalising G-SIBs. That is why there has been significant innovation in this area since 2007. It has not only proven difficult to measure global systemic importance, but also to define systemic risks quantitatively and define thresholds of systemic importance. Moreover, the standardised data, e.g. on bank interlinkages, required for profound analysis has only become available gradually. To date, there are no standard benchmarks in TBTF measurement.[28] Broadly categorised, there are two different approaches for the identification of systemically important banks:[29]

1. Indicator-based measurement approaches: Policymakers generally use some or all of the indicators introduced above. They are applied because they are simple to use

[25]Laeven, Ratnovski, and Tong (2016) and Rose and Wieladek (2012, 2038).

[26]Moyer and Lamy (1992).

[27]Carmassi and Herring (2014, 3).

[28]Cf. Hansen (2014).

[29]According to Bongini and Nieri (2014). Bisias et al. (2012) summarise many of the proposed measures. Molyneux, Schaeck, and Mi Zhou (2014) present a summary of different TBTF measures and thresholds applied between 1975 and 2011 in empirical studies conducted by academics and policymakers to assess systemic importance. The measures employed in these studies frequently include 'asset size, market capitalisation, market shares, and rating'. The more recent studies base their insights on the GFC and additionally consider a wider range of characteristics such as 'business complexity, wholesale banking activities, and substitutability of services'.

and because the permit consideration of subjective criteria. For instance, indicator-based approaches were implemented by the Basel Committee on Banking Supervision (BCBS) for FSB legislation.[30] These approaches rely mainly on accounting data, such financial statement data, transaction volumes and market shares.[31]

2. Market-based measurement approaches: Academics mostly base their approaches on market data, such as CDS prices, volatility measures, or bond spreads. Some authors argue that price distortions from IGGs are the right measure, while others use the implied price of insurance against financial distress.[32] Following the logic of the two origins of systemic risk (see Sect. 2.3), the approaches can be further distinguished into categories:
    a. Participation approaches: This group of methods assumes that an external systemic shock is exerted on the financial system and on the real economy (top-down shock). In this case a market participant's share of participation of the aggregated losses is measured and allocated to all members of the financial system. This means the more sensitive to shocks an institution is, the higher its share of the aggregated economic losses and its systemic importance.[33]
    b. Contribution approaches: This group of methods assumes that the systemic shock is exerted by the market participant itself or at least that it contributed to the shock (bottom-up shock). This means, this approach focuses on a single institution and measures the probability that shocks will spill over to other member of the financial system.[34]

Regardless of the approach of identifying G-SIBs, the simplistic measure of bank's size is believed to result (mostly) to the identical TBTF categorisation—correlating close to one—as large players are responsible for a larger share of banking output. The size in this regard is normally specified as a bank's total assets.[35] When generalising, research suggest that being a G-SIB starts at total assets exceeding US$ 100 billion.[36]

[30]Sect. 7.4 introduces the detailed methodology of the BCBS in order to identify G-SIBs.

[31]Cf. DeFerrari and Palmer (2001, 50) and Iwanicz-Drozdowska (2014, 147–48).

[32]E.g. Huang, Zhou, and Zhu (2009).

[33]Such measures include SRISK from Brownlees and Engle (2017) or systemic expected shortfall (SES) from Acharya et al. (2017).

[34]Such measures include CoVar from Adrian and Brunnermeier (2016).

[35]Cf. Schildbach (2017). The tougher regulatory supervision for the largest banks under the Dodd-Frank Act in the US and the Single Supervisory Mechanism (SSM) in the EU, is indeed only effectively dependent on the size indicator of bank's total assets.

[36]Monopolkommission (9 July 2014, 530).

3.4 The History of TBTF

The US as the Prototype of TBTF History

This section presents a chronology of TBTF, beginning shortly before the events that seeded the foundation of TBTF in banking.[37] Economists largely agree on the event coding presented here, although there is some disagreement regarding the exact dates and the impact of some of the events. The aim here is to illustrate the stylized way of how TBTF has emerged and how history repeats itself with regard to the concept of TBTF.

The evolution of TBTF is similar in all western countries. European banking history, however, is more fragmented and not as well-documented in English. The US serves as a prototype when it comes to TBTF, which is why the focus in this overview is on the US. The history of TBTF in the US goes back furthest in history, unsurprisingly so, as this country is commonly referred to as having the most advanced banking system in the world. The US banks were the biggest for many decades and it was not until the financial crisis of 2007–2009 when TBTF became a major topic in Europe.

The chronology begins prior to the TBTF doctrine, i.e. before 1913, when only limited regulation and supervision of banks in the US can be observed (see Sect. 3.4.1). The deregulation of the banking sector, accompanied by an increased government intervention in the period between 1913 and 1933, acted as the first breeding ground of TBTF (see Sect. 3.4.2). This contradicting regulatory environment in the free market consequently led to creating disincentives to banks to become TBTF[38] and to the first major bailouts (see Sect. 3.4.3). The following regulatory efforts to abandon TBTF (see Sect. 3.4.4) were quickly forgotten after a period of prosperity and stability in the banking system. It was not until the global financial crisis and its massive bailouts that the dramatic increase of TBTF risks during the previous decade was uncovered (see Sect. 3.4.5).

3.4.1 Banking Without Bailouts (Before 1913)

The over 100 years of banking history prior to the creation of a central bank in 1913 can be loosely described as the era of 'free banking and the gold standard'[39] in which there was no federal regulation and in which the states enacted their own banking rules. State supervision and state regulation of banks were very limited. The two main restrictions

---

[37]In their historical account of TBTF, Leathers and Raines (2004, 5–16) provide evidence of the existence of TBTF in the eighteenth century UK and they describe in detail the relationship between the British government and three large private joint-stock companies, including the Bank of England.

[38]Cf. Leathers and Raines (2004, 3).

[39]Sennholz (1992, 427–28). Cf. Rolnick and Weber (1982, 18–19).

that determined the banking environment were the 'unit banking system'[40] and the 'asset-backed currency'[41]. Consequently, banks remained relatively small in size and undiversified in their operations. Banks issued their own currency or accepted checking deposits against which checks or drafts could be written. Banks jointly created their own clearinghouses to settle balances and lend to each other on an interbank basis. Neither federal deposit insurance nor official lenders of last resort existed. Liquidity assistance to struggling banks 'was frequently provided by the local clearinghouse of which they were a member, financed by the other member banks'.[42]

The Panic of 1907

The banking sector in general was characterized by frequent crises in this period. Banks typically operated for only approximately five years. In case of insolvency, a bank was simply liquidated at a discount to creditors or taken over by stronger competitors. Bank insolvency spread not only within the banking sector, but it also led 'to a disruption in the payments system and a tightening of available credit, with adverse macroeconomic impact'.[43] The worst crisis scenario occurred during what is known as the panic of 1907.

---

[40]According to the National Bank Act of 1853, public state policy enforced the unit banking system. In other words, banking corporations were generally restricted to a single office or branch. This legislation intended to exclude out-of-state banks and to ensure some monopoly for local banks (cf. Federal Reserve Committee on Branch, Group, and Chain Banking (1930) and Hetzel (1991, 4)).

[41]A legal obligation existed to back the issued bank notes by means of precious metals, redemption, and state or federal treasuries. The exact legislation on this matter changed over time. Thus, the money supply was not controlled by the government, but driven by trade needs. Hence, the asset-backed currency is often considered to be the primary reason for long periods of deflation and frequent crises, since the money supply could not be influenced exogenously, i.e. it could not increase in times of crisis and prevent illiquidity (see Bernanke and Harold (1991, 33) and Shachmurove (2011, 219–20)).

While the data from the period does not distinctly confirm that this restriction caused the typical sequence in a banking crisis (see Sect. 2.6), in retrospect, the chain of events is much clearer: First, illiquidity and devaluation of assets: Since the issued bank notes were linked to treasuries, a large fraction of banks' total assets comprised those bonds. The value of state bonds was quite volatile at the time. These fluctuations regularly caused large losses for banks, and, therefore, to prevent illiquidity, banks had to recall loans or draw liquidity from other banks or clearinghouses. This system resulted in seasonal liquidity spikes. One such spike, for instance, occurred in the planting season, when rural banks withdrew their deposits from larger banks. Second, bank runs from depositors or noteholders: When depositors or noteholders believed that their bank was under threat of illiquidity, a typical cascade of a bank run occurred as a result (see Sect. 2.3). Third, insolvency: While in some US states many banks were forced to close down at the time and noteholders reportedly suffered, other states saw very few bank closings and managed to maintain a very stable financial environment (Rolnick and Weber (1982, 18–19)).

[42]Kaufman (2002, 425).

[43]Barth, Prabha, and Swagel (2012, 267).

3.4.2 The Breeding Ground of TBTF (1913–1933)

In hindsight, the regulatory changes during the short period of twenty years (1913–1933) acted as a crucial turning point that enabled the creation of the TBTF doctrine. The foundation of TBTF was laid with two major changes of banking legislation in the US in the period, which subsequently triggered the increased government intervention: (i) the creation of a central bank in the US and (ii) the introduction of the federal deposit insurance. Both were introduced in direct reaction on behalf of the regulatory authorities to severe banking crises that resulted in the gradual abandonment of normal bankruptcy arrangements for banks. In addition, the only two main restrictions that prevailed during the previous era of 'free banking and gold standard'—(i) the asset-backed currency and (ii) the unit banking system—have been abandoned or at least mitigated. The former resulted in the forming of a very lively expansion of the US banks during the first three decades of the century with banks reaching sizes never before seen.[44]

The Creation of the Federal Reserve System (1913)
At the time, the US was the last large country to establish a central bank. Bankers and government officials yearned for more stability in the economy and the banking system. They argued that the decentralized banking system could not regulate itself without a powerful intervening authority. Hence, and largely in response to a series of financial panics, particularly the severe panic of 1907, the Federal Reserve System (Fed), which became the central US bank, was formed on December 23, 1913, with the enactment of the Federal Reserve Act. As a consequence, the asset-backed currency principle was abandoned and the Fed became the lender of last resort.

The major purpose of the Fed was to establish an absolute monopoly over the money supply by monetary policy in a fractional-reserve banking system.[45] Bank notes were

[44]With banking corporations limited in general to one office, branch banking, i.e. expansion, was very restricted in the US. However, in the beginning of the twentieth century, several mitigations of this legislation for the state and national banks prevailed in the US. In 1900, there were 87 banks with a total of 119 branches. In 1915, the number increased to 397 and 785, respectively. The surge stagnated for some time in 1930 at 750 banks and 3,518 branches (Federal Reserve Committee on Branch, Group, and Chain Banking (1930, 1–7)). The 1933 Glass–Steagall Act limited diversification of banks by prohibiting universal banks, i.e. combined commercial and investment banks. The Act was created in the believe that deposit-taking banks could be using their securities businesses 'to underwrite security issues by their low-quality borrowers, and so to ensure that their loans were repaid' (Morrison (2011, 504–5)).

[45]The first step in controlling the money supply was to install the Office of the Comptroller of the Currency (OCC) as part of the National Currency Act of 1863. The American Civil War (1861–1865) triggered this legislation. The ultimate aim of the OCC was to keep the troops paid and provisioned. The banks were legally required to purchase US bonds to back the bank notes that they would then be allowed to issue. If a bank failed, depositors would be reimbursed from profits made from the sale of the bonds. The OCC was designed to monitor and control the soundness and safety of banks on a federal level. However, until the installation of the Fed, banks were still

no longer asset-backed and money supply was not regulated by demand and supply. Although the Fed considers itself to be an independent central bank from its constitution, it has to help promote national economic goals and is thus indirectly controlled by the government. Critics argue that the Fed produced an excessive monetary supply early on, which ultimately led to creating inflated deposits in the banking system. This in turn resulted in the practice of establishing very large banks and to miscalculated incentives for investments.[46] Moreover, the Fed was now effectively able to act as LOLR (see Sect. 2.4) by providing liquidity against good collateral to solvent but illiquid banks.[47]

The Great Depression (1929–1933)

Although the Fed had been in existence for nearly two decades by 1929, it could not address the widespread problems that existed in the banking sector at the time, in other words, it could not prevent bank runs and failures of solvent banks.[48] This can perhaps be explained by the fact that it did not expand the money supply during this period to meet the illiquidity shocks to banks and the declining economic activity. Acting as LOLR, the Fed seemed to have mismanaged this tool and subsequently to have amplified bank failures.[49]

The continuous bank runs and failures paved the way for the creation of the Reconstruction Finance Corporation (RFC) and the Federal Deposit Insurance Corporation (FDIC).

allowed to issue their own asset-backed currency alongside the US tenders (cf. US Department of the Treasury (2011) and Sprague (1988, 18)).

[46]Sennholz (1992, 427).

[47]Barth, Prabha, and Swagel (2012, 267–68). Cf. Friedman and Schwartz (1963).

[48]See Friedman and Schwartz (1963) and Bordo and Landon-Lane (2010) for examples of several bank panics that happened in the US in the early 1930s.

The most prominent was the failure of the Bank of United States (BUS), which did not trigger other bank failures, but was nonetheless considered to have contributed significantly to the economic downswing of the time. On December 11, 1930, during a severe bank run, the bank was closed. It was the largest bank in terms of total assets to fail in the US history to date and the twenty-eighth largest US commercial bank with deposits of US$ 238 million in September 1930. The mitigation of the unit banking system policy allowed banks to grow so large, which in turn contributed to the development of economic recessions (Trescott (1992, 384)).

[49]Sennholz (1992, 427). A likely cause of this was that even the highest Fed officials at the time did not fully understand the connections between bank insolvencies, bank runs, bank funding, etc. Bank failures were generally regarded as consequences of internal bank issues and bad bank management, but not as caused by the ongoing financial and economic crises (Friedman and Schwartz (1963, 358)).

The Establishment of the Reconstruction Finance Corporation (RFC) (1932)
At this time, the Fed was not authorized to provide liquidity against collateral other than genuine bills or treasuries and to lend for longer than fifteen days. This was the birth of the RFC, whose main purpose was 'to make loans to banks and financial institutions which cannot otherwise secure credit where such advances will protect the credit structure and stimulate employment'[50]. When the RFC was created on 22 January 1932, it effectively became the main government bailout agency for banks from 1932 to 1947. In March 1933, the Emergency Banking Act further authorised the RFC to purchase newly issued preferred stock from banks that required capital. This represented the first government bailouts of banks to stem financial and economic turmoil. 'Until 1945, the RFC purchased the preferred stock of 4,202 banks' with 'roughly 9,000 of 25,000 banks that failed during the 1930s'[51]. 'Almost all large banks funded themselves through the RFC'[52], which also indicates the beginning of the TBTF doctrine.

The Establishment of the Federal Deposit Insurance Corporation (FDIC) (1933)
Given that even solvent banks were the target of bank runs and creditors often suffered losses from bank failures, bank deposit insurance (see Sect. 2.4) in the US was increasingly organised on a state-by-state basis. The most important structural change in the banking system at the time was the implementation of a federal deposit insurance, the purpose of which was to lessen the incentive among depositors to make sudden withdrawals—an action that reflected depositors' diminishing confidence in banks as institutions—and ultimately to reduce the probability of bank runs. 'The US was the first country to introduce a national deposit insurance system', 'after decades of debate and largely adverse experiences with moral hazards in state-level schemes'[53]. This change resulted from bank panics that occurred in earlier periods. In June 1933, the FDIC was created under the Banking Act of 1933. The agency guaranteed deposits up to the amount of $2,500.

The federal deposit insurance from 1933 was indeed successful in achieving its main goal of preventing bank runs. Before 1934, frequent banking crises triggered by bank runs were the norm not only in the US, but in all advanced economies. However, it is widely acknowledged that a bank run of the same magnitude has not occurred since the Great Depression—including during the US savings and loan (S&L) crisis of the 1980s and 1990s.[54]

---

[50]Hoover (1952, 98).

[51]Barth, Prabha, and Swagel (2012, 267–68).

[52]Todd (1992).

[53]Demirgüç-Kunt and Kane (2002, 176).

[54]Cf. Cooper and Ross (2002), Diamond and Dybvig (1983, 401), Friedman and Schwartz (1963, 440), and Mishkin (2004, 526).

3.4.3 The First Major Bailouts (1934–1984)

The Evolution of the FDIC's Power for Interventions

The FDIC has evolved over time. At its inception, it was an insurance company that repaid insured deposits in failed banks. The deposit insurance, however, was an incentive to ensure the solvency of insured banks and to prevent their failure. Hence, the FDIC ultimately in effect assumed responsibility for preventing failures by protecting all creditors from loss. Hence, it acted as a substitute for the RFC until it was effectively abolished in 1954.

In 1950, the FDIC was bolstered by the Federal Deposit Insurance Act (FDIA). The scope of the agency's operations was extended to permit it 'to infuse funds into a bank to keep it open'[55]—this type of assistance, called 'open-bank assistance', could be implemented if 'the continued operation of the failed bank was essential to provide adequate banking services in the local community'[56]. This marks the introduction of the so-called 'essentiality doctrine'. The relatively loosely defined essentiality doctrine effectively removed the previous requirement to choose the less costly method of resolution. The FDIA was amended despite Fed opposition, which considered the amendment an infringement on its LOLR function.[57]

Now the FDIC had three basic actions it could take in response to a failing bank:[58]

1. Payout: It could apply the simple resolution method by liquidating a bank. This implies that it could 'appoint a receiver, sell its assets, protect insured deposits by having them assumed at par by another bank, and permit uninsured depositors and other unsecured creditors to share in any losses'.[59] This action terminates the bank's charter.
2. Purchase and assumption:[60] It could arrange the bank's acquisition by a solvent bank, while 'effectively assuming some or all of the bad loans or paying the assuming bank for any loss it incurred'[61], and supporting it with open-bank assistance. This action

[55]Barth, Prabha, and Swagel (2012, 268).

[56]Federal Deposit Insurance Corporation (FDIC) (1998, 742).

[57]Cf. Federal Deposit Insurance Corporation (FDIC) (1984, 81), Federal Deposit Insurance Corporation (FDIC) (23 December 2014, 12), Friedman and Schwartz (1963, 434), Sennholz (1992), Hetzel (1991, 6), Kaufman (2002, 425), Sennholz (1992, 428), and Sprague (1988, 23).

[58]Cf. Sprague (1988, 22).

[59]Kaufman (2002, 423).

[60]The authority was explicitly granted to the FDIC by the Garn–St. Germain Depository Institutions Act of 1982, although it was already heavily in use prior to this year.

[61]Kaufman (2002, 425).

also terminates the bank's charter, but transfers some of the bank's assets and other liabilities to a successor charter.

3. Bailout: It could prevent the bank from failing by declaring the bank essential and providing comprehensive open-bank assistance. This action keeps the bank's charter intact.

Figure 3.1 shows the development of FDIC-insured bank failures in the US in the period 1934–2016, including which of the three actions listed above was taken.

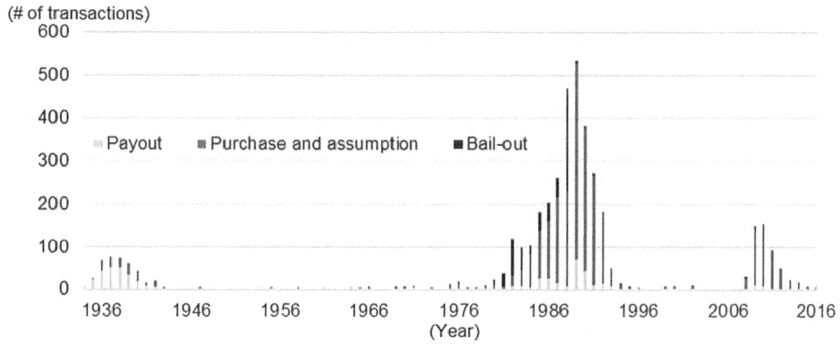

Fig. 3.1 Method Used by FDIC for Failing Banks in the US (1934–2016). (Source: FDIC)

Increasing Safety Nets for Banks

From its beginning, on January 1, 1934 until April 3, 1986, FDIC assisted 908 failed or failing banks.[62] In this time, the FDIC protected almost all affected creditors—also to the benefit of the shareholders. The FDIC 'protected both insured and uninsured depositors, guaranteed bank debt, insured risky assets, provided liquidity for exceptionally long periods and against collateral of depressed value, and injected public capital to the benefit of shareholders of banks that would otherwise have failed'.[63]

While, in its early years, the FDIC most commonly simply paid out insured deposits, its primary modus operandi gradually changed to purchase and assumption.[64] Starting in

[62]Sprague (1988, 8).

[63]Barth, Prabha, and Swagel (2012, 266). Cf. Sprague (1988, 242).

[64]One of the largest banks resolved by purchase and assumption was the Franklin National Bank (New York) in 1974. It was a regional bank, but with an international presence and ownership, and the twentieth largest bank in the US (Kaufman (2002, 425)).

1970, the FDIC declared four commercial banks essential and saved them by providing long-term assistance, in other words, by bailing them out.[65]

Unrestricted Growth

Several factors might have facilitated the immense growth and size of banks during the period of FDIC coverage. First, the McFadden Act of 1927 effectively restricted the size of banks until mid-1970s. During this period, average bank sizes in the US roughly increased in line with the nominal GDP. The act was partly born out of the motivation to protect the competition between smaller and larger banks and to avoid dangerous concentration within the industry. The Garn–St. Germain Act of 1982 and the Riegle-Neal Act of 1994 subsequently removed restrictions on bank size. The banking industry lobby successful argued that restrictions led to high private costs that exceeded social benefits. As restrictions fell, average bank sizes rapidly increased by multiples.[66]

Second, at the beginning of the 19th century, shareholders were generally fully liable for their banks and, on average, up to half of a bank's funding consisted of equity. To remove the risk of personal bankruptcy among bank owners, which frequently happened, and to increase the supply of credit, owners' liability beyond the paid-in equity capital was gradually abolished. The asymmetric payoff schedule of shareholders incentivised the rise in the volatility of the bank's assets.[67] In combination with the privilege of tax-deductibility of debt financing, it facilitated banks' leverage build-up. Due to the deposit insurance, high leverage was not prevented by soaring risk premiums for the deposits and effectively suspended the theorem of Modigliani–Miller that the overall cost of capital stays the same regardless of the leverage.

Altogether, this fragile construct enabled strong growth of the overall economy for many decades, to a degree at the cost and to the benefit of the public, but primarily to the benefit of shorter-term investors and bank management.[68]

The Bailout of Continental Illinois National Bank and Trust Company (1984)

As different authors identify different reasons for the development of the TBTF doctrine, they also identify different bailouts as the first precedents of G-SIBs. Nevertheless, the majority of academic studies agree that the bailout of the Continental Illinois National

---

[65]Sprague (1988, 4). The first three bank bailouts were: (i) Unity Bank (Boston) in 1971, (ii) Bank of the Commonwealth (Detroit) in 1972, and (iii) First Pennsylvania Bank in 1980. The FDIC justified the first two bailouts based on the uniqueness of the banks, while the bailout of First Pennsylvania Bank, the 23rd largest bank at the time, was justified mainly on the basis of bank's size (cf. Federal Deposit Insurance Corporation (FDIC) (1984, 94–95), Barth, Prabha, and Swagel (2012, 267–68), Kaufman (2002, 425), Sennholz (1992, 426), Hetzel (1991, 6), and Sprague (1988)).

[66]A. G. Haldane (30 March 2010).

[67]Merton (1974).

[68]Haldane (2012).

Bank and Trust Company represents a key turning point of the TBTF doctrine.[69] The reasons for this are fourfold:

1. The US$ 4.5 billion bailout of the Continental Illinois[70] was much larger than all previous bailouts. The bank was the seventh largest bank in the US and heavily interconnected with thousands of other US banks via interbank deposits. The regulators were unprepared for a threatening failure of this magnitude[71] and they decided to protect all creditors against loss. In addition, shareholders were not expropriated, at least not initially.[72]
2. The case had attracted the interest of the general public and, for the first time, government officials had to testify in front of a commission.[73]
3. It marked the birth of the easily comprehensible term 'TBTF', the genesis of which is widely attributed to the hearings before the House of Representatives and to the words of Congressman Stewart McKinney who described the bank as 'a new class of bank in the United States of America, a TBTF—too big to fail'.[74]
4. This was the first public acknowledgement of the TBTF doctrine. On September 19, 1984, during the testimony of C. Todd Conover, the Comptroller of the Currency of the US Treasury at the time, Fernand St. Germain, the chairman of the committee concluded: 'The fact of the matter is, as a practical matter, neither you nor your successors are ever going to let a big bank the size of Continental Illinois fail.'[75] On September 20, 1984, the 11 largest banks that were considered also classified TBTF during the hearing were listed in an article in the Wall Street Journal.[76]

---

[69]This case is analysed in detail by, for example, Federal Deposit Insurance Corporation (FDIC) (1997), Kaufman (2002), and Swary (1986); among others, these studies shed light on the market reactions, the shareholder compensation, and the costs accrued for the taxpayers.

[70]Stern and Feldman (2009b).

[71]Sprague (1988, 10): 'what were the real reasons for doing the [...] bailouts? Simply put, we were afraid not to.'

[72]Kaufman (2002, 423).

[73]Apart from the sheer size of the bailout, the respective decision attracted attention due to the fairness of treatment by the FDIC. 'To give large depositors an incentive to monitor and discipline their banks once again and reduce the costs of failure, the FDIC experimented in 1983–1984 with allowing banks to fail and not protecting uninsured depositors' (Kaufman (2002, 426)).

[74]Committee on Banking, Finance and Urban Affairs (18–19 September and 4 October 1984, 89).

[75]Committee on Banking, Finance and Urban Affairs (18–19 September and 4 October 1984, 300).

[76]Carrington (20 September 1984).

3.4.4 The First Regulatory Efforts to Restrict Bailouts (1985–1998)

Growing International Linkages and Systemic Complexity

In 1974, financial market turmoil followed the breakdown of the Bretton Woods system of managed exchange rates which had supported almost three decades of monetary stability. Many banks suffered large losses from foreign currency trades. As a consequence, two large international banks, Bankhaus Herstatt in West Germany in June of the same year and Long Island's Franklin National Bank in the US in October, became insolvent. The liquidation processes were intricate and the failures in turn triggered further losses for banks worldwide from unsettled trades with the respective counterparties. This incident showed (i) how interconnected banks had become on an international level and (ii) that even with proper domestic bank regulation, cross-border activities lacked supervision. Although not directly linked to the TBTF doctrine, this was one of the first major indicators of growing international linkages and systemic complexity.

In the early 1980s, the Latin American debt crisis forced governments to back their key international banks such as Citicorp. These actions further heightened concerns that the capital levels of very large banks were insufficient at the time.[77]

Introduction of the Basel Accords (Since 1988)

By the end of 1974, against the backdrop of the disruption in the international financial system, the Basel Committee on Banking Supervision (BCBS) was established under the sponsorship of the Bank for International Settlements (BIS) by the Group of 10 countries (G-10). Their aim was to establish a global regulatory framework that would strengthen the stability of the international financial markets. It was not until July 1988 that the first substantial agreement known as the Basel Accord or Basel I was reached. It was legally enforced in the G-10 countries in 1992 and more than 100 other countries later adopted the agreement.

The BCBS was particularly engaged with setting standards for large and diversified financial conglomerates. Hence, the focus soon became capital adequacy and the 'weighted approach to the measurement of risk, both on and off banks' balance sheets'[78].[79] If anything, the substantial increase of capital at large banks that resulted from the requirements imposed by Basel I reduced the TBTF problem. By holding more capital, a bank was provided with a thicker cushion against unexpected losses. Research suggests, however, that Basel I encouraged regulatory capital arbitrage techniques, such as securitisation, and that it, subsequently, in fact, further increased risk-taking.[80]

[77]Basel Committee on Banking Supervision (BCBS) (October 2015, 2).

[78]Basel Committee on Banking Supervision (BCBS) (October 2015, 2).

[79]Basel I required a minimum capital ratio of capital to risk-weighted assets of 8 percent for international banks. Assets of banks were classified and grouped into five categories according to credit risk, carrying risk weights between 0 and 100 percent (cf. Basel Committee on Banking Supervision (BCBS) (October 2015, 1–2) and Jablecki (2009, 16–18)).

[80]Cf. Mishkin (2006, 996), Jablecki (2009, 16), and Blundell-Wignall and Atkinson (2010).

Massive Bank Failures During the S&L Crises

A steep incline of bank failures occurred between 1980 and 1992 (see Fig. 3.1), as a result mainly of excessive risk-taking[81] and deregulation[82] of the previous years. The S&L institutions were affected in particular and about 40 percent of them failed, which is why this period is commonly referred to as the S&L crisis.

The FDIC suffered substantial outflows from its fund to pay off insured deposits, including those above US$ 100,000.[83] This was the first time that the Fed supported the banking system and consequently the entire economy by significantly reducing the Fed Funds Rate.[84]

The FDIC Improvement Act (FDICIA) (1991)

In December 1991, following the large losses incurred by the FDIC and the taxpayers during the S&L crisis, the FDIC Improvement Act (FDICIA) was enacted. Its two main purposes were (i) to reduce the incentive problems of the deposit insurance and (ii) to eliminate the TBTF doctrine. The main introduced amendments were:[85]

---

[81]The emergence of information and communication technology in the 1960s marked the foundation of non-bank financial institutions, such as money market funds, as well as innovative financial products, such as swaps and futures. They represented a growing competition for banks in their traditional businesses and gradually stole market share. This in turn meant a fall in banks' profitability (cf. Federal Deposit Insurance Corporation (FDIC) (1997)). In the mid-1980s, banks were increasingly searching for higher yielding assets to compensate for the emerged situation. Banks invested in much riskier businesses than before, such as leveraged loans for real estate and M&A transactions. The safety net established by the FDIC probably worsened the situation rather than helped preventing it. Financial innovations helped further lift the risk-return profile of the banks' balance sheets. Since deposit insurance premiums for banks were independent from the inherent bank risk, there was a strong incentive to do so.

[82]Due to the belief that the banking system was safe and the good experiences of the past 50 years, the government provided assistance in this regard with several initiatives: First, the Depository Institutions Deregulation and Monetary Act of 1980 increased the insured amount of deposits from US$ 40,000 to US$ 100,000 and phased out Regulation Q, which capped deposit rates. This effectively triggered a struggle for deposits to fund the fast balance sheet growth in order to maintain profitability (cf. Allen and Gale (2004)). Second, the deregulation of the savings & loan (S&L) institutions in 1980 and 1982 enabled the institutions to invest in the same risky asset classes as commercial banks. In the following years, the lack of competence in assessing risks associated with these investments was evident on the regulatory side and the bank management side.

[83]Until the Federal Savings and Loan Insurance Corporation (FSLIC) declared insolvency in 1989, deposits to S&L institutions were insured here, with the government assuming the remaining losses to insured depositors. In late 1993, the FDIC ultimately took over the deposit insurance for the S&L institutions.

[84]Cf. Hetzel (1991, 4), Mishkin (2004, 526–27), Shachmurove (2011, 224–25), and Kaufman (1994, vii).

[85]Cf. Mishkin (2004, 527–28), Angbazo and Saunders (1996, 4, 27), Barth, Prabha, and Swagel (2012, 270), Kaufman (2015, 2), and Strahan (2013, 48–49).

- Risk-based and burden-sharing deposit insurance premiums: Risk-based premiums were invented to reduce the moral hazard problem caused by flat-rate insurance. This instrument, however, was not effective because it was poorly implemented and most banks had to pay an equal amount in relative terms. Additionally, the FDIC was required to claw back fund outflows from bailouts with the help of high premiums whenever the reserve-to-insured deposits ratio fell below the threshold of 1.25 percent.[86]
- Limits on interbank credit exposure: The new 'Regulation F' was developed out of the FDICIA, which restricted a bank's total exposure to a counterparty to 25 percent of the bank's capital, the exception being when the counterparty is 'at least adequately capitalized'. However, this generous regulation failed to reduce interbank exposure.[87]
- Capital requirements: Capitalization levels became the subject of much closer attention. First, FDICIA required federal banking regulators to take 'prompt corrective action' when a bank's equity decline to less than 2 percent of its on-balance sheet assets. This trigger was installed to identify and address capital deficiencies and to minimize potential FDIC losses. The provisions required immediate recapitalization, restrictions on deposit gathering, and prompt closure of continuously undercapitalised banks. Second, the FDICIA placed new limitations on Fed loans to undercapitalized banks.
- Resolution procedure: With the previously facilitated 'lower-than-liquidation method', the FDIC was relatively unrestricting in finding a resolution method. The FDICIA imposed on the agency the choice of the 'least costly option'. The computation procedure for estimating the present value basis when resolving a failing bank was now explicitly defined.[88] The act required also an ex-post review of any failure causing significant losses to the FDIC.

Although the final legislation was watered down and some parts proved insufficient, as discussed above, the general opinion was that it achieved its goals by and large—at least in the years directly after its enactment. It is believed that the banking industry became financially healthier and that the legislation positively changed the behaviour of the regulators. While 'the FDIC imposed losses on uninsured depositors in costly resolutions in only 17 percent of all failed banks' in 1991, the numbers grew to 54 percent and 88 percent in 1992 and 1993 respectively. The investors pressured banks to improve capitalisation and 'banks raised record amounts of new capital in 1992 and 1993 and their capital ratios climbed to the highest levels since the 1960s'.[89]

[86]Kaufman (2002, 428).

[87]Jordan (2014, 454) and Wall (2010, 9).

[88]Kaufman (2002, 427).

[89]Kaufman (1995, 722).

Systemic Risk Replaces Bank Size

In 1993, another amendment followed: The Resolution Trust Corporation (RTC) Completion Act specifically prohibited the FDIC from protecting shareholders during a bailout.[90] Furthermore, the 'systemic risk exemption' replaced the previous exemption known as the 'essentiality condition', i.e. it was finally recognized that systemic relevance is a much better indicator of risk than bank size by itself. The 'systemic risk exemption' became more relevant than the choice of the 'least costly option' if a failure would cause 'serious adverse effects on economic conditions and financial stability'. The hurdles were just a bit higher and a bailout became a much more visible political process as it now required a joint decision to be made by the FDIC, Fed, and the Treasury Secretary in consultation with the President. Nevertheless, this was an indirect admission that the TBTF doctrine still survived and that the credibility problem could not simply be legislated away. Studies indeed prove 'that the systematic risk estimate for large banks declined'[91] after implementation.[92]

Amendment of the Basel Accords (2004)

Regulatory capital arbitrage techniques and financial innovations established after the introduction of the Basel Accords in 1988 were to be tackled by the revised capital framework, which was released in June 2004. The revision was prolonged considerably as there was no crisis that made a regulatory response imminent. The new framework, dubbed Basel II, extends beyond capital requirements, but still focuses on the underlying credit risks.[93]

---

[90]Kaufman (2002, 427).

[91]Angbazo and Saunders (1996, 27).

[92]Akhigbe and Whyte (2001, 393). Cf. Angbazo and Saunders (1996, 4–5), Benston and Kaufman (1997, 156), and Kaufman (1995, 722). The near failure of the hedge fund Long-Term Capital Management (LTCM) in 1998 is often mentioned in the context of systemic risk and TBTF. While not a genuine bank, this large financial entity, which was highly interconnected with financial institutions, collapsed following massive losses resulting from Russian debt crisis. While LTCM was not bailed out directly by the Fed, regulators forced the banks, that were LTCM creditors, to do so in order to avoid a messy liquidation of the hedge fund. This incident appears to have again strengthened the TBTF doctrine, nullifying some of the positive effects of FDICIA. Following this incident, large banks that were not creditors to LTCM experienced a decline in rates for unsecured funding, which is yet another sign of a strengthening TBTF doctrine. This case illustrated that TBTF is about the feared contagion effects and less about the failure of a bank (cf. Furfine (2006, 593), Strahan (2013, 49), Shachmurove (2011, 224–25), and Johnson and Mamun (2012, 376)).

[93]In addition to the fixed minimum capital requirements of Basel I, the framework comprises two additional pillars: Pillar 2 requires banks to monitor risk and calculate capital adequacy with an internal assessment process, which is then reviewed by the regulatory supervisor. Pillar 3 enables market participants to assess the soundness of a banks risk and capital by extending disclosure requirements (cf. Basel Committee on Banking Supervision (BCBS) (October 2015, 3)).

The US postponed Basel II adoption until 2008 and instituted a longer transition period, while in other countries implementation was phased in from the end of 2006 until the end of 2007. This

3.4.5 TBTF Grows Up (1999–2009)

The Rise of Global Systemic Risks

The late '1990s and early 2000s were generally characterized by high profits for the financial services industry'[94] driven by a strong economy, technological change, and financial innovation.[95] As a result, no case of bank failure occurred that could test TBTF theory for many years. Hence, after the S&L crisis and some regulatory efforts, a new wave of deregulation again followed in the US. The breeding ground of TBTF—a large and complex banking system with deposit insurance and extended authorities of the LOLR—was now the norm across the globe and incentivised banks for further growth accordingly.[96]

All categories of potential sources of systemic importance of banks (see Sect. 3.3) we know of today had been worsened in the time before 2007 on a global scale:

- Increasing linkages: Financial globalization is most apparent based on observations of how direct international interbank relationships gradually increased in the years leading up to 2007.[97] Moreover, financial markets and banks also grew increasingly interconnected.[98] The rapid growth of investment banking activities resulted in deep interconnections among banks with capital markets, not only with regard to funding. Banks facilitated financial markets to hedge their risks and open up new sources of refinancing, such as the 'originate-to-distribute' securitisation model.[99]
- Increasing size: The impulse for banks to grow was particularly apparent during this period. Not only did high profitability help banks to increase their balance sheets, but also increased leverage facilitated by cheap and easy access to international funding. Banks additionally widened the scope outside of traditional bank lending, for instance to insurance and market-based activities. They formed increasingly large universal banks,[100] '[t]hus possibly expanding the government safety net to nonbank activities

difference is often interpreted as providing competitive advantage to internationally operating US banks (Demirgüç-Kunt, Detragiache, and Merrouche (2013, 1150)).

94Strahan (2013, 49).

95Stiroh (2000).

96Cf. Demirgüç-Kunt and Kane (2002) and Mishkin (2006, 989).

97McGuire and von Peter (2009) and Fender and McGuire (2010).

98Song and Thakor (2010) and Stern and Feldman (2009b, 68).

99van Rixtel and Gasperini (2013).

100In the US this was partly possible due to the Gramm–Leach–Bliley Financial Services Modernization Act of 1999, which repealed large portions of the Glass–Steagall Act.

of these financial conglomerates.'[101] M&A activities helped to create a number of new megabanks.[102] This consolidation was not unwanted by the political powers. They attempted to have a national champion in the now increasingly global competition and a megabank that is able to absorb other failing banks during crises. 'At the end of 2008, 30 publicly listed banks worldwide held liabilities exceeding half of their country's GDP' and 'twelve of these had total liabilities exceeding one trillion dollars'[103].[104]

- Increasing concentration and decreasing substitutability: Not only did the increasing size result in greater concentration, but the advances in information technology also made it possible that even smaller players were now increasingly difficult to replace. This development was especially noticeable in payment services.[105]
- Increasing complexity: Banks grew significantly more complex, in particular in regard to their corporate structure,[106] as evidenced by a sharp increase in the majority-owned subsidiaries of the largest banks, mainly driven by their M&A transactions.[107]
- Increasing liquidity risk: The massive diversification of funding via interbank and capital markets (including repo markets) increased the banks' liquidity risks and made them more vulnerable to liquidity shortages. Both funding sources are generally short-term (often overnight) and less sticky than traditional retail deposit funding.[108]

The US Financial Crises (2007–2009)

The financial turmoil of 2007 had its origins in the US regional housing and mortgage market[109] and was the most severe financial crisis in the US since the Great Depression. The above-subsumed criteria of significantly increased systemic risk facilitated the pace of the spread and the global scope of the crisis. In the US, the crisis was marked by the following major events:

- First major bank failure: On September 15, 2008, Lehman Brothers filed for bankruptcy under Chapter 11, due to heavy asset devaluations and mounting funding

---

[101]Mishkin (2006, 996). Boyd, Graham, and Hewitt (1993) find that mergers of banks with insurance firms may reduce risk, but mergers of banks with securities firms or real estate firms would likely increase risk.

[102]Cf. Mishkin (2006, 994) and Weiß, Neumann, and Bostandzic (2014).

[103]Demirgüç-Kunt and Huizinga (2013, 875).

[104]See also Gandhi and Lustig (2015) for their findings regarding the cost of capital distortions that possibly 'contributed to the pre-crisis growth in the size of the financial sector relative to the overall economy'.

[105]Cf. Mishkin (2006, 994).

[106]Mishkin (2006, 994).

[107]Cf. Carmassi and Herring (2013).

[108]Stern and Feldman (2009b, 70) and Mishkin (2006, 994).

[109]See Laeven and Valencia (2013a, 233) for a synopsis.

problems. The banking sector had grown extremely fragile the previous year following the open-bank assistance to Bear Stearns.[110] Regulators were unwilling to bail out the investment bank after Barclays and Bank of America ultimately declined to acquire it with the assistance of the Fed. The regulators underestimated the aftermath of the insolvency. Lehman was not the largest bank but it was one of the most interconnected and complex investment banks in the world. This situation with expected large losses for all kind of uninsured creditors came as a surprise to investors. It had a major impact with chaotic conditions on the money and interbank funding markets. In hindsight, although the losses were manageable, due the complexity of the situation it would take a decade to resolve it.[111]

- First 'systemic risk exception': The unexpected but legally imposed losses on Washington Mutual's[112] creditors as well as the decision to let Lehman Brothers go bankrupt led to surging funding problems at banks with perceived similar levels of risk, such as Wachovia. On the weekend of September 27–28, 2008, in order to avoid the same fire sale-like situation at Wachovia, the FDIC decided to facilitate the 'systemic risk exception' of the FDICIA. This had not been invoked since the enactment in 1991. Hence, it was the first ever use and triggered what would become a massive government assistance to convince financial markets that the government would not allow another major bank to fail.
- Capitulation for TBTF: On October 3, 2008, as a response to the very recent bank failures, which quickly caused high volatility or even dry-up of all kind of financial markets, the Troubled Asset Relief Program (TARP) connected to the Emergency Economic Stabilization Act (EESA) was enacted in the US. The TARP initially enabled the US Treasury to purchase and insure distressed assets valued up to US$ 700 billion. Ultimately, TARP was mainly used to inject capital into banks.[113] This

---

[110]In March 2008, the Fed and the US Treasury negotiated an acquisition of Bear Stearns by J.P. Morgan. In order to facilitate the transaction, the Fed agreed partly to provide a guarantee for the purchased assets. Other large investment banks like Morgan Stanley and Lehman Brothers had assets on their balance sheets which were similar to Bear Stearns and they were also heavily dependent on short-term interbank markets. The regulators feared that the failure of Bear Stearns could spill over to these competitors and that the failures would, consequently, become impossible to handle.

[111]Strahan and Tanyeri (2015), Kacperczyk and Schnabl (2010), and Brunnermeier and Pedersen (2009).

[112]On September 25, 2008, due to a heavy bank run following the Lehman Brothers bankruptcy, the FDIC was willing to place Washington Mutual Bank into receivership. The bank was perceived as one with the highest risks of failure. The assets were subsequently sold to J.P. Morgan, but uninsured creditors suffered significant losses in line with the FDICIA.

[113]Barth, Prabha, and Swagel (2012, 270–71). Eventually, '707 banks received capital injections from the government, amounting to US$ 245 billion. [...] Fannie Mae and Freddie Mac received government capital injections amounting to US$ 180.4 billion as of early 2012 under the Housing and Economic Recovery Act of 2008 (HERA). The fact that 89 percent of the TARP's capital purchase program funds went to 32 big banks, while the other 11 percent went to the 675 smaller

massive government intervention reduced market turmoil. Additionally, the statutory maximum on insured deposits was increased to US$ 250,000, while '100% of money market mutual funds and transactions deposits were guaranteed, and all bank liabilities were guaranteed on a temporary basis'.[114]

Global Dimension of the Financial Crisis (2007–2009)

The crisis that originated in the US rapidly developed into a global financial crisis (GFC). Considering that banks in the western world now had similar asset and funding characteristics and that balance sheets were increasingly less influenced by regional factors, TBTF was no longer restricted to the US alone. Governments across the globe extended extensive liquidity support and guarantees to all banks, regardless of their size, similarly but more quickly to previous crises.[115] Banking systems in several countries completely collapsed in 2008 as a result, due to the 'burden of public debt and the size of fiscal contingent liabilities'.[116] Iceland serves as the prime example where the size of the banking system in terms of overall liabilities was approximately nine times as large as the country's GDP, according to the figures from the end of 2007.[117]

3.4.6 TBTF Lessons Learnt

Regulatory efforts as the driving forces of TBTF

The regulatory system for banks in the US and worldwide was created piecemeal through over a century of lawmaking.[118] Each peace followed an economic crisis serious enough to muster the support for enactment.[119] This was the case with deposit insurance and the LOLR as well. Both were implemented separately after crisis experiences with the purpose of stabilising the banking system. In hindsight, both met their original objectives. However, a change occurred when the deposit insurance was handled by an institution that also had the authority to intervene with failing banks short-term (LOLR) and subsequently also longer-term (open-bank assistance). The federal government had a natural incentive to keep banks alive to limit the losses from insured events.

institutions, again focused substantial attention on the TBTF issue.' (Barth, Prabha, and Swagel (2012, 270–71)).

[114]Strahan (2013, 49).

[115]Laeven and Valencia (2013a, 232). Molyneux, Schaeck, and Mi Zhou (2014) introduces a list of banks rescued in EU countries between October 2008 and June 2009.

[116]Laeven and Valencia (2013a, 232).

[117]Demirgüç-Kunt and Huizinga (2013, 875).

[118]Sprague (1988, 17).

[119]Sprague (1988, 18).

Now large banks were bailed out, while smaller ones were not. This practice created clear incentives in the banking market and changed the banking system. Large banks, as a consequence, tended to become insolvent more often than before the federal deposit insurance.[120] Moreover, the increased size and complexity of the banks, driven by deregulation and regulatory incentives, complicated their timely resolution.[121] A bank failure put the stability of the banking system at risk. Consequently, the criteria for receiving bank assistance were increasingly loosened and the scope was extended—a vicious circle. Hence, TBTF became gradually 'embedded in banking regulation through the precedent of saving one troubled bank at a time, rather than being a result of a conscious decision'.[122] That means each of the regulatory events can be interpreted as a swing of the pendulum that triggered successive events.[123] Ultimately, the regulatory efforts exerted on each other and resulted in the TBTF doctrine.[124]

The regulation of TBTF

As the saying goes, history repeats itself. Most efforts to restrict TBTF were mitigated after a period of economic prosperity when the TBTF problem was almost forgotten. The Lehman case illustrates how systemically relevant many international banks have become and how quickly a dry-up of the wholesale liquidity markets can lead to catastrophic events. The fact that the largest banks, in particular, were forced to accept capital injections and that the majority of funds went to the largest banks underscore the dangers of the TBTF doctrine. Events needed to escalate before academics (see Chap. 6) and regulators (see Chap. 7) were again convinced of the existence of TBTF and began developing new concepts to regulate the TBTF doctrine. This promoted not only domestic regulatory efforts in the EU (see Sect. 7.1) and the US (see Sect. 7.2) and a further amendment of the Basel Accords (see Sect. 7.3), but also initial globally coordinated regulatory efforts by the newly established Financial Stability Board (FSB) (see Sect. 7.4).

---

[120]Kaufman (2002, 425).

[121]Cf. Ennis and Malek (2005, 22).

[122]Hetzel (1991, 6).

[123]Bordo (2003, 160).

[124]Sprague (1988, 49): "The important precedent was, of course, the irreversible turn we had taken with Unity, away from our historic narrow role of acting only after the bank had failed. […] Now we were in the bailout business, how deeply no one could then tell."

4 TBTF Causal Chain: Explicit and Implicit Government Guarantees

The history of TBTF (see Sect. 3.4) illustrates how governments, due to conflicting goals and responsibilities such as providing deposit insurance and resolving banks, can unintentionally manoeuvre themselves into providing safety nets to banks. Banks are naturally incentivised to grow to exploit these public subsidies and increase the chances of benefitting from a government safety net. Once banks grow large and complex enough to be considered TBTF, a cascade of mechanisms of disincentives results that can hardly be corrected. This section reviews theoretical and empirical research into this causal chain or even vicious circle of TBTF to highlight related moral hazards in the banking system. Figure 4.1 presents a graphical and stylised form of the TBTF doctrine circle.

There are two natural causes of G-SIBs: explicit government guarantees (EGG) and implicit government guarantees (IGG). Section 4.1 explains the motivation, scope and methods of EGG, including how debt- and shareholders are affected by a public bailout. Section 4.2 explains the origin and strength of IGG, which derive from expected EGG. It also discusses how IGGs create disincentives for the various stakeholders of a bank: i.e., the creditors, the bank management, and the shareholders. Overall, research identifies inherently consistent mechanisms of creditor and bank moral hazards that ultimately increases the probability of future crises and EGG.[1] However, there is less clarity around how various distortions, including additional TBTF regulations, create potential shareholder moral hazard. To fill this research gap, this phenomenon is analysed empirically in Pt. II. Superficially, the illustration appears to present a chronology of events and causes, but in reality precise distinctions are impossible because the effects interact cyclically.

[1] Hoggarth, Jackson, and Nier (2005).

T. F. Lesche, *Too-Big-to-Fail in Banking*, Finanzwirtschaft, Banken und Bankmanagement I Finance, Banks and Bank Management, https://doi.org/10.1007/978-3-658-34182-4_4

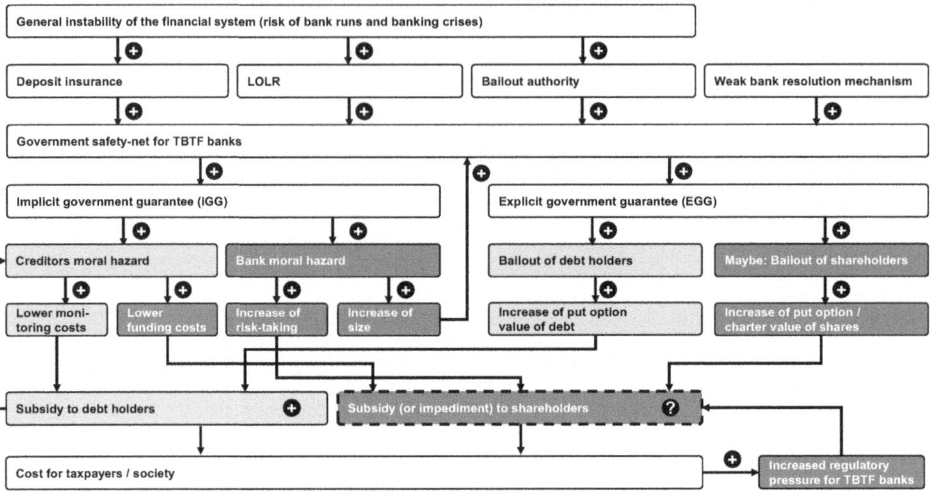

Fig. 4.1 Graphical Illustration of TBTF Causal Chain

4.1 Explicit Government Guarantees (EGGs) (Bailout)

To influence economic growth and stability, the government has, in general, two intervention tools: (i) monetary policy, which is primarily concerned with money supply and is generally carried out indirectly by central banks; and (ii) fiscal policy, which is primarily concerned with taxation and spending actions and is generally carried out directly by the government itself.

This dissertation is limited by design to the fiscal side of interventions—more precisely, to the direct bailout of banks to prevent their bankruptcy and liquidation. This section describes in detail the different dimensions of an EGG: that is, why governments bail out banks (see Sect. 4.1.1), who is guaranteed (see Sect. 4.1.2), how is it executed (see Sect. 4.1.3), and how the various stakeholders are affected.

4.1.1 EGG Motivation

When extending EGGs to banks, policymakers, including regulators, weigh the expected total costs and benefits of the measure compared to the bankruptcy costs (see Chap. 5). At the time of a failure, the benefits of EGGs tend to be overestimated and the costs underestimated. This phenomenon, called time-inconsistency (see Sect. 5.4), tends to be more pronounced the larger the crisis is.[2] G-SIBs often invoke fear to demand the

[2]Kaufman (2015, 5).

privilege and increase the probability of receiving EGG.[3] Policymakers might act as agents on behalf of the public, a fraction of the public, certain governmental institutions, or just themselves. Ideally, from a social-cost point of view, policymakers act on behalf of the group of people who provide the money they use for the bailout: namely, the taxpayers or public.

In considering EGG, policymakers may consider the following non-exclusive and interconnected motivations:

1. Economic stability: The reason most often given is to safeguard the country's economic growth and stability, which is considered greatly dependent on a well-functioning financial system (see Sect. 2.1). Hence, the systemic potential of a bank to disrupt the whole financial system is the subordinated objective in this context (see Sect. 3.3).
2. Direct credit allocation: This motivation might be present in developing countries where the government intervenes in the credit allocation. These banks are either directly government owned or operated, or they are indirectly government controlled. Banking regulation by those countries might function to force banks to give loans to targeted borrowers. By bailing out banks, policymakers intend to retain their power of directing credit rather than admit that banks go bankrupt because of the bad loans they were forced to originate.[4]
3. Competition between legislators: Since not all banks within a country serve the same regions or markets, a variety of legislators might protect their re-maintenance. These guardians may want to ensure that banks in their sphere of influence receive the same benefits as other banks, which automatically results in competition for TBTF support.[5] Furthermore, legislators could feel more responsible towards their own constituency, e.g., by saving jobs locally by a bailout and by neglecting the overall public.
4. Short-term votes: Under this perspective of the political economy, policymakers are primarily oriented towards gaining popularity among voters in order to get (re-) elected.[6] This means, they are aligned with the taxpayers' interests, however only on a very short-terms basis. Voters can also relate to a variety of bank stakeholders, such as depositors, borrowers, or employees.
5. Save deposit insurance funds: This is the crucial case when deposit insurance and bailout authority are united in the same hands of policymaker. The incentives might contradict each other, and a policymaker could encourage a bailout to avoid having to

[3]Moosa (2010, 319).

[4]See Stern and Feldman (2009b, 56–57).

[5]See Kaufman (2015, 4).

[6]Cf. Kaufman (2015, 5).

justify an outflow of deposit insurance funds or when the statutory deposit guarantee scheme is insufficient to protect depositors.[7]

6. Personal welfare: The policymaker might act to his own benefit, i.e., like a free agent.[8] He might advance his career to maximise his personal gain[9] or react to public pressure he is unable to resist. This is truer for policymakers than career regulators, who are more independent and do not need to be re-elected.[10] The public has a limited ability to assess the decisions of legislators and may judge externally visible outcomes. Thus, an absence of crisis or bank failure might be interpreted as a positive outcome and offers personal and bureaucratic rewards.[11] Furthermore, the "quiet-life" or hubris hypothesis may motivate the behaviour of avoiding potential litigation from bondholders in case of a bail-in instead of a bailout.[12]

Subsequently, for the sake of simplified reasoning, it is assumed that the policymaker's sole objective is to safeguard economic stability.

4.1.2 EGG Scope

There are no fixed criteria for a bank bailout. If a government's objective is to safeguard economic stability and avoid disruption of the financial system, it will aim to keep the bank's business operations alive. In a market economy, the government does not intend to nationalise a bank long-term; it will therefore try to avoid a situation in which a bank depends completely on direct government funding. Hence, it is crucial that the bank have continued access to various funding markets to continue its operations, such as lending to the real economy. Unhindered access to funding sources is conditional upon the trust of the bank's creditors. To be precise, it is conditioned upon the trust that they will neither cause a credit loss[13] nor a liquidity loss[14]. The government achieves this trust by guaranteeing prompt repayment of a bank's uninsured liabilities through certain bailout

[7]Most notable is the case of the FDIC, which during some period was responsible for both deposit insurance and deciding on public bailouts (see Sect. 3.4.2).

[8]Niskanen (1994).

[9]See Stern and Feldman (2009b, 44).

[10]See Mishkin (2006, 993).

[11]Kane (2001, 281).

[12]The use of opportunistic forbearance methods (see Sect. 4.1.3) for the bailout is connected with this motivation.

[13]Credit loss is defined as the legally entitled share of the insolvent bank's realised recovery value minus the repayment value under no bank distress (i.e., the value at par) (Kaufman (2014, 216)).

[14]Liquidity loss is defined as delays in the receipt of the proceeds of realised recovery amounts. This delay can be caused by the attempt to avoid larger fire-sale losses or by the legal prohibition of withdrawals over a certain period (Kaufman (2014, 216–17)).

methods (see Sect. 4.1.3). The policymaker's discretionary decision concerning which classes of liabilities to protect (such as deposits and debt issuances) and which not to protect[15] may depend on the expectation of how potential losses born on certain holders of these liabilities (or bank counterparties) will result in economic damage.[16] Generally, policymakers, however, have not quantified these public costs and benefits rigorously during past bank bailouts, but rather using subjective broad generalizations.[17]

The scope of protection, which equals the strength of TBTF policy, is illustrated in Table 4.1.[18] The columns represent simplified and stylised items of a bank's liabilities. From left to right, they range from insured deposits, over uninsured short-term and long-term deposits and debt, to shareholdings. This means they are shown in order of their legal liquidation priority; that is, the creditors are entitled to the value of the bank's assets based on where they appear in this hierarchy from left to right. For example, short-term debt holders are entitled to a pay-out only after all long-term depositors are paid out. In practise, however, this order is not necessarily the allocation mechanism in a bailout. Furthermore, there is a fluent passage between the debt and equity instruments of a bank. So-called hybrid instruments are not clearly identifiable as debt or equity instruments.

The strength of TBTF depends on the protection, which is measured from 0 to 13 in the column on the very left. The dots represent the protection of the respective liability. If only insured depositors are protected from credit loss, the strength rating is 0 or 0 percent, because deposit insurance covers such losses. If all creditors, i.e., all deposits and debt classes, as well as shareholders protected, the TBTF strength is 13 or 100 percent. The more accounts partially or fully protected against more types of loss, i.e., credit or liquidity loss, the stronger the TBTF regime.[19]

In practise, coverage tends to be fairly comprehensive for deposits and less so for other debt instruments:[20] i.e., around a strength rating of 8. The underlying assumption is that the contagion comes primarily from defaulting bank bonds held by other financial intermediaries (see Sect. 3.3) and from runs of uninsured depositors at other banks. Equity instruments are generally not guaranteed, as their holders are expected to be better prepared to bear substantial losses.[21]

[15]Cf., bail-in, where liability holders are forced to have (a portion) of their debt written off (see Sect. 6.3).

[16]Cf. Strahan (2013) and Kaufman (2014).

[17]Kaufman (2015, 4).

[18]Derived from Kaufman (2014, 220).

[19]Kaufman (2014) discusses in detail when and which creditors are protected.

[20]Stern and Feldman (2009b, 17).

[21]Notable exceptions have been made to this generalisation (Stern and Feldman (2009b, 17)), and shareholders have also been fully protected. Often policymakers do not want to fully take over a bank as this involves further responsibility and the later public offering of a privatised bank might prove difficult. Udell (2010) argues that one reason governments do not wipe out shareholders—even if this is economically reasonable—is to avoid committing an act which could be negatively perceived by the public as communistic in nature.

Table 4.1 Strength of TBTF: protection against credit and liquidity losses

Strength rating	Insured deposits		Sel. S-T deposits		All S-T deposits		All L-T deposits		All S-T debt		All L-T debt		Share-holdings
	Cred.	Liq.	Cred.	Liq.	Cred.	Liq.	Cred.	Liq.	Cred.	Liq.	Cred.	Liq.	
0 / 0 %	●												
1		●											
2	●	●											
3	●	●	●										
3	●	●		●									
4	●	●	●	●									
5	●	●	●	●	●								
5	●	●	●	●		●							
6	●	●	●	●	●	●							
7	●	●	●	●	●	●	●						
7	●	●	●	●	●	●		●					
8	●	●	●	●	●	●	●	●					
9	●	●	●	●	●	●	●	●	●				
9	●	●	●	●	●	●	●	●		●			
10	●	●	●	●	●	●	●	●	●	●			
11	●	●	●	●	●	●	●	●	●	●	●		
11	●	●	●	●	●	●	●	●	●	●		●	
12	●	●	●	●	●	●	●	●	●	●	●	●	
13 / 100 %	●	●	●	●	●	●	●	●	●	●	●	●	●

Sel. = selective; S-T = short-term; L-T = long-term; Cred. = credit loss; Liq. = liquidity loss

Source: Derived from Kaufman (2014, 220).

Empirical studies have shown that a more accommodative protection of liability holders during a banking crisis increases the fiscal costs involved in solving the crisis.[22] Although some bailout funds (such as private deposit insurance) might be provided by private sources, a complete private bailout is not considered a TBTF resolution in the above-described sense. TBTF costs are, by definition, borne primarily by the public.

4.1.3 EGG Methods

These are the known modes of fiscal intervention for banks in distress[23] where the bank survives either as an independent entity or as a melded part of an existing bank[24]—some require more than one method of intervention:

1. Liquidity support: Liquidity support is support with liquidity without provision of the usual collateral. Liquidity can be provided through loans, loan guarantees, or access to the central bank's discount window. This is often part of the open-bank assistance.[25]
2. Forbearance and delay: Forbearance describes a policy of leniency or indulgence in enforcing regulatory standards—particularly minimum capital requirements. It can also comprise an injunction to delay certain actions[26]. By applying methods of forbearance, the insured creditors receive an implicit claim on the deposit insurance fund[27]. This measure is the result of hope and uncertainty surrounding a bank's solvency when the regulators need more time to determine the foundations of a final decision.[28]
3. Bad banks: The nonperforming assets or risks of a distressed bank can be transferred into another entity called a 'bad bank'. This bank acts as special-purpose vehicle

[22]Honohan and Klingebiel (2003).

[23]Based on Gup (2004, 38–42).

[24]Udell (2010, 466).

[25]Gup (2004, 41).

[26]See Gup (2004, 40).

[27]See Kane (1996).

[28]In the worst case, it can be the result of a personal motivation of the policymaker to delay a critical decision that might also penalise his or her personal career. Kane (1996), one of the most prominent sceptics of this method, states that forbearance always leads to sub-optimal results. Whenever going-concern value can be preserved, efficient contracting would be more favourable than such lenient treatment, as the public assumes all of a bank's future losses whereas the gain is limited to recovering the opportunity cost of the risk capital, if any supplied. When the government grants an insolvent bank the right to operate further, it in fact creates zombies.

(SPV) that has been set-up solely for this purpose and is ultimately owned or guaranteed by the government.[29]
4. Bridge banks: A bridge bank is a temporary form of conservatorship, where the distressed bank is merged with the bridge bank. The bridge bank operates until the bank is sold.[30]
5. Purchase & assumption: This term refers to the purchase of almost all (distressed) bank assets and the assumption of its liabilities by a third-party bank. The negative value difference assets and the liabilities are covered by a payment of the government to the acquiring bank.[31]
6. Nationalisation: Nationalisation is also referred to as conservatorship. It is used to transfer ownership or operations of banks to the government.[32]

The method selected depends not only on the individual situation of the bank and the market environment play a role, but also on the visible costs to the public.[33]

4.1.4 EGGs and Stakeholders

The various alternatives are listed here concerning what happens to the three major groups of bank stakeholders during a bailout: namely, to creditors, bank management, and shareholders.

Creditors

The compensation of debt holders after a bailout is relatively straightforward. Insured debt is assumed at par in any case. There are three possible financial outcomes for the uninsured liabilities of the bank. The two latter procedures of burden-sharing of losses with debt holders are called a bail-in (see Sect. 6.3) and are the exception for G-SIBs:

1. At par: Liabilities are fully assumed to promote confidence in the capital markets. This is the standard procedure in banking history.
2. Haircut: A so-called haircut can be applied: i.e., the liabilities are assumed at a discount to par.
3. Debt-to-equity swap: Debt is converted into equity in a debt-to-equity swap. Some new forms of subordinated debt have predefined conversion ratios in their terms for this purpose (see Sect. 6.1.4).

[29]Gup (2004, 39–40).
[30]Gup (2004, 40).
[31]Gup (2004, 42).
[32]Gup (2004, 41).
[33]Kaufman (2015, 4).

Bank Management

What happens to bank management during a bailout is not as relevant with regard to the main objective to protect the maintenance of the essential services of the bank and the value of the bank's liabilities.[34] In a bailout, there are four basic options with respect to the bank's senior management:[35]

1. Management survives,
2. Management is fired and gets a severance package,
3. Management is fired without severance, or
4. Management is fired and receives sanctions (see Sect. 6.3).

Shareholders

The various bailout measures can have the following financial outcomes for equity holders:

1. No compensation payment: In an expropriation, the government confiscates all shares by applying laws for special circumstances. The shareholders lose their property rights at the bank, which equals a complete loss.
2. Compensation payment: In the case of complete and long-term takeover by the government or a third-party bank facilitated by the government, the bank's common shares can be either confiscated or acquired by the government. The latter procedure is normally executed by raising capital with relatively low subscription prices to get a sufficient shareholding for a subsequent squeeze-out. The price offered at squeeze-out can be considered a compensation payment to the former shareholders. Depending on the national law, the government may also confiscate the common shares against compensation. A compensation or squeeze-out payment is frequently defined by an independent valuator. This payment can be seen as an example of the put-option value and theory of TBTF shareholders.[36] With this direct compensation payment, the old shareholders no longer participate in the bank.
3. Dilution: For a more temporary takeover, the government could subscribe to newly issued securities to inject capital and recapitalise the bank. This results in dilution of ownership for the old shareholders—comparable to a haircut of debt instruments. Hybrid securities are often facilitated in this context, such as preferred shares, subordinated debt, or mandatory convertible debt. These instruments can combine, depending on their terms, the stable income stream of bonds, the potential appreciation of

[34]See Kaufman (2015, 3).

[35]See also Udell (2010, 466).

[36]Kane (2015, 12–13) argues that, for truly G-SIBs, the government will effectively cede the value of its loss-stopping rights back to the shareholders. He notes the bailout of AIG as a suitable example.

common shares, or the superior rights versus common shares to limit the upside or voting rights of the old shareholder base.[37]

4. No dilution: When debt capital is injected, i.e., capital for supporting primarily liquidity, no losses accrue for the shareholders, even if the government later imposes charges for support.[38] Shareholders benefit across the board, as the charter value of the bank is preserved. When capital forbearance is applied as a bailout measure, the returns are attributed solely to the old shareholders[39] because losses are limited to the shareholding, while the upside of potential gain is unlimited. This is the strongest TBTF resolution because shareholders remain in full control of the bank.

4.2 Implicit Government Guarantees (IGGs)

An IGG extends deposit insurance to uninsured bank liabilities without payment of any insurance premium by the insured G-SIB. This is why the fundamental consequences of deposit insurance (see Sect. 2.5) are also applicable here, only more strongly. The first two subsections explain why (see Sect. 4.2.1) and how (see Sect. 4.2.2) banks receive IGGs and are able to shift the liability for their potential losses to the state. This expected government intervention on a selective basis in a free-market economy results *per definitionem* in the distortion of market forces and incentives—more precisely, in moral hazards. The subsequent sections discuss how the behaviour of various bank stakeholders changes—namely, that of the creditors (see Sect. 4.2.3), the bank (management) (see Sect. 4.2.4), and the shareholders (see Sect. 4.2.5). Empirical evidence, where available, complements the findings.

4.2.1 IGG Origin

An IGG has two possible origins:

1. An official government statement designates a bank TBTF for two possible reasons:
   a. to pre-emptively give certainty to bank stakeholders and other market participants, and to stabilise the overall banking system, or
   b. to impose special regulatory requirements on the bank.

[37] M. R. King (2009b).

[38] See Kaufman (2015, 3).

[39] Cf. Kane (1996).

2. The market perceives a bank to be TBTF. This, in contrast, is based on the expectation of potential public bailout measures. The market participants that would potentially benefit from an EGG know what motivates policymakers to opt for a bailout (Sect. 4.1.1). Hence, even if a bank is not officially designated as TBTF, market participants will treat a bank as such if they are aware of the systemic importance and react to it by reasonably anticipating the EGG.[40]

4.2.2 IGG Strength

Even if a bank has been officially designated TBTF, the scope of any potential bailout will rarely be defined *ex ante*. This said, the strength of the IGG—and so the moral-hazard effect—depends in general again on market expectations: i.e., on the expected probability and scope of EGGs (see Sect. 4.1.2). These expectations are usually derived from past public interventions and bailout experiences.[41]

The value of such an IGG for a bank and its counterparties is not only dependent on the strength of the expected bailout, but also on the condition of the financial system. The more uncertainty or volatility there is in a market (such as during a banking crisis), the higher the value of a potential protection. This free insurance works like a put option getting closer to the money.[42]

It is worthwhile to note several factors that mitigate the strength and value of IGGs:

1. <u>TBTF regulation:</u> TBTF regulations constitute additional regulation and supervision of G-SIBs. These may include legislation concerning the contractual liability write-offs during a bailout—a so-called bail-in (see Sect. 6.3).[43]
2. <u>'Too-big-to-save':</u> The public finance capacity of some countries is insufficient to credibly protect G-SIBs. In such situations, banks may be called 'too-big-to save', which implies that TBTF failures can cause national insolvency.[44]
3. <u>'Too-many-to-fail':</u> This term names a general weakness of an entire banking sector that implies that a government is less likely to protect one bank because

[40]Monopolkommission (9 July 2014, 530).

[41]In a comprehensive study of the international banks of 104 countries over the period of 1989–2007, Cubillas, Fernández, and González (2016) find that IGGs are stronger in countries that did not impose losses on depositors in previous banking crises.

[42]Tsesmelidakis and Merton (July 2013). Schich and Lindh (2012) present evidence that the strength of the IGG increased at the beginning of the financial crisis of 2007–2009 but has decreased over time again.

[43]See, e.g., Schich and Lindh (2012).

[44]See Demirgüç-Kunt and Huizinga (2013), Schich and Lindh (2012), and Cubillas, Fernández, and González (2016). Recent examples are Iceland in 2008, Ireland in 2010, and Cyprus in 2013.

it cannot protect all similarly weak G-SIBs.[45] This scenario is also known as a 'too-many-to-fail'.[46]

Due to the above-named complexities, the extent of IGGs differs across countries and across banks within one country.[47]

4.2.3 Creditor Moral Hazard

The creditor moral hazard (see Sect. 2.5) extends simply from the depositors, who are already covered by the statutory deposit insurance, to all liability holders that are expected to be protected under a bailout of a G-SIB. Ultimately, creditor moral hazard leads to lower funding costs and larger counterparty positions for G-SIBs. This is the result of the lower return requirements of the creditors and is driven by the following:

- Lower default probability of bank liabilities: In event of bank bankruptcy, liabilities are generally repaid out of the insolvency estate. For the creditors, the IGG works like a double bottom and results in a downward shift in the probability of the default of the respective liabilities, including counterparty risk of derivative contracts.[48] Bank creditors not only lend at a lower rate according to the fundamental risk/return trade-off, but bank counterparties are also willing to accept larger positions and to price in lower counterparty risk. Two main approaches are analysed in the literature to support the foundation of the lower default probability:[49]
  - An 'objective argument', mostly measured by market CDS spreads, and
  - A 'subjective argument', measured by credit rating differences.
- Lower bank monitoring costs: The IGG partly replaces the necessity of monitoring the counterparty bank, which results in a decrease in associated costs.

Economic costs, or negative public economies, accrue when investors come to regard a bank as TBTF. These equal the total costs the bank and its creditors save due to its TBTF status: viz., the asserted argument of lower funding costs and lower bank-monitoring costs. What follows are the empirical results of different studies and methods analysing the above theoretical assertions with regard to the lowered default probability measured by credit ratings and CDS spreads. The lower monitoring costs and the larger counterparty positions are not as well analysed empirically. It also seems unclear to what degree the creditors versus the banks benefit from creditor moral hazard. Studies of the overall

[45]Brown and Dinç (2011).

[46]Cf. Acharya and Yorulmazer (2007).

[47]Schich and Lindh (2012).

[48]Schweikhard and Tsesmelidakis (1 November 2012).

[49]Araten and Turner (2013).

funding cost advantage of G-SIBs dominate this research field. All studies, regardless of the method applied, find very large and significant funding cost advantages of G-SIBs.

Stronger Credit Ratings

Rating agencies publish a variety of credit ratings about banks' creditworthiness, the issuer itself, and certain (classes of) financial obligations. Credit ratings represent the probability of default on the rating agency's own rating scale. Such credit ratings are a subjective assessment and do not always prove accurate. Nevertheless, to some degree, the rating also reflects and influences the market view of a bank's solvency because debt holders often base their investment and pricing decisions to a significant degree on such ratings. Hence, a better rating generally leads to cheaper funding conditions. Moreover, external ratings of bank debt are often a benchmark for central banks and wholesale operations and define minimum collateral requirements. This also means that better ratings indirectly result in better funding conditions in this case as well.

The three major credit-rating agencies—Standard & Poor's (S&P), Moody's, and Fitch—calculate and publish two (or more) separate issuer ratings that are of particular interest for our purposes: (i) a stand-alone issuer rating,[50] that reflects a bank's intrinsic capacity to repay its obligations, and (ii) an overall issuer rating,[51] that reflects a bank's capacity to repay its obligations with potential external support.

In order to measure the TBTF effect, several studies simply compare both ratings.[52] The difference reflects the impact or value of possible external support, primarily by the government. All of the studies find that banks considered TBTF receive overall rating uplifts—i.e. credit rating upgrades—compared with other banks.[53] This rating "bonus" varies: it is stronger after government interventions[54] and ranges from one to four notches. Furthermore, it is found that, higher IGGs are driven by a lower stand-alone rating of a bank,[55] a larger domestic market share of the bank, and greater solvency of the bank's sovereign.[56]

---

[50]Other terms that have been used over the years include 'Standard & Poor's Underlying Rating' (SPUR), Moody's 'Bank Financial Strength Rating' (BFSR) or 'Baseline Credit Assessments' (BCA), and Fitch's 'Bank Individual Rating' or 'Viability Rating' (VR).

[51]Other terms that have been used over the years include S&P 'Long-Term Issuer Credit Rating', Moody's 'Long-Term Issuer Credit Rating', and Fitch's 'Long-Term Rating' or 'Issuer Default Rating' (IDR).

[52]Some more sophisticated studies apply regressions and control for several factors other than TBTF.

[53]E.g. Soussa (2000), A. G. Haldane (30 March 2010), Rime (9 May 2005), Stern and Feldman (2009b, 38), and Schich and Lindh (2012).

[54]Morgan and Stiroh (2005, 18) and Schich and Lindh (2012).

[55]Rime (9 May 2005).

[56]Schich and Lindh (2012).

Lower CDS Spreads

Credit default swaps (CDSs) are credit derivatives used to insure against default of debt instruments. That means that CDSs securitise and reflect the default risk, while debt instruments also comprise interest rate risks in their market prices. Because IGGs only affect default risk, CDS are an intuitive measure for teasing out the insurance costs of an IGG. CDS investors might also rely on credit ratings; however, CDS markets are dominated by institutional investors that are potentially able to independently and accurately assess a bank's probability of default.[57] Moreover, market discipline in the CDS market is usually strong.

Many studies have illustrated that TBTF status affects CDS prices.[58] One study using regression analyses finds that 'a one percentage point increase in size reduces the CDS spread of a bank by about two basis points'. However, scholars agree that IGGs have a threshold, above which some banks are considered 'too-big-to-be rescued'[59]. Event studies identify widening CDS spreads prior to government interventions at other banks that are followed by narrowing CDS spreads around and after events.[60]

Lower Funding Costs

Funding costs reflect investors' assessment of risk levels. Risk is measured in terms of spreads above the risk-free rate, which is normally defined as the rate on bonds fully guaranteed by the government, such as government bonds. This is why spreads are generally aligned with credit ratings and CDS spreads. However, systemic market factors and issue-specific factors (such as liquidity) also affect bond prices and yields.[61]

When investors perceive a bank as TBTF, the risk is primarily in the probability that the government will unexpectedly not rescue the bank weighted by the likelihood of a threatening default. The funding-cost advantage is calculated by translating the rating[62] or CDS[63] uplift associated to TBTF into the yields paid on banks' liabilities. Alternatively, some authors apply econometric models[64] and control for factors other than TBTF. Other event studies that observe sudden credit-spread changes such after merger-related events[65] or government interventions[66]. Regardless of the research

---

[57]Flannery (2001).

[58]A noteworthy caveat is that CDSs only exist for the very large banks, and that investors have a preference for more liquid instruments, which in turn are frequently issued by larger issuers.

[59]Völz and Wedow (2011, 195).

[60]E.g. Araten and Turner (2013), Schweikhard and Tsesmelidakis (1 November 2012), M. R. King (2009b), and Panetta et al. (2009).

[61]Araten and Turner (2013)

[62]E.g. Ueda and Weder di Mauro (2013), Soussa (2000), and Schich and Lindh (2012).

[63]E.g. Araten and Turner (2013), Schweikhard and Tsesmelidakis (1 November 2012), and Panetta et al. (2009).

[64]E.g. Hughes and Mester (1993, 293) and Flannery and Sorescu (1996, 1373).

[65]E.g. Penas and Unal (2004, 149)

[66]E.g. Veronesi and Zingales (2010, 339), Balasubramnian and Cyree (2011, 21), and Furfine (2006, 593).

methodology, the observed yield difference—also called the spread—is an estimate of the monetary measure of IGGs. It is denoted in relative terms as a credit spread or in absolute terms as a monetary amount[67] and it represents the reduction of funding costs. This funding-cost advantage comprises both the structural strength of the IGG and the time-varying market valuation of the IGG.[68] A wide range of studies illustrate robust and very large funding benefits for banks considered TBTF of up to 600 basis points or several-hundred billion US$ per year per bank.[69] The relative and absolute funding advantages change materially over time and across banks and jurisdictions.[70] Only explicit guarantees to (partially) government-owned banks are stronger than IGG.[71] In other words, empirical studies, as a whole, suggest that even the uninsured liabilities of G-SIBs exhibit little sensitivity to banks' risk-taking.[72] It is noteworthy that G-SIBs are also more flexible in their funding strategies and more readily change their funding mix compared to non-G-SIBs.[73] This is why the full funding advantage extends beyond a simple comparison of the yields of the same debt instruments.

4.2.4 Bank Moral Hazard

The increased creditor moral hazard caused by the extension of guarantees of the retail depositors (see Sect. 4.2.3) to quasi all creditors of G-SIBs—even if only implicit—also exacerbates bank moral hazards.[74] Banks exploit IGGs in terms of (i) increased risk-taking and (ii) increased growth.[75]

Increased Risk-Taking

There are two reasons increased risk-taking is caused by creditor moral hazard stemming from the TBTF doctrine:

---

[67]Cf. A. G. Haldane (30 March 2010).

[68]Ueda and Weder di Mauro (2013).

[69]The various research methods do not necessarily determine the same strength of the IGG. Araten (2014) observe that bond-market implied ratings are two to three notches more conservative than issuer ratings for G-SIBs. The relationship between ratings and funding costs are also unstable and vary over time (Noss and Sowerbutts (2012)). This is not surprising, as (i) the value of the IGG (i.e., the cheaper funding) is stronger, and (ii) the spreads between higher-rated and lower-rated banks are wider during times of higher macroeconomic uncertainty.

[70]A comprehensive literature overview of relative and absolute funding advantages is published by the Federal Deposit Insurance Corporation (FDIC) (August 2014).

[71]Cf. Wolgast (2001, 361) and Gropp, Gruendl, and Guettler (2014, 457).

[72]Gorton and Santomero (1990, 119–20).

[73]See Araten and Turner (2013) on how the funding mix of G-SIBs differs.

[74]A general bank moral hazard exists, as most banks operate with a legal form according to which shareholders' liabilities are limited to the paid-in capital.

[75]Moyer and Lamy (1992) and Ennis and Malek (2005).

- Less monitoring: The typically well-informed and fast-moving institutional market participants are the driving forces behind a bank's market discipline. Without sufficient monitoring, engagement and signalling from creditors, bank management increasingly works to benefit shareholders and increase profitability by increasing risk, according to the risk-return principle.
- Lower funding costs: G-SIBs pay lower funding costs for a given level of risk and capital. This makes investment projects profitable at a lower return level: i.e., the relationship of risk and return worsens.

Concerning the increase in risk-taking, ample empirical studies exhibit several different forms of risk-taking:

- Higher leverage: Holding less equity in relation to total assets or liabilities incurs greater risk.[76]
- Higher asset risk: Engaging in high-risk investments with higher default rates[77] and tail risk results in higher asset risk.[78]
- Higher liquidity risk: G-SIBs take on liquidity risk by pursuing a higher risk funding strategy and holding less stable funding.[79]
- Higher operational risk: Poor management of all other operational risk categories results in operational risk.[80]

Higher riskiness of a bank's overall activities leads to a higher variance in returns.[81] This, in turn, results in higher potential losses[82] and higher stress to the economy. This suggests that G-SIBs 'may have a distinct, possibly more fragile, business model'.[83] In addition, non-G-SIB competitor banks are also indirectly encouraged to keep the pace with regard to profitability and increased risk.[84]

---

[76]Cf. Stan and McIntyre (2012) for the period from 2001 to 2008, Moyer and Lamy (1992) for the period from 1960 until the beginning of the 1990 s, and Bhagat, Bolton, and Lu (2015, 520). Cf. the agency-costs hypothesis, according to which 'high leverage or a low equity/asset ratio reduces the agency costs of outside equity and increases firm value by constraining or encouraging managers to act more in the interests of shareholders' (Berger and Bonaccorsi di Patti (2006)).

[77]Bhagat, Bolton, and Lu (2015, 533) and Gropp, Gruendl, and Guettler (2014, 457), and Kareken and Wallace (1978).

[78]Gandhi and Lustig (2015).

[79]Laeven, Ratnovski, and Tong (2016)

[80]O'Hara and Shaw (1990).

[81]Stan and McIntyre (2012).

[82]Boyd and Gertler (1993) provide empirical evidence for the mid to late 1980 s, and Boyd and Heitz (2016) provide empirical evidence for the financial crisis of 2007–2009.

[83]Laeven, Ratnovski, and Tong (2016, 25).

[84]Gropp, Hakenes, and Schnabel (2010).

Market Discipline and Charter Value

A bank is endogenously incentivised by its creditors and shareholders to exercise market discipline—i.e., to implement prudent risk management. Creditors want to ensure the repayment of their borrowings at par. Shareholders want to ensure that the bank maximises the profits after (re)paying the creditors, but without breaching regulatory requirements—i.e., without losing the banking license.[85] This charter value is the shareholders' value generated by the ownership of the banking license, which is foregone after a bank bankruptcy. Hence, the charter value has an importance for G-SIBs depending on the expected EGG. When creditor monitoring is weak, charter value is the intrinsic motivation to exercise market discipline that most reduces the moral hazard of risk-taking by G-SIBs. There is a trade-off between preserving a bank's charter value, which decreases as bank risk increases, and maximising the put option value from the IGG, which increases as bank risk increases.[86] This implies that the optimal risk management strategy is to increase risk either when the bank's charter value declines[87] or when the risk of losing it declines, and vice versa[88]. That means the cross-sectional distribution of bank risk-taking is non-uniform. Empirical studies confirm that higher capital levels are associated with higher charter value and lower risk, and vice-versa.[89] However, it seems that charter value and risk only exhibit a strong, inverse relationship during economic expansion; the opposite holds during economic contradictions.[90] Furthermore, due to higher regulatory capital requirements, the disciplining effect of charter value diminishes.[91] Findings[92] suggest that charter value has been declining over time, contributing to the increase in risk-taking in the years before the GFC.[93]

---

[85] Marcus (1984), Keeley (1990), and Park (1997).

[86] Ritchken et al. (1993) and Park and Peristiani (2007).

[87] Keeley (1990).

[88] Panageas (2010).

[89] Palia and Porter (2004).

[90] Saunders and Wilson (2001)

[91] Furlong and Kwan (April 2005).

[92] By Jones, Miller, and Yeager (2011).

[93] In strict contradiction to this mainstream moral-hazard argument, Cordella and Yeyati (2003) present the unorthodox hypothesis that public safety nets offered during crises help banks to survive and may increase banks' franchise value. This, in turn, leads to stronger risk aversion because they have more to lose if they fail (Demsetz, Saidenberg, and Strahan (1996)). However, Stern and Feldman (2009b) disqualified this argumentation, in particular with regard to G-SIBs, as government guarantees level out this relationship. Moreover, the conditions under which franchise value limits risk-taking may not exist when needed. In this context, Kauko (2014) notes that the recent GFC was less severe in countries where the government had offered more generous protection in previous crises, which may be interpreted as a sign of stronger risk aversion during the build-up phase. Moreover, losses suffered by depositors in past crises made the more recent crisis worse. This line of argument extends the described charter value hypothesis to a more comprehensive franchise value hypothesis.

Increase of Size

There are basically two reasons why banks increase in size because of the TBTF doctrine:

- Increasing systemic importance: Several studies show that banks sometimes grow larger than the size providing the greatest scale and scope economies (social optimum), especially to achieve or extend TBTF status and thereby exploit IGGs. Deposit insurance only incentivises extending the magnitude of insured deposits to benefit from cheaper deposits, as deposit insurance is generally underpriced. The relatively stable retail deposits are, per se, beneficial to the stability of the financial system. The TBTF doctrine, however, not only incentivises increasing the ratio of liabilities to insured deposits but also incentivises increasing the entire balance sheet to thereby increase IGGs. There are also other categories of achieving systemic importance (Sect. 3.3), but size remains the most prominent. Also, regarding motivations for M&A activities (i.e., to grow inorganically), TBTF is among the most relevant.[94]
- Increase of risk-taking: Firm size and risk-taking among banks are highly positively correlated.[95] Banks manage risk increase mostly through increased leverage, which means balance-sheet expansion. Moreover, more risky and more profitable banks are also able to grow faster.

4.2.5 Shareholder Moral Hazard

Banks have many stakeholders—such as management, employees, and creditors—that urge them to adhere to market discipline. The incentives of the direct decision-makers of a bank—i.e., the bank management and the bank shareholders—are generally best aligned, as the shareholders legally own the bank and appoint its operational representatives (i.e., its managers). The more the creditor's monitoring function is weakened by the moral hazard from TBTF, the more weight shareholder monitoring receives.

The origins of creditor and bank moral hazards are relatively simple and straight-forward. Whether shareholder moral hazard[96] exists from TBTF is less clear in both theory and practice. The theoretical incentives and disincentives for shareholder moral hazards are discussed below. Both the proprietary empirical study and related empirical studies on this matter are discussed in detail in Pt. II. In practice, and according to the equity valuation principles (see Sect. 2.2), shareholder moral hazard must lead to higher relative and absolute market-equity valuation, as investors prefer G-SIBs over non-G-SIBs.[97]

---

[94]Benston, Hunter, and Wall (1995) and DeYoung, Evanoff, and Molyneux (2009, 87).

[95]Bhagat, Bolton, and Lu (2015, 520).

[96]Cf. M. R. King (2009b, 2).

[97]Cf. Varmaz, Fieberg, and Prokop (2015).

According to the risk-return trade-off, an increase in the (relative) equity valuations of G-SIBs depends on higher profits, while risk (volatility) does not rise on a proportional basis. Non-G-SIBs are assumed not to benefit from TBTF subsidies and remain unchanged in their valuation.[98]

These are the public subsidies or incentives that could lead to a shareholder moral hazard and could positively impact shareholder wealth:

1. Competitive advantage from EGGs: Shareholders can absorb the EGG either indirectly through capital injections during a bailout or directly through compensation payments. The outcome of EGGs for stockholders is, however, uncertain, and the event experiences have been mixed (Sect. 4.1.2).
   a. Affecting creditors: If the government supports liability holders (see Sect. 4.1.4), the shareholders also benefit from lower cost of debt and preserving the bank's charter.
   b. Affecting shareholders: Shareholders can benefit from government interventions (Sect. 4.1.4) either by receiving compensation payments above market levels (put option value) when the government takes over the bank, or by preserving the bank's charter value upon government capital injections.
2. Competitive advantages from IGGs: The shareholders can absorb the IGG from creditor and bank moral hazard, as described above:
   a. Lower funding costs: For a G-SIB, creditor moral hazard leads to lower funding costs, a stronger position as counterparty, and greater flexibility and readiness with respect to funding activities.[99] All of these factors lower the overall cost of debt and subsequently improve overall bank profitability.
   b. Increase of risk-taking: When a G-SIB's funding costs are no longer tied to the riskiness of its operations, shareholders have the incentive to transfer wealth from the IGG by pushing the management to take on more risk,[100] which ultimately leads to higher profitability.[101]

---

[98]O'Hara and Shaw (1990).

[99]See Jayaratine and Morgan (2000) and Kashyap and Stein (2000).

[100]Cf. Park and Peristiani (2007).

[101]Cf. O'Hara and Shaw (1990). Stern and Feldman (2009b, 24) state that only the creditors cash in on the benefit of TBTF. Saunders, Strock, and Travlos (1990) present evidence for the hypothesis that shareholder are even more risk-affine than bank managers. Banks in which the management holds a larger equity stake, exhibit higher-risk behaviour than banks in which the management has only a small shareholding. Cheng, Hong, and Scheinkman (2015) prove that institutional investors encourage banks to take on higher risks and reward them with better compensation and higher bank valuations.

On the other side, the following factors discourage shareholders from investing in G-SIBs and can put a strain on their equity valuations:

1. Higher volatility: An increase in bank risk, or profitability, will generally make future earnings streams more uncertain or volatile. This means shareholders will discount future cash flows with their higher inherent cost of equity.
2. Less efficiency: Due to creditor and bank moral hazards, corporate governance mechanisms and market discipline are weakened. Both can lead to increased bank inefficiency, which results in reduced profitability.
3. TBTF regulation (before bailout): G-SIBs are increasingly exposed to regulations that selectively target them. These additional regulatory costs may reduce profitability in various ways (Chap. 7).
4. Burden-sharing (after bailout): Even if shareholders retain bank ownership after a direct bailout, the government can put several strains or conditions on the future profitability of a G-SIB.

In summary, while some of the competitive advantages gained through TBTF status should generally improve bank valuations, other outcomes, such as those derived from a risk increase, are much more uncertain. Overall, the net effect of TBTF on G-SIBs' stocks. Part II sheds light on this question.

5 Public Costs and Benefits of TBTF

This chapter analyses the welfare perspective of TBTF: i.e., it examines how EGGs and IGGs impact society at large. The previous chapter analysed the impact of EGGs and IGGs on private individuals or bank stakeholders. It identified the moral hazards that lead to monetary effects for G-SIB stakeholders. These public subsidies for G-SIB stakeholders, whether implicit or explicit, come at a cost to society. Moreover, when there are differences between private and social costs or private and social returns, the market economy does not deliver an outcome that maximises overall efficiency. This so-called market failure leads to deadweight losses. The social optimum—that is the optimal promotion of the well-being of all economic agents—is achieved by maximising social returns and minimising social costs. This implies that all costs and benefits need to be internalised by households and firms making production decisions. G-SIBs that do not internalise all the costs of IGGs and EGGs are sources of inefficiency in this context. Their actions make other members of society worse off, which makes G-SIBs a negative externality of systemic risk. By definition, this leads to overproduction:[1] i.e., to a market outcome that is less than optimal in terms of a society's overall condition. It can be called 'banking pollution'[2] in the logic of environmental economics.

The intention here is to quantify (or at least name) the sources of this imbalance. A cost-benefit analysis is particularly relevant to estimating how a balance—the social optimum—can be re-achieved and before discussing the regulatory efforts on TBTF in subsequent chapters. However, a cost-benefit analysis of the TBTF doctrine is widely acknowledged to be very difficult. One main reason is the emergence of a financial crisis cannot be attributed solely to G-SIBs nor can the bailout of a G-SIB be attributed

[1]Cf. Denk, Schich, and Cournède (2014, 64) with regard to credit overexpansion.

[2]A. G. Haldane (30 March 2010).

T. F. Lesche, *Too-Big-to-Fail in Banking*, Finanzwirtschaft, Banken und Bankmanagement I Finance, Banks and Bank Management, https://doi.org/10.1007/978-3-658-34182-4_5

directly to the avoidance of a financial crisis. Hence, the costs and benefits of TBTF are highly subjective and may also vary across countries and over time.[3]

The first section, Sect. 5.1 sheds light on bank's economies of scale and scope—in particular on limitations and who is benefitting from them. Section 5.2 compares the public costs of EGGs—i.e., the direct bailout costs from public finances—with the public benefits of EGGs: i.e., the avoidance of output losses from a financial crisis. Along the same lines, Sect. 5.3 compares the public costs of IGGs—which are the benefits G-SIB stakeholders derive from moral hazard taking (see Sect. 4.2)—with the public benefits of IGGs, which are minimal. Finally, Sect. 5.4 concludes that the TBTF doctrine does not have any value for society, but that it is hard to abolish because of the time-inconsistency of policymakers' decision-making.

5.1 Economies of Large Banks (Incentives for Scale and Scope)

This section is a preparation for the analysis of public costs and benefits of IGGs (see Sect. 5.3). There is a potentially important trade-off inherent in G-SIBs with respect to overall economic efficiency: systemic importance and economies of scale (and scope). Both depend on various criteria (see Sect. 3.3), but a bank's size is believed to be one of the best measures for both—the correlation is close to one—as large players are responsible for a larger fraction of banking output (see Sect. 7.4). In this regard, size is normally measured as the sum of a bank's total assets.

Intuitive questions arise in this context: First, what is the socially optimal bank size? In other words, up to which size are banks able to achieve economies scale and scope (see Sect. 5.1). This is equivalent to the size limit banks are incentivised to grow to while increasing public welfare. Second, are there super-scale economies (efficiency gains for G-SIBs) or any diseconomies (inefficiencies) beyond the socially optimal bank size? Answers to these questions are important for the later cost-benefit analysis: i.e., the question of whether being TBTF has any value to the public (after deducting the public subsidy due to TBTF). Answers are also crucial for regulatory considerations such as potential regulatory limits on bank size.

Economic Efficiency of Banks

In a competitive banking system, economic efficiency[4] is based upon the competition, regulation and economies of the firm, with various trade-offs between them. The focus here is on the economies of the firm: i.e., on how a bank itself can increase efficiency.

[3]Kaufman (2014, 218).

[4]The economic efficiency of firms can be decomposed into the following: (i) technical or productive efficiency (i.e., producing bank services for the lowest cost, that is, in the 'right way'); and (ii) allocative or price efficiency (i.e., the optimal distribution and allocation of bank services in society, which is to say producing the 'right amount').

The efficiency function of a bank is potentially U-shaped. On the one hand, the sub-optimal size of a bank may be such that input or output quantities are chosen inefficiently. On the other hand, very large banks that compete only with a small number of banks could encourage X-inefficiency and diseconomies. Here we want to understand the socially optimal bank size. To achieve this goal, only studies excluding externalities such as the TBTF doctrine from their analyses were considered.[5]

Table 5.1 summarises and briefly explains the ways banks can increase their efficiency[6] that have been identified in the literature. Besides X-efficiency, all listed sources imply some sort of growth—whether in scale, scope or any other dimension of expansion. In principle, efficiency gains increase the welfare of the public, the shareholders and the managers at the same time. They 'are made by changing input or output quantities in ways that reduce costs, increase revenues, and/or reduce risks to increase value for a given set of prices'.[7] However, agency conflicts between bank stakeholders can also lead to misalignment among incentives. Gains are then made by banks by exploiting other stakeholders. This is why the sources of efficiency are here divided into (i) economies of scale, (ii) economies of scope, (iii) other economies that increase public welfare (X-efficiency), and (iv) other economies that exploit public welfare. On this broader topic, there is a large body of literature on bank M&A and bank consolidation, most of which relies on data about U.S. banks. The primary research focus is on cost efficiencies on an organic scale—in particular, bank-wide cost functions. The focus is much less on scope, in part because of the difficult empirical issues involved.[8]

---

[5]Cf. Qayyum, Khan, and Ghani (2006, 733–34) and Dermine (2014, 103–4).

[6]Cf. Dermine (2014, 108).

[7]Berger, Demsetz, and Strahan (1999).

[8]Schmid and Walter (2009, 214). All published studies on the economies of banks have in common that they include many caveats because of the overall complexity of the analysis. At the same time, it is not unproblematic to compare the research results. The challenge for statistics is to consider and measure all the factors that need to be included and excluded (such as TBTF doctrine). However, the relevant statistical techniques have improved over time and better account for extreme variations in the sample (for instance Mester (2010, 11)). The main challenges are the following factors in the underlying data of the studies:

Bank-internal factors: <u>(i) Bank size:</u> 'The distribution of bank size is severely skewed' (DeYoung (2010)). <u>(ii) Banking services offered:</u> Because of the lack of data on banking products, the analysis is generally conducted on bank-wide data (Dermine (2014, 104–5)). However, the banking services and products banks offer can differ significantly. For instance, custody services with high standardisation and automatization enjoy different economies than more complex services such as M&A advisory. Moreover, small and large banks generally operate in different banking fields and make money in different ways (DeYoung (2010)). <u>(iii) Risk-taking:</u> Different levels of risk-taking add complexity, as better diversification (e.g., resulting from larger scale) incentivises greater risk-taking. When this additional risk-taking is viewed as a cost, it can lead to misleading econometric results (Hughes and Mester (2013, 559)).

Environmental factors: <u>(i) Country characteristics:</u> A country's public policy determines a bank's geographic and product expansion potential and the costs attributable to regulation, such

Table 5.1 Summary of Scale and Scope Economies of Banks

Source	Short-description	Significance	Beneficiary
Economies of scale:			
Cost-based economies of scale	Achieved by lowering the average cost per unit of output by expanding a single line of business	Low	Shareholders (by increasing public welfare)
Brand-based economies of scale	Achieved by lowering the marketing costs per unit of product sold	NA	Shareholders (by increasing public welfare)
Revenue-based economies of scale	Size and a large capital base make it possible to underwrite large loans and securities	Large in capital market activities	Shareholders (by increasing public welfare)
Economies of scope:			
Cost-based economies of scope	Cost efficiencies can be achieved by offering a broad range of products or services to a customer base	Low	Shareholders (by increasing public welfare)
Revenue-based economies of scope	Cross-selling new products to an existing customer base	NA	Shareholders (by increasing public welfare)
Financial diversification-based economies of scope	A portfolio of imperfectly correlated risks will reduce the overall volatility of profit	Large	Shareholders (by increasing public welfare)
Other economies that increase public welfare:			
X-efficiency	Degree of efficiency under conditions of imperfect competition	Large	Shareholders (by increasing public welfare)
Other economies that exploit public welfare:			
Market power	Reduction of banks operating in an individual market, may lead to less competition and higher margins	Large	Shareholders (by exploiting public welfare)
Safety net-based (TBTF) economies of scale	Increased likelihood of IGG and EGG	Large	Shareholders / management (by exploiting public welfare)
Political and regulatory power	More influence on decisions of political and regulatory authorities	NA	Shareholders / management (by exploiting public welfare)
Defence-based economies of scale	Achieving a certain size (capital clout) can act as a defensive measure against takeover	NA	Management (by exploiting public welfare)
Expense-preference-based economies of scale	Higher profit captured by management in the form of higher salaries or perks	Large	Management (by exploiting public welfare)
'Quiet life'-hypothesis-based economies of scale	Reduction of risk for management	Large	Management (by exploiting public welfare)
'Hubris'-hypothesis-based economies of scale	Excessive overestimation by the management	NA	Management (by exploiting public welfare)

Source: derived from Dermine (2014, 103–9).

Economies of Scale

Economies of scale are marginal production efficiencies achieved by increasing bank size and resulting in cost savings, better brand recognition, or revenue expansion. The scale effects generally account for less than 5 percent of costs, while revenues increase slightly with bank size (by approximately 1 to 4 percent)—but only at smaller banks[9] or banks with capital market activities. Most studies focus on the broader and traditional definition of cost-based economies of scale.[10] Overall, 'there is little agreement regarding economies of scale' for banks[11]. This might equally be due to statistical complexities and to constantly evolving bank characteristics. It appears that advances in information and communication technologies have been the fundamental impact factor.[12] This development favours larger banks because larger banks can spread increasing fixed technology costs among more customers.[13] As a result, economies of scale have risen steadily over the last decades, even centuries.[14] Ideal bank size has grown accordingly.[15] As recent technological advancements are sometimes considered to have revolutionised the banking landscape, it has even 'been argued that reliable estimates of scale economies for very large banks cannot be obtained in the current environment'[16].

Relatively better agreement can be found with regard to smaller banks—a research focus of older studies. It is widely accepted that 'very small banks (less than a few hundred million US$ in assets) are generally inefficient'. The minimum efficient scale has

---

as consumer protection (Mester (2010) and Wheelock and Lopez (2012, 11)). (ii) Information and communication technology advancements: Bank operations depend increasingly and to a large extent on information and communication technology. This field has seen significant technical advancements in recent decades. Consequently, other factors, such as the proximity to clients and personal client relationships, are increasingly less important.

To account for the above considerations as well as possible, the results of the latest general studies on (large) universal and commercial banks that offer a wide range of products and services are presented. Geographically, only studies on the US and European banking sectors are considered; these studies arrive at similar conclusions about scale and scope economies and efficiencies (Berger and Humphrey (1994, 2)). Lower economies are typically found in smaller financial systems (Beccalli, Anolli, and Borello (2015, 243)).

[9]Berger and Humphrey (1994, 2).

[10]Cost-based economies of scale are measured with respect to costs and refer to how size is related to costs (Mester (2010, 10–11)).

[11]Boyd and Heitz (2016, 251).

[12]Hughes and Mester (2013, 584).

[13]Wheelock and Lopez (2012, 11).

[14]Cf. Mester (2010).

[15]For a literature review of scale economies in international and US banking see Berger and Humphrey (1997, 175) and Mester (2010), respectively.

[16]Boyd and Heitz (2016, 251).

increased rapidly from the beginning of the millennium from US$ 0.5 billion to US$ 25 billion today—an amount that may still be rising[17].

More recent studies tend to look at larger banks and so-called economies of super-scale.[18] The most recent literature uniformly concludes that economies of scale are achievable for banks with total assets of up to US$ 100 billion.[19] This is much less than the median size of large international banks. Above this level there is mixed evidence concerning whether scale economies,[20] constant average costs or slight diseconomies of scale prevail. The results depend to a great extent on the variables that have been controlled for, such as market power and diversification of risks.[21] Even when explicitly controlling for TBTF factors—in particular for the funding cost advantage—evidence has been found for[22] and against[23] scale economies at very large international banks. Proponents of super-scale economies argue that they exist for banks that emphasise investment banking[24] to service large and global non-financial businesses.[25]

Economies of Scope

Economies of scope are marginal production efficiencies achieved by extending bank activities and resulting in cost savings, revenue expansion, or better financial diversification. The scope effects generally account for less than 5 percent of costs when multiple products are produced jointly, while revenues appear to be less affected by product

[17]Dermine (2014, 104–5), Hughes, Mester, and Moon (2001), and Feng and Serletis (2010).

[18]Boyd and Heitz (2016, 251).

[19]A. G. Haldane ((30 March 2010, 11) and Vander Vennet (2002). Earlier studies for the US and Europe from the mid-1990 s (Berger and Mester (1997)) and early-2000 s (Amel et al. (2004)) report that economies of scale in banking are exhausted at around US$ 5–10 billion.

[20]Cf. Mester (2010), Wheelock and Wilson (2012, 171), and Kovner, Vickery, and Zhou (2014, 1).

[21]Cf. Berger, Demsetz, and Strahan (1999, 135).

[22]Hughes and Mester (2013, 584).

[23]Davies and Tracey (2014, 243–44).

[24]Beccalli, Anolli, and Borello (2015, 243).

[25]The literature measures scale economies either by analysing 'the cross-sectional efficiency of banks of different sizes, or the time-series efficiency of banks on either side of a merger'. Nevertheless, both methods seems to yield similar results (A. G. Haldane (30 March 2010, 11)). In studies looking at inorganic growth through M&A, gains are mostly due to the previous inefficiency of the banks (X-inefficiency). This means the merger itself was a wake-up event for improving bank management (cf. DeYoung (1993, i) and Shaffer (1993, 434–35)). There is very little evidence that the M&A of large banks positively affects bank efficiency (Berger and Humphrey (1997, 204)) or economic value (DeLong (2001) and A. G. Haldane (30 March 2010, 11)). The stock market can also serve as an indicator that efficiency gains are believed to be very limited: 'On average, at the announcement of a transaction, the combined value of the firms involved does not vary much, as it should if significant benefits were expected' (Amel et al. (2004, 2513)). Literature overviews in this context are presented by Amel et al. (2004, 2513) and DeYoung, Evanoff, and Molyneux (2009).

mix.[26] Overall, empirical studies of these scope economies are even more inconclusive than those conducted into scale economies.[27] Most of the them tend towards insignificant scope economies based on costs or revenues. Scope economies from financial diversification, however, are of special and larger importance to banks, as, according to standard portfolio theory,[28] 'a portfolio of imperfectly correlated risks will reduce the overall volatility of profit',[29] which in turn increases shareholder value (see Sect. 2.2). There is evidence of financial diversification gains from multiple business lines or loan portfolios.[30] The reduced risk and volatility, however, 'may be more than counter-balanced by heightened exposures to volatile income-generating activities, such as trading',[31] and lower capital ratios of the larger banks.[32]

Other Economies

Economies other than those described above include economies that increase public welfare and economies that exploit public welfare. The former includes only

- X-efficiency: X-efficiency is the observed degree of efficiency maintained by a bank in practice under conditions of imperfect competition compared to efficient behaviour derived from economic theory. For example, banks may 20 to 30 percent higher costs than the industry minimum for the same scale and product mix.[33] The ability of management to control these costs is believed to be much more important than scale economies and scope economies.[34] X-efficiencies are not limited to certain bank sizes but to the lack of competitive pressure; they thus concern rather large banks.[35]

Economies that exploit public welfare are either pursued to the benefit of shareholders or management, or both. Besides safety-net (or TBTF) economies of scale (see Sect. 4.2.4), other examples include:

---

[26]Berger and Humphrey (1994, 2).

[27]Amel et al. (2004, 2513).

[28]Based on Markowitz (1959).

[29]Dermine (2014, 107).

[30]Cf. Dermine (2014, 107).

[31]A. G. Haldane (30 March 2010, 11).

[32]Demsetz and Strahan (1997) and Stiroh and Rumble (2006, 2131). See Sect. 12.2.4 for a discussion of equity valuation discounts on banks with diversified banking activities—also referred to as a holding discount. This is could be interpreted as evidence of diseconomies of scope in banking (A. G. Haldane (30 March 2010, 12–13)).

[33]Berger and Humphrey (1997).

[34]Berger and Humphrey (1994, 2).

[35]Consolidation and M&A are often-cited means to change managerial behaviour and thereby improve X-efficiencies. Berger, Demsetz, and Strahan (1999) present a literature overview of empirical findings in this context.

- Market power: According to traditional economic theory,[36] a lack of competition leads to unfair market power, monopolisation and collusion. This causes less efficient allocation of resources. Antitrust regulation establishes effective frameworks and maintains balance in the system: i.e., facilitates the free entry of banks and restricts the market powers of banks.
- Expense-preference-based economies of scale: The argument is that higher profit driven by larger scale or market power can be captured by management in the form of higher salaries or perks.[37]
- 'Quiet life'-hypothesis-based economies of scale: The argument is that higher profit driven by larger scale or market power can be captured by management in the form of reduction of risk and less need for innovation.[38]

These bank economies are not limited to certain sizes of banks and are believed to greatly significantly bank behaviour—though the impact has not been sufficiently quantified.

Results

Research indicates that the maximum efficient scale of banks could be somewhere around US$ 100 billion in total assets. This is a size that is still beneficial for the public and for bank stakeholders. Beyond this point, further economies are assumed to be exhausted, while there is at least the possibility of X-inefficiency or diseconomies of scale and scope that lead to deadweight costs.[39] This means that the incentives for banks to grow further at this point are driven by management or shareholder self-interest—they are not beneficial to the public welfare. One of the primary drivers is considered to be TBTF scale economies (see Sect. 4.2.4).

Coincidentally or not, research suggests that banks with totals assets of more than US$ 100 billion can be considered TBTF (see Sect. 3.3). Although both quantitative

[36]There are two competing hypotheses on the market structure and performance of firms: the traditional structure-conduct-performance (SCP) paradigm and the newer efficiency-structure (ES) hypothesis. The latter's proposition is that more efficient firms will better compete and grow in scale, thereby resulting in an increase in the degree of market concentration. An implication of the SCP paradigm is that a higher market concentration has harmful effects on social welfare. According to the ES hypothesis, on the other hand, the greater the degree of market concentration, the more efficient the market. Cf. Homma, Tsutsui, and Uchida (2014, 143).

[37]Dermine (2014, 109). Denk, Schich, and Cournède (2014, 63) argue that IGGs even strengthen increased income inequality in the financial sector, which is also called 'financial-sector wage premia'. Employees are considered to benefit from more and cheaper bank funding.

[38]Dermine (2014, 109).

[39]A. G. Haldane (30 March 2010, 12–13).

thresholds might be just rough approximations, G-SIBs can be considered to operate at a size that is too large both from a micro-level perspective on bank efficiency and from a macro-level perspective on systemic risk.[40]

5.2 Public Costs and Benefits of EGGs

Costs of EGGs (Bailout Costs)

The costs of EGGs are defined here in the context of narrow fiscal interpretation: that is, the wealth transfer from the public to the G-SIBs as a result of a bailout.[41] They comprise the direct cash flow used in the various methods of bank bailouts (see Sect. 4.1.3) while direct administrative expenses also accrue. The costs of the intervention generally roughly equals the subsequent increase in value of debt and/or equity issued by the respective banks.[42] In addition, there may be indirect opportunity costs from EGGs either because the bailout funds cannot used for other purposes or because a government needs to borrow, raise taxes[43], or print money to finance the bailout. While an increase of debt relative to GDP negatively affects a country's sovereign debt rating, an expansionary monetary policy can cause inflation and depreciation of a country's currency.[44] There is even more uncertainty about the eventual loss the public may eventually face from EGGs: First, government investment into G-SIBs or their associated bad banks might lead them to swiftly increase in value or make profits after the banking crisis is resolved. Second, as EGGs are measurable and visible to the wider public, G-SIBs are often obliged to repay some or all of the direct bailout costs.

Studies show that generous rescue measures, with blanket guarantees, open-ended liquidity support, and repeated recapitalisations can lead to budgetary outlays, whether immediate or deferred, that exceed a country's GDP or even result in public bankruptcy (see Sect. 3.4.5).[45] In the GFC, the direct costs for EGGs were on average approximately

[40]Cf. Laeven, Ratnovski, and Tong (2016, 3) and Boyd and Heitz (2016, 251). Anginer, Demirgüç-Kunt, and Zhu (2014a, 1) 'show a robust negative relationship between bank competition and systemic risk'. They argue that 'greater competition encourages banks to take on more diversified risks, making the banking system less fragile to shocks'.

[41]A. G. Haldane (30 March 2010, 1).

[42]Cf. van Bekkum (2016).

[43]Morrison (2011, 502).

[44]Stern and Feldman (2009b, 28).

[45]Honohan and Klingebiel (2003, 1539).

one[46] to five[47] percent of a country's GDP[48]. This compares to ten percent in previous crises on the back of less swift direct policy actions and indirect expansionary monetary and fiscal support.[49]

Benefits of EGGs (Avoidance of Bankruptcy Costs and Economic Output Losses)
A banking crisis can be triggered or strengthened by the failure of a G-SIB, as a relatively small number of G-SIBs are central to finance (see Sect. 2.6). The benefit of an EGG is basically the avoidance of the economic costs of bankruptcy (see Sect. 2.3) of a G-SIB. It is difficult to study the benefits of bailouts of G-SIBs, as the failures of G-SIBs are low-probability events and data is scarce.[50] Studies investigating this context usually look at the (potential) foregone output losses (value of goods and services not produced) that (would) have been created (without a bailout) (see Sect. 2.6).[51] This can be quite costly, as it includes large and long-lasting 'declines in employment, household wealth, and other economic indicators'.[52] Moreover, governments face 'greater fiscal challenges, in part because of reduced tax revenues from lower economic activity and increased spending to mitigate the impact of the recession',[53] and increased public debt.

The relative costs of modern financial crises 'are computed as deviations of actual GDP from its trend'. On average, they seem 'to be large and long-lived, often in excess of ten percent'[54] and on median at 25 percent[55] of pre-crisis GDP.[56] This compares with

[46]A. G. Haldane (30 March 2010).

[47]Laeven and Valencia (2013a, 232).

[48]Total direct assistance to the financial sector has amounted to over 80 percent of GDP in the UK and nearly 75 percent of GDP in the US when monetary measures by the central banks are also considered (Huertas (2014, 11–14)).

[49]Laeven and Valencia (2013a, 232).

[50]Ennis and Malek (2005).

[51]Cf. Federal Reserve Bank of Minneapolis (16 November 2016). Laeven and Valencia (2013b, 225) present a comprehensive database on systemic banking crises during 1970–2011 which includes information about costs and policy responses associated with banking crises.

[52]Cf. Hoggarth, Reis, and Saporta (2002, 851–52), Boyd, Sungkyu, and Smith (2005), and Huertas (2014, 4–5).

[53]U.S. Government Accountability Office (GAO) (16 January 2013, 17).

[54]A. G. Haldane (30 March 2010) and Reinhart and Rogoff (2011).

[55]Laeven and Valencia (2013a, 232).

[56]In absolute terms, studies estimate the losses associated with the GFC could range from a few trillion dollars to over US$ 14.8 trillion (U.S. Government Accountability Office (GAO) (16 January 2013) and Boyd and Heitz (2016)).

a median of 20 percent of GDP in historical crises, partly due to an increase in the size of the financial systems and the initial shocks to the financial system.[57]

Conclusions

Two general conclusions can be drawn from the above discussion: First, the increasing sophistication and expansion of financial systems has made financial crises more disastrous. At the same time, the magnitude of the fiscal costs of EGGs is significantly reduced by the regulatory preparation of G-SIBs in distress, such as the design of crisis containment and resolution policies (see Sect. 6.3). Second, the costs of EGGs are short-term, while G-SIBs often are able to repay some or all of it. The benefits of EGGs are long-term and significant, because GDP losses from a banking crisis are usually permanent or at least persistent. This is why, from a present value perspective, it can be generalised that EGG benefits exceed EGG costs.[58] This confirms a government's justification of a G-SIB bailout using taxpayers' money.

5.3 Public Costs and Benefits of IGGs

Costs of IGGs (Inefficiencies)

G-SIBs can cause two types of inefficiencies (see Sect. 5.1):

- TBTF diseconomies of scale: These are the result of the IGG (see Sect. 4.2) and concern only banks considered TBTF. The three fundamental moral hazards from IGGs—creditor moral hazard (see Sect. 4.2.3), bank moral hazard (see Sect. 4.2.4), and shareholder moral hazard (see Sect. 4.2.5)—represent the cost of TBTF diseconomies of scale. Altogether, these diseconomies of scale have massive indirect social costs. Generally, it is proven that the larger the IGG, the larger the economic inefficiencies.[59]
- X-inefficiencies and diseconomies of scale and scope: Generally, these inefficiencies concern all (large) banks. However, some researchers argue that in particular G-SIBs face diseconomies, i.e., they do 'not operate in a cost-efficient manner and also may innovate less', as inefficient G-SIBs are not forced out of the markets by market forces.[60] Empirical evidence of this reasoning is, however, not available.

[57]Laeven and Valencia (2013a, 232).

[58]Cf. A. G. Haldane (30 March 2010).

[59]Cf. Black, Collins, and Robinson (2000, 42).

[60]Mishkin (2006, 991).

Hence, the total public costs of IGGs are very significant. It can be argued that the total costs of IGGs must be at least equal the benefits of EGGs: i.e., the anticipated costs from a potential banking crisis triggered by the TBTF doctrine.

Benefits of IGGs

There is very little evidence of public (efficiency) gains from having G-SIBs.[61]

Results

Section 5.1 shows that there is no (significant) trade-off between systemic importance and economies of scale (and scope). Systemic importance is believed to start somewhere substantially above US$ 100 million of a bank's total assets, while economies are believed stop somewhere below this threshold. That means that there are no substantial benefits of G-SIBs to be taken into consideration—if any, there might be only operational inefficiencies in addition to the systemic risk inefficiency of G-SIBs. Consequently, the social costs of increased systemic risk resulting from IGGs always substantially exceeds any IGG benefits.

5.4 Overall Results

Public Costs and Benefits of EGGs and IGGs

Section 5.2 shows that EGG benefits outweigh EGG costs in particular, because potential GDP losses from the absence of G-SIB rescue measures are sustained while bailouts are one-off. In other words, EGGs are probably cost effective when executed.[62] Section 5.3 shows that massive IGG costs far outweigh nearly non-existent IGG benefits. This is intuitive, as there is no public benefit from the existence of G-SIBs, though there is a public imperative for their rescue. Both taken together, show that, even under extreme assumptions, the total costs of EGGs and IGGs always exceed the total benefits of EGGs and IGGs.[63]

The real social costs of a TBTF policy appear to incur *ex ante* and indirectly, due to IGG, 'in the form of distorted incentives in the financial sector'[64] or equivalently, in the form of anticipated crisis costs. The problems arise in the IGG rather than in the EGG, as the IGG is the breeding ground for the EGG. This means the social costs are higher than the private costs, as 'individually rational bank management may lead to a higher level of systemic risk than would be socially optimal'.[65] This clearly points to the fact that there

[61]Cf. Hughes and Mester (2013, 584)

[62]Morrison (2011, 502).

[63]Boyd and Heitz (2016).

[64]Morrison (2011).

[65]De Bandt and Hartmann (2000, 16).

is market failure in which the government should intervene via regulation. This means that the IGG should be contained by forcing banks to internalise the social costs of being TBTF via regulation (see Chap. 6).

Time-inconsistency

The motivations of policymakers for EGGs are described in Sect. 4.1.1, while the public necessity is explained in Sect. 5.2. For IGG, there are no such motivations (see Sect. 4.2), while the lack of value to the public is explained in Sect. 5.3. This begs the question why governments do not pledge no future bailouts? And why the TBTF doctrine still prevails?

The fundamental reason is called 'time-inconsistency' or the 'this-time-is-different syndrome'[66] and is one key difficulties of banking regulation (see Sect. 2.7). According to this phenomenon, policymakers only consider part of the impact of government guarantees: namely, the short-term impact of EGGs. The short-term perspective is not only easier to comprehend and to project, but also leads to a mostly positive conclusion, because benefits are recognised immediately and decline over time. The social costs of IGGs behave the other way around. This classic problem in economics (time inconsistency and credibility)[67] is very serious with respect to the TBTF doctrine. It makes a government pledge unlikely to succeed because governments' economic planning is against rational economic counterparties who act on the basis of expectations rather than against something of a stiff nature.[68]

Time-inconsistency is sometimes also understood to include the political economy aspect of short-term oriented need to win votes and get (re-)elected. Voters can also relate to a variety of bank stakeholders, such as depositors, borrowers, or employees for whom the EGG is particularly beneficial. Moreover, the frequencies of legislative periods considerably exceed those of potential banking crises triggered by G-SIBs. No politician will find himself or herself bound to long-term promises of former governments if the impact of a bailout is positive in the narrow view encompassing his or her legislative period. Consequently, any government pledge is obstructed from the beginning by its time-inconsistent nature and is not credible for rationally acting bank stakeholders.[69,70]

[66]Reinhart and Rogoff (2011).

[67]See Kydland and Prescott (1977, 473) and Calvo (1978, 1411).

[68]See Grochulski (2011, 149) and Kaufman (2015, 5).

[69]Cf. Stern and Feldman (2009b, 19–20).

[70]Cf. how discretion of the FDIC has undermined the effectiveness of strict policies for bailouts (see Sect. 3.4.3).

Some authors[71] argue that the time-inconsistency problem can be mitigated by the appointment of a 'conservative' regulator, who acts on a long-term basis and independently from the ruling government. Such a differentiation between legislative and regulatory bodies, however, seems problematic, because elected politicians ultimately rule the entire system in a democracy.[72] History has shown that governments tend to override regulators during crisis times—in particular, to prevent bank failures[73].[74]

[71]E.g. Rogoff (1985).

[72]Cf. Mishkin and Westelius (2008).

[73]Brock (2000, 69) confirms this practise by analysing Chile's banking history.

[74]A further discussion in the context of time-inconsistency concerns the application of discretion versus rules when handling banking crises from systemic risk. While banking crises (see Sect. 2.6) are per se unexpected with causes often not seen before, discretionary policies might be more adequate for crisis responding than rigid rules. Similarly, Freixas (23 June 1999) promotes a strategy of "creative ambiguity" of regulators that depends on the social costs of bank bankruptcy. Discretionary policies, however, tend to promote the time-inconsistency problem, as they 'lead to a sequence of policies that are suboptimal' (Mishkin (2006, 995)).

TBTF Policy Recommendations 6

The GFC and the Policy Responses

The GFC was the largest wave of banking crises since the Great Depression. A common feature of these recent crises is that mainly advanced economies hosting G-SIBs were affected. The empirical evidence provided in Chap. 5 paints a clear and consistent picture of the implicit and explicit costs that result from the negative externalities of the TBTF doctrine. Arguably, G-SIBs have either been the causes of or major contributors to the crises (see Sect. 3.4.6).[1] The dramatic GFC caused renewed interest not only with respect to the workings of banking crises (see Sect. 2.6) but also with respect to optimal policy responses. Traditional bank regulation (see Sect. 2.7)[2] is considered insufficient given these historical experiences.

The proposals concerning regulatory requirements and fiscal interventions aim at banking crises that emerge at the individual bank level, whereas proposals for monetary interventions—such as standard stabilisation measures—are best for macro problems.[3] Given that bank characteristics have changed significantly (see Sect. 3.4.5) and the acknowledgement of the emergence of G-SIBs, academics and regulators have not only formulated new general banking regulations but also new ones specifically for G-SIBs. These TBTF policy recommendations are intended to capture the systemic risk profile that leads to negative externalities[4] to reduce the probability or severity of future crises. Many of the proposals were made already after previous crises, such as after the S&L

[1]See Laeven and Valencia (2013a, 233).

[2]Or existing competition or antitrust law (see Monopolkommission (9 July 2014, 535)).

[3]De Bandt and Hartmann (2000)

[4]Laeven, Ratnovski, and Tong (2016).

T. F. Lesche, *Too-Big-to-Fail in Banking*, Finanzwirtschaft, Banken und Bankmanagement I Finance, Banks and Bank Management, https://doi.org/10.1007/978-3-658-34182-4_6

crisis, and did not make it into legislation or were subsequently abolished. Chapter 7 presents the policy initiatives that have been realised since the GFC.

Newly Proposed TBTF Regulation

This chapter introduces the most relevant and most frequently proposed regulatory measures specifically targeted at G-SIBs and their likely impact.[5] The chapter is organised in the sequential order of the three pillars of banking crisis policy:[6] crisis prevention (see Sect. 6.1), crisis management (see Sect. 6.2), and crisis resolution (see Sect. 6.3).

An intuitive approach would be to turn back the hands of time of the banking regulations that laid the foundations for the build-up of G-SIBs (see Sect. 3.4.2) and reconsidering (risk-taking) distortions directly. This would include, for instance, abolishing deposit insurance, the LOLR, the limited liability of shareholders, and the tax deduction of debt.[7] Such fundamental and rigorous changes are, however, rarely called upon—except to impose certain restrictions of size and scope (see Sect. 6.1.3). The regulators see themselves in the "financial trilemma"[8]. They have three regulatory objectives: financial stability, financial integration, and national financial policies; but only two of them can be achieved at the same time.

Hence, instead of abolishing G-SIBs, the main goal of current proposals is to reduce the probability of banking crises induced by G-SIBs by forcing G-SIBs to internalise some of the social costs of their existence and thereby penalising banks that have grown too systemically important. That means the dominant research focus is on crisis prevention.[9] However, measures of crisis management and resolution also indirectly prevent crises through signalling. Last but not least, it must be noted that it is not unproblematic to compare various proposals and that there is little agreement on the right regulatory path. Just one example is the difference apparent in the regulatory targeting: some

[5]Comprehensive proposals comprising a wealth of measures have been compiled, partly in response to government requests. The most prominent ones are as follows: the Turner Review (Financial Services Authority (FSA) (March 2009)), the Liikanen Report (Liikanen (2 October 2012)), the Vickers Report (Independent Commission on Banking (September 2011) and Edmonds (30 December 2013)), the Minneapolis Plan (Federal Reserve Bank of Minneapolis (16 November 2016)), and the Squam Lake Working Group on Financial Regulation (Squam Lake Working Group on Financial Regulation (2009), French et al. (2010b), French et al. (2010a), and Baily et al. (2013)).

[6]According to Bordo (2003).

[7]Haldane (2012) estimates that lowering the tax shield on debt by five percentage points could have the same impact as Basel III, which lowers banks' required debt-to-asset ratio by around three percentage points.

[8]Schoenmaker (2011).

[9]In the classical theory according to Musgrave and Musgrave (1989), there are three different functions of public policies: (i) the allocation function, (ii) the stabilisation function, and (iii) the distribution function. It appears that systemic risk is most relevant for allocation policies that allocate public goods through crisis-prevention regulation (De Bandt and Hartmann 2000, 16).

policies aim to reduce the fiscal costs of banking crisis while others aim to reduce the economic costs of lost output.[10]

6.1 Crisis Prevention (*ex ante*)

Measures intended to prevent a crisis aim to reduce the systemic risk of G-SIBs: i.e., to reduce their systemic risk contribution or their systemic sensitivity (see Sect. 2.3). Recommendations focus on the systemic importance of the banking market participants rather than on the transmission, since interlinkages in the financial market are not intrinsically bad (see Sect. 3.3). As with any pollution problem in economics, there are market-based and government-based solutions:

Market-Based Solutions (Market Discipline)

Strengthening market discipline is the first line of defence against TBTF,[11] as it is empowering a better functioning of the intrinsic motivation of the bank stakeholders to manage and control a bank. As a result, business is conducted in a safer, sounder and more efficient manner. Because market discipline imposes strong incentives, it is less subject to subsequent problems of bank regulation such as regulatory arbitrage (see Sect. 2.7). There are two basic ways to strengthen market-based crisis prevention, which should be viewed as complementary rather than mutually exclusive:

- Corporate Governance (see Sect. 6.1.1): Better market discipline is achieved through techniques that remove the information asymmetries and price distortions that lead to moral hazard problems in the first place. Examples include measures to improve corporate governance, public disclosure, or risk-based pricing of deposit insurance. Better market discipline can also comprise deregulatory measures. Indirectly, it provides incentives for banks to maintain stronger capital, funding and liquidity positions.[12]
- Supervision (see Sect. 6.1.2): Enhanced supervision by third parties—i.e., financial regulatory bodies—complements and promotes the intrinsic monitoring of traditional bank stakeholders by a adding a further, particularly knowledgeable control.

[10] Laeven and Valencia (2013a, 233). The main difficulties of banking regulation are summarised in Sect. 2.7.

[11] Meyer (14 June 1999).

[12] Cf. Barth, Caprio, and Levine (2004, 205) and Basel Committee on Banking Supervision (BCBS) (June 1999, 17–18).

Government-Based Solutions

Although there might be some room for market-based corrective solutions, banks may require government intervention in order to internalise all externalities resulting from TBTF. In accord with the economic theory of pollution, either the government can itself undertake the respective activities (as is the case for police and defence) or the can entrust the activities to private banks but regulate them by one or more of these three means:

- Restrictions (see Sect. 6.1.3): Restrictions are also known as (or at least are very similar to) command and control regulations, quantity regulations or prohibitions. Such direct, quantitative regulations impose outright limits on certain bank activities, such as structural limits on the size and scope of a bank's assets and business operations. The social benefits of this kind of regulation are particularly present in complex adaptive systems or 'where the assessment of risk and its regulation and supervision are inherently difficult'.[13] Restrictions have the advantage that they can withstand even the failure of another component of regulation, which increases the likelihood that the regulation will work when needed.[14] A potential downside in banking, however, is that these strict ceilings 'inhibit a bank's ability to realise scale and scope economies, which could contribute to higher costs and other externalities'.[15] Furthermore, it can create motivations to redirect risk-taking outside of the banking sector into the unregulated shadow banking market, which would not reduce systemic risk.[16]
- Price-based regulations (see Sect. 6.1.4): Price-based regulation is also called (Pigouvian[17]) taxation. It is meant to discourage certain banking practices by creating external diseconomies to force banks to internalise the externality. These price-based regulations can comprise the same regulatory measures other banks face but in a stricter form for a selective group, such as G-SIBs. Most frequent are surcharges to liquidity and capital requirements for unexpected events, which in turn also increase market discipline. An advantage of this approach is that it provides efficient incentives by aligning banks and regulators while working hand in hand with market forces. G-SIBs internalise the social cost of TBTF by choosing the efficient amount of production themselves. A potential disadvantage of this method is that it is hardly possible to internalise the tail risk of TBTF. In other words, no capital level will be high enough to avoid the failure of a G-SIB given the risk-seeking nature of banking.

---

[13]Viñals et al. (2013, 23).

[14]A. G. Haldane (30 March 2010) calls these the advantages of modularity and robustness of prohibition.

[15]Beccalli, Anolli, and Borello (2015, 243).

[16]Mester (2010).

[17]Pigou (1920).

- Cap-and-trade regulations: Cap-and-trade regulations are examples of the so-called Coasean[18] approach. The government assigns property rights to banks, e.g., for the right to achieve greater size. Subsequently, banks negotiate among themselves to find the lowest cost solution to TBTF. This process aligns private and social costs by pricing the social costs. The common example of such application is the emission trading of allocated CO2 reduction certificates. In theory, regardless of the initial allocation of the property rights, the overall economical outcomes are identical; however, the profits on the individual bank level are, of course, not identical.[19] There are no known policy proposals for G-SIBs that take this approach, likely due to major roadblocks to the practical implementation in the real world. Global governments are likely to disagree on how to implement tradable systemic risk certificates and on initial allocation to banks. There is also no guarantee that banks will bargain successfully even if a mutually beneficial agreement is possible.

Restrictions Versus Price-Based Regulations

In contrast to market-based solutions, government-based solutions do not complement each other. The question concerning the optimal public choice of quantitative restrictions versus price-based regulations has been considered frequently. The classic public-goods framework of Weitzman (1974) is a useful lens to consider this question. 'Under this framework, the optimal amount of pollution control is found by equating the marginal social benefits of pollution-control and the marginal private costs of this control. With no uncertainty about either costs or benefits, a policymaker would be indifferent between taxation and restrictions when striking this cost/benefit balance'. In the context of TBTF, the precise costs and benefits are very difficult to estimate and hence are uncertain (see Chap. 5). When uncertainty prevails, only one of the methods 'is likely to deliver the better welfare outcome', depending on the relationship of social benefits and private costs. 'If the marginal social benefits foregone of the wrong choice are large, relative to the private costs incurred, then quantitative restrictions are optimal'. This is true because 'fixing quantities to achieve pollution control, while letting prices vary, does not have large private costs'. On the contrary, 'if the private costs of the wrong choice are high, relative to the social benefits foregone, fixing these costs through taxation is likely to deliver the better welfare outcome'. In other words, 'when the marginal social benefit curve is flatter than the marginal private cost curve, taxation dominates', and vice versa.[20]

Chapter 5 concludes that the main private costs are lost economies of scale and scope. These, however, do not exist in banking beyond a moderate threshold. That said, the social benefits of avoiding a banking crisis from TBTF and avoiding G-SIB bailouts appear to be high. For these reasons, this theoretical perspective on social welfare

---

[18]Coase (1960).

[19]Cf. Autor (2004).

[20]A. G. Haldane (30 March 2010, 4).

suggests that the imposition of quantitative restrictions to abolish the TBTF problem may be justified.

6.1.1 Corporate Governance (e.g., Compensation and Disclosure)

Strengthened corporate governance improves market discipline which acts as a natural restraint on excessive risk-taking and other inefficiencies of G-SIBs. This measure generally affects all banks regardless of their size. Nevertheless, the measures that particularly impact G-SIBs are listed here. Measures can be grouped into those which reduce information asymmetries between a bank and its investors by facilitating the monitoring of banks, and those which reduce disincentives that lead to creditor and bank moral hazards (see Sect. 4.2). In general, the purpose is to strengthen the principle of fiduciary duty of various bank stakeholders to avoid or minimise conflicts of interest.[21]

Reducing Information Asymmetries

- Enhanced Information Systems, transparency and disclosure: The GFC revealed significant gaps in the information provided by G-SIBs for their proper monitoring. This applies not only to data available to investors in the public domain, but also for supervisors in the private domain. The information and risk-management infrastructure has simply been outpaced by increasing bank complexity.[22] The non-existence and disclosure of appropriate information exacerbated the negative effects of financial contagion. The key information gaps are in sectoral, market, cross-border, and off-balance sheet items; in transparency in complex derivative and OTC products; and in data on interconnectedness and financial stability.[23] Hence, to strengthen the ability of market participants to assess and compare a banks' exposures, scholars and regulators[24] demand a more timely, uniform, transparent[25], simple, and accurate presentation of G-SIBs' financial conditions.[26] New and improved information infrastructures would

[21]De Bondt (2010, 148). Sometimes the term *corporate* (or *bank*) *governance* is used in a broader sense with regard to regulation and includes measures on bank capital, resolution regimes, etc. (cf. Ellis, Haldane, and Moshirian (2014, 175)).

[22]Cf. Ötker-Robe et al. (2011, 15–16).

[23]Johnston et al. (2009, 3).

[24]E.g. Ötker-Robe et al. (2011, 17), De Bondt (2010, 147), French et al. (2010b, 17), and Johnston et al. (2009, 3).

[25]Cf. Landier and Thesmar (2014) for the trade-off between the benefits of transparency and the costs of public disclosure of financial data, as increasing transparency may also reduce welfare.

[26]Ötker-Robe et al. (2011, 17)

be better able to foresee and prevent potential disruptions of the financial systems and to build trust and understanding.[27]

Reducing Disincentives, Conflicts of Interest and Moral Hazards

- Compensation: Conflicts of interest at G-SIBs have emerged especially with regard to employee compensation. Remuneration of senior bank managers and traders is widely seen as excessive by virtue of the fact that it exploits the hold-up problem between bank managers and shareholders.[28] Moreover, the major part of it, bonuses, is defined based on short-term goals and paid out too quickly without liability.[29] Thus it is demanded to stretch, limit and re-base the compensation.[30] The payoff can depend on a bank's probability of survival and so, for example, on capital ratios and risk-adjusted performance or risk management targets.[31] The overall objective is to better align the interests of the various stakeholders. This can be achieved by paying bonuses in the form of vested bank shares or subordinated debt over longer periods.[32] Moreover, G-SIBs should be required to retain or claw back a substantial share of variable remuneration until uncertainty about employee performance is largely resolved.
- Improving risk management: A criticism frequently heard after the GFC is that not just banks but also bank products (e.g., CDS, OTC derivatives and prime brokerage) and regulation have grown too complex[33] in the wake of decentralized clearing. Hence, it is postulated that regulation should be simplified to avoid regulatory arbitrage (for example, through difficult risk-weighting approaches) and that the banks' risk management be strengthened.

---

[27]French et al. (2010b, 17).

[28]There is a fundamental trade-off between bank managers' hold-up problem and bank managers' rents. The hold-up problem arises because bank managers accumulate specific valuable knowledge while working for a bank. This acts as a threat in compensation negotiations with their banks' financiers and lets managers extract a part of their added value. If, however, the hold-up problem gets mitigated to the benefit of the banks' financiers, the managers' rents subsequently diminish, which also diminishes the managers' incentives to properly monitor borrowers and contribute to overall efficiency (Fecht and Wagner (2009)).

[29]Cf. De Bondt (2010, 147).

[30]Financial Services Authority (FSA) (March 2009).

[31]Baily et al. (2013). E.g., instead of the commonly used measure return on equity (RoE), Haldane (2012) proposes return on assets (RoA) as one appropriate underlying performance measure.

[32]Bhagat, Bolton, and Lu (2015, 533) prove that these measures are connected with a de-risking of bank activities.

[33]Cf. French et al. (2010b, 17).

6.1.2 Supervision (e.g., Supranational Regulator)

Supervisors seek to regulate and correct faults in the existing system. In hindsight, it seems that various supervisors who had dealt with the health of the financial system in the wider sense had focused too narrowly on their specific mandate: e.g., central banks focused too narrowly on controlling inflation and security regulators focused too narrowly on disclosure and market conduct.[34] However, as banks 'have become more complex, government supervisors have found it more difficult to monitor them in a timely manner'.[35] Consequently, neither predicted the depth of the GFC and neither was held responsible for the overall health of the financial system and for specific excesses that had not previously been on the regulatory radar. Regulators were perceived to be relatively lenient towards banks, possibly because they were reluctant to be perceived as hurting the real economy by imposing sanctions in the banking landscape. This is why there are two central proposals with regard to future supervision:[36]

- Creation of a macro-prudential supervisor: A systemic risk regulator is to be established which pools all responsibilities 'for overseeing the health and stability of the overall financial system' in each country.[37] This financial watchdog should hold the power both during the crisis management and resolution of banks (see Sect. 6.3) and for unregulated and non-bank financial intermediaries: i.e., by following the principle of economic substance rather than of legal form. In addition to national super-regulators, there are many calls for a supranational regulator that connects all country supervisors. Through global agreements, such a regulator could also cover offshore financial centres.[38] In particular, with regard to cross-border contagion and resolutions, a supranational regulator is optimal, whereas national regulators often have diverging objectives and information asymmetries.[39]
- Stricter micro-prudential supervision: The fact that creditors of G-SIBs conduct less monitoring than creditors of non-G-SIBs (see Sect. 4.2.3) should be (partly) compensated by stricter supervision by third parties. This would mean not only stricter regulation in traditional key areas (e.g., capital, liquidity and provisioning) but also more pro-active, independent and adaptive regulation of G-SIBs' business models[40] because earlier interventions can substantially reduce costs caused by the TBTF doctrine.

[34]Huertas (2014).

[35]Bliss (2001, 24).

[36]See also Huertas (2014, 50–81) on supervision of G-SIBs.

[37]French et al. (2010b, 17). Cf. Huertas (2014) and De Bondt (2010, 147).

[38]Financial Services Authority (FSA) (March 2009).

[39]Górnicka and Zoican (2016, 53).

[40]Cf. Viñals and Fiechter (2010) and Financial Stability Board (FSB) (2 November 2010).

6.1.3 Restriction (e.g., Limitations of Size and Scope)

There are three broad categories of proposed limits affecting TBTF institutions:[41]

- Limits to size: In October of 2009, Alan Greenspan noted that, 'if [banks] are too big to fail, they are too big.'[42] It is logical to demand that banks avoid TBTF status by breaking up or downsizing to a specific level.[43] As evaluated in Sect. 5.1, banks game the financial system and achieve sizes far beyond the social optimum. The associated benefits of the TBTF status appear to be the preeminent reason for banks to do so. Nevertheless, any quantitative restriction imposed by the government involves the significant challenge of choose the right sized cap: i.e., to satisfy the economies of all individual G-SIBs and to produce the social optimum. As discussed above, size is typically measured by the sum of total assets. Alternative limitations recently proposed include limits on market concentration, which would also reduce the size gap between small and large banks and thereby increase the stability of the entire banking system.[44]
- Limits to scope (ring-fencing): The call to limit or separate banks' business activities has several motivations. First, it indirectly leads to an overall decrease in the size of banks because most can usually only achieve TBTF size by combining several financial businesses. Second, such structural measures separate activities with disparate risk characteristics that generate conflicts of interest, or activities that might be inherently difficult to regulate and supervise.[45] The classical example is ring-fencing: i.e., creating separate legal entities for a bank's capital-market activities, including proprietary trading,[46] and its unrelated activities of deposit taking and lending to small and medium-sized enterprises (SMEs) and retail clients.[47] When such business activities are combined, distress in the globally connected capital markets business can swiftly leapfrog to the rather domestic activities that are refinanced with insured retail deposits.[48] Third, such stand-alone operations are easier to resolve in a bankruptcy proceeding than TBTF conglomerates, which tend to be very complex to resolve.[49]

---

[41]Limitations of risk are generally achieved with price-based regulation (see Sect. 6.1.4).

[42]De Bondt (2010, 147).

[43]Cf. Federal Reserve Bank of Minneapolis (16 November 2016).

[44]Tabak, Fazio, and Cajueiro (2013, 3855).

[45]Viñals et al. (2013, 23).

[46]De Bondt (2010, 147).

[47]Cf. the unintended consequence of the 1933 Glass–Steagall Act that outlawed universal banking in the US (see Sect. 3.4.2) and prohibited deposit-taking banks from operating in the securities business (Morrison (2011, 504–5)).

[48]Blundell-Wignall and Atkinson (2012).

[49]E.g., Viñals et al. (2013, 6).

A functional ring-fencing, for instance of payment and lending functions,[50] could facilitate the continuation of certain activities after the failure of other affiliated businesses. Fourth, legally mandated subsidiarisation leads to overall higher capital and liquidity levels when all subsidies need to comply with capital requirements on a stand-alone basis.[51]

There are also downsides of such restrictions. Economies of scope between various banking operations, even if they are controversial and not really measurable, might exists and could be lost (see Sect. 5.1). Furthermore, such restrictions may lead banks to pull out completely from certain activities.[52]

- Limits to interlinkages: Despite the distinct advantages of interlinkages in the financial system and between banks in particular (see Sect. 3.3), there are also calls for setting strict limits on such interconnections to limit the potential of contagion. This concerns direct interlinkages of interbank exposures[53] and indirect linkages of correlated bank portfolios. Limits could be achieved through the mandatory deduction of such portfolios from banks' equity capital positions.

6.1.4 Price-based regulations (e.g., Capital Surcharges and Contingent Capital)

Price-based regulations, also called (Pigouvian)[54] taxation, creates external diseconomies to force banks to internalise the targeted externality. Indirect taxation, such as surcharges on capital or liquidity requirements, additionally creates greater bank-internal cushions for risks from unexpected events. Direct taxation, such as tax on size, in contrast, additionally compensates the public budget for EGGs and IGGs. Capital requirements,[55] in the form of capital surcharges and additional contingent capital, and a tax on size will now be analysed in detail. Liquidity (or funding) requirements are only infrequently demanded to be increased specifically for G-SIBs.[56]

---

[50]Cf. Mishkin (2006, 1001).

[51]Chow and Surti (2011, 4).

[52]Zulauf (2 April 2016) reports that banks' withdrawals from market-making and proprietary trading have significantly impaired the liquidity and market-pricing situation of previously hyper-liquid markets in Switzerland, such as for sovereign debt.

[53]Todd and Thomson (1990, iii).

[54]Pigou (1920).

[55]Bhagat, Bolton, and Lu (2015, 533) find that the positive association between firm size and risk-taking is not driven only by size per se but also by the unusually high leverage of the larger banks. This is why they suggest that risk-mitigating regulations of banks should focus more on capital requirements rather than on bank size alone.

[56]This is the case, although the GFC revealed that liquidity risk was underestimated, playing a major role in contagious effects. Liquidity requirements can be as effective as capital requirements in preventing contagious failures (Cifuentes, Ferrucci, and Shin (2005)). Liquidity requirements

Capital Surcharges

Equity capital is generally invested with the liability limited to the paid-in capital, while profits are not capped. This asymmetric payoff schedule, in combination with the ability to obtain high and cheap leverage through deposit insurance, leads to the strong incentives to increase the asset risk to increase profits and equity value (see Sect. 2.2). Because it is acknowledged that banks' private optimal leverage is higher (or capitalisation is lower, respectively) than the leverage at social optimum, banks are subject to capital requirements to internalise the costs of their insolvency. The incentive to increase asset risk is strengthened by the TBTF doctrine because not only deposits, but also all liabilities are insured indirectly (see Sect. 4.2.4). This is why higher equity requirements for G-SIBs are widely seen as panacea and have received the most attention.[57] The incentive to take excessive risk resulting from TBTF status, however, cannot be removed by higher capital cushions alone.[58]

There are several dimensions to stricter capital requirements[59] for banks[60]. For G-SIBs, higher minimum risk-based capital ratios have dominated scientific

mandate maintaining a buffer of liquid assets sufficient to meet the net-cash short-term outflows in certain scenarios. The focus here is on withdrawals. Funding requirements mostly refer to potential outflows on a longer-term basis. The focus here is on stability and access to funding (cf. Naqvi (2015), Financial Services Authority (FSA) (March 2009), and Ötker-Robe et al. (2011, 14)).

Moreover, Imbierowicz and Rauch (2014, 242) present evidence that liquidity risk and credit risk do not have an economically meaningful relationship: i.e., they both increase a bank's probability of default (PD), but separately. It can be concluded that surcharges on liquidity requirements for G-SIBs should also be considered a regulatory short-term measure.

[57]Cf. Monopolkommission (9 July 2014).

[58]Only a change of the legal forms of banks that make shareholders liable for losses beyond the paid-in capital would completely remove the incentive of excessive risk-taking. Such a fundamental change of business conventions, however, does not appear feasible (in the mid-term).

[59]Capital requirements are commonly calculated as the ratio of regulatory-recognised capital to risk-weighted assets (RWA). RWA are meant to reflect the different inherent risk levels of a bank's balance sheet. Pre-GFC regulatory minimum requirements for all banks in countries which adopted Basel II were four percent core capital, which comprises mainly genuine common equity (see Fig. 7.2). In the post-GFC period, Basel III has roughly doubled this minimum requirement for all banks.

[60]Capital requirements can be adjusted via the following dimensions (cf. Huertas (2014), Freixas (2010, 386), and Financial Services Authority (FSA) (March 2009, 7)): (i) increasing capital (ratios); (ii) provisioning for business-cycle risk through maintaining conservation or countercyclical capital buffer; (iii) hardening the definition or calculation of capital (i.e., to limit the ability of instruments other than common equity to be part of the regulatory capital); (iv) tighter dividend and provisioning policy (i.e., restrictions of dividend payments when losses are widely anticipated, and exclusion of provisions from regulatory equity as provisions are meant to bear the risk of more or less expected losses) (cf. Freixas (2010, 385)); (v) tightening the regulations for calculating the value of certain (risk-weighted) assets; (vi) computing risks (RWA) through the cycle rather than at one point in time; and (vii) introducing additional complementary capital ratios

and regulatory proposals. The proposed requirements range from 10 to 38 percent.[61]

The impacts of higher capital requirements are controversial[62]—the complexity is particularly reflected in the potential trade-off between bank-failure risk and bank-loan origination:

- Failure risk: Equity capital is immediately and infinitively available and is meant to act as a buffer for unexpected events—especially from credit risks. This is the direct effect of equity that unambiguously decreases the probability of bank default and 'reduces the expected liability of the deposit insurance system'.[63] The indirect effect of capital is its effect on bank risk-taking.[64] The mainstream academic reasoning is that value-maximizing banks with more 'skin in the game' reduce asset risk.[65] Consequently, more capital decreases systemic risk and IGG, and increases market discipline.[66] However, many academics argue that the opposite is the case.[67] 'Higher

which involve less discretion, such as a leverage ratio, to act as a kind of backstop and to prevent banks from practicing regulatory arbitrage.

[61]E.g., 10 percent by Calomiris (2013), approximately 15 percent by Hanson, Kashyap, and Stein (2011), 15–23 percent by Dagher et al. (2016), 20 percent by Miles, Yang, and Marcheggiano (2011), 23.5–38 percent by Federal Reserve Bank of Minneapolis (16 November 2016), and 25 percent by Admati et al. (2013; Admati and Hellwig 2013). Federal Reserve Bank of Minneapolis (16 November 2016, 19) calculate the probability of future banking crisis based the capital requirements.

[62]Plantin (2015, 146) argues that tighter capital regulation incentivises the shift of (systemic) risk into an opaque shadow-banking sector, while looser requirements dry up liquidity in the shadow-banking sector.

[63]Furlong and Keeley (1989, 883). Jorda et al. (2017), however, argue that 'higher capital ratios are unlikely to prevent a financial crisis'. Their empirical evaluation of data on advanced economies between 1870 and 2013 shows that capital indicators have 'no value as a crisis predictor', while liquidity ratios do have such value. Nevertheless, they attribute social benefits, including macro-stability from quicker recoveries from financial crises and recessions, to capital buffers.

[64]Cf. Sect. 4.2.4 which discusses the impact of funding, monitoring and charter value on bank risk-taking. VanHoose (2007) and Iwanicz-Drozdowska (2014, 149–50) provide overviews of studies of bank behaviour and risk-taking under capital regulation.

[65]E.g., Furlong and Keeley (1989, 883). Peek and Rosengren (2005, 1144) prove that the 'ever-greening' behaviour of lending 'to severely impaired borrowers in order to avoid the realisation of losses on their own balance sheets' 'is more prevalent among banks that have reported capital ratios close to the required minimum'.

[66]Laeven, Ratnovski, and Tong (2016).

[67]E.g., Gennotte and Pyle (1991, 820).

capital may have an unintended effect of enabling banks to take more tail risk'[68], or 'if raising equity is excessively costly, the only possibility to increase equity tomorrow is to increase risk today'[69]. Calem and Rob (1999) combine both contrasting theories by formulating a U-shaped relationship of the banks' risk-taking and capital positions. Their model predicts that at low capital levels, risk-taking is a decreasing function of capital, while at high capital levels the opposite is the case.

- Loan origination: The above proposed capital levels were mostly calculated by looking at what would have been sufficient in the past financial crisis to avoid the majority of bank failures. However, it is rarely the case that such high capital buffers are needed. Moreover, since capital ratios decrease during recessions, the cyclical effect of capital requirements hampers the banks' lending activity. This is why the pervasive argument is that increased capital requirements are a constraint on banking output and are thus costly to society. The claim is based on the view that equity is expensive and is only limitedly available. That said, the retained capital might be used inefficiently most of the time and might be scarce during crisis times.[70] Empirical research proves, however, that banks' cost of equity works in the traditional logic of capital costs of Modigliani and Miller (1958), even despite of the distorting deposit insurance. Thus, 'the return on equity contains a risk premium that must go down if banks have more equity'.[71] Moreover, it seems that better capitalised banks pay better attention to stable loan origination and cause less disruption of lending during crises because they can better shield their lending from (monetary policy) shocks.[72] In summary, while an increase in capital requirements is indeed associated with a reduction of loan growth, this effect is small[73] and is completely offset if banks hold moderately high levels of capital[74].

With respect to the overall public costs and benefits of higher capital requirements in general, or capital surcharges for G-SIBs in particular, there has apparently been a shift in the view of academics. This is presumably the case because the cost of banking crises

[68]Perotti, Ratnovski, and Vlahu (2011).

[69]Blum (1999, 755).

[70]Blum and Hellwig (1995, 739).

[71]Admati et al. (2013). Cf. Toader (2015). Besanko and Kanatas (1996, 178–79) report an exemption in which the 'issuing equity may dilute the ownership of bank insiders sufficiently to reduce their incentives to expend effort on behalf of the bank's stockholders'. This means the 'dilution effect can overcome the chief benefit of capital standards'. This leads to 'the perverse effect of reducing the market value of their equity'. Fig. 12.3 illustrates how equity requirements (calculated as the equity / total assets (E/A) ratio) impact equity profitability (RoE) at various asset-return (RoA) levels.

[72]Gambacorta and Mistrulli (2004, 454).

[73]Noss and Toffano (2016, 15).

[74]Deli and Hasan (2017).

and bankruptcies have risen over time. While earlier studies[75] recognise deadweight costs of stricter capital standards, most academics today recognise welfare gains[76].

Contingent Capital

The disadvantages of higher capital requirements discussed above—the inefficiently used capital during economic expansion and the cyclical effect during economic contraction—have spawned calls[77] for a new class of financial instruments specifically designed for large banks. These instruments, called contingent capital or contingent convertible securities (CoCos or CC), are issued by banks as subordinated bonds with a fixed maturity during normal times. When a predetermined crisis trigger event occurs, their principal and scheduled coupon payments are automatically converted or (temporarily) written down into equity (without maturity).[78] CoCos are complex hybrids that combine favourable characteristics of debt and equity instruments to realign the incentives of bank stakeholders, which is ultimately also beneficial to the public. The main general objective is to establish a contractual structure that increases core capital in adverse situations. This can occur either directly through converted CoCos or indirectly through incentives to raise new capital voluntarily.[79] The intended impact of CoCos depends crucially upon its contractual design, which specifically regulates the incentives to transfer wealth between debt and equity holders.[80] The three key parameters and trade-offs that determine CoCos are:

- Issuance amount: The amount of CoCos to be issued shall generally be sufficient to (entirely) recapitalise a bank and to dilute the old shareholders (depending on the conversion terms). It is possible either to issue one kind of CoCos with the same credit terms (i.e., the full amount will be converted at the same trigger event) or with various terms.
- Conversion trigger: The conversion can be either be triggered by a contractually fixed event or at the full discretion of shareholders or the supervisor. A fixed trigger event is frequently based on regulatory, accounting or market ratios.
- Conversion terms: This central parameter governs the wealth transfer from debt to equity holders or vice versa. The CoCos can either be written down (conversion ratio

[75]E.g., Gennotte and Pyle (1991, 820).

[76]E.g., Admati et al. (2013).

[77]E.g., De Bondt (2010, 147) and French et al. (2010b, 17).

[78]Pazarbasioglu et al. (2011, 4). Cf. Sect. 6.3, which describes a resolution regime in which usual bank debt can be converted into equity or written down at the discretion of the supervisor and without a bankruptcy proceeding.

[79]Calomiris and Herring (2013, 44).

[80]Maes and Schoutens (2012, 66–67) give many examples of the disadvantages of CoCos if their contracts are badly designed.

of zero; 'stock-friendly') or converted into equity. The conversion ratio can be fixed or flexible based on predefined market prices. The higher the conversion ratio, the higher the dilution of the incumbent shareholders, which corresponds to a motivation to decrease asset risk. At a conversion level of one ('CoCo-friendly'), the CoCo holders become the sole new shareholders.[81]

Depending on the above characteristics, CoCos can cover both extreme cases: It can be used as an early prevention tool (high trigger relative to the point of insolvency, low conversion into equity) or as an orderly resolution tool (low trigger, high conversion).[82] This is also referred to as conversion timing. CoCos can 'generate better risk incentives than either debt or equity in isolation'.[83] If the terms of CoCos are ill-designed, however, they can easily cause perverse incentives of bank stakeholders, which further promotes systemic risk. This is why the appropriate choice of parameters is crucial, which subsequently can lead to the following benefits of CoCos:

- Improved capital efficiency / mitigated capital-raising problems: Compared to the elevation of simple capital requirements, CoCos have several advantages. While both the build-up and holding of excessive equity can hamper a bank's loan origination, CoCos deliver the same equity cushion for loss absorption but at lower social and private cost of capital. CoCos can either indirectly encourage timely voluntary equity raisings or directly inject fresh capital into a bank. Raising external capital is often impossible when a bank is in distress. Shareholders typically want to avoid a capital increase and their connected heavy dilution due to the 'lemons problem'[84] of newly issued shares and the debt-overhang problem.[85]
- Mitigated time-inconsistency and forbearance problems: CoCo contracts with predefined trigger events before a crisis arises do not leave much room for the discretion of bank stakeholders. In particular, they help to prevent regulatory forbearance (see Sect. 4.1.3): that is, the supervisors' reluctance to recognise losses.[86] Albeit manipulable, market-based triggers are especially beneficial in the sense that they remove the

[81]Hilscher and Raviv (2014, 542).

[82]Calomiris and Herring (2013, 57–59) present a summary of CoCo term recommendations proposed in the literature with regard to the three parameters: issuance amounts, conversion triggers, and conversion terms.

[83]Haldane (2012, 56).

[84]Akerlof (1970).

[85]'If a bank carries substantial impaired assets and has a lot of debt relative to equity, the market value of debt will reflect the higher probability of default and any equity injection will benefit the debt holders by pushing up the market value of their claims. However, private investors are only willing to invest new capital in a bank if their investment does not instantly leak away to prop up the value of the debt holders' (Maes and Schoutens (2012, 65–66)).

[86]Calomiris and Herring (2013, 56).

time-inconsistency problem (see Sect. 5.4) of recapitalisation decisions and often signal distress well ahead of a crisis.[87]

- Reduced risk-taking: The risk-taking behaviour of banks can be decreased in several dimensions with the help of CoCos. First of all, outstanding subordinated debt in general enhances market monitoring and discipline,[88] as such debt has the lowest probability of all liabilities of being bailed out (see Sect. 4.1.2). Secondly, a credible threat of losses due to conversion and dilution helps to limit risk-taking on behalf of the shareholders.[89]
- Reduced failure risk: All of the above results in a reduced failure risk of banks when well-designed CoCos are issued, implying that they are an effective tool for stabilising banks.[90] The conversion of CoCos into equity well ahead of bankruptcy avoids deadweight and bankruptcy costs. Subsequently, less bailout money needs to be injected into these banks with such privately born self-insurance for distress.

G-SIB Levy Tax

The government provides two fundamental forms of relief to banks: under-priced deposit insurance (see Sect. 2.4) and tax-deductible interest on debt. Both have massively helped banks grow their balance sheets and risk exposure (see Sect. 3.4). This is why there are proposals to counterbalance these two reliefs by imposing a levy tax on G-SIBs. The reasoning is twofold: first, such a TBTF tax would by design discourage excessive risk-taking and to be systemically important; second, it would finance ex-ante the rescue of G-SIBs.[91] The tax works differently from a capital surcharge, as the capital is not retained on a company-level but in a fund or at the government-level, which can possibly be more capital-efficient. This means that it works like deposit insurance arrangements but in extended form only for G-SIBs and for a wider scope of creditors.[92] A tax is controversial, as the perception of paying an insurance premium against failure has the same major downsides as the deposit insurance: extended creditor and bank moral hazards. This is why a linkage to effective resolution mechanisms (Sect. 6.3) is even more important.[93]

---

[87]Cf. Sundaresan and Wang (2015) and Haldane (2012).

[88]Jagtiani, Kaufman, and Lemieux (2002, 559).

[89]Ötker-Robe et al. (2011, 14). This works like the threat of losing a bank's charter value (see Sect. 4.2.4).

[90]Hilscher and Raviv (2014, 542).

[91]Ex-post recovery charges are also possible but have significant drawbacks: (i) they impose a burden only on industry survivors, and (ii) they are pro-cyclical, demanding payments from banks when they are least able to make them (International Monetary Fund (IMF) (June 2010)).

[92]The International Monetary Fund (IMF) (June 2010) presents a report at the request of the G20 to examine options for bank levies. It comprises thoughts on the key operational characteristics.

[93]Cf. Ötker-Robe et al. (2011, 15) and Schich and Kim (2010, 2).

6.2 Crisis Management (*ex post*)

Once a crisis has erupted, crisis management comes into play. Crisis management typically involves relatively short-term government measures targeting either the organisation of liquidity support or capital forbearance (see Sect. 4.1.3). Hence, crisis management is primarily concerned with the rules and with the extent of government interventions and what signals it sends to the market. Generally, there is little room for crisis management of G-SIBs as truly G-SIBs will always be rescued.

- First G-SIB fails: This is the proposal for a policy pledge that only the first G-SIB fails.[94] The logic is to strengthen the market discipline of uninsured creditors, while the economic costs of just one major failure would outweigh the benefits of increased market discipline. In the eyes of proponents, a government pledge to allow only one G-SIB to fail appears more credible than a pledge to not bail out any bank.[95]
- International LOLR: An international LOLR[96] is an institution that undertakes concerted actions on an international level to support G-SIBs with liquidity. Since the interbank market is an international one, the contagion risk is also international. This is why proponents argue that an international LOLR is necessary for reducing international contagion.

6.3 Crisis Resolution

The objective of crisis resolution is to resolve the distress experienced by a G-SIB. By definition (see Sect. 3.1), it is not reasonable for a government to let a G-SIB fail and declare bankruptcy. The bankruptcy costs of a usual bankruptcy resolution regime (see Sect. 2.3), including the disruption costs of the economy, far exceed the bailout costs of a G-SIB (see Chap. 5). A G-SIB that almost failed—even with the measures in place to prevent and manage such a failure—should be considered inefficient and not be allowed to return to the market in its failed form[97].[98]

---

[94]Mishkin (2006, 1001) and Stern and Feldman (2009b).

[95]It should be noticed that the initial idea for such a policy comes from the pre-GFC era. The Lehman Brother's failure likely contributed significantly to the severity of the GFC (see Sect. 3.4.5).

[96]E.g., Goodhart and Huang (2000, 1).

[97]Cf. the creation of so called 'zombie' banks (Kane 1987) during the S&L crisis, which are mainly due to regulatory forbearance (see Sect. 3.4.4), which allows banks that are insolvent to continue to roll over their debt ((Kane 2015, 12) and Moyer and Lamy (1992)).

[98]There is considerable confusion in the academic literature over the use of the terms *rescue process* (or *bailout*) and *resolution process* (or *restructuring*). Changing the resolution regime does not affect the rescue process (Kaufman (2015, 3)).

A G-SIB in trouble will be rescued and stabilised with the methods described in Sect. 4.1.3. What follows is a discussion of how the government handles the G-SIB in the aftermath. It has frequently been proposed[99] that the government establish a strict resolution regime including heavy restructuring on the rescued G-SIB to prevent resulting moral hazards.[100] A resolution regime is preparation for the rare event that a G-SIB is rescued.[101] Such a light version of bankruptcy shows how a market exit of the G-SIB can be facilitated. This is also a powerful tool for policymakers to establish credibility—i.e., to avoid time-inconsistency (see Sect. 5.4)—by not providing an unlimited safety net.[102] Improving the ability of the government to maintain the vital banking functions makes resolution more feasible and credible.[103] This has the positive effect of reducing IGG, as bank stakeholders clearly understand how they will be penalised. 'Uninsured creditors will worry that large risk-taking banks will expose the [them] to losses.'[104] The proposed resolution regime fulfils two government objectives once the rescue of a G-SIB has been triggered:

- Living wills and bank resolution—protecting the financial system and vital banking functions
- Burden sharing and individual sanctions—minimising bailout costs and preventing future bailouts and IGG

Living Wills and Bank Resolution

One the hand, the goal is to restructure the rescued G-SIB—especially the business parts causing the initial distress—by shrinking those operations, breaking them into smaller entities or closing down and liquidating certain operations.[105] On the other hand, the continuity of all critical services performed by a G-SIB shall be ensured, thereby reducing risks to financial instability. Resolving a bank is lengthy and complicated (see Chap. 5) due to the complexities of G-SIBs (see Sect. 3.3). There are several components that could ease a resolution:

---

[99]E.g., by Squam Lake Working Group on Financial Regulation (2009) and French et al. (2010b, 17).

[100]Korte (2015, 213) finds that a relatively stronger implementation of bank resolution rules has a significantly positive effect on firm growth, particularly with regard to firms that are more dependent on financing from banks.

[101]Cf. Huertas (2014, 82–133) on bank resolutions.

[102]Jarque and Price (2015, 79).

[103]Ötker-Robe et al. (2011, 17–20).

[104]Mishkin (2006, 991). Ignatowski and Korte (2015, 264) find that only non-G-SIBs decreased their overall risk-taking as a result of the implementation of bank-resolution regimes (orderly liquidation authority) in the US.

[105]Federal Deposit Insurance Corporation (FDIC) & Bank of England (BoE) (10 December 2012, ii).

- Living wills: Banks shall be obliged to prepare themselves for a potential failure and resolution by writing their own so-called living will. These plans need to be approved by the respective supervisor. Thinking through the steps of resolving the bank prior to any crisis is not just prudent; it also enables the bank and supervisors to calmly consider what measures are likely to work best and disrupt normal operations least.[106] Living wills—also called bank-resolution or wind-down plans—can be split in three chronological parts: First, they highlight the key complexities of the bank's organisational and financing structures. In urgent, emergency situations, this information helps supervisors as lenders and other banks as acquirers to more swiftly assess the financial health of a G-SIB. Second, G-SIBs lay out a 'detailed strategic plan for a rapid and orderly resolution in the event of distress'. This comprises how the legal dismantling—also with respect to cross-border presences and burden-sharing—can be executed. A recovery capital and liquidity plan for stress situations ensures that the need for government assistance can be reduced to a minimum.[107] Third, G-SIBs lay out the foundations of how the resolution can be facilitated. This can be achieved by simplifying the legal structure and by making the legal entities commensurate with the functional business lines.[108] Overall, the production of living wills and the execution of structural changes to make a bank resolvable is very expensive. This can be seen as a further deliberate penalty for G-SIBs.[109]
- There are, however, also various pitfalls to establishing living wills. For example, G-SIBs operate in various jurisdictions with various supervisors and face incompatibilities with regard to the resolution plans of cross-border activities and different national regulators. Every national regulator might want to increase the number of assets that stay in national territory to protect local creditors (also called global asset grab).[110]
- Resolution authority: Given the formidable nature of G-SIB resolution, two main demands are usually made with regard to the respective supervisory body: First, a single public institution should have the power and authority to deal with all aspects of a G-SIB resolution, starting from the approval of the living wills, to the decision to bail out the G-SIB, to the execution of the wind-down. Such an institution shall be as independent as possible from national governments and act in the interest of global financial stability. Second, a supranational institution should oversee all G-SIBs—regardless of their home regulator—to overcome the cross-border challenges of resolution.[111]

[106]Huertas (2 October 2009).

[107]Jarque and Price (2015, 82–84).

[108]Avgouleas, Goodhart, and Schoenmaker (2013, 210).

[109]See Jarque and Price (2015, 84–85).

[110]Ford (17 April 2016).

[111]Cf. Carmassi and Herring (2013, 378).

- Resolution legislation: The government needs to establish a comprehensive legislative framework for a resolution regime that ensures that G-SIBs are resolvable in the smoothest way possible. Only a consistent legal regime on an international basis enables a fast and efficient resolution. The governmental efforts need to include the described living wills and resolution authority, as well as divesture rules. All of which must be regulated in accord with provisions on bank recovery and security mechanisms, such as institutional security and deposit insurance.[112]

Individual Sanctions and Burden Sharing (bail-in)
Bank rescues are expensive and resolution plans for G-SIBs should minimise these costs. Before taxpayers carry the burden of a rescue, bank stakeholders should cover the expenses:[113]

- Burden sharing with shareholders and creditors: Liability and shareholders can generally only be ousted legally if a bank declares bankruptcy. These legal complications are a major reason why creditors rarely faced losses and have not been prepared to bear losses in the past. For G-SIBs, however, the government is invested in avoiding bankruptcy to prevent major financial market disruption. This is why a key element of any proposed resolution regime is the statutory power of a resolution authority to restructure all the liabilities of a distressed G-SIB. This ensures that shareholders and creditors bear the losses of a G-SIB failure and provides additional loss-absorbing capacity during distress. Such discretionary restructuring—as opposed to contractual agreements with certain capital triggers (e.g., for contingent capital; see Sect. 6.1.4)—can be executed either by writing down the bank's unsecured debt or by converting it to equity. The legal foundations are not supposed to be included in liabilities credit terms, but in banking law. This is also called a bail-in of creditors.[114] The bail-in process should mirror the legal hierarchy of the claims under bankruptcy[115] and not be left to the discretion of regulators[116]. This gives certainty to the debt holders, who fare better than in a bankruptcy because the franchise value of the bank gets preserved.[117]
- Individual sanctions on the bank management: Bank moral hazard is ultimately to be accounted for by the bank management: i.e., by individuals that are incentivised mostly short-term and not bound long-term to a bank. After the GFC, G-SIBs were levied with heavy fines for bad behaviour; individuals were levied only on a very

112 Monopolkommission (9 July 2014)

113 Sect. 4.1.4 lists the ways stakeholders can contribute to bailout costs.

114 Zhou et al. (2012, 3) present a comprehensive review of how bail-in works and when it should be applied.

115 Huertas (2014).

116 Squam Lake Working Group on Financial Regulation (2009).

117 Cf. Kaufman (2014).

selective basis and for extreme wrong-doings, ethical failures and reckless risk-taking. Many reformers call for sanctioning individuals with fines and exclusion from working in banking.[118]

A resolution regime, if applied in a strict manner, in which nonviable G-SIBs can be resolved, shareholders wiped out, losses of unsecured creditors absorbed, and management sanctioned would increase market discipline and reduce the moral hazard risk posed by G-SIBs. Moreover, it would reduce the likelihood and amount of government funds needed.[119]

118 Kane (2015, 15).

119 Ötker-Robe et al. (2011, 17–20).

TBTF Policy Initiatives

7

Before 2009, there were very few policies against TBTF (see Sect. 3.4).[1] The efforts to tackle the TBTF problem during a phase without crises in the 2000s can be described as purposefully ambiguous: i.e., it concerned policy that was neither explicit about which banks were to be considered TBTF nor what should happen in the event of the insolvency of a G-SIB. The regulatory regime was not based on bank size but on bank type. Deposit-gathering institutions were regulated to minimise the costs and moral hazards stemming from deposit insurance.[2] It was not until the recent GFC that policymakers seriously focused on the matter of the TBTF doctrine. While the first policy recommendations were made quickly during and after the GFC from 2007–2009, the first policies to contain the systemic risk of banks were agreed upon in 2010. Most of them, in fact, came into force much later—many with bank-friendly phase-in periods until the mid-2020s. The US acted most resolutely and quickly, not only with regards to public bank recapitalisations, but also with regard to special legislation for G-SIBs. In general, bank regulation has become much more important since the GFC because it is now widely acknowledged that the TBTF doctrine is a real and massive problem for a well-functioning financial system (see Sect. 2.1). 'Next to monetary and fiscal policy, the promotion of safety and soundness of financial intermediaries has become the third major pillar of public policy'.[3] Ten years after the beginning of the GFC, there are still efforts underway, but with the focus now on the systemic risk of non-banks, such as asset managers. Due

[1]Mishkin (2006, 996).

[2]Labonte (30 June 2015).

[3]Deli and Hasan (2017, 217).

T. F. Lesche, *Too-Big-to-Fail in Banking*, Finanzwirtschaft, Banken und Bankmanagement I Finance, Banks and Bank Management, https://doi.org/10.1007/978-3-658-34182-4_7

to the booming global economy and the absence of major bank insolvencies, policymakers and bankers have increasing called for the reversal of G-SIB regulation.[4]

The recently implemented bank regulations comprise system-wide (or macro-prudential) and bank-level (or micro-prudential) regulation. These two complementary approaches correspond to the occurrence of systemic risk (see Sect. 2.3) in the form of systemic-risk sensitivity (from the macro to the micro level) and systemic risk contribution (from micro to the macro level), respectively. The focus is again on the micro level of bank regulation. Chapter 6 illustrates, foremost, the need to force banks to internalise the social costs of being TBTF: i.e., to make banks (implicitly) pay for EGGs and IGGs. In large part, policymakers have followed academics' and regulators' TBTF policy proposals, including: (i) reduce G-SIB risk-taking, (ii) minimise contagion risk, (iii) enact regulatory and supervisory integration, and (iv) improve the efficiency of resolution regimes.[5] These are mirrored in the initiatives that have been announced or implemented by legislators. The cornerstone of G-SIB regulation are capital requirements. Corporate governance and restrictions were less in focus on policy agendas.[6]

This chapter gives a brief overview of the key measures of local (euro area and US) and global policies since the GFC. The most important policies were adopted by the European Banking Union (see Sect. 7.1) and set forth in the *Dodd-Frank Act* in the US (see Sect. 7.2). The two major standard-setting bodies (SSBs) in banking are the BCBS and the FSB. Their major recommendations are the Basel III regulations (see Sect. 7.3) and the G-SIB regulations (see Sect. 7.4), respectively. These policies were not only implemented into domestic law by the EU and the US, their reach also extends across the globe. The G-SIB regulations are the first and only initiatives that include binding rules only for global G-SIBs.

7.1 European Banking Union

The European banking union has two main pillars:

- *Single Supervisory Mechanism* (SSM): 'The SSM is a new system of banking supervision for Europe. It comprises the ECB and the national supervisory authorities of the participating countries.' 'All euro area countries participate automatically in the SSM. Other EU countries that do not yet have the euro as their currency can choose to participate'.

[4]E.g., the President of the USA, Donald J. Trump (Jopson and Leatherby (13 March 2017))

[5]Blundell-Wignall and Atkinson (2010).

[6]Cf. Ellis, Haldane, and Moshirian (2014, 175).

- Single Resolution Mechanism (SRM): The SRM's purpose is to facilitate the more efficient resolution of failing banks and to centralising decision-making at the EU level. A *Single Resolution Board* (SRB) shall 'ensure swift decision-making procedures, allowing a bank to be resolved over a weekend', while forcing banks' creditors to share the burden. 'As a supervisor, the ECB will have an important role in deciding whether a bank is failing or is likely to fail. A *Single Resolution Fund* (SRF), financed by contributions from banks, will be available to pay for resolution measures.'

While the SSM applies only to large banks with total assets of € 30 billion or more, the SRM applies to all banks of participating EU countries. Both the SSM and the SRM were passed in 2014 and were subsequently implemented throughout the EU. 'The two pillars rest on the foundation of the single rulebook, which applies to all EU countries.'[7] The single rulebook harmonises European banking-supervision law—its key elements are the following:

1. the *Capital Requirements Regulation* (CRR) and the *Capital Requirements Directive IV* (CRD IV), which are based on the global recommendation of the BCBS (see Sect. 7.3);
2. the *Bank Recovery and Resolution Directive* (BRRD) and the *Deposit Guarantee Schemes Directive* (DGSD);
3. the regulatory technical standards (RTS) and implementing technical standards (ITS) issued by the *European Commission* (EC); and
4. the guidelines and recommendations of the *European Banking Authority* (EBA), which was established on 1 January 2011.

In summary, the European banking union established a large number of initiatives, as discussed in Chap. 6. It is certainly too early to assess the full impact of these measures—in particular with regard to future crises stemming from TBTF. However, it is already clear that the new and harmonised legal framework still leaves some potential for discretionary interventions by the governments of EU member states.[8] One example of such intervention was on the one hand, the wiping out of billions in debt during the financial disruption at *Novo Banco* in 2016 and at *Banco Populare* in 2017 marked 'a new era in which bank bondholders are no longer king', i.e. can no longer rely on the protection in the EU.[9] On the other hand, the case of *Banca Monte dei Paschi di Siena*

[7]European Central Bank.

[8]Zimmer, Weck, and Schepp (2015, 101).

[9]Jenkins (April 18, 2016). See also Hale (30 March 2016).

in the same period illustrates that one EU-country government can exert sufficient pressure on the newly established central institutions to avoid such burden-sharing with bank stakeholders while using taxpayers' money.

7.2 Dodd-Frank Act in the US

The *Dodd-Frank Wall Street Reform and Consumer Protection Act*, commonly referred to as the *Dodd–Frank Act* (or DFA), brought about the most significant changes to financial regulation in the US since the Great Depression. It affected all federal financial regulatory agencies and most of the US' financial services industry. It was signed into law on 21 July 2010. Although it targeted the entire US financial system, one of the express purposes of DFA, according to its preamble, is 'to end "too big to fail"'. The key DFA regulations specifically addressing TBTF include:

- Title I—Financial Stability: This *Financial Stability Act of 2010* established the Financial Stability Oversight Council (FSOC) to identify risks and respond to emerging threats to financial stability–in particular, from institutions deemed TBTF. The DFA itself effectively identifies so-called systemically-important financial institutions (SIFIs) as all banks or non-banks with assets of US$ 50 billion or more. According to Section 165, these SIFIs are supervised more closely and required to operate with higher levels of capital and to face further limitations on their activities. Section 171 of the DFA, the so-called *Collins Amendment*, sets a uniform-leverage and risk-based capital floor for all U.S. banks. Subsequently, the Basel III capital standards complemented these standards (see Sect. 7.3).
- Title II—Orderly Liquidation Authority: This part of the DFA extends the FDIC's authority to resolve failed firms designated as SIFIs. The newly established Orderly Liquidation Authority (OLA) repays the FDIC for any costs incurred by a SIFI resolution, and it is to be funded by all SIFIs. This means that the OLA provides a superior alternative to the only other choices: bailout or bankruptcy. To aid in this process, SIFIs are required to develop resolution plans in advance to facilitate the bank resolution.
- Title III—Transfer of Powers to the Comptroller, the FDIC, and the Fed: The *Enhancing Financial Institution Safety and Soundness Act of 2010* 'is intended to streamline banking regulation and reduce competition and overlaps between different regulators'.
- Title VI—Improvements to Regulation: Section 619 of the *Bank and Savings Association Holding Company and Depository Institution Regulatory Improvements Act of 2010*, which is also dubbed *Volcker Rule*, is particularly relevant. It generally 'prohibits any banking entity from engaging in proprietary trading or from acquiring or retaining an ownership interest in, sponsoring or having certain relationships with a

hedge fund or private equity fund'. 'The motivation for this type of institutional separation is the increased scope for conflicts of interest and risk-taking when banks are allowed to combine lending, securities underwriting, and market-making with proprietary trading and investment on their own account.'[10]

In summary, the significant reforms brought about by the DFA makes the US significantly better prepared, on paper, against systemic risks due to TBTF. Although the DFA 'presents unassisted bankruptcy as the preferred option', the OLA 'gives regulators the power to resolve large financial firms in distress through an administrative process' 'if they conclude that unassisted failure would threaten financial stability'. While this side door of financial assistance is initially funded with taxpayer money, the DFA obliges the SIFIs to fund the OLA *ex-post.*[11] However, 'the net effect of the OLA is likely to be that the moral-hazard problem prevails'.[12]

7.3 Global BCBS regulation: Basel III

While it took more than 15 years to rework the first Basel Accords, which culminated in Basel II (see Sect. 3.4.4), it took just above seven years for the next workover, thanks to reform pressure from the GFC. On 16 December 2010, the BCBS published its new regulatory framework, Basel III, which was finalised on 7 December 2017 after years of revisions. The overall objective 'is to create a more disciplined and less procyclical financial system that better supports balanced sustainable economic growth'. These global BCBS policies[13] are recommendations for the minimum standards 'to strengthen the regulation, supervision and risk management of the banking sector'. Subsequently, they need to be enacted into law by all participating countries. The BCBS comprises 45 members from 28 major developed countries. They consist of central banks and banking regulators. The application is, however, by far more far-reaching globally.[14]

Basel III essentially targets the two fundamental bank risks: credit risk (to be contained by capital regulations) and liquidity risk (to be contained by liquidity regulations) (see Fig. 7.1). Completely new are the rules on liquidity, which are in place due to the lessons learnt from the GFC when various bank funding markets dried up completely.

[10]Chow and Surti (2011, 13). This is similar to the *Glass–Steagall Act* of 1933 (see Sect. 3.4.2).

[11]Cf. Kaufman (2015, 6–7).

[12]Jarque and Price (2015, 80–81).

[13]Basel Committee on Banking Supervision (BCBS) (December 2017).

[14]Broadly speaking, Basel III includes Basel II and decisions taken since then by the BCBS. In particular, it includes a package of measures from 2009–2011 referred to informally as "Basel II plus" or "Basel 2.5" for strengthening the rules, especially for securitisations and market risk.

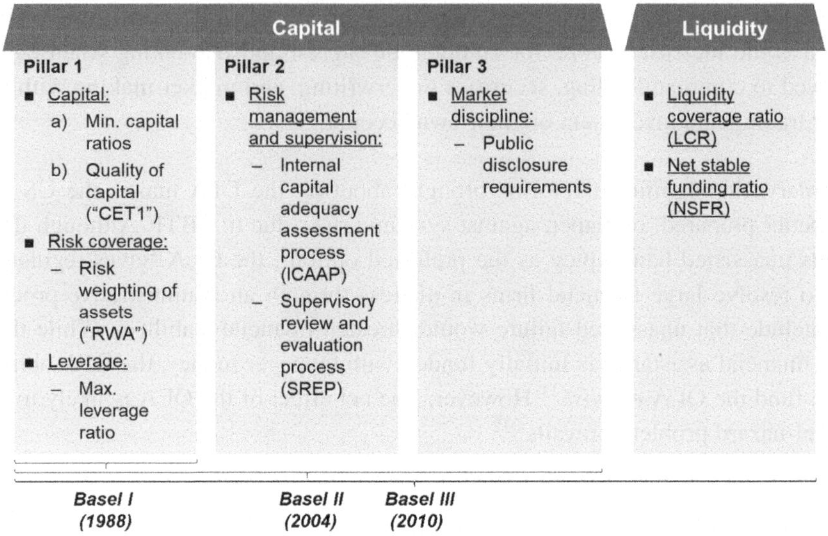

Fig. 7.1 Components of Basel I-III

Capital Regulations

The overall guideline of the Basel III capital regulation prohibits leverage from increasing to the extent that it did during the GFC. To this end, each of the three pillars introduced in Basel II was tightened. Pillar 1 represents the traditional approach of requiring banks to keep certain capital minimum ratios. Pillar 2 requires bank management (Internal Capital Adequacy Assessment Process (ICAAP)) and regulators (Supervisory Review and Evaluation Process (SREP)) to develop their own assessments of a banks' individual adequate capitalisation. The SREP may lead to discretionary capital surcharges relative to Pillar 1 for individual banks. The public disclosure requirements in Pillar 3 ensure that outsiders can also receive sufficient information to form their view and thereby improve market discipline.

The centrepiece of the reworked Basel regulation is Pillar 1's minimum capital ratio, which ensures that banks are sufficiently capitalised even after incidents from unexpected risks. The main capital ratio is defined as follows:

$$CET1\ ratio = \frac{CET1\ capital}{RWA}$$

This equation contains the following elements:

- Common equity tier 1 (CET1) capital: Basel I and Basel II focused on total capital, which comprises not only genuine equity capital but also some types of capital securities, such as subordinated debt. The GFC made it clear that only common equity could absorb losses on a going-concern basis. This is why the capital composition of Basel III's CET1 capital has become much narrower, as illustrated in Fig. 7.2.

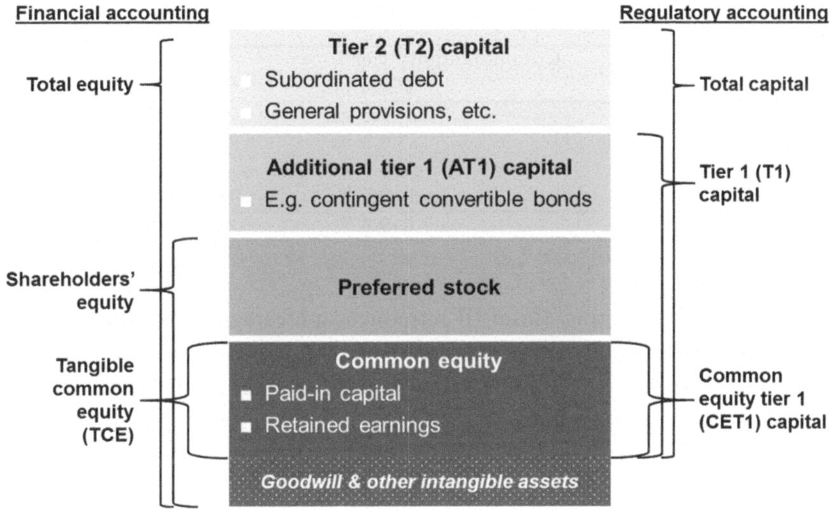

Fig. 7.2 Bank capital composition

- Risk-weighted assets (RWA): Basel I already mandated that bank assets were multiplied with risk-factors to take into account the different expected losses of bank exposures. To derive the respective risk-factors, banks are allowed to choose between a standardised approach with fixed risk buckets and two internal ratings-based approaches (IRBA) that require a bank's own estimation of risk factors.[15] This means that credit risk is generally the main inflation factor for RWA. In addition, trading risk and operational risk are also converted into an RWA measure. Under Basel III, the calculation of all three risk types was tightened while a minimum output floor of 72.5% for the total RWA amount was established.
- CET1 ratio: Under Basel I and II, the BCBS recommended at least eight percent total capital of RWA. The focus under Basel III is on CET1 capital, and additional buffers lead to a significant increase in the respective minimum ratios (see Table 7.1), which have to be fully complied with by 2019 at the latest. While the capital conservation buffer is fixed at 2.5 percent, a countercyclical buffer of up to 2.5 percent is imposed when authorities 'judge that credit growth is resulting in an unacceptable build-up of system-wide risk'. In addition to these capital ratio requirements, G-SIBs are obliged to keep additional CET1 of up to 3.5 percent (see Sect. 7.4).

[15]Under IRBA the expected losses of assets are generally calculated as: *Expected Loss* (*EL*) = *Loss Given Default* (*LGD*) × *Probability of Default* (*PD*) × *Exposure at Default* (*EaD*).

Table 7.1 Basel III minimum capital requirements

	Common equity tier 1 (CET1)	Tier 1 (T1)	Total capital (TC)
Minimum	4.5 %	6.0 %	8.0 %
+ Capital conservation buffer	2.5 %	2.5 %	2.5 %
+ Countercyclical buffer	0.0–2.5 %	0.0–2.5 %	0.0–2.5 %
Total	7.0–9.5 %	8.5–11.0 %	10.5–13.0 %

In addition to the capital ratios, Basel III introduces a leverage ratio, which aims to prevent banks from excessive leverage when risk-weightings are very low (e.g., for large government bond portfolios). It is also supposed to provide a much simpler way than capital ratios to avoid gaming behaviour. The minimum leverage ratio starts at 3.0 percent and was implemented starting in 2018.

Liquidity Regulations
Basel III implements two ratios with regard to the liquidity risk of banks: the liquidity coverage ratio (LCR), which covers a short-term, 30-day stress scenario; and the net stable funding ratio (NSFR), which is designed to ensure that banks will be funded in a 12-months crisis scenario.

7.4 Global FSB Regulation: G-SIBs

The G20 meeting in November 2008 took place amid the ongoing GFC. The participating members called for the prudential regulation of G-SIBs, which led to the establishment of the Financial Stability Board (FSB) in April of 2009 as the successor to the *Financial Stability Forum* (FSF). Like the FSF, but with a broadened mandate, the FSB enhances cooperation among the various national and international supervisory bodies so as to promote stability in the global financial system. It exemplifies the first approach to reducing systemic risk on a global level. After Basel III was agreed upon in 2010, which affects banks regardless of their size, the G20 leaders focused on the treatment of institutions deemed TBTF, which the FSB branded as global-systemically important financial institutions (G-SIFIs). Table 7.2 presents a chronology of the main events of the FSB's G-SIB regulation—also known as G-SIB regulation.[16] This G-SIB regulation is closely associated with Basel III because FSB and BCBS collaborate closely. As is the case in Basel III, the centrepiece of the G-SIB regulation are the capital requirements for targeted banks. In autumn 2011, the additional capital surcharges were endorsed and the first official list with 29 banks designated as G-SIBs was published by FSB and BCBS.

[16]Based on Moenninghoff, Ongena, and Wieandt (2015, 226) and updated for events until the end of 2015.

Table 7.2 Overview of FSB Event Dates (2008–2015)

#	Date	Event	Type	Description of event news
1	17-Nov-2008	1st G20 summit	General	Call for appropriate regulation and oversight
2	02-Apr-2009	2nd G20 summit	General	Establishment of the FSB
3	25-Sep-2009	3rd G20 summit	General	FSB tasked to develop G-SIB regulation incl. enhanced supervision, resolution tools, and additional loss absorbency requirements
4	30-Nov-2009	Financial Times publication	Designation	Publication of leaked FSB list of 24 G-SIBs by the Financial Times
5	28-Jun-2010	4th G20 summit	General	Reiteration of importance of enhanced supervision, resolution tools, and additional loss absorbency
6	01-Nov-2010	FSB report publication	Supervision	Report with concrete recommendations for enhanced supervision
7	10-Nov-2010	Financial Times publication	Designation	Republication of leaked FSB list of 24 G-SIBs by the Financial Times with specific reference to the new G-SIB regulation
8	12-Nov-2010	5th G20 summit	General	Endorsement of core elements for supervision and resolution regimes and principal need for higher loss absorbency
9	27-Jun-2011	BCBS proposal announcement	Loss absorbency	Proposal of additional capital surcharges of 1.0–2.5 % Common Tier 1
10	19-Jun-2011	FSB and BCBS report publication	Resolution	Consultative report with concrete measures (national resolution regimes, cross-border cooperation, resolution planning, enhanced resolvability)
11	28-Sep-2011	BCBS decision announcement	Loss absorbency	Endorsement of proposal on additional capital surcharges
12	04-Nov-2011	6th G20 summit	Designation	Publication of official list of 29 G-SIBs
13	01-Nov-2012	FSB report publication	Designation	Publication of official list of 28 G-SIBs
14	11-Nov-2013	FSB report publication	Designation	Publication of official list of 29 G-SIBs
15	06-Nov-2014	FSB report publication	Designation	Publication of official list of 30 G-SIBs
16	10-Nov-2014	FSB report publication	Loss absorbency	Consultative report with proposal of minimum Total Loss-Absorbency Capacity of 16–20 %
17	03-Nov-2015	FSB report publication	Designation	Publication of official list of 30 G-SIBs
18	09-Nov-2015	BCBS decision announcement	Loss absorbency	Endorsement of proposal on Total Loss-Absorbing Capacity (TLAC)

Source: Moenninghoff, Ongena, and Wieandt (2015, 226), Financial Stability Board (FSB) (1 November 2012, 226), Financial Stability Board (FSB) (11 November 2013, 226), Financial Stability Board (FSB) (6 November 2014, 226), Financial Stability Board (FSB) (10 November 2014, 226), Financial Stability Board (FSB) (3 November 2015, 226), and Financial Stability Board (FSB) (9 November 2015, 226).

In November 2012, the G20 also committed to implementing the recommendations of the BCBS on the prudential treatment of 'domestic-systemically important banks' (D-SIBs), also referred to as 'other-systemically important institutions' (O-SIIs). On 25 April 2016, the EBA published the first list of D-SIBs in the EU.[17] Named banks are required to hold additional CET1 capital of up to 2.0 percent after a phase-in period ending in 2019. The sole focus here, however, is on G-SIBs.

BCBS Assessment of G-SIBs

To identify G-SIBs, the BCBS has developed an indicator-based measurement approach (see Sect. 3.3). Table 7.3 shows a scoring system that uses twelve indicators across five equally weighted categories: cross-jurisdictional activity, size, interconnectedness, substitutability, and complexity.[18] These are broadly in line with the generally accepted catalysts of systemic risk. 'Each of the 12 indicators is scored on a scale from zero to 100 percent by taking each bank's reported value and dividing by the total value across a panel of 75 global banks'.[19] The selection of banks is based primary on size, i.e. on the financial year-end Basel III leverage ratio exposure, and secondarily on supervisory discretion. Banks are assessed only on a consolidated basis. The indicators are then combined into an overall score[20] The analysis and G-SIB designation is intended to be applied on a yearly basis.

Table 7.3 BCBS Indicator-Based Measurement Approach for Assessing G-SIBs

Category (and weighting)	Individual indicator	Indicator weighting
Cross-jurisdictional activity (20 %)	Cross-jurisdictional claims	10 %
	Cross-jurisdictional liabilities	10 %
Size (20 %)	Total exposures (Basel III leverage ratio definition)	20 %
Interconnectedness (20 %)	Intra-financial system assets	7 %
	Intra-financial system liabilities	7 %
	Securities outstanding	7 %
Substitutability / financial institution infrastructure (20 %)	Assets under custody	7 %
	Payments activity	7 %
	Underwritten transactions (debt and equity)	7 %
Complexity (20 %)	Notional amount of OTC derivatives	7 %
	Level 3 assets	7 %
	Trading and available-for-sale securities	7 %

Source: Basel Committee on Banking Supervision (BCBS) (July 2013, 6).

[17]European Banking Authority (EBA) (25 April 2016).

[18]See Basel Committee on Banking Supervision (BCBS) (July 2013, 6) for the latest comprehensive assessment methodology.

[19]Loudis and Allahrakha (2016, 3).

[20]See Basel Committee on Banking Supervision (BCBS) (November 2014) for the score calculation and Loudis and Allahrakha (2016, 2) who edited the data for a full list with scores for each bank and category.

The threshold of G-SIB designation (based on the overall score) is set by the FSB. Since the first publication of the official list of G-SIBs in 2011, the FSB has designated roughly 30 banks as G-SIBs every year, as illustrated in Table 7.4. This table including the lists for 2009 and 2010 based on a leaked preliminary and unofficial list of G-SIBs in those years published by The Financial Times. The composition of the G-SIB list

Table 7.4 G-SIB Designation 2009–2016

Publisher	FT	FT	FSB	FSB	FSB	FSB	FSB	FSB
Date	30-Nov-09	01-Nov-10	04-Nov-11	01-Nov-12	11-Nov-13	06-Nov-14	03-Nov-15	21-Nov-16
HSBC	●	●	●	2.5 %	2.5 %	2.5 %	2.5 %	2.0 %
JP Morgan Chase	●	●	●	2.5 %	2.5 %	2.5 %	2.5 %	2.5 %
Citigroup	●	●	●	2.5 %	2.0 %	2.0 %	2.0 %	2.5 %
Deutsche Bank	●	●	●	2.5 %	2.0 %	2.0 %	2.0 %	2.0 %
Barclays	●	●	●	2.0 %	2.0 %	2.0 %	2.0 %	1.5 %
BNP Paribas	●	●	●	2.0 %	2.0 %	2.0 %	2.0 %	2.0 %
Bank of America	●	●	●	1.5 %	1.5 %	1.5 %	1.5 %	2.0 %
Credit Suisse	●	●	●	1.5 %	1.5 %	1.5 %	1.5 %	1.5 %
Goldman Sachs	●	●	●	1.5 %	1.5 %	1.5 %	1.5 %	1.5 %
Mitsubishi UFJ FG	●	●	●	1.5 %	1.5 %	1.5 %	1.5 %	1.5 %
Morgan Stanley	●	●	●	1.5 %	1.5 %	1.5 %	1.5 %	1.0 %
Royal Bank of Scotland	●	●	●	1.5 %	1.5 %	1.5 %	1.0 %	1.0 %
UBS	●	●	●	1.5 %	1.5 %	1.0 %	1.0 %	1.0 %
Group Crédit Agricole			●	1.0 %	1.5 %	1.0 %	1.0 %	1.0 %
Bank of New York Mellon			●	1.5 %	1.0 %	1.0 %	1.0 %	1.0 %
Bank of China			●	1.0 %	1.0 %	1.0 %	1.0 %	1.0 %
BPCE			●	1.0 %	1.0 %	1.0 %	1.0 %	1.0 %
ING Bank	●	●	●	1.0 %	1.0 %	1.0 %	1.0 %	1.0 %
Mizuho FG	●	●	●	1.0 %	1.0 %	1.0 %	1.0 %	1.0 %
Nordea	●	●	●	1.0 %	1.0 %	1.0 %	1.0 %	1.0 %
Santander			●	1.0 %	1.0 %	1.0 %	1.0 %	1.0 %
Société Générale	●	●	●	1.0 %	1.0 %	1.0 %	1.0 %	1.0 %
State Street			●	1.0 %	1.0 %	1.0 %	1.0 %	1.0 %
Sumitomo Mitsui FG	●	●	●	1.0 %	1.0 %	1.0 %	1.0 %	1.0 %
Unicredit Group	●	●	●	1.0 %	1.0 %	1.0 %	1.0 %	1.0 %
Wells Fargo			●	1.0 %	1.0 %	1.0 %	1.0 %	1.0 %
Standard Chartered	●	●		1.0 %	1.0 %	1.0 %	1.0 %	1.0 %
ICBC					1.0 %	1.0 %	1.0 %	1.5 %
Agricultural Bank of China						1.0 %	1.0 %	1.0 %
China Construction Bank							1.0 %	1.0 %
BBVA	●	●		1.0 %	1.0 %	1.0 %		
Banca Intesa	●	●						
Commerzbank			●					
Dexia			●					
Lloyds Banking Group			●					
Royal Bank of Canada	●	●						
Nomura	●	●						
Total #	24	24	29	28	29	30	30	30

Source: Jenkins and Davies (30 November 2009), Jenkins (1 November 2010), Financial Stability Board (FSB) (4 November 2011), Financial Stability Board (FSB) (1 November 2012), Financial Stability Board (FSB) (11 November 2013), Financial Stability Board (FSB) (6 November 2014), Financial Stability Board (FSB) (3 November 2015), and Financial Stability Board (FSB) (21 November 2016).

changed only marginally from 2011–2015 with five banks changing after the first year of publication. Roughly half of the G-SIBs are headquartered in the EU, one third in the US, and the remaining in Japan and China. The largest global banks tend to dominate all twelve of the indicators. Collectively, they account for a very significant share of the global financial system. For instance, G-SIBs account for approximately 40 percent of banks' total Tier 1 capital and total assets; over 65 percent of the total assets under custody; over 90 percent of FX trading; and over 70 percent of total volume of loan syndication, bond underwriting and equity underwriting. At the same time, all G-SIBs are generally the leading players in their domestic retail markets and are also the principal participants in financial market infrastructures (FMIs) such as payment systems, trade settlement systems, and central counterparties (CCPs).[21]

Capital Regulations for G-SIBs

The FSB capital regulation has two components:

- CET1 capital surcharge: The primary measure is the surcharge to CET1 ratio under Basel III (see Sect. 7.3). Surcharges range from 1.0 percent to 3.5 percent, and 2.5 percent is currently the highest surcharge allocated, and depend on the risk bucket the G-SIBs are assigned to (see Table 7.4). The risk buckets depend on the systemic relevance assessed in the selection process. The requirement were phased in from 1 January 2016 to 1 January 2019.
- TLAC holdings: A second capital regulation is the requirement to have additional so-called total loss-absorbing capacity (TLAC). Besides common equity, TLAC-eligible instruments are certain kinds of equity-like capital and subordinated debt, such as CoCos (see Sect. 6.1.4). The TLAC ratio is calculated as a percentage of RWA. The minimum ratio is being phased in with a minimum of 16 percent from 1 January 2019 and 18 percent starting on 1 January 2022. It was mandated that TLAC be a minimum of 6 percent of the Basel III leverage exposure starting on 1 January 2019 and at least 6.75 percent starting on 1 January 2022. There are no different requirements with regards to risk buckets. However, there are weaker requirements and a prolonged phase-in period for G-SIBs headquartered in emerging markets, which are currently only the Chinese G-SIBs.[22]

Other Regulations for G-SIBs

In addition to Basel III, the enhanced regulatory framework for G-SIBs also includes:

- 'Tougher liquidity standards' and more 'proactive and intensive supervision consistent with the risks an institution poses to the financial system';
- 'An effective resolution framework with tools to enhance orderly recovery and wind-down in the event of failure, including effective burden-sharing with the private sector

[21] Huertas (2014, 9–10).

[22] Financial Stability Board (FSB) (9 November 2015).

through debt that can be bailed in, cross-border arrangements, and firm-specific structural measures as needed';
- 'Enhanced transparency and disclosure to improve market discipline and monitoring'; and
- 'Strengthened market infrastructure to limit the risks of contagion arising from interconnectedness and the limited transparency of counterparty relationships.'[23]

[23]Viñals et al. (2013, 5–6).

8 Conclusion

This final chapter summarises the previous chapters of Pt. I (see Sect. 8.1) and highlights the main future challenges with regard to TBTF in banking (see Sect. 8.2).

8.1 Summary

Chap. 3: Introduction to Too-Big-to-Fail in Banking

A bank is considered to be TBTF when a government believes that it must safeguard the country's financial system and economic activity from a significant disruption caused by the adverse effect of a possible default of that bank by guaranteeing the repayment of that bank's uninsured liabilities (see Sect. 3.1). This systemic risk of G-SIBs derives from the risk contribution to financial contagion or the risk sensitivity to macroeconomic shocks (see Sect. 3.3).

The US serves as a prototype when it comes to the history of TBTF (see Sect. 3.4), and the term TBTF is closely connected to the bailout of Continental Illinois National Bank and Trust Company in 1984 (see Sect. 3.2). However, the genesis of the TBTF doctrine occurred much earlier and in a similar form in all developed economies. Not only in the US, the regulatory system for banks was created piecemeal and was the accumulation of more than a century of law-making. Each piece resulted from an economic crisis serious enough to muster support for enactment. The most relevant examples are the deposit insurance and the lender-of-last-resort (LOLR) in the period between 1913 and 1933 in the US; both were implemented separately after experiences of relevant crises with the purpose of stabilising the banking system. In hindsight, both met their original objectives. However, a change occurred when the deposit insurance was handled by an institution that also had the authority to intervene with failing banks short term (LOLR) and subsequently also longer term (open-bank assistance). The federal government had a

T. F. Lesche, *Too-Big-to-Fail in Banking*, Finanzwirtschaft, Banken und Bankmanagement I Finance, Banks and Bank Management, https://doi.org/10.1007/978-3-658-34182-4_8

natural incentive to keep banks alive to limit losses from insured events. As a result, large banks were bailed out, while smaller ones were not. At the same time, the banking sector was increasingly deregulated and implicit size restrictions were repealed. This practice sent clear incentives to the banking market and changed the banking system. Moreover, the increased size and complexity of banks complicated their timely resolution and the potential failure of a large and complex bank was a threat to the stability of the banking system. Consequently, the criteria for banks to receive assistance were increasingly loosened and the scope was extended—a vicious cycle.

The deregulation of the banking sector, accompanied by increased government intervention, acted as the breeding ground of TBTF. This contradicting regulatory environment in the free market created disincentives for banks to become TBTF and led to the first major bailouts. Hence, 'over time TBTF became embedded in banking regulation through the precedent of saving one troubled bank at a time, rather than as a result of a conscious decision'.[1] Ultimately, the regulatory efforts exerted on each other and resulting in the TBTF doctrine. Moreover, regulatory efforts to abandon TBTF were quickly forgotten during periods of prosperity and stability in the banking system. It was not until the massive bailouts during the global financial crisis (GFC) that the dramatic increase of TBTF risks during the previous decade was revealed.

Chap. 4: TBTF Causal Chain: Explicit and Implicit Government Guarantees

The history of TBTF illustrates how conflicting goals and responsibilities often lead governments to manoeuvre themselves into providing safety nets to banks. Banks are naturally incentivised to grow to exploit these public subsidies and increase their chances of benefitting from such a safety net. Once banks have grown to such a magnitude that they are considered TBTF, the cascade of mechanisms of disincentives can hardly be corrected because TBTF breeds more TBTF. There are two natural causes of TBTF: explicit government guarantees (EGG) and implicit government guarantees (IGG).

There are no fixed criteria for the scope and practices of EGGs (see Sect. 4.1), which is called a G-SIB bailout. If a government's objective is to safeguard economic stability and avoid disruption of the financial system, it will aim to keep the bank's business operations alive. It is crucial that the bank have continued access to various funding markets to continue its operations, such as lending to the real economy. Unhindered access to funding sources is conditional upon the trust of the bank's creditors, and the government achieves this trust by guaranteeing prompt repayment of a bank's uninsured liabilities. In practise, coverage tends to be fairly comprehensive for deposits and less so for other debt instruments, due to the political economy of banking. Equity instruments are generally not guaranteed, as their holders are expected to be better prepared to bear substantial losses.

[1] Hetzel (1991, 6).

IGGs (see Sect. 4.2) extend deposit insurance to uninsured bank liabilities without payment of insurance premiums by the insured G-SIB. Banks which receive an IGG are able to shift the liability for their potential losses to the state. This expected government intervention on a selective basis in a free market economy results *per definitionem* in the distortion of market forces and incentives—more precisely, in moral hazards among various bank stakeholders. The creditor moral hazard extends simply from the insured depositors to all liability holders that are expected to be protected if a G-SIB is bailed out. Ultimately, creditor moral hazard leads to lower funding costs and larger counterparty positions for G-SIBs. This is the result of the lower return requirements of creditors and is extensively evidenced by stronger credit ratings and lower CDS spreads among G-SIBs. The bank moral hazard is exacerbated by IGG because G-SIBs face less monitoring from creditors and enjoy lower funding costs. Therefore, banks respond to IGGs with increased risk-taking and increased growth. Whether shareholder moral hazard exists due to IGGs is less clear both in theory and in practice, since bank equity is generally not protected and additional TBTF regulations drag down equity returns.

Chap. 5: Public Cost and Benefits of TBTF

While the previous chapter examines the impact of EGGs and IGGs on bank stakeholders, this chapter analyses the welfare perspective of TBTF, i.e. the impact of EGGs and IGGs on society. These public subsidies for G-SIB stakeholders, whether implicit or explicit, represent costs for society. In this context, G-SIBs that do not internalise all the costs of IGGs and EGGs are sources of inefficiency. This leads by definition to overproduction and to a suboptimal market outcomes in terms of a society's overall condition. Hence, the TBTF doctrine can be called 'banking pollution'[2] in the logic of environmental economics. A cost-and-benefit analysis of the TBTF doctrine, to quantify the sources of this imbalance, is widely acknowledged to be highly subjective and may also vary across countries and over time.

Current research indicates that the maximum efficient scale of banks could be somewhere around US$ 100 billion of total assets (see Sect. 5.1). This is a size that is still beneficial for the public and for bank stakeholders. Beyond this point, further economies are assumed to be exhausted, while there is at least the possibility of X-inefficiency or diseconomies of scale and scope that lead to deadweight costs. This means that the incentives for banks to grow beyond this size are driven by management or shareholder self-interest—and such growth does not benefit public welfare. One of the primary drivers of excessive growth is considered to be TBTF scale economies. Coincidentally or not, research suggests that banks with totals assets of more than US$ 100 billion can be considered TBTF. Although both quantitative thresholds might be just rough approximations, G-SIBs can be considered to operate at a size that is too large both from the

[2] A. G. Haldane (30 March 2010).

micro-level perspective of bank efficiency and from the macro-level perspective of systemic risk.

In general, once G-SIBs are in place, the benefits of EGGs outweigh the costs, particularly as potential GDP losses from the absence of G-SIB rescue measures are sustained while bailouts are one-offs (see Sect. 5.2). The real social costs of a TBTF policy appear to be incurred *ex ante* and indirectly, due to IGG, in the form of distorted incentives for banks or equivalently, in the form of anticipated crisis costs. The problems arise due to IGGs rather than EGGs, as the former is the breeding ground for the latter (see Sect. 5.3).

The fundamental reasons why the TBTF doctrine still exists can be found in the decision-making processes of governments, which are either influenced by the short-term-oriented desire to attract voters or by 'time inconsistency'. The 'time inconsistency' phenomenon describes a situation in which policymakers only take into account the short-term impact of EGGs and ignore previous pledges of no government intervention.

Chap. 6: TBTF Policy Recommendations

The previous chapter confirms that the social costs from TBTF are higher than the private costs, as individually rational bank management leads to a higher level of systemic risk than is socially optimal.[3] This clearly indicates that there is a market failure in which the government should intervene via regulation by forcing banks to internalise the social costs of being TBTF. In this regard, the main area of current proposals is the first of the three pillars of banking crisis policy, which are crisis prevention (see Sect. 6.1), crisis management (see Sect. 6.2), and crisis resolution (see Sect. 6.3).

Strengthening market discipline is the first line of defence in crisis prevention, as it improves the intrinsic motivation of bank stakeholders to manage and control a bank. Moreover, it is less subject to subsequent problems of bank regulation such as regulatory arbitrage. Improved corporate governance and supervision of G-SIBs are the two basic solutions to strengthen market-based crisis prevention.

Nevertheless, government interventions might be required for banks to internalise all externalities from TBTF. In line with the economic theory of pollution, this can happen either with the government itself running the respective activities (as is the case for police and defence) or with the government leaving the activity to private banks but regulating them using one of three methods: (i) restrictions, which impose outright limits on certain bank activities, such as structural limits on the size and scope of a bank's assets and business operations; (ii) price-based regulation, most frequent in the form of surcharges to liquidity and capital requirements, which is meant to discourage certain banking practices by creating external diseconomies to force banks to internalise the externality; and (iii) cap-and-trade regulation, where the government assigns property

[3]De Bandt and Hartmann (2000, 16).

rights to banks, e.g. for the right to achieve greater size, and banks negotiate among themselves to find the lowest cost solution to correct TBTF.

From a theoretical perspective on social welfare, the classic public-goods framework by Weitzman (1974) suggests that imposing quantitative restrictions may be the best solution to abolish the TBTF problem. The social benefits of this kind of regulation are particularly present in complex adaptive systems or where the assessment of risk and its regulation is inherently difficult. Restrictions have the advantage that they can withstand even the failure of another component of regulation, which increases the likelihood that the regulation will work when needed.[4]

In addition to crisis prevention, policy recommendations also focus on crisis resolution. The proposed resolution regimes prepare for the rare event of a G-SIB being rescued, aiming to minimise the costs associated with bankruptcy, such as the cost of economic disruption, and to facilitate the market exit of a failed G-SIB. These measures can be categorised into 'living wills and bank resolution' (to protect the financial system and vital banking functions) and 'burden sharing and individual sanctions' (to minimise bailout costs and prevent future bailouts and IGGs).

Chap. 7: TBTF Policy Initiatives

Before 2009, there were very few policies against TBTF. The efforts to tackle the TBTF problem during a phase without crises in the 2000 s can be described as purposefully ambiguous: i.e., the policy that was not explicit about which banks were to be considered TBTF nor about what should happen in the event of the insolvency of a G-SIB. The regulatory regime was not based on bank size but on bank type: deposit-gathering institutions were regulated to minimise the costs and moral hazards stemming from deposit insurance.

It was not until the recent GFC that policymakers seriously focused on the matter of the TBTF doctrine. In general, bank regulation has become much more important since the GFC, as it has been widely realised that the TBTF doctrine is a real and massive problem for a well-functioning financial system. 'Next to monetary and fiscal policy, the promotion of safety and soundness of financial intermediaries has become the third major pillar of public policy'[5]. Policymakers have largely followed academics' and regulators' proposals on bank-level regulation. Overall, the main objectives of the various TBTF initiatives are to: (i) reduce G-SIB risk-taking, (ii) minimise contagion risk, (iii) enact regulatory and supervisory integration, and, (iv) improve the efficiency of resolution regimes. The flagship of G-SIB regulation is the various requirements on capital.

The most prominent local policies have been made in the context of the European Banking Union (see Sect. 7.1) and the *Dodd-Frank Act* in the US (see Sect. 7.2). The two major global recommendations are the Basel III regulations (see Sect. 7.3) and the

[4]A. G. Haldane (30 March 2010, 4).

[5]Deli and Hasan (2017, 217).

G-SIB regulations (see Sect. 7.4). These policies are not only implemented into domestic law by the EU and the US, but also stretch across the globe. The G-SIB regulations by the Financial Stability Board (FSB) constitute a milestone by being the first and only initiative that comprises binding rules for global G-SIBs only. The centrepiece of these regulations is the capital surcharges for the circa 30 designated G-SIBs. Collectively, these banks account for a highly significant share of the global financial system.

8.2 Outlook

Improved Research on and Regulation of TBTF

First, the good news: the GFC triggered a major step forward in terms of understanding the TBTF problem and what can be done to solve it. Together with financial stability, TBTF has become one of the most important public policy issues. The GFC and the subsequent research on TBTF have convinced the majority of academics that TBTF is a negative externality in the financial system that contributed to the scope of the GFC and perhaps even triggered it. Some scholars still emphasise that the available evidence is far from conclusive, and that G-SIBs might have some social benefits. However, the bulk of the available literature is unambiguous, with gaps in only few areas, particularly where the banking landscape is evolving swiftly and measurement challenges prevail, such as mega-bank economies or the impact of TBTF on equity (holders) (see Pt. II). Further research in these areas is desirable given the massive costs that could be incurred by another financial crisis strengthened or triggered by TBTF. In particular, it remains completely unclear how effective the newly implemented policy tools are.

Since legislators implemented the proposed measures, by and large, during and directly after the GFC, banks are now less likely to fail and are generally safer because they are forced to have larger capital buffers and more resilient liquidity positions. Regulatory stress tests are now conducted frequently, demonstrating the improved resilience of the entire banking sector. G-SIBs have lost at least some of their public subsidies from IGG, as proven by decreasing funding benefits. This is driven by resolution regimes and burden-sharing arrangements. These implementations also decrease the potential bankruptcy costs of G-SIBs and thereby facilitate the process of inefficient banks exiting the market. In some cases, G-SIBs have responded by reducing certain activities. Furthermore, bank balance sheets around the globe have been shrunk since the GFC due to either statutory conditions following governmental capital injections or general increased capital requirements. Overall and preliminarily, the policy initiatives can be assessed as necessary and adequate to address the acute and short-term problems.

TBTF Has Not Been Abolished

Now, the bad news. First, G-SIBs obviously still exist, i.e. many banks remain very large and their business models are largely unchanged. Despite the best regulatory efforts, G-SIBs will still inevitably run into trouble sometimes. Moreover, the vastly different international bankruptcy laws and procedures hampers the efficient resolution of large international banks. Furthermore, where resolution regimes are in place, they remain unproven or inconsistently applied.[6] The exit of large inefficient banks most probably puts the overall health of the financial sector at risk, particularly under weak economic conditions, with potential disruption of the real economy. For mega-banks, even the most sophisticated resolution plan will always be difficult and time-consuming to execute. Some investors will bear heavy losses, which will inevitably affect other healthy institutions, if not the entire market. As the term TBTF implies, truly G-SIBs will never be allowed to fail.

Second, the current financial market regulation is more focused on financial stability than on the important policy task of establishing fair competition on a level playing field. After the GFC, regulators decided in favour of more regulation for increased safety instead of encouraging innovation.[7] Overall, the new regulation has sharply increased the regulatory costs not only for G-SIBs but for the entire banking sector. Smaller banks are disproportionally affected and the social optimal size of banks may even have increased.[8] Recollecting the pre-GFC era, the inflated banking industry in developed countries is plagued by overcapacity, exaggerated costs, and too little profit. In any other industry, this would mean that the strongest player would buy the weaker competitor and the weakest firm would be forced out of the market. However, this does not apply in banking as neither case is generally desired by regulators, who find themselves trapped between G-SIBs and bank bankruptcies.

Third, current regulation is not a robust solution for the long term: it is highly prone to a changing economic and financial environment. The new policies bring further complexity and regulatory inconsistences in the adaptive banking system, which will inevitably create new inefficiencies and future instabilities. For instance, it favours the shift of financial activities from the regulated (banking) to the unregulated (shadow banking) sector. In some expanding areas of loans, insurance companies and credit funds are already the only providers of debt capital. Moreover, the significant expansion of less regulated financial firms such as asset managers poses another worrying risk, for instance because an increasing share of the assets is only passively managed.

Finally, current TBTF regulation does not solve major problems stemming from political economy and time-inconsistency. Policymakers are driven by short-term interests and survival. Hence, they will always bail out banks to reap short-term benefits. In this perspective, it is doubtful whether the good intentions of abolishing TBTF will last. Ten

[6]A prime example in the EU is the public bailout of Italian bank Banca Monte dei Paschi di Siena (Cf. Lorz (22 December 2016)), while Spanish bank Banco Popular was denied public rescue measures (Cf. Sandbu (25 August 2017)).

[7]Blinder (2010, 893).

[8]Cf. U.S. Government Accountability Office (GAO) (16 January 2013), Monopolkommission (9 July 2014), and Varmaz, Fieberg, and Prokop (2015).

years after the onset of the GFC, the global economy has reached new heights and TBTF is no longer the centre of public attention. Governments around the globe show 'regulatory fatigue'[9] or pledge for a reversion of the heavy regulation of large banks, most notably in the US.

Breaking up G-SIBs Must be the Next Step

This is a word of caution and a call for fundamental reform. It would be tragic for the lessons of the GFC to be forgotten so soon because the economy has not been stressed by a G-SIB bailout for some time. 'There is no question that there will be another crisis; the question is only when, and if we will be prepared for it when it comes.'[10] While it is impossible to foresee the source of any future crisis, it is at least possible to make sure that it is not triggered or strengthened by the TBTF doctrine. One of the inescapable truths of banking history is that policies introduced to mitigate a crisis often bring about another one. Central banks have created an environment of ultra-low interest rates to stimulate the economy in reaction to the GFC. In response and in search for yield, investors have pushed up the value in many asset classes. These resulting asset bubbles can often trigger a crisis. Global debt is also at record heights, and much higher than before the GFC. Most of this growth and imminent threats seem to come from emerging regions, particularly China. These regions are now home to the largest banks worldwide, which are far less regulated and have some highly risky practises in place that were common in developed countries before the GFC.[11]

Hence, it is crucial that the strong capital regime be maintained and extended to developing countries and to non-bank financial firms. Moreover, a value-maximising bank is unable to internalise all social costs solely via incentives established by larger capital buffers. Larger capital buffer can only reduce the probability of G-SIB failures and banking crises. In other words, 'a well-run bank needs no capital. No amount of capital will rescue a badly run bank'[12]. Price-based regulation of capital surcharges has been chosen for political reasons and implemented more cautiously due to a weak economic environment.

The wider economy is now strong enough to calibrate the financial system on the long term. This is why it is now the right time for bolder and transformational actions to correct the source of the deep-rooted incentive problems of privatised returns and socialised risks.[13] TBTF means too-big-to-exist, as internalising all social costs is only possible in a break-up. As systemic risk is inseparable from bank size, this can only happen with smaller institutions that pose less systematic risk on the banking system. A regulation

[9]Binham (25 April 2017).

[10]Jordan (2014, 453).

[11]Jenkins (31 August 2017).

[12]Bagehot (1873).

[13]Cf. Haldane (2012) and Kashkari (16 February 2016).

can only be fully successful if it effectively stipulates a break-up of G-SIBs and thereby ends the TBTF doctrine. Restrictions are the optimal response to the TBTF problem in banking, because the social benefits of avoiding a banking crisis from TBTF are largely relative to the private costs of lost economies of scale and scope. It is important that banks can both go for risk to contribute to growth and innovation, and be able to fail to leave the market if they prove inefficient. Moreover, smaller, less complex banks pave the way for simplified, less complex regulation with more lasting impact on bank behaviour.[14] Nevertheless, the short-term implementation costs of such regulation, e.g. in the form of liquidity constraints, cannot be underestimated, and likely exceed the costs of stepping up capital buffers. The main question remains where to set the dynamic limit of size restrictions in the swiftly evolving banking industry. The answer needs to balance scale and scope benefits with increases in systemic risk. Hence, limits could be expressed in relation to a country's gross domestic product (GDP) which could trigger further financial integration among countries. The latest findings show that current bank sizes are a multiple higher than the higher end of estimated bank sizes that are socially beneficial. In any case and with regard to the TBTF doctrine, it is safer to have this question answered by regulatory bodies than to leave it to the free market forces.

[14]A. G. Haldane (30 March 2010).

Part II

Quantifying the Shareholder Value of Too-Big-to-Fail in Banking

9 Related Research

This chapter of the empirical part of this thesis, labelled Pt. *II*, summarises existing research specifically related to relevant quantitative analysis. The overall research question of this dissertation is:

What drives the valuation of stocks of G-SIBs compared to stocks of other banks over time?

Several research directions are relevant to this question: Sect. 9.1 relates to the content of question, i.e., what have similar studies concluded about the impact of the TBTF doctrine on bank equity and stocks? The following two sections relate to the research method: Sect. 9.2 summarises the latest recommendations on regression analysis that account for both a firm- and a time-effect; Sect. 9.3 summarises the latest research on the input factors of such a regression, i.e., what is considered the best relative valuation measure for banks (dependent variable) and how is this measure explained best by bank fundamentals (independent variables)?

9.1 Impact of TBTF on Equity

The behaviour of stakeholders of G-SIBs can be distorted by competitive advantages from EGGs and IGGs and by regulation that specifically targets G-SIBs (see Chap. 7). Many empirical studies have examined the impact of the TBTF doctrine on the behaviour of creditors (see Sect. 4.2.3) and banks (see Sect. 4.2.4), i.e., the impact on bank debt and asset risk, respectively. Creditor moral hazard and bank moral hazard have been extensively evidenced and quantified. However, studies of potential shareholder moral hazard resulting from TBTF are much rarer. There may be two reasons for this: First, in a bailout, creditors are primarily protected (see Sect. 4.1.2). The impact on shareholders is much more uncertain because there are competitive advantage and disadvantages

T. F. Lesche, *Too-Big-to-Fail in Banking*, Finanzwirtschaft, Banken und Bankmanagement I Finance, Banks and Bank Management, https://doi.org/10.1007/978-3-658-34182-4_9

associated with the equity of G-SIBs (see Sect. 4.2.5). Second, it appears to be easier to measure the relative impact on bank assets and on bank funding than on equity. In contrast to equity, loans granted and liabilities issued are normally repaid at par and are comparable across banks.

Two different sources of value impacts are conceivable from the TBTF doctrine: EGGs in case of bankruptcy,[1] or IGGs in case of a going concern. Empirical studies are only available on the latter source, and can be categorised according to the applied research methodology:

1. Translation of TBTF funding benefits (see Sect. 9.1.1): One study examines privileged funding as the only source of potential shareholder benefits from TBTF.
2. TBTF premiums in precedent M&A transactions (see Sect. 9.1.2): Three studies examine takeover premiums for large banks where the new combined entity became TBTF.
3. TFTF sum-of-the-parts (see Sect. 9.1.3): One secondary source, an equity research report, calculates the value of one G-SIB by comparing the valuation of its business units with average relative valuation measures (P/E) of non-G-SIB competitors.
4. Share-Price Reactions to TBTF Events (see Sect. 9.1.4): Many share-price reaction studies evaluate the positive or negative impact of certain events or periods on the absolute value of G-SIBs. Some of these studies analyse a comprehensive set of global G-SIBs by using the G-SIB designation.

These research approaches can be categorised according to their results and the applied methodology. The research in categories 1 and 2 quantifies the value impact in absolute terms. Both types of research conclude that conjectural TBTF guarantees have a positive overall impact on bank valuation. The secondary research source in category 3 compares the value of G-SIBs versus non-G-SIBs in relative terms and explores a negative relationship. The research in category 4 neither quantifies the value impact in absolute

[1]No research is available on compensation payments to shareholders of G-SIBs from governments after precedent bailouts or situations of distress. With respect to bank bailouts during the GFC, however, several general observations can be made: Governments tried to avoid taking over G-SIBs completely—at least initially. They preferred to inject preference shares rather than expropriate or inject common shares. M. R. King (2009b, 15) presents an overview of terms of government capital injections in the US and the EU. Shareholders of G-SIBs were likely to keep their (diluted) shares, receive a debtor warrant or similar. That means they retained the upside potential of a share price recovery, even though shares lost their value completely after some time in many cases. Only in the UK are there some prominent bailed-out banks whose shareholders were expropriated straight away. The most notable examples are Northern Rock on 22 February 2008 (UK Asset Resolution (1 February 2016a)); Bradford & Bingley on 29 September 2008 (UK Asset Resolution (1 February 2016b)); and Anglo Irish Bank on 21 January 2009 (Anglo Irish Bank (2009)).

nor relative terms but instead analyses movements of share prices with regard to certain relevant TBTF events. This line of research identifies advantageous and disadvantageous repercussions for the shareholders associated with G-SIBs.

9.1.1 Translation of TBTF Funding Benefits

As described in Sect. 4.2.3, G-SIBs generally enjoy lower funding costs.

- Tsesmelidakis and Merton (July 2013) analyse how funding benefits translate into shareholder and debtholder benefits. Their results indicate that banks not only benefit from better financing terms but also deliberately take advantage of their TBTF status in their funding strategies. They prefer short-term, fixed-rate debt over the usual behaviour of non-guaranteed terms to subscribe to long-term debt in uncertain circumstances. For a sample of 27 US banks for the period from January 2007 to September 2010, they calculate the model-market spread difference of CDS, which is interpreted as the value of the guarantee in basis points. The authors differentiate the benefits accrued to shareholders in the amount of US$ 121.3 billion at debt issuance (because of better terms) from the benefits to debtholders of US$ 202.9 billion which accrue over the life of the debt. Shareholders benefited most from bond issues in the period after the announcement of several rescue programs and market expectations of TBTF: i.e., between the fourth quarter of 2008 and the second quarter of 2009.

9.1.2 TBTF Premiums in Precedent M&A Transactions

As elaborated in Sect. 4.2.4, banks try to achieve TBTF status in order receive to associated TBTF benefits. Banks can achieve sufficient size through organic or inorganic growth, such as through M&A transactions. These studies analyse M&A precedents:

- Kane (2000) analyses bank mega-mergers between 1991 and 1998 in a share-price reaction-event study. He finds that 'stockholders of large-bank acquirers have gained value when a deposit institution target is large, and that acquirers gained more value when a deposit institution target was previously headquartered in the same state'. He concludes that the TBTF doctrine has 'distorted dealmaking incentives for megabanks and that the high leverage these firms maintain makes it easy for them to shift unaccounted risk onto taxpayers'.
- Brewer III and Jagtiani (2013) estimate the value of the TBTF subsidy by analysing data from 1991–2004. They find that 'banking organizations are willing to pay an added premium for mergers that will put them over the asset sizes that are commonly viewed as the thresholds for being TBTF'. This added premium is approximately US$

15 to 23 billion that 8 banks in the dataset were willing to pay for acquisitions that enabled them cross the established threshold of US$ 100 billion in total assets.

- Molyneux, Schaeck, and Mi Zhou (2014) analyse precedent European transactions between 1997 and 2008. Their results indicate that merger premiums 'are positively associated with a higher possibility of becoming TBTF'.

No studies of this research type decisively relate the premiums to the TBTF attribute. Other socially comforting explanations or synergies cannot be ruled out.[2] Furthermore, absolute amounts 'are likely to underestimate the total value of the benefits that accrue to TBTF' for two reasons: (1) Banks 'seeking to obtain TBTF benefits are not likely to be forced by the marketplace to pass on anywhere near the full value of these benefits to the shareholders of their acquisition targets; and (2) the TBTF benefits already obtained prior to the merger cannot be measured with these event studies.[3]

9.1.3 TBTF Sum-of-the-Parts

Banks achieve TBTF size not only by upscaling the volume of business activities in one segment, but also by extending the scope of business activities to include other segments. In many cases, each of the businesses would not individually be considered TBTF.

- In their equity research report, Goldman Sachs (5 January 2015) analyses the impact of the G-SIB designation on J.P. Morgan Chase. They calculate the potential value of the bank without the G-SIB status with the help of a sum-of-the-parts analysis which is based on the P/E ratios of the pure-play competitors of the various business units. Then they add the value generated from the return of excess capital due to lower capital requirements after a potential bank break-up. Finally, they deduct values related to lost synergies and to the execution risk of the bank split up. The difference between the calculated value and the actual market value is considered the potential G-SIB discount. It is in the range of 4 percent to 25 percent depending on the assumptions of the sum-of-the-parts analysis.

9.1.4 Share Price Reactions to TBTF Events

The research papers considered in this section are based on event study methodologies[4] that test the TBTF hypothesis. They focus on the abnormal stock returns of large banks

---

[2]Kane (2000, 496).

[3]Brewer III and Jagtiani (2013).

[4]Described by Fama et al. (1969) and MacKinlay (1997).

or a given set of G-SIBs versus a (random) control group around the date of specific TBTF events, such as government announcements or bailouts. These events contain information that is valuable to investors, and one would accordingly expect to see a reaction to these TBTF events. The available studies are categorised based on their research findings, which include four different primary effects (see Fig. 9.1):[5]

1. TBTF designation effect: Describes the direct or indirect designation of certain banks as TBTF by an official body and potential positive abnormal reactions of the banks' share prices.
2. TBTF effect: Describes a strengthening of the TBTF doctrine (e.g., because the bailout of a bank perceived as TBTF confirms market expectations) and potential positive abnormal reactions of the banks' share prices.
3. Reverse TBTF effect: Describes a weakening of the TBTF doctrine (e.g., because the failure of a bank perceived to be TBTF contradicts market expectations) and potential negative abnormal reactions to the banks' share prices.
4. Regulatory TBTF burden effect: Describes the announcement of additional regulatory measures targeting G-SIBs and potential negative abnormal reactions of the banks' share prices.

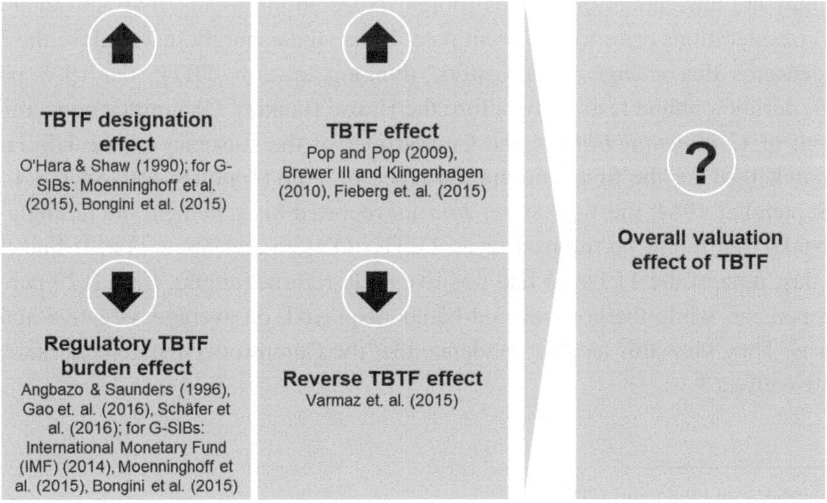

Fig. 9.1 TBTF Share-Price Reactions Summary

[5]Kleinow (2014, 1589–90) presents an overview of the statistical parameters of many of the event studies mentioned below.

None of these studies reveal the overall valuation effect of TBTF and extant research, by and large, does not consider other bank characteristics that could interact with the TBTF perception. There is just one study[6] that considers the capitalisation levels of G-SIBs, i.e., the need to raise additional equity to meet new capital requirements. This factor may have a major impact on the share prices because shareholders can anticipate future dilution through mandatory capital increases.

The research summarised below takes various approaches to distinguishing G-SIBs from non-G-SIBs. Nevertheless, all of the studies confirm the intuitive assumption that G-SIBs' share prices react to the events, as illustrated in the figure above. All evidence seems to be consistent with investors' reactions in an efficient market in an imperfect information setting.

9.1.4.1 TBTF Designation Effect

Studies that examine the TBTF designation effect are comparable to those that examine the effect of governmental deposit insurance, except that governmental deposit insurance is extended to all banks regardless of their size or importance.

- O'Hara and Shaw (1990) analyse the potentially first significant appearance of the TBTF-designation phenomenon on share prices. The study might be unique, as investors may not have intentionally incorporate expectations about TBTF into their valuation considerations prior to this event date. Later studies might just analyse the impact of measures that change the investors' thinking towards TBTF. On 19 September 1984, during a public testimony before the House Banking Committee concerning the bailout of *Continental Illinois*, the Comptroller of the Currency of the US Treasury acknowledged for the first time the existence of a TBTF policy (see Sect. 3.4.3). On 20 September 1984, the *Wall Street Journal* reported his statement, including a list of 11 banks that might be referred to as TBTF.[7] O'Hara and Shaw (1990) find that on that day, nine of the 11 banks had positive daily returns ranging from 0.29 percent to 5.65 percent, while the non-covered banks displayed, on average, negative abnormal returns. They view this as clear evidence that the Comptroller's statement had a large positive effect.[8]

[6]Bongini, Nieri, and Pelagatti (2015).

[7]Carrington (20 September 1984).

[8]Black et al. (1997, 405) examine how the Comptroller's acknowledgement impacted banking stocks in general. Their findings indicate that the market did not limit the event to G-SIBs. The results show that institutions significantly increase their ownership of a sample of random bank stocks following the event. Moreover, by examining the market's reaction to dividend cuts and omissions before and after the TBTF announcement, they find that the price response by the market is stronger in the pre-TBTF period. Consequently, the passage and expansion of the TBTF doctrine is interpreted as reducing the market's perception of the riskiness of all banks—even of those that were not considered TBTF.

9.1.4.2 TBTF Effect

In a way, the TBTF effect reconfirms the TBTF designation effect. Often, there is no specific point in time from which a bank is perceived as TBTF. Rather, becoming TBTF is a gradual process in line with a bank's growth. This is why the TBTF effect can be observed much more often in reality than is possible for the TBTF designation effect. Studies that examine the TBTF effect are also comparable to studies that examine the "flight-to-quality" effect in capital markets in crisis situations, as TBTF effects will be most likely be observed in crisis situations. The TBTF effect is triggered when a government's action strengthens the TBTF doctrine in the eyes of investors. However, the signal the government sends is not always clear. A G-SIB bailout, for instance, can theoretically be interpreted in two ways: Either it signals that the government might save another G-SIB (TBTF effect) if required, or it signals that the government will have fewer resources for rescuing other G-SIBs (resource crowding-out effect).[9] So far, studies confirm only the former effect:

- Pop and Pop (2009, 1429) document the TBTF effect in Japan after the government decided to bailout *Resona Holdings*, the fifth largest financial group in the country. They find significant a positive share-price reaction at large banks, while smaller bank stocks reacted negatively.
- Brewer III and Klingenhagen (2010) confirm the TBTF effect by examining events around the first TARP by the US government (see Sect. 3.4.5). The TARP was initially intended only to support the largest banks in the country. The authors measured cumulative abnormal stock returns after the TARP announcement on 14 October 2008, that were 'large, positive, and statistically significant not only for the banks included in the initial TARP assistance but also for those large banks that were not included'.
- Fieberg et al. (2015) analyse 'about 3,300 global bank rating changes before and after the *Lehman* bankruptcy in September 2008 to assess if differences in stock market reactions for small and big banks emerge'. They find a 'lack of a reaction to large banks' rating downgrades in the narrow event window'. The authors infer that even post-*Lehman*, the implicit TBTF guarantee may be a driving force behind this phenomenon.[10]

[9]Fratianni and Marchionne (2013).

[10]M. R. King (2009b, 28) reviews the equity market reaction of TBTF events on all banks regardless of their systemic importance in October 2008 and January 2009. He finds that, 'despite a brief positive reaction, bank stock prices continued to underperform in all countries except the United States where the generous terms of the government support allowed bank stocks to outperform'.

9.1.4.3 Reverse TBTF Effect

Like a TBTF designation event, it is rare that a government lets a bank fail that is widely considered TBTF. That is presumably a main reason why there is just one study confirming this phenomenon.

- Varmaz, Fieberg, and Prokop (2015) analyse two different shocks to equity investors' expectations in late 2008: The *Lehman* bankruptcy and the first announcement of the Capital Purchase Program (CPP) by the US government. For both events, the authors find negative returns on large banks' stocks: i.e., a reverse TBTF effect. Moreover, 'the authors observed significant spillover effects to both competitors and non-competitors of Lehman', and conclude that 'the Lehman event shook the widely held belief in' IGGs.

9.1.4.4 Regulatory TBTF Burden Effect

Most research analysing the impact of TBTF on share prices concentrates on the impact of regulatory measures. The regulatory TBTF burden effect is discoverable when an official body puts additional regulatory requirements on G-SIBs that reduce the benefits associated with TBTF status. The implementation of a resolution regime, for instead, could trigger the perception of a reduced likelihood or scope of a public bailout. Additional capital requirements could constitute additional burdens that lower the profitability of G-SIBs. Initial announcements and early proposal discussions towards TBTF regulatory actions normally have the greatest impact on share prices. Later regulatory implementations show limited stock reactions because the market has already priced in new reforms.[11]

- Angbazo and Saunders (1996) analyse stock-market reactions with respect to announcements concerning TBTF as part of the FDICIA of 1991 (see Sect. 3.4.4). They show that the initial release of the US president's plan to reduce the scope of TBTF protection, 'its initial approval in the House, and its passage by Congress generated negative abnormal returns limited for large banks'. 'The announcement of a less generous proposal by the Senate and the President's final approval produced positive returns'. The authors assess that distribution of these wealth effects consistently reflects the regulatory TBTF burden effect.[12]
- Gao, Liao, and Wang (2017) examine share-price reactions to the key events leading to the passage of the DFA (see Sect. 7.2). They find that large banks overall had negative abnormal stock returns, and they infer that the markets expect the act to be effective in reducing these banks' risk-taking. Furthermore, they test for two groups:

[11]International Monetary Fund (IMF) (April 2014, 118).

[12]The FDICIA had a generally positive effect on bank stock returns (Akhigbe and Whyte (2001, 393)).

(i) larger and more interconnected banks, and (ii) the largest six banks. They prove that the first group experienced more negative abnormal stock returns compared to the full sample; but these relations are not present during the final phase of the passage. Likewise, they find that the largest six banks' shareholders initially experienced significantly negative returns followed by insignificant returns during the final phase of the passage. The authors conclude that the markets are doubtful about the effectiveness of the final version of the act to end the TBTF doctrine in particular for the largest banks.

- Schäfer, Schnabel, and Weder di Mauro (2016) have analysed the effect of various regulatory reforms enacted in the US and European countries which host major financial centres on share prices. They 'find the strongest results for the DFA, and, in particular, in the Volcker rule', which led to a share-price decrease in most specifications, while the 'effects were stronger for investment banks, systemic banks, and weak banks'. 'The announcement of the Volcker rule also produced significant spillover effects to banks in the UK and Switzerland'. Similarly, the Vickers reform stream in the UK led to a marked decrease in share prices, while 'there were reversals when the reforms were watered down or postponed. Finally, in Switzerland, the TBTF regulation, which requires systemic banks to hold significantly higher levels of capital, lowered the share prices of systemic banks.'

9.1.4.5 G-SIB Designation

With regard to share-price reactions to TBTF events, most recent research considers events in the context of the FSB regulation (see Sect. 7.4).

Short-term reactions

- Moenninghoff, Ongena, and Wieandt (2015) analyse the share-price reactions of G-SIBs to many prominent FSB events, including designation events and regulatory events (see Table 7.2). Following the first three designation events (later designation events are not part of the study), they observe positive-aggregate absolute and relative abnormal returns for G-SIBs. Hence, they conclude that the designation as a G-SIB creates value for the affected banks' shareholders (a TBTF designation effect). They also observe negative absolute and negative relative abnormal returns for G-SIBs after the regulatory events (a TBTF regulatory burden effect). They infer that the new FSB regulation comes at a cost for the designated banks.
- With regard to the TBTF designation effect, Abreu and Gulamhussen (2013), Bongini, Nieri, and Pelagatti (2015), and Dewenter and Hess (October 2013) analyse only the market reaction to the official FSB designations—in particular, to the first designation on 4 November 2011. In contrast to Moenninghoff, Ongena, and Wieandt (2015), Abreu and Gulamhussen (2013) and Dewenter and Hess (October 2013) do not find significant abnormal returns surrounding the announcement date. Moenninghoff, Ongena, and Wieandt (2015), however, also consider the unofficial designation list

leaked by the *Financial Times* in the two previous years (precisely on 30 November 2009 and 10 November 2010), which cover almost the same banks as the later official FSB list. Across these two designation events, the abnormal positive returns for G-SIBs are much more significant, according to the authors.

- Bongini, Nieri, and Pelagatti (2015) recognise a differentiated reaction of G-SIBs' share prices to the first official FSB designation. G-SIBs with lower capital adequacy (i.e., lower Tier 1 ratios and/or higher leverage) apparently suffered negative abnormal returns, while their more-capitalised and less-leveraged peers enjoyed positive cumulative abnormal returns. This is consistent with the regulatory TBTF burden effect and the TBTF designation effect, respectively, because the designation was also connected to expected materially higher capital requirements.

Long-term Development

For longer periods after the first FSB events, two research papers agree that G-SIBs lost equity market value compared to competitor banks.[13]

- For the timeframe from the beginning of the regulatory process on 17 November 2008 to the endorsement of the FSB regulation on 4 November 2011, Moenninghoff, Ongena, and Wieandt (2015) calculate an underperformance of 21.2 percent, compared to an overperformance of 42.0 percent and 63.2 percent for non-G-SIBs whose size would in principle merit G-SIB categorisation, and approximately 250 other banks, respectively.
- Dewenter and Hess (October 2013) calculate that the average change in market value from 1 November 2009 to 31 October 2012 is -24.8 percent for G-SIBs, compared to+0.7 percent for other large banks.

Reactions to Other Regulatory Events

- The International Monetary Fund (IMF) (April 2014, 118–19) examines the effect of various regulatory measures on G-SIBs using the FSB designation to identify G-SIBs. In the US, they find that the announcement of the Volcker Rule (see Sect. 7.2) negatively affected G-SIBs equity returns, thereby implying that it was seen as negative for the G-SIBs' profitability. In the euro area, they prove that the European Commission's proposal for a BRRD and the DGSD (see Sect. 7.1) had a significantly

[13]De Vincentiis (2013) does a simple analysis of average annual stock returns for G-SIBs and non-G-SIBs for the period from January 2006 to November 2012. She finds that both the sign and the magnitude of returns is similar and concludes that the difference between the groups is not statistically significant.

positive impact on G-SIBs' equity returns but that the SRM did not. Furthermore, they discover that 'the Eurogroup's approval of the European Financial Stability Facility's assistance (subsequently taken over by the European Stability Mechanism) for recapitalising Spanish banks reduced the equity value of G-SIBs in the euro area.'

9.2 Two-Way Fixed-Effect Regression Analysis

This section and the following Sect. 9.3 prepare for the discussion of the methodology of the quantitative part of this dissertation. In empirical economics, the workhorse of methodologies is still the single-equation linear model.[14] For panel data—also known as longitudinal or cross-sectional time-series data—that contains, for example, complete observations on multiple firms and multiple periods, the basic regression model is:

$$Y_{it} = \beta_1 X_{it} + u_{it} \tag{9.1}$$

where Y_{it} is the variable to be explained by the regressor X_{it}. If X_{it} is observed for all firms (i) and periods (t), then the entire model can be treated as an ordinary linear model. The coefficient(s) (β) will be estimated by the method of ordinary least squares (OLS). OLS standard errors are unbiased when the residuals (u) are independent ($Cov(X_{it}, u_{it}) = 0$) and identically distributed ($u_{it} \sim N(0, \sigma^2)$).

If the residuals of a given firm are correlated across periods (time-series dependence), this is called an unobserved firm effect. If the residuals of a given year are correlated across different firms (cross-sectional dependence), this is called an unobserved time effect.[15] This means that, in the presence of a firm- and/or time-effect, the standard errors are biased and contain unused additional information. Hence, at least one explanatory factor is omitted, and the coefficients are over- or under-estimated.

Although the analysis of panel data is common in finance papers, the 'literature has proposed and used a variety of methods for estimating standard errors when the residuals are correlated across firms or years'.[16] There are basically two different main approaches: Either one dimension can be addressed parametrically (e.g., by adding binary variables, which are also called dummy variables) with estimated standard errors clustered on the other dimension, or both dimensions can be addressed parametrically. When there is a sufficient number of clusters in each dimension, standard errors are unbiased and produce correctly sized confidence intervals whether the firm and time-effect is permanent or temporary.[17]

[14]Wooldridge (2001).

[15]Wooldridge (2001).

[16]Petersen (2009, 475).

[17]Petersen (2009, 475). Petersen (2009) evaluated the approaches of papers with panel data and within-cluster correlation: '42 percent of the papers did not adjust the standard errors for possible dependence in the residuals.' '34 percent of the remaining papers estimated both the coefficients and the standard errors using the Fama-MacBeth procedure (Fama and MacBeth (1973)).

Most of the recent advanced econometric guides propose the latter method. Most of the recent advanced econometric guides propose the latter method. This type of regression is then called an entity-and-time-fixed effects model[18] or a two-way fixed-effect model[19]. The coefficients in these models are sometimes referred to as difference-in-differences estimators.[20] This regression model can be formalised (where α_i is the entity-fixed effect, λ_t is the time-fixed effect, and u_{it} is the error term):

$$Y_{it} = \beta_1 X_{it} + \alpha_i + \lambda_t + u_{it} \tag{9.2}$$

Equation 9.2 can equivalently be represented using $n - 1$ entity binary indicators and $T - 1$ time binary indicators (along with an intercept and unknown coefficients $\beta_0, \beta_1, \gamma_2, \ldots, \gamma_n$, and $\delta_2, \ldots, \delta_T$):

$$Y_{it} = \beta_0 + \beta_1 X_{it} + \gamma_2 D2_i + \cdots + \gamma_n Dn_i + \delta_2 B2_t + \cdots + \delta_T BT_t + u_{it} \tag{9.3}$$

The coefficients can be estimated using the least squares dummy variables (LSDV) method.

9.3 Relative Bank Valuation and Explaining Factors

The previous Sect. 9.2 lays out the framework for a regression model and this section discusses the potential input variables. The dependent factor is a relative bank-valuation measure (see Sect. 9.3.1). To explain such a measure—i.e., the P/BV—the literature provides theoretical (see Sect. 9.3.2) and empirical (see Sect. 9.3.3) models. The latest research suggests that these identified value drivers can potentially be refined for practical use by considering banks' intangible assets (see Sect. 9.3.4).

Twenty-nine percent include dummy variables for each cluster (e.g., fixed effects or within estimation). The next two most common methods use OLS (or an analogous method) to estimate the coefficients but report standard errors adjusted for the correlation within a cluster (e.g., within a firm or industry). Seven percent adjust the standard errors using the Newey-West procedure (Newey and West (1987)), modified for use in a panel data set, while 23 percent report clustered standard errors (Liang and Zeger (1986), Moulton (1990), and Andrews (1991)), which are White standard errors (White (1980)) adjusted to account for the possible correlation within a cluster. These are also called Rogers standard errors in the finance literature.'

[18]Stock and Watson (2012, 402).

[19]Thomas (2003).

[20]Wooldridge (2001). Cf., for technical explanation and matrix notation Thomas (2003, 39–51).

9.3.1 Market-oriented bank valuation

Section 2.2 shows the common valuation methods for banks. According to the overview of bank-valuation methods provided in Table 2.1, banks can be valued on a relative-market basis—that is, without further strategic value considerations—with the help of either market multiples or regressions based on market multiples.

Market Multiples (*P/BV* vs. *P/E*)

In a relative valuation, prices have to be standardised, usually by converting prices into ratios. The two most common relative-valuation measures for banks are the price-to-earnings ratio (P/E) and the price-to-book value ratio (P/BV). These ratios are also called trading or market multiples. The following equation, in accordance with Dermine (2014), shows the close relation between the two ratios (where n is the number of shares, PPS is the price per share, EPS is the earnings per share, and BVS is the book value per share, which equals $equity/n$):

$$\frac{P}{BV} = \frac{PPS \times n}{BVS \times n} \times \frac{PPS \times EPS}{BVS \times EPS} = \frac{PPS}{EPS} \times \frac{EPS}{BVS} = P/E \times RoE \tag{9.4}$$

The P/BV is the product of P/E and return on equity (RoE). P/E and RoE are both, to a large extent, based on the expected future (growth of) earnings. Earnings is a financial-reporting measure defined under bank accounting rules (see Sect. 2.2) and is therefore biased by management discretion and accounting-related issues. Moreover, it is subject to high fluctuations that are not directly related to the underlying firm value. In a way, P/BV complements P/E, as it also takes into account the earnings level by adding RoE. Book value of equity (BV), the denominator of RoE, is also a less-sensitive metric that does not merely follow the rigour of accounting rules.[21] P/BV represents the expectations about the firm's ability to generate excess profits from its capital base along with future growth expectations.[22] This is why P/E is only considered adequate for banks in which growth is the main value driver.

Tobin's Q

Tobin (1969) was the first to reveal the usefulness of the ratio of the market value of assets and liabilities to its replacement or reproduction costs. This ratio was accordingly baptized Tobin's q (quotient). In practice, however, it is at least difficult to obtain replacement or reproduction costs.[23] Since it is a relative metric, it is crucial to apply it to many firms to achieve comparability and meaningfulness. Hence, for practical use, many authors have subsequently modified Tobin's q. First, instead of relying on replacement

---

[21] Huizinga and Laeven (2012, 532).

[22] Cf. Jordan et al. (2011, 2049), Dermine (2014), and Fairfield (1994, 30).

[23] Tobin and Brainard (1977).

or reproductions costs, accounting book values are often drawn on because they are easily obtainable and are arguably the best proxies.[24] Second, the value of liabilities is excluded, which results in P/BV: that is, the market valuation of the firm to the net-asset value perspective of an accountant (i.e., the difference between the book value of assets and the book value of liabilities). Some authors have promoted the reverse writing as book-to-market value (BV/P). Both P/BV and BV/P can be seen as equivalent measures for value creation measured by Tobin's q, which has been proven empirically.[25]

Price-to-Book Value Ratio (*P/BV*)

The P/BV is commonly understood as the best valuation measure for banks in terms of prediction accuracy for profitability, earnings and stock returns.[26] The P/BV is applied especially to banks because the book value of bank assets generally have a high explanatory power. A substantial share of the assets are either marked-to-market or precisely valued with internally sophisticated models.[27] The P/BV can be seen as a measure of how efficiently a firm's equity is used to generate profits. A ratio below one indicates that the market believes that the firm will not be able to turn the assets on the balance sheet into profits: i.e., that the firm is expected to make losses on a going concern which will decrease the book value. A ratio in excess of one, ceteris paribus, indicates high franchise value that can be unlocked within the company and its assets and liabilities. Even if these are stylised conclusions from the ratio, investors often use this ratio for banks because of its intuitive application—even when earnings streams are expected to be (temporarily) negative.[28]

Price-to-Book Value Regression (*P/BV* − *RoE*)

When applying the relative P/BV valuation metric, it is crucial to choose similar banks—in particular, with regard to profitability, risk, and growth (see Sect. 9.3.2 and Sect. 9.3.3). Since not two firms are identical, it is essential to control for their differences. To this end, financial analysts often conduct regression analyses. The most common is the simple bivariate $P/BV - RoE$ regression, with P/BV being the dependent

[24]Cf. Branch et al. (2014). The book value of an asset is the original price paid for the asset minus any allowable depreciation of the asset. This means that the book value of an asset tends to decrease over time. Similarly, the book value of a liability represents the value of a liabilities when issued. The book value of an asset generally has the potential to deviate much more from its market value than the book value of a liability. This is the case, as the market value of an asset value mirrors the asset's earning expectations, which may change significantly. A liability generally has to be repaid at par (Damodaran (2012)).

[25]Varaiya, Kerin, and Weeks (1987, 496). Cf. Damodaran (2012).

[26]Cf. Park and Lee (2003, 331) and Imam, Barker, and Clubb (2008, 517).

[27]Barth (1994)

[28]Damodaran (2012).

variable explained by *RoE*. It is used to explain whether a bank appears fairly valued compared to other banks.[29] Fig. 9.2 plots such an illustrative graphical regression analysis. Hence, Eq. 9.4 can be understood as a regression function with P/E being the slope of the regression line. Banks above the regression line appear overvalued compared to peers in the sample, and vice versa. The regression analysis takes advantage of the strong empirical correlation of market valuation (P/BV) and profitability (RoE). The following examines this relationship in more detail.[30]

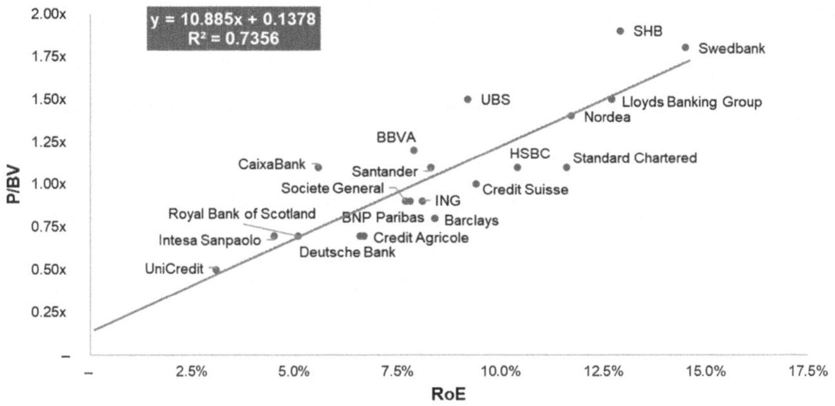

Fig. 9.2 Illustrative Graphical $P/BV - RoE$ Regression

9.3.2 Theoretical Decomposition of P/BV

Explaining valuation—in particular, in terms of P/BV (or BV/P)—is one string of research in a long history of asset pricing: a core focus of capital markets research.[31]

Foundation—Gordon Growth Model

Williams (1938) is widely considered to be the first to formulate an essential relationship that every investor nowadays acts upon naturally:

---

[29] Cf. Damodaran (2012, 453–67).

[30] The $P/BV - RoE$ regression is explained in detail by Wilcox (1984) and Wilcox and Philips (2005).

[31] An historical overview of asset pricing is provided by e.g., Dimson and Mussavian (1999), Çelik (2012), Royal Swedish Academy of Sciences (14 October 2013), and Shih et al. (2014).

A stock is worth the present value of all the dividends ever to be paid upon it, no more, no less... Present earnings, outlook, financial condition, and capitalization should bear upon the price of a stock only as they assist buyers and sellers in estimating future dividends.

Gordon and Shapiro (1956) rediscovered the sentinel work of Williams (1938) and built on it to develop the framework commonly known as the dividend discount model (DDM) or the Gordon growth model. Gordon and Shapiro (1956) formalise the above cited paradigm as follows:

$$P_0 = \sum_{t=1}^{\infty} \frac{DV_t}{(1 + CoE)^t} \tag{9.5}$$

where price, P_0, is the value of the firm, asset or stock at $t = 1$; DV_t is the dividend expected at time t; and cost of equity, CoE, is the investors' required rate of return which equates the asset's expected future payments with its price. To reformulate mathematical Eq. 9.5 more easily, it can be rewritten when the dividend is assumed to be received and discounted on a continuous basis:

$$P_0 = \int_0^{\infty} DV_t e^{-CoE \times t} dt \tag{9.6}$$

Two further assumptions are introduced: First, a firm is expected to retain a fraction b (retention rate; (1-payout ratio)) of its net income, E_t, and to pay out the remaining in the form of a dividend, DV_t:

$$DV_t = (1 - b)E_t \tag{9.7}$$

Second, a firm is expected to earn a return, RoE, on its book value, BV_t:

$$RoE = \frac{E_t}{BV_t} \tag{9.8}$$

Assuming a constant RoE over time, the income, E, at time t is the income at $(t - 1)$ plus RoE percent of the income at $(t - 1)$ retained:

$$E_t = E_{t-1} + RoE \times bE_{t-1} \tag{9.9}$$

Equation 9.9 is simply a compound interest expression so that, if E_t grows continuously at the rate $g = RoE \times b$,

$$E_t = E_0 e^{gt} \tag{9.10}$$

Eq. 9.7 and 9.10 results in

$$DV_t = DV_0 e^{gt} \tag{9.11}$$

Substituting this expression for D_t in Eq. 9.6 and integrating gives the formula that is known in finance as perpetuity:

$$P_0 = \int_0^\infty DV_0 e^{gt} g^{-CoE \times t} dt = DV_0 \int_0^\infty e^{-t(CoE-g)} dt = \frac{DV_0}{CoE - g} \tag{9.12}$$

Decomposition of Price-to-Book Value (*P*/*BV*)

To arrive at P/BV, book value, BV, is added in the next steps.[32] We can substitute the dividends, DV_0, with Eq. 9.7 and receive,

$$P_o = \frac{E_0(1-b)}{CoE - g} \tag{9.13}$$

Equation 9.8 can be rewritten as $E_0 = BV_0 RoE$, and inserted into the following term:

$$P_o = \frac{BV_0 RoE(1-b)}{CoE - g} \tag{9.14}$$

Equation 9.14 can be rewritten to represent the so-called residual-income model (RIM) or the economic-value added model (EVA), in which the firm distributes the amount that it earns above its cost of capital:

$$P_o = BV_0 + \frac{BV_0 RoE - BV_0 CoE}{CoE - g} \tag{9.15}$$

Equation 9.14 can also be rewritten in terms of the P/BV:

$$\frac{P_0}{BV_0} = \frac{RoE(1-b)}{CoE - g} \tag{9.16}$$

Here it can be seen that the P/BV is an increasing function of the return on book equity, RoE; the payout ratio, $(1-b)$; and the growth, g. And it is a decreasing function of the riskiness of the firm, CoE. It is possible to simplify the formula even further. Growth, g, can be defined as retained earnings over book value, BV; while $E = BV \times RoE$:

$$g = \frac{bE}{BV} = \frac{b \times RoE \times BV}{BV} = b \times RoE \tag{9.17}$$

When substituting b with g/RoE,

$$\frac{P_0}{BV_0} = P/BV = \frac{RoE - g}{CoE - g} \tag{9.18}$$

Since the growth rate is the same in the numerator and the denominator, the market value will be greater than the book value ($P/BV > 1$) if the return on equity, RoE, exceeds the cost of equity, CoE, and vice versa. Finally, a formal expression of P/BV is derived with just three independent variables (RoE, CoE, and g) that are observable in company

[32] In accordance with Damodaran (2012) and Dermine (2014).

disclosures or market statistics. Due to the use of one-stage inputs, it is valid only for a stable firm, however.

Decomposition of Return on Equity (*RoE*)

RoE is an accounting term that can be used for financial and non-financial firms in general. When decomposing *RoE* into its components, there are fundamental difference between banks and non-banks, however, because banks' only genuine source of income is interest income. Subsequently, the most detailed formal *RoE*-breakdown for banks[33] shall be derived with using commonly used performance metrics based on standard accounting terms. Equation 9.19 presents a bank's income statement (see Sect. 2.2) in a formalised form (*II* be interest income, *IE* be interest expense, *LLP* be loan-loss provisions, *OE* be operating expenses, and *t* be tax-rate):

$$RoE = (II - IE - LLP - OE) \times (1 - t)/BV \tag{9.19}$$

To receive a formula that consists only of ratios instead of absolute numbers, interest income on total assets ($IIoA = II/A$), cost of debt ($CoD = IE/D$), cost-income-ratio ($CIR = OE/(II - IE)$) and cost of risk ($CoR = LLP/A$) are introduced, while total assets equal debt plus book value of equity ($A = D + BV$):

$$\begin{aligned} RoE &= [IIoA \times A - CoD \times D - CIR \times (II - IE) - LLP \times A] \times (1 - t)/BV \\ &= \{IIoA \times (D + BV) - CoD \times D - CIR \times IIoA \times [(D + BV) - CoD \times D] - CoR \times (D + BV)\} \times (1 - t)/BV \\ &= [IIoA \times (1 - CIR) - LLP] \times (1 - t) + [(IIoA - CoD) \times (1 - CIR) - CoR] \times (1 - t) \times D/BV \end{aligned} \tag{9.20}$$

This formula essentially represents the flow through a general bank income statement where the topline revenue, in form of interest income earned on total assets (*IIoA*), is diminished by cost for debt funding (*CoD*), operational costs (*CIR*), and costs to account for potential loan-losses (*CoR*). The resulting profit before tax is taxed ($1 - t$) to result in net income to shareholders. Finally, it is multiplied by a bank's capital structure ratio (D/BV) to receive the return on the capital invested by shareholders' only. Generally, it is not practical to further break down the resulting ratios in Eq. 9.20, due to the standard availability of bank disclosures.

Decomposition of Cost of Equity (*CoE*)

Cost of equity represents the return an investor would normally expect to receive from another asset with the same perceived risk. To break down *CoE*, Eq. 9.12 can be rewritten as follows:

$$CoE = \frac{DV_0}{P_0} + g \tag{9.21}$$

[33]Based on Dermine (2014).

Equation 9.21 works in a perfectly priced market where all assets with the same risk have the same price. Since this is normally not the case, the capital asset pricing model (CAPM) is the most widely used model to derive the theoretically appropriate return the market would expect. It was the first formalised model to analyse asset pricing, and it is based on the findings of Markowitz (1959) and Tobin (1958). Markowitz (1959) developed a new approach to compiling portfolios, introducing the use of portfolio diversification to optimise the risk-and-return profile of a portfolio (r_m). The correlation characteristics between assets are utilised for this purpose and are expressed by the assets' beta (β). Tobin (1958) extends this approach with the possibility of adding a risk-free asset to the portfolio, which is not correlated to other portfolio assets and yields a fixed rate. The CAPM was independently developed by Sharpe (1964), Lintner (1965), and Mossin (1966). The model is based on two further fundamental conditions: (i) investors have the same information about and expectation of the risks and returns of the assets, and (ii) investors have the ability to borrow at the risk-free rate (r_f). The overarching assumption is that the higher the risk of an asset, the higher the investors' compensation for that risk (i.e., the yield). It can be formalised as follows:

$$CoE = r_f + \beta(r_m - r_f) \tag{9.22}$$

The arbitrage pricing theory (APT), developed by Ross (1976), extends the strict one-factor CAPM. It makes it possible to input further factors that explain the riskiness of an asset. The different factors can be understood as 'special portfolios of stocks that tend to be subject to a common influence'. The APT does not tell what these factors are, unlike the CAPM.[34]

$$CoE = r_f + \beta_1(r_{factor\ 1} - r_f) + \beta_2(r_{factor\ 2} - r_f) + \ldots + \beta_n(r_{factor\ n} - r_f) \tag{9.23}$$

Decomposition of Growth (g)

Growth is mathematically the same for net income, Y, dividends, DV, or book value, BV. But there is also a possibility to observe growth without looking at two different points in time, as seen in Eq. 9.17: $g = b \times RoE$. Since RoE was decomposed and explained in Sect. 9.3.2, retention rate, b, is the only variable left. In practice, it is common to use $(1 - b)$: the dividend payout ratio (PO). PO seems to be relatively stable. A company's management has a good degree of discretion over this ratio, as it is not governed by accounting rules. Management often gives out a public dividend payout guidance to meet investors' preferences for planning certainty. When Eq. 9.7 is reorganised, it results in the following:

$$b = 1 - \frac{DV}{Y} = 1 - PO \tag{9.24}$$

[34] Brealey and Myers (2003, 206).

9.3.3 Empirical Explanation of P/BV

Sentinel empirical studies were conducted after the Center for Research in Security Prices (CRPS) compiled its database in 1960 and the Compustat database was compiled in 1962. For the first time, both provided a wide-range and long-reaching time series of financial and market data—in particular, on share prices. Banks, however, were, at least at the beginning, treated as an orphan by these databases because of their financial characteristics—in particular, because of their high leverage—which made them less comparable to firms of other industries.[35]

To anticipate the major conclusions, the subsequent empirical studies generally confirm the factors derived from theory (see Sect. 9.3.2). It becomes apparent, however, that these factors cannot be isolated as well as in the theoretical considerations. The main superior factors—profitability (*RoE*), risk (*CoE*) and growth (*g*)—seem to explain each other in many studies, while many additional factors cannot be derived from theory. This might, to a good extent, be due to the statistical challenges of factor controlling.

Explaining Stock Returns and Market Value

The first large wave of empirical studies explained stock prices and equity values. In an initial study, Ball and Brown (1968) empirically confirmed the strong relationship between the basic accounting measure earnings and market equity value described in the theoretical Gordon growth model (formalised in Eq. 9.5). Beaver, Clarke, and Wright (1979) and Collins and Kothari (1989) corroborate this elementary relationship, while Mukherjee and Dukes (1989) confirm the relationship explicitly for (small) banks. They add that the certainty (risk), payout ratio and growth of the earning streams are approximating values.

Chan, Hamao, and Lakonishok (1991) were among the first to prove that the BV/P has significant explanatory power for cross-section stock returns. Ohlson (1995) confirms the residual-income concept (formalised in Eq. 9.15) that relates equity value to book value and earnings. This means that it is possible to shift value analysis away from discounting dividends to book value plus the present value of expected abnormal earnings. Beltratti and Paladino (2015) subsequently confirmed that this holds true for banks.

However, the success of the P/BV is consistent with two very different models of stock prices:[36] In an inefficient market, P/BV helps to identify stocks that are mispriced relative to their fundamental characteristics. Lakonishok, Shleifer, and Vishny (1994) discovered that, since temporary mispricing is eliminated, underpriced stocks (those with low P/BV) deliver high excess returns while overpriced stocks (those with high P/BV) deliver low excess returns. On the other hand, in an efficient market, P/BV forecasts returns because it is a proxy for the unobserved *CoE*, according to Fama and French (1992).

---

[35]Cooper, Jackson III, and Patterson (2003, 818).

[36]Bulkley, Harris, and Herrerias (2004).

Explaining Price-to-Book Value (*P*/*BV*)

Hence, there are two groups of academics with opposing interpretations of the difference in the market and book value of equity:[37] One group sees the ratio primarily as a measure of profitability (efficiency of invested capital, *RoE*) and growth;[38] the other group sees it primarily as a proxy for risk (variation in market returns, beta, *CoE*).[39] Though both perspectives are theoretically sound (formalised in Eq. 9.18), many empirical studies have shown that the former interpretation has far more explanatory power, also for banks.[40] This could also be interpreted as evidence that stock markets function efficiently at most times.

Varaiya, Kerin, and Weeks (1987, 496) empirically clarifies the fact that none of the three input factors (*RoE*, *CoE*, and *g*) should be analysed separately. The spread between *RoE* and *CoE* (i.e., profitability adjusted for opportunity costs) explains more than each factor alone. Moreover, a positive spread ($RoE > CoE$) is more important for value creation than growth (*g*).[41] On a separate basis, it generally appears that the explanatory power has the following descendent order when the spread is positive and the competitive environment is stable: *RoE*, *g*, and *CoE*.[42] Furthermore, Fama and French (1995) empirically confirm the theoretical assumption that, in a rational market, valuation measures such as *P*/*BV* are driven by long-term expectations of *RoE* while short-term changes have only limited impact. Brief and Lawson (1992) confirms that, even given the accounting nature of the term, *RoE* is the best proxy for profitability.

Beyond the three exclusively theoretical impact factors, many authors have found additional relationships of *P*/*BV* with various financial and non-financial factors. Most importantly, Fama and French (1992) discover that size, in terms of the market value of equity, has a significant impact on *P*/*BV* for non-financial firms. Barber and Lyon (1997) subsequently document that this relation holds true for banks as well. Non-financial factors on bank valuation that have been found are, for instance, larger cash-flow rights of shareholders and stronger shareholder-protection laws.[43]

The most recent and sophisticated studies that are regressing *P*/*BV*, or *P*/*TBV* respectively, are interested in changes of bank valuations due to the GFC. Jordan et al. (2011) use this method to test for the impact of TARP-injections and Calomiris and Nissim (2014) use it to test for changes in the general explanatory factors from the pre- to the post-crisis period.

---

[37]Sharma et al. (2013) present a review of the available literature regarding the explanation of *P*/*BV*.

[38]E.g., Fama and French (1995).

[39]E.g., Sharma et al. (2013).

[40]Cf. Bertsatos and Sakellaris (2016).

[41]Cf. Niu (2016).

[42]Cf. Harris and Marston (1994, 18) and Hammami and Lindahl (2014).

[43]Caprio, Laeven, and Levine (2007).

Explaining Return on Equity (*RoE*)

Several empirical studies have investigated what drives profitability, beyond the theoretical framework (see Sect. 9.3.2).[44] Empirical research confirms that the disaggregated-earnings components of non-financial firms explain more of the variation in returns[45] and profitability[46] than aggregated earnings alone. The incremental predictive content of the disaggregated earnings is not limited to extraordinary items and discontinued operations but to the quality of the measurement of the more granular line items.

The research findings on factors driving profitability—particularly for banks—can be split into three categories:[47]

1. Primary internal (or bank-specific) factors: These factors confirm the theoretical decomposition of *RoE* (see Sect. 9.3.2) into various ratios consisting of accounting measures. There are studies which simply confirm that the decomposition of *RoE* also improves the explanatory models for banks.[48] The relevant factors include: diversification of business, growth of total loans,[49] credit and liquidity risk,[50] market risk exposures,[51] capitalisation,[52] asset structure and asset quality.[53] Empirical studies find that particularly operational efficiency, which is generally understood as the ratio of operating costs to operating income (cost-income-ratio or *CIR*), has a significant impact on profitability.[54] Some studies disaggregate costs further and identify ratios on funding costs[55] and labour costs[56] as major factors. There is no agreement in the

[44]Cf. Pasiouras and Kosmidou (2007). *Efficiency* and *profitability* are sometimes used interchangeably. In this context, *efficiency* concerns how efficiently the invested capital is used to generate profits. *RoE*, which is post-tax profitability of invested equity capital, is the adequate technical term which is also most often used in literature. The term return on assets (*RoA*) is also frequently used for banks, as it is meaningful for banks due to the interest-bearing assets on their balance sheets. Cf. Imam, Barker, and Clubb (2008, 515).

[45]Lipe (1986) and Ohlson and Penman (1992).

[46]Fairfield, Sweeney, and Lombardi Yohn (1996).

[47]Based on Petria, Capraru, and Ihnatov (2015).

[48]E.g., Ming-Li and Liang (2005) and Alam and Brown (2006).

[49]E.g., Dietrich and Wanzenried (2011).

[50]E.g., Petria, Capraru, and Ihnatov (2015).

[51]E.g., Molyneux and Fiordelisi (2010).

[52]E.g., Athanasoglou, Brissimis, and Delis (2008).

[53]E.g., Tomuleasda and Cocris (2014).

[54]E.g., Molyneux and Fiordelisi (2010).

[55]E.g., Dietrich and Wanzenried (2011).

[56]E.g., Athanasoglou, Brissimis, and Delis (2008).

literature about the impact of the line items below profit before tax: i.e., about taxation and minority interest.[57]

2. Secondary internal (or bank-specific) factors: In contrast to the above primary factors derived from accounting concepts, the underlying or secondary internal factors only indirectly impact earnings and profitability. This might be why Molyneux and Fiordelisi (2010) find a greater influence of most of these factors with a lag of one to two years. The most notable factors include bank ownership, size,[58] and underlying legal and institutional indicators.[59]
3. External (or industry-specific and macroeconomic) factors: External factors are those which impact the banking industry or the entire economy or country. Industry-specific factors include, first and foremost, bank concentration and other competitive factors.[60] Macroeconomic factors primarily include economic (GDP) growth and inflation[61] and country-level characteristics relating to location, regulation, and legal tradition.[62]

Tomuleasda and Cocris (2014) note that the factors explaining bank profitability have a rather heterogeneous impact due to particularities of the countries they operate in. This may be because banks are subject to different national regulations and are heavily dependent on their macroeconomic environments.

Explaining Cost of Equity (*CoE*)

Black, Jensen, and Scholes (1972) were the first to perform empirical tests of the CAPM. Their evidence, however, indicates that the expected return on an asset is not strictly proportional to its beta: the measurement of risk. There had to be other significant factors influencing the asset pricing. Many authors identify various factors that have explanatory power for *CoE*. Prominent examples include Basu (1977) (P/E) and Banz (1991) (market value). The major breakthrough was the so-called three-factor model by Fama and French (1992). It added the two variables size and value effect (BV/P) to the CAPM, which they observed to be most influential. This model can be understood as a special case of the APT:

---

[57]Cf. Demirgüç-Kunt, Kane, and Huizinga (1999) and Alam and Brown (2006).

[58]E.g., Barros, Ferreira, and Williams (2007).

[59]E.g., Demirgüç-Kunt, Kane, and Huizinga (1999).

[60]E.g., Molyneux and Thornton (1992) and Bourke (1989) in line with the SCP paradigm, while Athanasoglou, Brissimis, and Delis (2008) proves the opposite in line with the ES hypothesis, according to which concentration is not related to profitability once the other effects are controlled for.

[61]E.g., Tomuleasda and Cocris (2014) and Petria, Capraru, and Ihnatov (2015).

[62]E.g., Barros, Ferreira, and Williams (2007) and Demirgüç-Kunt, Kane, and Huizinga (1999).

$$CoE = r_f + \beta_{market}\left(r_{market|factor}\right) + \beta_{size}\left(r_{size|factor}\right) + \beta_{book-to-market}\left(r_{book-to-market|factor}\right) \tag{9.25}$$

'At this juncture, the critical issue is encountered again, which remains unresolved, [as to] whether size and BV/P are proxies for unidentified risk factors (as suggested by Fama and French (1993)) or security mispricing (as suggested by Lakonishok, Shleifer, and Vishny (1994)).'[63] It is clear, however, that the three-factor model significantly improves the explanatory power compared to the one-factor model.[64] Last but not least, M. R. King (2009a) notes that only a handful of studies provide estimates of the *CoE* for banks.

Explaining Growth (*g*)

To date, no studies have proven the existence of any further factors driving growth beyond the theoretical framework of profitability and profit retention.

9.3.4 Intangible Assets and Bank Valuation

Definition of Banks' Intangible Assets

Intangible asset is an accounting term ruled by the respective accounting norm, while *franchise value* is the respective term from an economical perspective (see Sect. 2.2).[65] US GAAP and IFRS have similar rules on intangible assets and define intangible assets as non-monetary assets without physical substance.[66] The recognition criteria of both accounting principles require probable future economic benefits and costs that can be reliably measured. Examples for banks include patented technology, bank reputation, computer software, trademarks, mortgage servicing rights, licenses, franchise agreements, and customer relationships. Most intangible assets are internally developed by the banks, in particular competences and the proper use of resources in certain banking fields. Due to the strict GAAP for the valuation and recognition of these intangible assets, the majority of them are not recorded on the balance sheet. Intangible assets shown on the balance sheet are normally either purchased separately, in particular

[63]Barber and Lyon (1997, 883).

[64]Dimson and Mussavian (1999) and Royal Swedish Academy of Sciences (14 October 2013).

[65]Sharma (2012) provides an overview of international accounting norms and valuation methods of intangible assets. PricewaterhouseCoopers (September 2015) provides an overview of differences between US GAAP and IFRS with regard to intangible assets.

[66]'Under US GAAP and IFRS, the primary sources of guidance on the recognition, measurement, amortization, and impairment of goodwill and other intangible assets are ASC 350 and both IAS 36, Impairment of Assets, and IAS 38, Intangible Assets.' Harasim (2008, 47) presents an overview of features that distinguish intangible assets from tangible assets at banks.

software, or, most commonly, purchased in the context of the acquisition of another firm. Intangibles recognised as part of a business combination are then shown as goodwill on the acquirer's balance sheet.[67] 'Intangible assets meeting the relevant recognition criteria are initially measured at cost or subsequently measured using the revaluation model and amortised on a systematic basis over their useful lives (unless the asset has an indefinite useful life, in which case it is not amortised)'. Goodwill must not be amortised and is carried as an asset and evaluated for impairment at least once a year.

Valuation of Intangible Assets Recorded on Banks' Balance Sheets

When banks invest in intangible assets, they undoubtedly (should) expect a return above its cost. Hence, intangible assets should have a substantial value.[68] From a theoretical point of view, the cash flows generated from intangibles are more uncertain compared to other assets, for instead retail loans with fixed income streams. On the other hand, to compensate for this higher risk, the return of intangible assets should be higher compared to that of tangible assets consistent with the uncertainty hypothesis. Consequently, its value should not be significantly different.[69]

Since goodwill is normally the largest fraction of the recorded intangible assets, most research is devoted to it.[70] Chauvin and Hirschey (1994, 176), McCarthy and Schneider (1995), and Jennings et al. (1996, 513) find a strong positive relation between equity values and recorded goodwill-asset amounts, while goodwill numbers exert just a small positive influence on profitability in the non-manufacturing sector. However, when comparing banks over a longer period of time, there are several reasons why attributing value to intangible assets as a whole is difficult for investors:

1. Uncertainty: The future economic benefits resulting from intangibles are significantly more uncertain,[71] and value attributed to intangible assets changes greatly depending on the economic circumstances or company success. For instance, lower base rates to counter economic recessions reduce the intangible franchise value of the banks' core deposits. Recorded goodwill captures just the differences in the acquisition history of banks. Many studies confirm that a good proportion of M&A transactions cannot deemed successful.[72] Hence, Bugeja and Gallery (2006, 519) find that only recently acquired goodwill has information content. This means intangibles cannot readily be turned into cash and are particularly prone to write-offs.

---

[67]Cf. Calomiris and Nissim (2014).

[68]Chauvin and Hirschey (1994, 177).

[69]Cf. Choi, Kwon, and Lobo (Cf. 2000, 44).

[70]Cf. McCarthy and Schneider (1995).

[71]Choi, Kwon, and Lobo (2000, 35).

[72]Cf. Beccalli and Frantz (2009) and Berger and Humphrey (1994).

2. Disclosure: Investors have only little information about intangible assets other than goodwill. In particular, the most valuable intangible assets are not reflected in the financial statements. Only a few banks voluntarily provide value estimates in their accounting notes. Hence, the market has only very limited information about intangible assets.[73]
3. Valuation: Valuing intangible assets appears to be extremely difficult even for bank insiders, and there is no consistent method of valuation across banks.[74]

Overall, including intangibles just adds another variable that is non-comparable across banks. Intangibles are already captured indirectly in the earning streams they generate and in other bank characteristics, such as the size and yield of loans.[75] Only the disaggregation of intangible assets and inclusion of separate disclosure of intangibles helps preserve the relation with the share price.[76] In practise, however, this is rarely achievable.

From an empirical perspective, Calomiris and Nissim (2014) report that, in particular, during the financial crisis of 2006–2012, investors associated little value with the intangibles of US banks for this reason. Hirschey and Richardson (2002, 173) and Churyk (2005, 1353) find more explanatory power in intangibles on bank valuation, but during previous periods with potentially less economic uncertainty.

Tangible Book Value (*TBV*)

Consistent with the above findings, Calomiris and Nissim (2014, 433) find that the substantial decline in P/BV is mostly explained by the declining value perception of intangibles rather than by unrecognised losses only. For the purpose of a valuation regression, Bernstein Research (2003, 53) confirms that RoE has a stronger relationship in explaining P/TBV than P/BV. Consequently, Barba (2015) finds, following the downturn, that investors increasingly based their valuations on tangible-book-value ratios (*TBV*). Major global banks, such as Goldman Sachs and Deutsche Bank, followed this investor demand and changed their financial reporting accordingly. Furthermore, TBV, which is sometimes also referred to as net tangible assets (NTA), can be considered a good proxy for regulatory capital: i.e., the capital available to absorb losses while the bank remains a going concern.[77] Some controversially consider it a liquidation value in a true bank wind-up.[78]

[73]Kohlbeck (2004).

[74]Sharma (2012, 61).

[75]Calomiris and Nissim (2014).

[76]Ely and Waymire (1999, 41).

[77]Demirgüç-Kunt, Detragiache, and Merrouche (2013, 1149).

[78]Cf. Deutsche Bank (4 April 2016).

Hypothesis Development 10

Based on the literature review of related research developed in (see Chap. 9), Sect. 10.1 works out the research gaps while providing objectives for this quantitative study. Subsequently, Sect. 10.2 develops and formalises the research hypotheses. Hypotheses 1–3 are related to the content of the overall research question (What drives the valuation of stocks of G-SIBs compared to stocks of other banks over time?), which represents the primary research interest of this thesis. Hypotheses 4–6 are related to the regression method, which represents the secondary research interest.

10.1 Research Gaps vs. Research Objectives

The following highlights of this empirical study point out the research gaps and the main characteristics of the analysis undertaken to close them:

- Analysing the relative difference of G-SIBs by using an advanced valuation measure (dependent variable: P/TCE): Existing research (see Sect. 9.1 shows that G-SIBs are valued differently by the market than non-G-SIBs. These studies apply a variety of research approaches and mainly assess single effects that are exerted by the TBTF doctrine on respective banks, such as funding benefits, TBTF designation effects, or regulatory TBTF burden effects. The results are either calculated in absolute or directional terms when associated with certain TBTF events. There is, however, not a single primary research study on the valuational differences of G-SIBs compared to non-G-SIBs. Therefore, this study applies a refined version of P/BV, the most common relative valuation measure for banks. As elaborated in Sect. 9.3.4, intangible assets, which are included in the BV metric, seem to add a non-comparable variable to P/BV. Hence, a regression based on tangible book value (*TBV*) should improve

T. F. Lesche, *Too-Big-to-Fail in Banking*, Finanzwirtschaft, Banken und Bankmanagement I Finance, Banks and Bank Management, https://doi.org/10.1007/978-3-658-34182-4_10

regression results. Moreover, tangible common equity (*TCE*) is considered here to be an even more precise measure than *TBV*. *TCE* excludes equity-like instruments that are not captured in the market price (*P*). These are all instruments other than common equity listed on the stock exchange, such as minority interest or hybrid capital. It is assumed that the explanatory power of regressing *P*/*TCE* is stronger than regressing *P*/*BV* or *P*/*TBV* with the same explanatory variables (see below). No previous primary studies have used *P*/*TCE* in their research methodology, but practitioners in investment banking do.

- Using the distinct definition of G-SIBs by the FSB: There is no generally accepted definition of G-SIBs. The FSB, however, has designated approximately 30 global banks as G-SIBs—a designation connected with significant additional regulatory requirements. Several studies (see Sect. 9.1.4.5) consider this connection in their analyses of G-SIBs.
- Controlling for 'noise' with decomposed fundamentals deduced from theory (explanatory variables: *RoE*, *CoE*, *g*): Available studies on the impact of TBTF on equity do not control for exogenous factors, mainly due the short-term nature of their analyses. When analysing relative differences (over a period time), however, it is crucial to exclude impact factors other than the G-SIB designation. The large amount research into this matter shows a wealth of findings, and the empirical explanation of *P*/*BV* (see Sect. 9.3.3) is anything but decisive. Two superior observations can be made, however: First, the main factors at the highest level are profitability (*RoE*), risk (*CoE*), and growth (*g*), which are the same as those deduced from theory (see Sect. 9.3.2). In many studies, these factors seem also to explain each other. Second, when decomposing the factors—in particular *RoE*—the explanatory content of any regression can be further improved. Hence, this study uses a structured approach to finding the best explanatory variables by strictly decomposing *P*/*TCE* according to theory while also considering off-balance sheet bank income.
- Analysing a long and continuous period (2008–2015) by using an advanced econometric model (two-way fixed-effect regression): The related empirical studies on the impact of TBTF on equity analyse only isolated points in time. This study, in contrast, analyses a long and continuous period with quarterly frequencies, which equals the financial-reporting frequency of many banks. The period shall cover at least the period from the time before the FSB establishment (17 November 2008) until before the first publication of the list of O-SIIs in the EU by the EBA on 26 April 2016 (see Sect. 7.4).[1] This period comprises several relevant designation and regulation events

[1]Due to the introduction of O-SIIs, much of the distinction of G-SIBs is lost. It adds to the confusion that, for some banks, the O-SII (D-SIB) surcharge is higher than the G-SIB surcharge (for instance, ING and Nordea with a 2 percent D-SIB surcharge against a 1 percent G-SIB surcharge). In some cases, it is lower (for instance, BNP Paribas with a 1.5 percent D-SIB surcharge against a G-SIB surcharge of 2 percent).

for G-SIBs (see Table 7.2). In order to identify entity- and time-fixed effects (i.e. valuation developments of a subset of banks per quarter), a two-way fixed-fixed regression model (see Sect. 9.2) shall be applied. To date, no academic research has utilised this approach in finance research.

- Analysing a global bank sample by using a financial database with most sophisticated data (SNL): Empirical studies that collectively explain P/BV predominantly use bank samples restricted to certain regions—mostly the US or Europe. Time periods of the studies of more than three years are the exception. Both can be explained by the use of antiquated databases, limited data availability, and the intention to increase the explanatory power in any regression model. Given the assumed improved robustness of the regression, through the above refinements, this study shall utilise a global sample in order to cover as many G-SIBs and their peers as possible. This shall be achieved by using the state-of-art database, SNL Financial, which is used mainly by professional bank analysts and has rarely been used by the academic research community.

10.2 Research Hypotheses

There is no academic source—only one equity research source[2]—on the relative valuation of G-SIBs. Also, theoretical considerations about how the potential impact factor IGGs distorts relative valuation are not definite. This is because IGGs involve both TBTF advantages, such as funding benefits, and TBTF disadvantages, such as additional regulation. Hence, the results of this dissertation are guided by the following, non-directional hypothesis:[3]

- Hypothesis 1: G-SIB designation distorted G-SIBs' *P/TCE* from Q2 2008 to Q3 2015.

With regard to the evolution of the hypothesised valuation difference, two further hypotheses shall be established:

One event study[4] shows that G-SIBs' share prices have received the largest abnormal gains after the first (inofficial) designation event on 30 November 2009. This result may have been driven by the so-called TBTF-designation effect, while abnormal losses from regulatory events occurred later. Based on these findings, the directional hypothesis is:

[2]Goldman Sachs (5 January 2015).

[3]Cf. Creswell (2014).

[4]Moenninghoff, Ongena, and Wieandt (2015).

- Hypothesis 2: G-SIBs' P/TCE is more favorable in Q4 2009 than non-G-SIBs' P/TCE in the same quarter (i.e. G-SIBs' P/TCE improved more than non-G-SIBs' P/TCE in Q4 2009)

One academic working paper[5] calculates that the average G-SIBs' long-term share-price development lags significantly behind that of non-GIBs' between 1 November 2009 and 31 October 2012—i.e., after the first designation event—however the calculation does not control for fundamentals. The potential reasoning is that the increasing clarity of additional regulatory requirements for G-SIBs (such as capital surcharges), is mainly driving the underperformance of G-SIBs. Hence, the following directional hypothesis is:

- Hypothesis 3: G-SIBs' P/TCE worsened more than non-G-SIBs' P/TCE between Q4 2009 and Q4 2011.

There is a wealth of previous research studies concerning theoretical (see Sect. 9.3.2) and empirical (see Sect. 9.3.3) explanations of P/BV and its components RoE, CoE, and g. Based on these findings, and incorporating the more recent findings concerning the absence of the explanatory power of intangible assets (see Sect. 9.3.4), the research method of this dissertation is guided by the following three directional hypotheses:

- Hypothesis 4: A bank's P/TCE is positively associated with the decomposition of $RoTCE$. It is
  - positively associated with interest margin ($IIoTA$),
  - negatively associated with cost-income ratio (CIR),
  - negatively associated with cost of risk (CoR),
  - negatively associated with loans-to-tangible assets (L/TA),
  - negatively associated with cost of debt (CoD),
  - positively associated with leverage (D/TCE), and
  - positively associated with percentage of non-interest income ($NonII/OpI$)[6].
- Hypothesis 5: A bank's P/TCE is positively associated with the decomposition of g: i.e.,
  - negatively associated with payout ratio (PO).
- Hypothesis 6: A bank's P/TCE is negatively associated with the decomposition of $CoTCE$: i.e.,
  - negatively associated with dividend yield (DY).

[5] Dewenter and Hess (October 2013).

[6] With tax considered to be insignificant.

11 Empirical Methodology and Data

Section 10.2 briefly discussed how an empirical study must be structured to answer the primary research question (What drives the valuation of stocks of G-SIBs compared to stocks of other banks over time?). The approach is based on the cross-sectional relationship between P/TCE and various bank fundamentals derived from accounting concepts. This chapter describes how a suitable regression model was devised and the sample data was compiled. All variables are developed, leading to the regression formula. The dependent variable is P/TCE, explained by the mathematical decomposition of RoE, CoE, and g, along with the G-SIB designation and some other fundamental bank characteristics. The chapter ends by describing the sample characteristics and the regression function.

11.1 Regression Framework

The underlying assumption of the forthcoming multivariate regression is that at each moment in time the average empirical relationships between the impact factors (financial metrics) and the firm value are reflected in observed P/TCE values. The regression model estimates the coefficients of each of the input factors under this principle. In this special case, a regression is developed that is able to analyse a certain impact factor (i.e., G-SIB designation) that changes over time (i.e., per quarter) and only affects some entities of the sample (i.e., the G-SIBs). This type of multivariate regression is called a

Electronic supplementary material The online version of this chapter (https://doi.org/10.1007/978-3-658-34182-4_11) contains supplementary material, which is available to authorized users.

T. F. Lesche, *Too-Big-to-Fail in Banking*, Finanzwirtschaft, Banken und Bankmanagement I Finance, Banks and Bank Management, https://doi.org/10.1007/978-3-658-34182-4_11

two-way fixed-effect regression model and serves to discover the so-called difference-in-difference (see Sect. 9.2) by inserting binary variables instead of running separate regressions. In other words, it is assumed that some omitted variables vary over time and also across entities (here G-SIBs or non-G-SIBs) while others are constant across entities but vary over time (such as macroeconomic trends or major bank-relevant events). The latter assumption is necessary to separate the G-SIB impact from other interference factors in each quarter. Hence, all variables keep their impact factor through all quarters, and only the G-SIB quarter variable and the time quarter variable can change each quarter.

Equation 11.1 summarises the basis relationship:

$$\begin{gathered}\text{Re}\mathit{lative}\ \widehat{\mathit{bank}}\ \mathit{valuation} = \\ \mathit{Various\ financial\ metrics} + \mathit{Fixed\ GSIB\ time\ effects} + \mathit{Fixed\ time\ effects}\end{gathered} \tag{11.1}$$

11.2 Dependent Variable: Price-to-Tangible Common Equity (P/TCE)

P/TCE is defined as the valuation measure and dependent variable. It is the ratio of the intrinsic value of equity to its book value (see Sect. 9.3.1). However, since intrinsic values are unobservable, market values (*P*) are used instead. This is legitimate as long as the market prices equity efficiently on average and price deviations are not related to fundamentals. In this case, pricing deviations are visible in the error term of the regression, which is then normally distributed and subsequently tested for (see Sect. 12.1). If equity is systemically mispriced, the model's coefficients are biased.[1] Tangible common equity (*TCE*) is used as substitute for the simpler book value. Below, the nominator *P* and denominator *TCE* are developed to ensure that both are related to the same kind of equity instruments.

Price (*P*)

Price, *P*, is defined as the market value of common shares traded on the stock exchange. Ideally, this market capitalisation would be calculated as share price multiplied by the fully diluted number of outstanding common shares. This means that shares resulting from exercisable options or in-the-money convertibles would be added to outstanding shares. However, this computation of management options and conversion plans is only feasible for small samples. Instead, the conventional measure of outstanding shares is used here, where treasury shares and authorised capital are already excluded.

[1] Cf. Calomiris and Nissim (2007, 26).

For the large sample used in this analysis, the options issue is deemed to be of minor significance.[2]

Tangible Common Equity (*TCE*)

The equivalent of the market variable price (*P*) is the accounting variable common equity (*CE*). All outstanding common shares together securitise the common equity of a firm. This means that all additional equity-like components, such as preferred equity and all variations of hybrid capital, are excluded from this definition. Furthermore, not included is equity that is not owned by the parent company, i.e., minority interest. This must all be deducted from the book value of equity to derive the common equity.

Furthermore, intangible assets including goodwill are deducted from common equity to derive *TCE*. There are two main reasons to use this approach (see. Sect. 9.3.4). First, including intangibles would mainly add a non-comparable variation as mainly goodwill from previous business combinations would be recognised. Second, investors often do not attribute any imminent value to these more subjective assets that cannot be capitalised easily. This is particularly true during downturns, when earnings are typically volatile and bank investors focus on more stable book values for valuation purposes. The time period of the present study spans at least one recession. Due to concerns about capital and asset quality during these times, regulators also focus on this core capital. For example, the new Basel III capital regulations (see Sect. 7.3) have a much more rigorous focus on genuine equity, and the Federal Reserve has used the *TCE* measurement as a gauge for bank health.[3] Hence, *TCE* is a good proxy for regulatory capital as well. Figure 7.2 reconciles the accounting and regulatory concepts of how to derive *TCE*, starting from total equity. The formal definition is

$$\begin{aligned} TCE &= BV - (intangible\ assets - goodwill) \\ &-(preferred\ equity - hybrid\ capital) - (minority\ interest) \\ &= total\ assets - total\ liabilities - (intangible\ assets - goodwill) \\ &-(preferred\ equity - hybrid\ capital) - (minority\ interest) \end{aligned} \tag{11.2}$$

Hereafter, the established mathematical explanation and decomposition of P/BV (see Sect. 9.3.2) will be amended to reflect the substitution of *BV* by *TCE*. Adapting Equation 9.18 results in

$$P/TCE = \frac{RoTCE - g}{CoTCE - g} \tag{11.3}$$

where *RoTCE* is the net income attributable to TCE holders over *TCE*, and *CoTCE* is the return expectations of TCE holders.

---

[2]Cf. Damodaran (2012).

[3]Enrich and Langley (23 February 2009).

11.3 Explanatory Variables

This study follows a few principles on the inclusion of explanatory variables:[4]

- All variables included are commonly used and interpretable;
- Variables are derived from theory as far as possible; and
- The number of variables is restricted to permit sufficient degrees of freedom in estimation.

11.3.1 Return on Tangible Common Equity (RoTCE)

RoTCE is decomposed to improve the explanation power of the regression model. The separate income statement items that lead to net income can be rewritten as ratios, and this study employs ratios that are widely used in the academic and professional world.

Equation 9.20 is amended to reflect that the return is now based on *TCE* (*IIoTA* is the interest income over tangible assets, *TA* is tangible assets, and debt (*D*) can be calculated as $TA - TCE$).[5] Hence, depreciation and amortisation expenses are also excluded.

$$\begin{aligned} RoTCE &= (II - IE - LLP - OE) \times (1 - t)/TCE \\ &= [IIoTA \times (1 - CIR) - LLP] \times (1 - t) + [(IIoTA - CoD) \times (1 - CIR) - CoR] \times (1 - t) \\ &\quad \times D/TCE \end{aligned} \tag{11.4}$$

Equation 11.4 is then extended to reflect that banks also conduct off-balance-sheet activities, i.e., they do not only grant loans. This means that *CoR* is based more precisely only on gross loans (*L*) ($(LLP/L) \times (L/TA) = CoR \times L/TA$), and non-interest income (*NonII*) is added and calculated as ($(NonII/OpI) \times OpI$, with operating income as $OpI = II - IE + NonII$). This is the common ratio for considering non-interest income. However, it unfortunately leads to circularity, and *NonII* cannot be perfectly integrated into the above equation since *NonII* is already included in *OpI*:

$$\begin{aligned} &RoTCE \\ &= [IIoTA \times (1 - CIR) - LLP] \times (1 - t) + [(IIoTA - CoD) \times (1 - CIR) - CoR \times L/TA] \\ &\quad \times (1 - t) \times D/TCE + (NonII/OpI) \times OpI \times (1 - t) \times (D/TCE)/D \end{aligned} \tag{11.5}$$

From the decomposition of *RoTCE*, the following six major key factors have been derived that represent more than the resulting profitability: *IIoTA*, *CIR*, *CoR*, L/TA, *CoD*, D/TCE, $NonII/OpI$ and t. Figure 3.1 graphically illustrates the decomposition. The arrows symbolise whether an increasing ratio is considered to be associated with an increasing *RoTCE* and

[4]Cf. Cohen (1990), who gives useful guidance with regard to the practical application of regression analysis.

[5]For the income statement items, see Sect. 2.2.

P/TCE. Taxes are considered to be insignificant as tax rates are generally the same for all banks within a jurisdiction and cannot be influenced on bank-level.

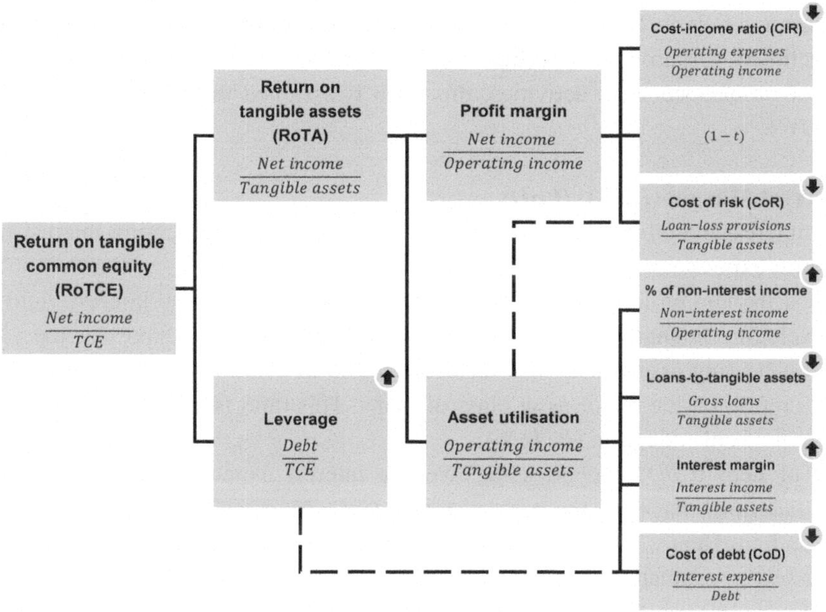

Fig. 11.1 Graphical Illustration of *RoTCE* Decomposition. Source: Similar to Saunders and Cornett (2008, 1)

Business Model ($NonII/OpI$) (L/TA)

$NonII/OpI$ and L/TA are considered to represent a bank's overall business model from a P&L and from a balance sheet perspective, respectively.

Non-interest income (*NonII*) is generally the second most important source of income at banks. It includes fee and commission income from loan products and other cross-selling products, such as insurance policies. Large banks, particularly, generate trading income in their global investment banking arms. These income sources are also called off-balance-sheet activities, as they do not directly depend on interest-bearing assets that normally sit on the balance sheet in the long term. The ratio of non-interest income over total operating income ($NonII/OpI$) represents the reliance on these activities and a bank's business model. In general, as off-balance-sheet activities by definition require only few tangible assets, a return on assets or equity perspective is often inadequate. Instead, the efficiency of off-balance-sheet activities is much better captured by P&L margins, in particular *CIR*. Due to asset lightness, off-balance-sheet activities mostly generate higher returns on equity than on-balance-sheet activities do. With regard to risk, off-balance-sheet activities are a double-edged sword: on the one hand, they offer diversification benefits; and on the other hand, their income streams are normally more volatile.[6] Overall, it is expected that a higher share will lead to higher valuations (*P*/*TCE*).

The loans-to-tangible assets ratio (*L*/*TA*) reflects how much of all assets are invested in gross loans (*L*), which represent the on-balance-sheet activities and normally by far the largest asset class. This class is the source of interest income and thus captures most cross-sectional variation of tangible assets (*TA*). With the above reasoning of lower returns of on-balance-sheet activities, this ratio is assumed to be negatively associated with *P*/*TCE*.

Net Interest Margin (*IIoTA*) (*CoD*)

The net interest margin (NIM) is determined here as ratios representing interest income and interest expense.

Interest income on tangible assets (*IIoTA*) expresses the average interest yield on all assets excluding intangible assets. Multiplied by *L*/*TA*, this ratio expresses the yield on all interest-bearing assets. It is then also referred to as gross interest margin and shows the gross return on the major asset class of loans. This ratio is expected to be positively related to the bank valuation (*P*/*TCE*).

Cost of debt (*CoD*) expresses the average interest expenses paid on all interest-bearing liabilities that fund the granted loans. *CoD* measures how much the bank pays for its funding. Hence, it is also a risk measure as debtors will monitor the riskiness of banks' assets to estimate the default probability of their exposure. This is why, it can be assumed that *CoD* has a negative relationship with *P*/*TCE*.

Cost Efficiency (*CIR*)

The cost-income ratio (*CIR*) expresses how much a bank has to spend to generate its operating income. These non-interest or operational expenses are mainly related to income-generating operations, either for the acquisition and servicing of loans and deposits or for stimulating non-interest income business. It does not, however, include costs for loan-loss provisioning which is considered in *CIR*. *CIR* is the most commonly used indicator of a bank's cost efficiency and has a large impact on the overall bank profitability. Amortisation and impairments of intangibles are excluded, since intangibles are excluded throughout this study. Consequently, this ratio is considered to be strongly negatively associated with *P*/*TCE*. Recorded intangibles other than goodwill are amortised as costs through the income statement, as per GAAPs. Sometimes the disclosed P&L does not allow for the segregation of these expenses from other costs. However, this is not considered to be an issue, because in the vast majority of cases amortisation expenses are highly limited compared to all other expenses.

---

[6] Williams and Prather (2010, 220)

Asset Quality and Risk (*CoR*)

Cost of risk (*CoR*) is considered to represent a bank's risk and asset quality. *CoR* puts the loan-loss provisioning (*LLP*) of one period into relation with the total of gross loans (*L*) granted, i.e. all loans before deducting loan allowances. *LLP* not only tends to greatly fluctuate over time, but is also discretionary in large parts. It is an adjustment to the loan allowances on the balance sheet and does not directly indicate anything about the actual loan losses. As worsening asset quality decreases profitability, *CoR* is expected to be negatively related to bank valuation.

Leverage and Capital (D/TCE)

This measure of debt-to-tangible common equity (D/TCE) can be interpreted in two distinct ways. Either valuation can be assumed to be positively associated with higher leverage, i.e. less equity financing, which results in better capital utilisation that consequently leads to a higher (but more volatile) profitability; or valuation can be assumed to be positively associated with stronger capitalisation, i.e. more equity financing, which makes a bank more resilient against the loss of the charter value according to the bankruptcy costs hypothesis (see Sect. 4.2.4),[7] and more flexible in its operations and the growth of the loan book according to the signalling hypothesis. Excess capital can also be considered as market power, since banks with greater market power hold more capital as they have more to lose.[8] When the focus is on leverage, it is commonly referred to as the leverage ratio; and when on capital, it is commonly referred to as the capital ratio.[9] *TCE* is thereby a good proxy for regulatory capital (see Sect. 11.2). Based on the desired meaning, the common representation of the measure often varies. The representation of (D/TCE) is here imposed from the mathematical decomposition. Following the strict theoretical framework, which does not consider the charter value aspect of banks, it is assumed that (D/TCE) is positively associated with bank valuation (P/TCE).

11.3.2 Opportunity Costs (CoTCE)

Equation 9.23 must be rewritten to reflect the amended equity definition of *TCE*:

$$CoTCE = DY + g \tag{11.6}$$

Equation 11.6 represents the dividend yield plus the rate at which the dividend is expected to grow (if $CoTCE > g$, otherwise P_0 would be infinite or negative). Hence, dividend yield *DY* is added to the regression variables.

7 Cf. Berger (1995, 454–55) and Berger and Bouwman (2013, 146).

8 Cf. Keeley (1990) and Goddard, Molyneux, and Wilson (2004).

9 Cf. Calomiris and Nissim (2014, 414–15).

Substituting *CoTCE* in Eq. 11.3 results in

$$P/TCE = \frac{RoTCE - g}{DY} \tag{11.7}$$

DY is calculated as paid dividends per share over the latest share price. It is a measure that is to a great degree at the management's discretion. Banks often give guidance for this measure or at least envisage keeping *DY* stable to give investors some planning certainty.[10] Hence, it represents a partly forward-looking measure that reflects the long-term expectations of the bank management. *DY* represents the opportunity costs minus the expected growth rate of a bank. As *DY* supplies the denominator of the above fraction, it is assumed that there is a negative association between *DY* and P/TCE. The higher the long-term expectations are, the more difficult it is for banks to exceed those expectations.

11.3.3 Growth (g)

There are generally two ways of estimating growth. The first is to look at two different points in history and measure how certain accounting measures have grown between them. This is biased not only by the chosen time period but also by the chosen bank fundamental. The second way is to look at the reinvestment rate or payout ratio. This measures how much a bank is ploughing back to future growth. Hence, it is also forward-looking from an insider's perspective.[11]

Adapting Eq. 9.17 to *TCE* and integrating Eq. 9.24 results in

$$g = (1 - PO) \times RoTCE \tag{11.8}$$

Hence, *PO* is added to the regression variables. Substituting *g* in Eq. 11.7 results in

$$P/TCE = \frac{RoTCE - (1 - PO) \times RoTCE}{DY} \tag{11.9}$$

The payout ratio (*PO*), as earnings distributed over total period earnings, is a measure that can be greatly influenced by the management. There are different lines of thought for its association with bank value. On the one hand, a larger payout is positively associated with *DY*, which results in lower P/TCE. Larger payouts, however, can also represent positive signalling effects about bank health, particularly during times of distress, when other banks are obliged to stop distributing earnings to their shareholders to keep the capital requirements.[12] On the other hand, when payout is low, i.e. when earnings are retained within the bank, this can be interpreted as a signal that a bank sees great

[10]Cf. Lintner (1956).

[11]Cf. Damodaran (2012, 291).

[12]Calomiris and Nissim (2014, 415).

potential for attractive investment opportunities. Higher and profitable earnings growth ($RoE > CoE$) drives higher valuations.[13] Hence, from a theoretical reasoning, *PO* is ambiguous in sign, but from a mathematical perspective it is assumed that *PO* is negatively associated with P/TCE.

11.3.4 Further Control Variables

It is not feasible to practically further decompose Eq. 11.9. Nevertheless, for the purpose of removing further extraneous influences from the regression, the following variables are controlled for as well. These few variables are not directly linked to the mathematical explanation but rather arise from the nature of the sample and precedent empirical tests (see Sect. 9.3.3).

Size ($ln(A)$)
The sub-sample containing G-SIBs is dominated by very large banks, since it is biased against size due to the identification criteria of G-SIBs.[14] On the other hand, the full sample also contains the smallest traded banks as it is not conditioned to avoid any other bias. Hence, this control variable removes the 'noise' from the G-SIB designation dummy, which represents the pure TBTF characteristic of a bank. Total assets seem to be the most common and unbiased indicator for bank size. Since the intention is to avoid any absolute measure in the regression, the natural logarithm of total assets ($ln(A)$) is applied. The above arguments indicate a positive relationship of size ($ln(A)$) and bank value (P/TCE).

Asset Quality/NPL Ratio (*NPL*)
Quarterly loan provisioning levels (*CoR*) are to a great degree at the management's discretion while likewise often greatly varying over time. Hence, their meaningfulness is limited[15] and it is reasonable to complement *CoR* with another, more stable credit risk measure. Moreover, the period of this analysis spans over a recession, when equity investors focus increasingly on asset risks and their own judgement of adequate loan provisioning. The non-performing loans ratio (*NPL*) is the most common risk measure of overall credit risk. It is calculated as non-performing loans over gross loans (loans before loan-loss reserves). The standard definition of *NPL* is applied here, where loans are considered non-performing when payments are overdue for 90 days or longer. The higher the threat of defaults is, the higher the likelihood is of decreasing equity, which clearly suggests a negative association of *NPL* with P/TCE.

---

[13]Cf. Varaiya, Kerin, and Weeks (1987, 496).

[14]For the G-SIB selection process, see Sect. 7.4.

[15]Cf. Beaver et al. (1989) and Elliott and Douglas (1991).

Region (λ_R–Dummy Variable)
This dummy variable controls for any possible omitted effect that operates at the regional level. Among others, this can include the following impact factors or regional differences: macroeconomic shocks, policy response to a crisis, regulatory definition of capital, type of listed company, accounting standard, tax level, bank penetration, and bank concentration.[16] A distinction is made between these regions: Asia-Pacific, Europe, Latin America and the Caribbean, and the US and Canada.

Unobserved Quarter-Constant Variables (λ_Q–Dummy Variable)
It is assumed that even with the aforementioned explanatory variables, there are unobserved effects on the dependent variable that are uncorrelated with all explanatory variables. Furthermore, it is assumed that these unobserved effects are time-invariant. Hence, an own dummy variable is added to the regression function for each quarter.

11.3.5 Test Variable: Unobserved G-SIB-Constant Variable ($\lambda_{G\text{-}SIB}$ –Dummy Variable)

The TBTF status is derived from the FSB's G-SIB designation (see Sect. 7.4). It is most convenient to use the prominent G-SIB designation when analysing G-SIBs for two main reasons:

- Precise G-SIB definition: There is no need to develop a new methodology of defining G-SIBs that could potentially deviate from investors' views. Through the FSB designation, the scope of G-SIBs is defined precisely. G-SIBs are chosen based on comprehensible and market-accepted criteria. The FSB, and thus also the G-SIB designation, is backed and originated by the G20, and many more countries have implemented the FSB regulations in their domestic framework. Furthermore, the official G-SIB list is transparently and frequently published, and actively followed by the market.
- Congruent G-SIB regulation: The designated G-SIBs are obliged to comply with certain regulatory measures, in particular with regard to regulatory capital. This means that the exact same group of banks is impacted not just by the TBTF designation effect, but also by the regulatory TBTF burden effect.[17]

A dummy variable during each quarter reflects whether a bank has been declared a G-SIB. In the two years prior to the official designation by the FSB, the *Financial Times* published a leaked G-SIB list; this list is used for that period (see Table 5.2). Prior to

[16] Cf. Barros, Ferreira, and Williams (2007) and Demirgüç-Kunt, Detragiache, and Merrouche (2013, 1151–2).

[17] Both terms are explained and empirically confirmed in Sect. 9.1.4.

that, it is assumed that banks are G-SIBs if they were considered as such by the FSB and the *Financial Times* in every disclosure.

11.4 Sample Data

11.4.1 Database Requirements

This empirical study requires two types of micro data for banks:

1. Market data is necessary for share prices, i.e., for the *P* in the dependent variable.
2. Fundamental data, in particular balance sheet and income statement information, is necessary for all remaining inputs.

This mix of market and accounting measures is per se not ideal because accounting measures can often be adjusted at the bank's discretion, while market measures cannot. Hence, the analysis is determined by two underlying assumptions.[18] First, accounting measures are well-defined and understood by investors. Second, accounting measures are good approximations for true banking operations. Both assumptions are generally accepted as valid in financial research. Although accounting data is presumed to have noise, it is assumed to be unbiased. Ultimately, market value and dividends, which are real cash flows to shareholders, are dependent on the distributable profits from an accounting perspective.

Furthermore, there are two availability requirements with regard to market and fundamental data:

1. Data should be available at least since the first official call of the G20 for appropriate regulation of G-SIBs on 17 November 2008. Data reaching back further would permit a comparison of the pre- and post-FSB regulation eras.
2. Data should be available for (large) banks around the globe and all banks affected by the G-SIB legislation. Ideally, all listed global banks should be included to avoid any data selection bias.

Three databases broadly satisfy the above criteria regarding data type and availability: Bankscope, SNL Financial, and Compustat Bank in connection with CRSP. Table 11.1 provides an overview of the respective strengths and weaknesses of these databases. Compustat Bank and CRSP have been the choice for academic studies over the last decades. CRSP was founded by economists at the University of Chicago in 1960 and has been customised to meet the needs of academics. Financial bank analysts at central

[18]Gorton and Santomero (1990).

banks and investment banks increasingly use the state-of-the-art database SNL Financial, which provides in-depth financials, but which does not extend back as long as the other two databases. Due the focus of the present empirical study on large global banks with a limited time period but high demands regarding comprehensive and detailed financials, SNL Financial best satisfies the database requirements.

Table 11.1 Overview of Financial Databases for Banks

Database	Bankscope	Compustat Bank / CSRP	SNL Financial
Advantages			
	• Widest coverage universe (>32,000 banks) • Data is available for up to 16 years • Widely used in banking	• Most comprehensive market database • Very long data range dating back to 1950 • Widely used in academia	• Superior data quality • In-depth data and coverage of most financial items and ratios • Ability to track where data comes from and how ratios have been calculated • Excel add-in facilitates data download • Most user-friendly interface and support • Widely used in investment banking
Disadvantages			
	• Old-fashioned user interface • No Excel add in available	• Focus on North America • Data is not traceable	• Focus on large banks • Non-US banks only available starting from 2005

11.4.2 Data Characteristics

When compiling the required data, several trade-offs exist. For the sake of transparency, the following discusses the most relevant decisions made with regard to the data characteristics.

Balanced Data (vs. Unbalanced Data)

For the purpose of this analysis with the utilisation of the two-way fixed-effect regression, a balanced panel data sample is used. In balanced panel data, in contrast to unbalanced panel data (pooled data), all variables are observed for a given entity (bank) during one observation (quarter). Particularly in small samples, the explanatory content of balanced panels is higher. However, this proceeding has a main disadvantage: a substantial amount of data must be excluded because one or more variables in a given observation are missing, so the entire entity cannot be included in the sample for that observation.[19] This is not considered a problem in this case as the sample is still very large. Moreover, it is assumed that the reason for the missing data lies solely in the disclosure practises of a given bank and in the step-by-step inclusion of banks into the databank at the random discretion of the database provider. This means that it is assumed that the missing data for some banks is not correlated with the idiosyncratic errors. Moreover, it is worth mentioning that there is no survivor bias within the balanced panel, as banks that failed at any time during the full period are not excluded from the full sample.

Period-End Data of Balance Sheet Items (vs. Period Averages)

Balance sheet items represent period-end values, while income statement items represent values accumulated during an entire period. When calculating ratios that include both income statement and balance sheet data, it would be methodologically most correct to use the period average for the balance sheet item. Some banks occasionally provide this type of data themselves. In practice, it is common to calculate the mean of a given period and the previous period to receive an approximation of the period average. In this analysis, however, only period-end data is compiled to avoid further limiting the (G-SIB) sample due to the balanced data constraint. The disadvantage, i.e. the risk of over- or understating certain ratios, is considered negligible.

Historical Data (vs. Forecasted Data)

This study uses historical (or backward-looking) data mainly due to data availability. However, valuation (or more precisely the valuation metric P/TCE) reflects future return expectations of the investor community. Hence, focusing on current profitability measures can lead to significant valuation errors when the competitive environment is changing.[20] Moreover, it is proven that explanatory variables that (try to) forecast the future have higher explanatory power than historical financials.[21] In practice, these forecasts are made by equity research analysts and are often combined by consensus by major database providers. However, there are three material disadvantages and biases of forecasted (or forward-looking) data: (i) it is only provided for the largest listed banks, (ii) it is only published on an irregular basis by various analysts, and (iii) the number of balance sheet and income statement items that are predicted varies greatly.

Multiplying Market Capitalisation with Cumulative Stock Returns (vs. Publication Lag of Accounting Data)

Accounting data is generally prepared for each quarter-, half year-, or year-end depending on the respective GAAP, listing requirements, and firm discretion. In the

---

[19]Cf. Greene (2002).

[20]Cf. Damodaran (2012).

[21]Brown and Rozeff (1978).

vast majority of cases, the data is published within the following quarter. This is why for P/TCE the P, i.e. the market capitalisation of the end of a given quarter, is multiplied with the cumulative stock returns over the subsequent quarter. This assumes that accounting data is published, on average, one quarter after its preparation. This method is in line with other academic studies in this field.[22] In contrast to taking actual market capitalisations, this approach of using cumulative stock returns is unsusceptible to certain events that affect a bank's *TCE*, such as capital increases, share repurchases, or dividend distributions.

11.4.3 Process of Generating Data

All data was downloaded from SNL Financial into Microsoft Excel 2016 (Excel)[23] using SNL's proprietary Excel add-in SNL Office. The sample data was generated in five steps:

1. A list of companies was generated that match the following criteria: (i) industry is bank, savings bank/thrift/mutual, or global investment bank; (ii) listed on a stock exchange; (iii) full coverage level of SNL; (iv) consolidation entity; (v) subsidiaries shown separately when separately listed; (vi) operating company as of now, i.e. not acquired or defunct; and (vii) all geographies.
2. The data for the above filtered financial institutions was downloaded with the following attributes: (i) quarterly data from Q1 2008 until Q2 2015 for accounting information and from Q2 2008 until Q3 2015 for market information; (ii) as originally reported, i.e. no restated data; (iii) reported in euros or converted into euros (balance sheet data was converted as of the date of the end of the period, and income statement data was converted using the average exchange rate over the period).[24] The analysis does not go back earlier than Q1 2008 because accounting information on G-SIB is increasingly limited for earlier years (see Table 11.2).
3. The panel data was organised in the form of unstacked data, i.e. only one case (row) per bank and quarter. Market data, i.e. price P, was matched with accounting data. This resulted in about 60,000 cases.
4. If possible, missing data for G-SIBs was complemented manually to increase subsample size, which is crucial for the analysis given the small G-SIB sample size. For this purpose, individual balance sheet data items of G-SIBs were assumed to be constant for up to 4 quarters, if deemed appropriate and not disclosed otherwise. This proceeding is considered unbiased as investors would make the same approximating assumption if no financial data was published.

---

[22]Cf. Calomiris and Nissim (2007) and Calomiris and Nissim (2014) who use 75 days.

[23]Only the 64-bit program version is capable of handling the large amount of data.

[24]SNL Financial (28 September 2015).

5. The data was solely edited in Excel to calculate ratios and insert dummy variables for the regression. Subsequently, cases with incomplete data were removed resulting in about 27,000 cases. The dependent variable, P/TCE, was then truncated at the one percent level, and all explanatory variables were winsorised at the one percent level. Table A.1 in the electronic supplementary material provides a detailed explanation of how the variables were sourced and calculated.

11.5 Sample Characteristics

The following analyses were conducted using IBM SPSS Statistics 23 (SPSS). All sample characteristic tables differentiate between the full sample, the G-SIB sample, and the non-G-SIB sample. The following describes the sample in terms of its constituents, the development of certain bank fundamentals, and its overall statistical characteristics. The average and median results must be interpreted with some caution since the same banks are not always part of the sample in each quarter. As a further caveat, the sharp change in business environment played into the numbers during the analysed period. Overall, the data reveals that G-SIBs and non-G-SIBs have different financial characteristics, presumably due their distinct business models and size differences.[25] Moreover, it can be observed more broadly that there are also differences between large and small banks which are statistically significant but relatively small. For this reason, this study uses and discusses the full sample of banks for which complete data sets are available.

Region

Table 11.2 describes the sample characteristics by region. The balanced sample contains 27,071 data sets, of which 357 are attributable to G-SIBs. The majority of banks included are headquartered in the US and Canada. Latin America and the Caribbean only contribute a low number of banks, and none of the G-SIBs are based there.

Table 11.2 Sample Characteristics by Region

	Total sample	G-SIB sample	non-G-SIB sample
Asia-Pacific	1,888	60	1,828
Europe	1,677	155	1,522
Latin America and Caribbean	114	0	114
United States and Canada	23,392	142	23,250
Sample size	27,071	357	26,714

[25]Loudis and Allahrakha (2016) report very similar findings and further identify that 'borderline non-G-SIBs are similar to G-SIBs on some indicators for systemic importance, but starkly different on others'.

Quarter

Table 11.3 complements Table 11.2 by showing the evolution of the sample constituents over time. During the analysed period from Q2 2008 to Q3 2015, the number of genuine banks is between 762 (in Q4 2008) and 1,055 (in Q1 2015), while the number of included G-SIBs per quarter varies between 5 (e.g., in Q2 2008) and 18 (e.g., in Q4 2014).

Table 11.3 Sample Characteristics by Quarter

Metric	Total sample	G-SIB sample	non-G-SIB sample	Total P/TCE (mean)	G-SIB P/TCE (mean)	non-G-SIB P/TCE (mean)	Total RoTCE (mean)	G-SIB RoTCE (mean)	non-G-SIB RoTCE (mean)
2015Q3	684	15	669	1.33x	1.32x	1.34x	9.8 %	13.1 %	9.8 %
2015Q2	986	18	968	1.23x	1.40x	1.22x	8.4 %	11.2 %	8.4 %
2015Q1	1,055	17	1,038	1.38x	1.55x	1.37x	7.7 %	6.1 %	7.7 %
2014Q4	992	18	974	1.29x	1.42x	1.29x	8.5 %	12.0 %	8.4 %
2014Q3	988	17	971	1.32x	1.49x	1.32x	8.6 %	9.4 %	8.6 %
2014Q2	981	17	964	1.28x	1.44x	1.28x	8.3 %	11.1 %	8.2 %
2014Q1	1,005	15	990	1.26x	1.42x	1.25x	7.0 %	3.1 %	7.0 %
2013Q4	934	16	918	1.23x	1.42x	1.22x	8.3 %	9.9 %	8.2 %
2013Q3	946	16	930	1.17x	1.37x	1.16x	8.5 %	12.9 %	8.4 %
2013Q2	944	16	928	1.12x	1.27x	1.12x	7.5 %	11.6 %	7.5 %
2013Q1	947	14	933	1.14x	1.29x	1.14x	6.1 %	5.1 %	6.1 %
2012Q4	925	12	913	1.01x	1.15x	1.01x	7.2 %	7.6 %	7.2 %
2012Q3	945	15	930	1.04x	1.01x	1.04x	7.1 %	9.1 %	7.1 %
2012Q2	961	14	947	1.07x	1.06x	1.07x	7.3 %	10.7 %	7.2 %
2012Q1	989	13	976	1.00x	1.04x	1.00x	2.6 %	5.7 %	2.6 %
2011Q4	978	15	963	0.96x	0.94x	0.96x	4.9 %	9.6 %	4.9 %
2011Q3	983	10	973	0.99x	1.04x	0.99x	4.8 %	10.1 %	4.7 %
2011Q2	950	7	943	1.04x	1.58x	1.04x	4.5 %	18.0 %	4.4 %
2011Q1	897	9	888	1.00x	1.51x	1.00x	-0.2 %	9.4 %	-0.3 %
2010Q4	870	11	859	1.05x	1.47x	1.04x	2.8 %	5.2 %	2.8 %
2010Q3	868	10	858	0.91x	1.52x	0.90x	2.0 %	15.8 %	1.9 %
2010Q2	859	10	849	1.13x	1.68x	1.12x	2.9 %	18.6 %	2.7 %
2010Q1	848	9	839	1.13x	1.80x	1.12x	-3.7 %	3.2 %	-3.7 %
2009Q4	809	9	800	1.02x	1.56x	1.01x	-1.1 %	8.9 %	-1.2 %
2009Q3	795	7	788	1.05x	1.99x	1.04x	-2.0 %	9.6 %	-2.1 %
2009Q2	801	7	794	1.00x	1.51x	1.00x	2.6 %	4.6 %	2.6 %
2009Q1	820	4	816	1.03x	0.96x	1.03x	-1.3 %	1.5 %	-1.3 %
2008Q4	762	6	756	1.20x	1.08x	1.20x	3.3 %	-1.9 %	3.3 %
2008Q3	769	5	764	1.53x	2.29x	1.52x	5.5 %	9.3 %	5.5 %
2008Q2	780	5	775	1.33x	1.68x	1.33x	8.2 %	-6.4 %	8.3 %
Total	27,071	357	26,714	1.14x	1.37x	1.14x	5.0 %	9.1 %	5.0 %

Table 11.2 presents an overview of the G-SIB data availability from Q1 2006 until Q3 2015. Most of the around 30 G-SIBs are part of the sample for multiple quarters during the analysed period.

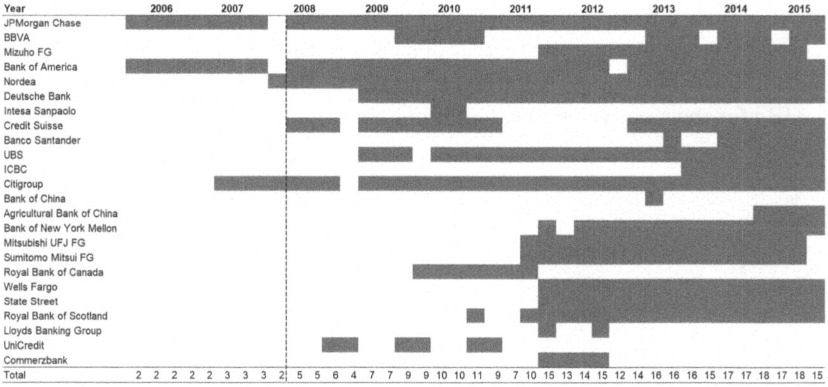

Fig. 11.2 Constituents of G-SIB Sample Over Time

Size (*ln*(*A*))
Table 11.4 presents the characteristics of the overall sample and the two sub-samples, G-SIBs and non-G-SIBs, as mean and median values. G-SIBs and non-G-SIBs show an extreme size difference in terms of total assets and market capitalisation. The smallest bank in the sample has just € 11 million in total assets, while the largest has more than € 3 trillion. This is because all available listed banks were included without any cut-off point. G-SIBs exceed non-G-SIBs by more than 80 times in terms of average total assets, and by more than 1,000 times in terms of average market capitalisation. This is a first indicator that G-SIBs conduct many more off-balance-sheet activities than non-G-SIBs do.

P*/*TCE
The metric *RoTCE* is not part of the regression—only its components are—but it is shown to easily grasp overall profitability. The overall RoTCE of G-SIBs during the full time period is much higher than that of non-G-SIBs.[26] Figure 11.3 visualises the developments of average profitability and valuation levels (see Table 11.3). In most quarters, the average *RoTCE* of G-SIBs is much higher than that of non-G-SIBs. There is a general trend of decreasing valuations in terms of *P*/*TCE* during the period of the GFC (from the beginning of the study until Q4 2011) and the recovery thereafter. This is especially the case for G-SIBs and might come from several factors, such as uncertainty, regulatory requirements especially on trading activities, and higher loan defaults from weaker economic prospects. On average, G-SIBs exhibit stronger relative valuation

[26]This holds on an unadjusted *RoE*-basis as well, although it is not as pronounced. *RoE* s are per se lower because the denominator is inflated by goodwill. G-SIBs appear to have much more intangibles on their balance sheet, particularly goodwill from M&A activities.

than non-G-SIBs do, while this relationship is inverted in the year 2012. Taken together, this is an early indication that the market does not reward the profitability of G-SIBs and non-G-SIBs in the same way. After 2011, it seems that investors expect higher returns from G-SIBs for the same relative valuation.[27]

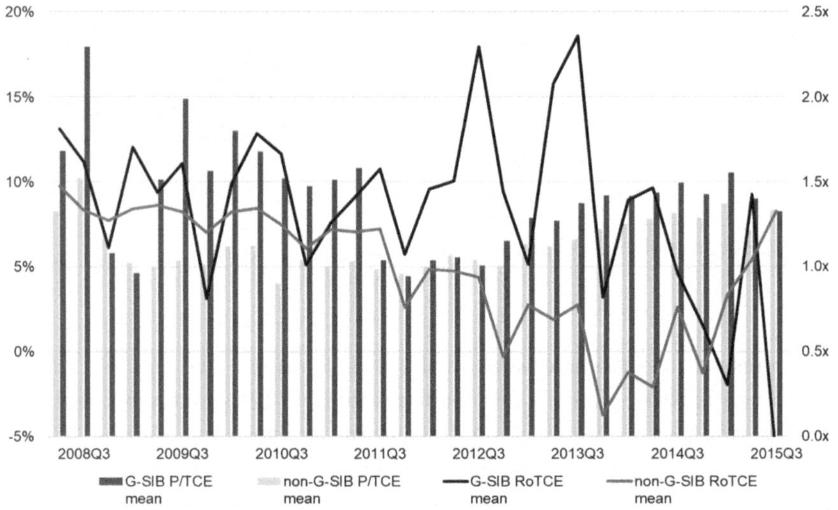

Fig. 11.3 Quarterly Development of *RoTCE* and *P/TCE*

Business Model (*NonII/OpI*) (*L/TA*)

On average, G-SIBs generate half of their operating income from non-interest-bearing activities, while for non-G-SIBs such activities contribute just 21 percent. The total balance sheet consists of only 40 percent loans at G-SIBs, while non-G-SIBs invest two thirds of their assets into loans. Both confirm the greater importance of off-balance-sheet activities for G-SIBs. In fact, only very large global banks run investment banking arms that generate substantial fee and trading income from capital market advisory and trading.

Net Interest Margin (*IIoTA*) (*CoD*)

The net interest margin is determined by the gross interest margin (*IIoTA*), i.e. a bank's ability to charge for loans, and the cost of debt (*CoD*), i.e. a bank's ability to gather

[27]Bassett and Brady (2001, 728) analyse the profitability of small and large banks between 1985 and 2000. They report higher net interest income (*NII*) and a higher share of loans from total assets (*L/A*) of small banks throughout all periods; large banks showed average *RoE* s of about 15 percent throughout the latter half of the 1990 s after previous high fluctuation, while small banks had steady returns of roughly 8–12 percent.

Table 11.4 Sample Characteristics by Variable

Metric	Total sample mean (median)	G-SIB sample mean (median)	non-G-SIB sample mean (median)
Total Assets (in € billions)	31.3 (0.6)	1,229.7 (1,292.1)	15.2 (0.6)
Market capitalisation (in € billions)	2.19 (0.05)	67.35 (46.19)	0.05 (0.05)
Price-book value ratio (*P/BV*)	0.98x (0.91x)	0.89x (0.82x)	0.98x (0.91x)
Price-tangible common equity ratio (*P/TCE*)	1.14x (1.02x)	1.37x (1.23x)	1.14x (1.02x)
Return on equity (*RoE*)	4.5 % (6.5 %)	6.3 % (7.5 %)	4.5 % (6.4 %)
Return on tangible common equity (*RoTCE*)	5.0 % (7.4 %)	9.1 % (11.0 %)	5.0 % (7.4 %)
Interest margin (*IIoTA*)	4.5 % (4.3 %)	2.4 % (2.0 %)	4.5 % (4.3 %)
Cost of debt (*CoD*)	1.4 % (1.0 %)	0.9 % (0.7 %)	1.4 % (1.0 %)
% of non-interest income (*NonII/OpI*)	21 % (19 %)	50 % (48 %)	21 % (19 %)
Cost of risk (*CoR*)	0.7 % (0.3 %)	0.8 % (0.3 %)	0.7 % (0.3 %)
Loans-to-tangible assets (*L/TA*)	67 % (69 %)	40 % (38 %)	67 % (69 %)
Cost-income ratio (*CIR*)	72 % (69 %)	68 % (64 %)	72 % (69 %)
Leverage ratio (*D/TCE*)	12x (10x)	25x (24x)	12x (10x)
Payout ratio (*PO*)	28 % (0 %)	28 % (2 %)	28 % (0 %)
Dividend yield (*DY*)	2.0 % (1.7 %)	2.5 % (2.4 %)	2.0 % (1.7 %)
NPL ratio (*NPL*)	3.1 % (2.1 %)	3.2 % (2.2 %)	3.1 % (2.1 %)

inexpensive funding. The net interest margin represents the gross profitability on assets before costs for operations and risk provisioning. On average, G-SIBs have a much lower gross interest margin, which is partly compensated because they pay less on their debt compared to non-G-SIBs.

Cost Efficiency (*CIR*)

In terms of the CIR, G-SIBs operate marginally better on average, paying 68 cents for every unit of earnings versus 72 cents paid by non-G-SIBs. Without explicitly considering the business model, this is consistent with the predominant view that there are no economies of superscale (see Sect. 5.1).

Asset Quality and Risk (*CoR*) (*NPL*)

In the asset quality and risk categories—cost of risk (*CoR*) and NPL ratio (*NPL*)—G-SIBs take more risks than non-G-SIBs, with both ratios being slightly higher on average. This is consistent with the risk-taking hypothesis of G-SIBs (see Sect. 4.2.4). Furthermore, G-SIBs' *CoD*, which generally also serves as an external risk measure (in contrast to the internal risk measures *CoR* and *NPL*), is lower than that of non-G-SIBs. Without explicitly considering the funding mix, this is consistent with the hypothesis of TBTF funding benefits (see Sect. 4.2.3).

Leverage and Capital (*D*/*TCE*)

On average, G-SIBs' level of leverage, in terms of *D*/*TCE*, is more than twice as high as that of non-G-SIBs. This further strengthens the hypothesis of TBTF funding benefits, i.e. G-SIBs have lower funding costs despite their higher asset risk. It also shows that capital ratios are not a good predictor of risk premiums on bank debt[28]—at least across G-SIBs and non-G-SIBs.

Opportunity Costs and Growth (*PO*) (*DY*)

The G-SIB and the non-G-SIB sub-samples have, on average, the same profit distribution (*PO*) of 28 percent, which suggests that the overall long-term growth rates are entirely dependent on return levels since the same share of profits is retained for future growth. Because the return levels (*RoTCE*) of G-SIBs are higher, G-SIBs also grow at a higher rate. Furthermore, G-SIBs have higher shareholder returns in terms of dividend yield (*DY*): 2.5 percent compared to 2.0 percent for non-G-SIBs. This is consistent with the higher return levels of G-SIBs at slightly higher valuation levels. This indicator for opportunity costs suggests that stock investors expect higher returns from G-SIBs for the same relative valuation due to increased risk, i.e. that overall there is no shareholder moral hazard regarding G-SIBs (see Sect. 4.2.5).

The following test whether the variables meet certain requirements to consider the regression results valid.

Assumption #1: Sample Size Has Sufficient Statistical Power

As a rule of thumb, in terms of adequacy in degrees of freedom, the sample required to detect a significant R-square at a specified significance level should include at least 20 times more cases than independent variables.[29] To determine the minimum sample size more accurately, Cohen (1988)'s methodology has been applied has been applied. With very high requirements on the robustness of the regression, i.e. small expected effect ($R^2 = 0.02$), low Type I error probability ($\alpha = 0.01$),[30] and low Type II error probability

[28]Cf. Rubens and Corrigan (1990).

[29]Cohen and Cohen (1983).

[30]Probability of incorrectly claiming statistical significance.

($\beta = 0.01$; $power = 1 - \beta = 0.99$),[31] and anticipating 73 predictors in the regression, the software application *GPower 3* calculates a minimum sample size of 3,799. With more than 27,000 data sets in the generated sample, the sample size is more than sufficient.

Assumption #2: Variables Are Measured at the Continuous Level

All variables are measured at the continuous level as there are only three types of variables in the analysis: absolute measures are either converted into (i) ratios or (ii) logarithmised variables; and discrete variables with more than two categories (quarter, region, G-SIB quarter) are converted into a set of (iii) dichotomous variables by binary variable coding.

Assumption #3: Variables Have No Significant Outliers

SSNL Financial is generally a more reliable database than others.[32] However, in some extreme cases, ratios can have very limited meaning. To improve the robustness of the regression, these outliers were removed. The dependent variable was truncated at the one percent level to avoid having to explain extreme cases with the model. Furthermore, the independent variables that are ratios were winsorised at the one percent level (see Sect. 11.4.3).[33] The winsorisation was tested at different levels with similar regression results, which suggests that the applied outlier removal does not bias the sample.

Assumption #4: Explanatory Variables Are Not Correlated

Empirical studies have shown several interrelationships among some of the ratios used. For example, correlations are proven between profitability and risk-taking, leverage and profitability, efficiency and risk-taking, growth and efficiency (see Sect. 9.3.3), cost of debt and NPL ratio,[34] and business model and profitability.[35] However, this multicollinearity is limited and thus is not problematic in this analysis since the tolerance values[36] for all variables are above 0.20[37] and the variance inflation factor (VIF) values are below 10.[38] In addition, graphical tests that plot all independent variables against each other suggests that there are no serious intercorrelations.

---

[31]Probability of incorrectly claiming no statistical significance.

[32]Evidence for the data reliability is the award of US$ 50 that SNL pays for each error spotted.

[33]Winsorisation has the advantage vis-à-vis truncation that it is less arbitrary and does not the reduce sample size.

[34]E.g. Arping (2017).

[35]E.g. Nguyen (2012).

[36]Tolerance is defined as $1 - R^2$, where R^2 is calculated by regressing the independent variable of interest onto the remaining independent variables included in the multiple regression analysis. This means that the higher the value of tolerance is, the less overlap there is with other variables and the more useful the predictor is for the analysis.

[37]As suggested by Tabachnick and Fidell (2007).

[38]As suggested by Pituch and Stevens (2016).

11.6 Regression Function

Inserting all variables into the regression framework results in Eq. 9.2.

$$\begin{aligned} P/TCE_i = {} & \beta_0 + \beta_1 IIoTA_i + \beta_2 CoD_i + \beta_3 NonII/OpI_i + \beta_4 CoR_i + \beta_5 CIR_i \\ & + \beta_6 D/TCE_i + \beta_7 L/TA_i + \beta_8 PO_i + \beta_9 DY_i \\ & + \beta_{10} ln(A)_i + \beta_{11} NPL_i \\ & + \sum_{R}^{3} \lambda_R REGION\ DUMMY + \sum_{Q}^{29} \lambda_Q QUARTER\ DUMMY \\ & + \sum_{G-SIB}^{29} \lambda_{G-SIB} G-SIB\ QUARTER\ DUMMY + \varepsilon_i \end{aligned} \quad (11.10)$$

where $i = 1, ..., 27001$ and where the residual ε_i by definition obeys $\varepsilon_i \sim N(0, \sigma^2)$. Subsequently, the following ensures that the statistical requirements for this multivariate regression model are met.

Assumption #5: Linear Relationship Between the Dependent Variable and Each of the Explanatory Variables

Derived from theory and empirical evidence, there is a linear relationship between P/BV and *RoE*, *CoE*, and g (see Sect. 9.3). Hence, it can be inferred that all of the decomposed parts of *RoE*, *CoE*, and g also have a linear relationship with P/TCE. Visual tests for linearity and unusual cases, in particular scatter plots of single variables, have highly limited meaningfulness due to the very large sample size. A scatterplot of standardised residuals against the standardised predicted values shows no relationship pattern. Furthermore, non linear relationships were tested for by running non-linear regressions and by transforming all individual variables into logarithmic and exponential functions. All of these tests weaken the explanatory power of the overall model.

Assumption #6: Observations Are Independent

There is independence of residuals as assessed by the Durbin-Watson statistic. The test statistic value of 1.887 (see Table 12.1) suggests no linear auto-correlation in the data, as values in the range of 1.5 to 2.5 can be considered normal, and it is common with time-series data for this value to be below 2.[39]

---

[39]Field (2009).

Results and Discussion

12

This chapter explains the results with regard to the residuals and the independent variables of the regression, but most importantly with regard to the G-SIB dummy and its development. Moreover, further variables will be elaborated that have been tested to improve the explanatory power of the regression. What follows is a content-related conclusion based on the empirical results. The chapter closes with recommendations for future research.

12.1 Results

The regression and associated tests were conducted using SPSS. The linear regression was calculated using the method of least squares dummy variables (LSDV), and all predictors were forced into the model simultaneously.

Assumption #7: Residuals Are Equal

Heteroscedasticity occurs when the errors in the regression equation correlate to the size of the independent variables. Here, size was controlled for by adding the natural logarithm of total assets.[1] Furthermore, only scaled dependent variables were used in the regression model, which by nature has the advantage of eliminating or at least reducing the statistical problem of heteroscedasticity. Homoscedasticity was visually confirmed by plotting the standardised residuals against the standardised predicted values, which resulted in no clear relationship pattern, thereby confirming the assumption.

[1] As recommended by Abrams (2012).

T. F. Lesche, *Too-Big-to-Fail in Banking*, Finanzwirtschaft, Banken und Bankmanagement I Finance, Banks and Bank Management, https://doi.org/10.1007/978-3-658-34182-4_12

Assumption #8: Residuals Are Normally Distributed

Both applied visual tests, i.e. the histogram with a superimposed normal curve and the normal probability-probability plot, suggest normal distribution of residuals.

Regression Characteristics

Overall, the results are promising in the sense that this approach explains a substantial amount of the cross-sectional variation in observed P/TCE values while being statistically significant at the same time. Table 12.1 summarises the statistical model.[2]

Table 12.1 Regression Model Summary

N	27,071
R^2	.413
F-value	260.440*
Significance	.000*
Durbin-Watson	1.887

* Statistical significance at the one percent level.

12.2 Discussion

12.2.1 Regression Coefficients

Standard coefficients or beta weights express the strength of their independent relationship with the dependent variable. Table 12.2 shows all regression coefficients and their statistics,[3] except for G-SIBs and quarters, which were developed (see Sect. 11.3) and

[2]A brief explanation of the regression statistics shown:

- The coefficient of determination, R^2, indicates the goodness of fit of the model or, more precisely, how much of the total variation in the dependent variable can be explained by the independent variables. An R^2 of 0.413 is indicative of a large effect size in this context (according to Cohen (1988)'s classification). Comparable peer-reviewed regression models with price-to-book value ratios as the dependent variable have been conducted by Jordan et al. (2011) and Calomiris and Nissim (2014). Their R^2 is even slightly higher due to the narrower focus of their samples, which include US banks only and span a shorter time period.
- The F-value (with $df = K, N - K - 1$) and its significance (or p-value) test the overall significance of the regression model. They test the null hypothesis that all of the regression coefficients are equal to zero. The null hypothesis of R can be rejected, since the F-value ($F(73, 26997) = 260.440, p < .01$) is larger than the F-critical value (or F-statistic of 1.42). Since the p-value is less than the significance level set at 1%, it can be concluded that the coefficients are statistically significantly different than zero.
- The Durbin-Watson test statistic tests for lag 1 autocorrelation. The resulting value ranges from 0 to 4, while a value near 2 indicates non-autocorrelation.

[3]A short explanation of the regression statistics that are shown:

described above (see Sect. 11.5). The following discusses how each of the factors is associated with the relative bank valuation measure (*T*/*TCE*) and whether the direction of the relationship matches the research hypotheses (see Sect. 10.2). Overall, all coefficient signs conform to expectations, except for one (*PO*), and all estimates are statistically significant.

Table 12.2 Regression Coefficients of Explanatory Variables

Independent variables	Unstd. coefficients	Std. error	Std. coefficients	t-value	Significance*
Intercept	-.829	.044		-18.869	.000
Interest margin ($IIoTA$)	18.690	.421	.430	44.432	.000
Cost of debt (CoD)	-14.320	.544	-.279	-26.304	.000
% of non-interest income ($NonII/OpI$)	.453	.023	.106	19.344	.000
Cost of risk (CoR)	-4.816	.297	-.091	-16.195	.000
Loans-to-tangible assets (L/TA)	-.536	.024	-.113	-21.926	.000
Cost-income ratio (CIR)	-.191	.017	-.066	-11.415	.000
Leverage ratio (D/TCE)	.008	.001	.080	14.404	.000
Payout ratio (PO)	.090	.006	.076	14.349	.000
Dividend yield (DY)	-.007	.002	-.024	-4.176	.000
Size ($ln(A)$)	.148	.002	.527	69.752	.000
NPL ratio (NPL)	-4.397	.108	-.231	-40.701	.000
Europe	-.402	.016	-.160	-25.516	.000
Asia-Pacific	-.392	.015	-.165	-26.637	.000
Latin America and Caribbean	.244	.047	.026	5.219	.000

* Statistical significance at the 0.01 level.

- The unstandardised coefficient is the constant that represents the rate of change of the respective explanatory variable (measured on different scales) to estimate the dependent varyiable.
- The standard error represents the standard deviation of the estimate of a regression coefficient.
- The standardised coefficient or β-coefficient removes the unit measurement from the regression coefficient to compare the relative effects of the explanatory variables. It refers to how many standard deviations a dependent variable will change per standard deviation increase in the explanatory variable.
- The t-value is calculated by dividing the coefficient by its standard error. Thus, the t-statistic measures how many standard errors the coefficient is away from zero. In general, any t-value greater than + 2 or less than –2 is acceptable. The higher the t-value is, the greater the confidence in the coefficient as a predictor.
- The p-value (or significance probability) tests the null hypothesis, i.e. that the coefficient is equal to zero. The threshold value for p (significance or α level) to conclude that the coefficient is significantly different from zero is traditionally set at the five or one percent level (cf. Wasserstein and Lazar (2016)).

Region

The region dummy represents the P/TCE premium or discount compared to US banks.[4] Banks in Europe and Asia-Pacific have a discount of 0.402 and 0.392, respectively, while those in Latin America and the Caribbean enjoy a valuation upside of 0.244 P/TCE. The signs are not unexpected: banks are generally more heavily regulated in Europe and customer protection laws are stricter. In addition, the low interest rate environment and the recent European sovereign debt crisis have lowered valuations in Europe.[5] The Latin America and Caribbean region is still underbanked compared to first-world countries. Hence, margins and growth rates are significantly higher here.

Quarter

The analysed period includes the GFC. Hence, changes in the impact of the regressors are likely and supposed to be jointly reflected in the quarter dummy. This means that changes in individual regressors cannot be tracked; this is due to the anatomy of the regression, which entirely focuses on the G-SIB impact over time.[6] As assumed, unobserved effects are uncorrelated with all explanatory variables and are time-invariant without a recognisable trend. The statistical significance is very strong in all quarters.

Size ($ln(A)$)

Size, in terms of total assets, is the largest impact factor on P/TCE and, as expected, has a positive association with bank valuation. There are two fundamental explanations. First, increasingly large banks could benefit from more market power or scale and scope economies (see Sect. 5.1). However, many of these benefits should already be explained by the other input metrics, especially *CIR*, which largely reflects the cost efficiencies. An example of such an omitted factor are high-margin investment banking activities reserved for larger banks. Second, previous research in this area (see Sect. 9.3.3) identifies size as a preeminent factor explaining risk and return. This means that some sort of risk is not represented by the standard risk metrics that are part of the regression. Fama and French (1993) regard size as proxy for non-diversifiable factor risk, i.e. in the covariance structure of firms' returns. Gandhi and Lustig (2015) find that the size factor is a measure of bank-specific tail-risk.[7]

---

[4]Since most banks are headquartered in the US, an additional dummy for the US is redundant.

[5]Cf. Allegret, Raymond, and Rharrabti (2017).

[6]Cf. Calomiris and Nissim (2014), who conducted 55 quarterly regressions for the period from 2000 until 2013 to examine the evolution of P/TBV regressors.

[7]Interestingly, Demirgüç-Kunt and Huizinga (2013) find a negative relationship between P/BV and banks' total assets, i.e. the direct opposite of the present findings. They infer that many banks have grown too large to be rescuable. The reason for this contrary result might lie in the fact that the coefficient in the present study excludes the characteristic of being TBTF, which is separately captured by the G-SIB designation coefficients.

Business Model (*NonII/OpI*) (*L/TA*)
With regard to the business model, i.e. the sources of income, both regressors (*NonII/OpI*; *L/TA*) are in line with expectations: the higher the share of non-interest income (over operating income) and the lower the share of loans (over tangible assets) are, the higher the valuation is. Both measures have roughly the same impact on valuation (*P/TCE*) and complement each other. This means that the market rewards off-balance-sheet activities more than traditional banking services.[8] However, it is widely evidenced that banks with higher levels of non-interest income are riskier.[9] The two main sources of non-interest income are trading activities and commission and fee activities. Lepetit et al. (2008a) show that 'the positive link with risk is mostly accurate for small banks and essentially driven by commission and fee activities'. Stiroh (2006) finds that no significant valuation benefit remains from an increased stream of non-interest income when taking into account the higher risk associated with it. In this analysis, however, risk and opportunity costs are kept separate.

Net Interest Margin (*IIoTA*) (*CoD*)
After size, gross interest margin and cost of debt are the strongest regressors of valuation. Both NIM measures are associated with *P/TCE* as expected: positive with regard to *IIoTA* and negative with regard to *CoD*. Gross interest margin is assumed to have a stronger impact than cost of debt because the former also determines non-interest income from cross-selling activities.[10]

Cost Efficiency (*CIR*)
As expected, the efficiency measure (*CIR*) has a clear negative connection with *P/TCE*. As extensively evidenced,[11] stocks of more cost-efficient banks outperform those of their peers.

Asset Quality and Risk (*CoR*) (*NPL*)
As expected, both internal risk measures, cost of risk (*CoR*) and the NPL ratio (*NPL*), have a negative impact on valuation. *NPL* has an even higher explanatory power than *CoR*, as assumed, due to its less volatile nature and its better comparability across banks.

---

[8]Cf. Sawada (2013). Calomiris and Nissim (2014) present hypotheses on the change of market perceptions on a variety of different bank income sources. For instance, they argue that 'loan relationships that were valuable prior to the crisis may have declined in value or even become a net cost during the crisis' when banks themselves were scrambling for liquidity.

[9]E.g., Baele, De Jonghe, and Vander Vennet (2007).

[10]Cf. Lepetit et al. (2008b). Calomiris and Nissim (2014) argue that 'core deposit relationships that were valuable as a source of interest expense saving prior to the crisis also may have become less valuable as a result of monetary policy changes that resulted in the decline in market interest rates on non-core deposit liabilities of banks during and after the crisis'. Demirgüç-Kunt, Detragiache, and Merrouche (2013, 1155) argue the opposite: that deposit funding became much more rewarded throughout the GFC due to the disruption in the wholesale funding markets.

[11]Cf. Beccalli, Casu, and Girardone (2006, 258).

Leverage and Capital (*D/TCE*)

During the analysed period (2008–2015), investors (on average and without differentiating changes over time) reward higher leverage (and hence less capitalisation) with higher bank valuation.[12] While leverage is not a large impact factor compared to other regressors, it is still highly statistically significant. The findings suggest that investors approve sufficient regulatory capital levels as efficiently avoiding distress at bank level. In other words, sufficient capital is viewed as a hygiene factor and overly generous capital cushions are not rewarded by the market.

The relationship of *P/TCE* and *D/TCE*, or bank valuation and capital in general, is controversial in the academic community (see Sect. 4.2.4).[13] The currently prevailing theory[14] about the relationship of valuation and leverage (or capital, respectively) is not static, however. It describes a high-valuation (or low-risk) anomaly that is fundamentally based on the logic of the charter value of banks and depends on the degree of severity of financial distress in an economy. When default risk is low and equity financing is relatively expensive, investors will focus on higher leverage and profitability. On the other hand, in economic downturns, additional capital buffers will be more appreciated. This signals not only a lower default probability, but also a lower risk of dilution from raising equity at distressed valuation levels.[15] Overall, however, such a dynamic impact of leverage on valuation, which changes in scale and sign over time, cannot be tracked by the constructed regression model.

Opportunity Costs and Growth (*PO*) (*DY*)

The payout ratio (*PO*) is positively associated with shareholder wealth (*P/TCE*), while dividend yield (*DY*) is negatively associated with it. This effect direction was anticipated by the mathematical decomposition of *P/TCE*, for *DY*, but not for *PO*. *DY* can be simply interpreted as a measure that represents shareholders' return expectations and

---

[12]Consistent with e.g. Bhandari (1988).

[13]This discussion is often intertwined with bank risk-taking and opportunity costs (*CoE*), which are analysed as separate regressors here.

[14]E.g. Diamond and Rajan (2000). According to traditional capital structure theory based on Modigliani and Miller (1958), reducing banks' leverage decreases the risk and cost of equity but does not change the weighted average cost of capital.

[15]This effect is very similar to the relationship of bank risk-taking and capital in different states of the economic cycle described Calem and Rob (1999). Their model predicts that at low capital levels, risk-taking is a decreasing function of capital, while at high capital levels the opposite is the case.

This U-shaped relationship between leverage and valuation is empirically confirmed by Calomiris and Nissim (2014), who define leverage as *TBV/TA* in their study. They find that higher leverage positively impacted valuation before the crisis (between Q1 2000 and Q2 2007). Thus, leverage gradually increased in the years before 2007 (e.g., Acharya and Richardson (2009)). During and after the crisis (between Q3 2007 and Q3 2013), however, they find the reverse, potentially because the asset quality concerns recalibrated investors' focus on the ability of banks' equity to absorb stress.

opportunity costs, which always drag down valuation as they increase. Many authors[16] have confirmed this strong empirical evidence that *DY* represents equity risk premiums.[17]

With regard to *PO*, it appears that the signalling effect of financial strength has overweighted the growth (or mathematical) effect.[18] Especially during the GFC, financial watchdogs around the globe forced banks to build up higher capital cushions, while rising default rates simultaneously eroded capital reserves. This is because financial regulators have insider knowledge about banks' assets and hold the ultimate decisional power over any profit distribution, which represents additional signalling. Moreover, because *PO* reflects management expectations, it is clearly an even better indicator of financial strength than capital ratio during times of uncertainty.

12.2.2 Further Tested and Excluded Variables

In contrast to most previous studies that use similar regression models to explain banks' book value ratios, the present work deduces most regressors from a theoretical framework. Nevertheless, to test the validity of this approach, several other factors have been tested that could theoretically have an impact on *P*/*TCE*. The following variables, sorted in the frequently used CAMEL bank rating methodology, were tested and discarded in unreported tests as they were unable to explain more of the cross-sectional variation with statistical significance:[19]

- Capital: This study uses *D*/*TCE*, imposed by the mathematical decomposition of *RoTCE*, to capture the leverage and capital adequacy of banks. Although not a regulatory measure, TCE is a good proxy for the narrowest regulatory definition of capital, known as CET 1 capital (see Fig. 7.2). A variety of other (non-)regulatory capitalisation measures were tested, such as total capital, tier 1 capital, and tier 1 common equity as percentage of risk-weighted assets (RWA). The two major findings confirm previous studies.[20] First, the power of simpler accounting or market measures describing capital levels in explaining bank valuation (or in predicting bank defaults) is much greater than the power of more complex regulatory ones. Risk-adjusted capitalisation measures seem to add more noise to any analysis, which suggests that market participants do not view the risk adjustment under Basel as truly informative in capturing the true risk in bank portfolios. Second, ratios with the strictest definition of capital explain most of the cross-section of bank valuation. This suggests that market

[16]E.g., Rozeff (1984) and Hodrick (1992).

[17]However, Goetzmann and Jorion (1993) state the opposite, blaming prior studies' failure to recognise the biases arising from regressions on lagged explanatory variables.

[18]This is in line with the empirical results of Calomiris and Nissim (2014, 400–401, 433).

[19]The parameter is a standardised coefficient above 0.20 at a significance of at least 0.000.

[20]Cf. A. G. Haldane and Madouros (August 31, 2012) and Blankespoor et al. (2013).

participants focus more on the capital that is available to absorb losses while the bank continues as a going concern.[21]

- Assets: To measure the scale of banks, this study uses the natural logarithm of total assets (*ln*(*A*)). Different scaling methods were also tested, such as size deciles, as were different underlying size characteristics, such as market capitalisation. In addition, concentration measures, such as domestic market shares or liabilities as a percentage of the country of origin's GDP, were unable to improve the model. To measure the asset quality of banks, the NPL ratio (*NPL*) was chosen despite several weaknesses: in particular, it is biased by management discretion and is backward-looking at only one point in time.[22] This is why other measures were also considered that take into account the coverage of NPLs with loan-loss reserves and the ratio of net loan charge-offs to gross loans.
- Management: As a rather qualitative characteristic of banks, management is probably one of the most difficult impact factors to measure. This study assumes that the management quality is eventually reflected in the quality of financials. Nevertheless, different types of corporate governance structures[23] were tested, such as bank type (private bank, savings bank, mutual banks) and legal form, as were different ownership structures,[24] such as economic interest held by governments and insiders.
- Earnings: The model reflects the quality, growth, and risk of the earnings by several measures. With regard to the earnings quality, it was found that the measures that exclude intangibles (*L*/*TA*; *IIoTA*) improved the model significantly. Likewise the payout ratio (*PO*) is derived from the Gordon growth model to measure growth. In contrast, more traditional measures such as growth rates from period to period of assets or loans were unable to improve the model. The cost of equity (*CoE*) in the model is covered by the dividend yield (*DY*), while other risk measures such as the market beta had less explanatory power.
- Liquidity: The liquidity and funding situation, which is determined by a bank's asset and liability management, is represented by cost of debt (*CoD*). Other measures that reflect the funding structure, such as the loan-to-deposit ratio (LDR), could not improve the robustness of the model.
- Other external factors: Factors that are potentially dependent on the location of a bank are collectively described by a dummy that represents four different global geographies (Asia-Pacific; Europe; Latin America and the Caribbean; the US and Canada). Further dummy variables that take into account regional differences on an even more

[21]Demirgüç-Kunt, Detragiache, and Merrouche (2013, 1157).

[22]Cf. Calomiris and Nissim (2014, 411).

[23]Cf. Caprio, Laeven, and Levine (2007).

[24]Cf. Garel and Petit-Romec (2017).

granular basis, such as for every country or accounting standard,[25] do did not change the standard errors substantially.

12.2.3 G-SIB Dummy

The results of this study show that, as hypothesised, the *P*/*TCE* of the sample banks is distorted by the G-SIB designation. Table 12.3 presents statistics for the G-SIB dummy for every quarter. The sign of the G-SIB dummy is negative for all quarters. The significance is strong for most of the quarters, but less robust for some earlier quarters. There might be two main reasons for the weaker significance at the beginning of the analysed period. First, the market might have needed some time to foresee and incorporate the effects of the FSB regulation on all G-SIBs.

Table 12.3 Regression Coefficients of G-SIB Quarter Dummies

Independent variables	Unstd. coefficients	Std. error	Std. coefficients	t-value	Significance	95.0 % Conf. int. Lower	Upper
2015Q3 G-SIB	-.747	.122	-.029	-6.116	.000	-.986	-.507
2015Q2 G-SIB	-.686	.111	-.029	-6.162	.000	-.904	-.468
2015Q1 G-SIB	-.673	.114	-.028	-5.885	.000	-.898	-.449
2014Q4 G-SIB	-.683	.111	-.029	-6.139	.000	-.902	-.465
2014Q3 G-SIB	-.630	.114	-.026	-5.502	.000	-.854	-.405
2014Q2 G-SIB	-.686	.114	-.028	-5.992	.000	-.910	-.462
2014Q1 G-SIB	-.696	.122	-.027	-5.721	.000	-.935	-.458
2013Q4 G-SIB	-.636	.118	-.025	-5.388	.000	-.867	-.405
2013Q3 G-SIB	-.645	.118	-.026	-5.467	.000	-.876	-.414
2013Q2 G-SIB	-.754	.118	-.030	-6.389	.000	-.985	-.522
2013Q1 G-SIB	-.770	.126	-.029	-6.113	.000	-1.017	-.523
2012Q4 G-SIB	-.721	.136	-.025	-5.311	.000	-.988	-.455
2012Q3 G-SIB	-.866	.122	-.034	-7.107	.000	-1.104	-.627
2012Q2 G-SIB	-.911	.126	-.034	-7.234	.000	-1.158	-.664
2012Q1 G-SIB	-.901	.131	-.033	-6.901	.000	-1.157	-.645
2011Q4 G-SIB	-.890	.122	-.035	-7.307	.000	-1.129	-.651
2011Q3 G-SIB	-.863	.149	-.027	-5.812	.000	-1.154	-.572
2011Q2 G-SIB	-.559	.177	-.015	-3.159	.002	-.907	-.212
2011Q1 G-SIB	-.477	.157	-.014	-3.049	.002	-.784	-.170
2010Q4 G-SIB	-.398	.142	-.013	-2.807	.005	-.677	-.120
2010Q3 G-SIB	-.327	.149	-.010	-2.199	.028	-.618	-.035
2010Q2 G-SIB	-.448	.149	-.014	-3.011	.003	-.739	-.156
2010Q1 G-SIB	-.266	.157	-.008	-1.702	.089	-.573	.040
2009Q4 G-SIB	-.382	.157	-.011	-2.435	.015	-.689	-.074
2009Q3 G-SIB	-.059	.177	-.002	-.333	.739	-.407	.289
2009Q2 G-SIB	-.595	.178	-.016	-3.352	.001	-.943	-.247
2009Q1 G-SIB	-1.097	.234	-.022	-4.696	.000	-1.555	-.639
2008Q4 G-SIB	-1.132	.192	-.028	-5.910	.000	-1.508	-.757
2008Q3 G-SIB	-.332	.209	-.007	-1.584	.113	-.742	.079
2008Q2 G-SIB	-.583	.210	-.013	-2.782	.005	-.994	-.172

[25]Cf. Clarkson et al. (2011).

Second, it appears that the statistical significance of the coefficients, represented by the p-value, is dependent on the size of the sub-sample comprising G-SIBs (see Fig. 12.1). In some early quarters, its size and significance are not satisfying. Notable is Q3 2009, which seems to be an outlier in every dimension. From Q4 2010 onwards, however, the statistics are convincing. It should be mentioned that the explanatory content of the model could not be improved by differentiating between the different G-SIB buckets (see Sect. 7.4).

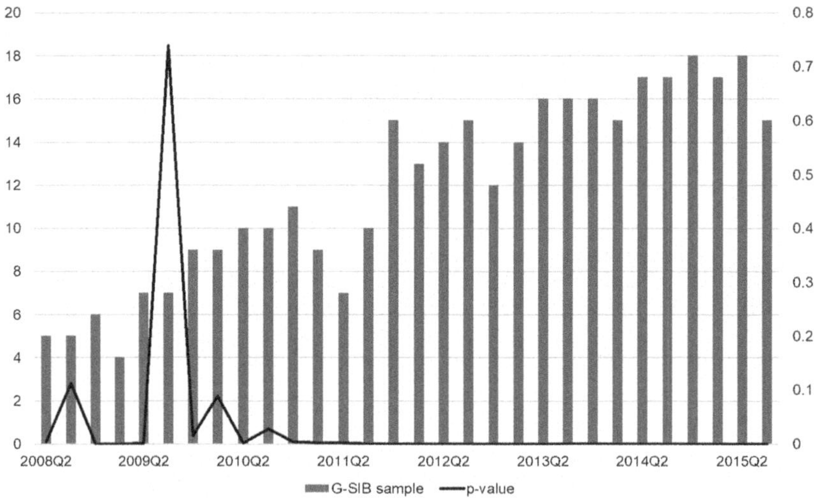

Fig. 12.1 G-SIB Sample Size and p-Value Over Time

Interpretation of Coefficient

The G-SIB dummy variables reveal that a G-SIB valuation discount exists of between about 0.3× and 1.1× P/TCE during the examined period. Figure 12.2 shows the development of the P/TCE discount of G-SIBs over the quarters (Q2 2008–Q3 2015) in a line chart that includes the upper and lower bound of the coefficients with 95 percent confidence.[26] The ranges basically confirm the general trend.

[26]These intervals are related to the p-values such that the coefficient will not be statistically significant if the confidence interval includes 0.

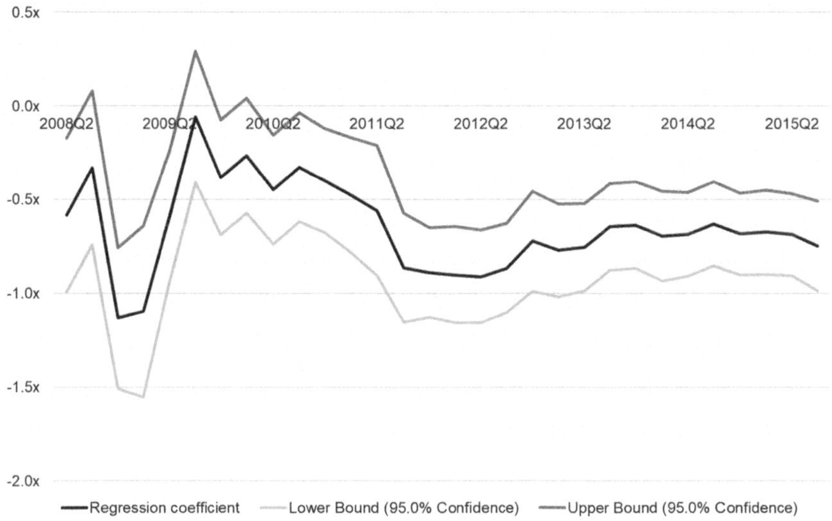

Fig. 12.2 Development of G-SIB Discount Over Time

Interpretation of *P/TCE* Discount

The market value of banks can be split into liquidation value and franchise value.[27] On a gone-concern basis, a bank's value consists only of the liquidation value, i.e., the current value of assets minus the current value of liabilities. *TCE* is often considered a reasonable proxy for liquidation value if the majority of a bank's assets are valued at fair value or at historical costs with adequate provisions for losses. On a going-concern basis, the franchise value has to be added to the liquidation value. With traditional bank activities, franchise value can be generated by granting loans above market rate and by receiving deposits below market rate.

When a bank's *P/TCE* is below one, the market value of equity is below its *TCE*. This is an interesting threshold when assuming the liquidation value, i.e. the value if a bank were to close today, equals roughly a bank's *TCE*. It indicates that investors assume that a bank will not earn its opportunity costs (*CoE*) or even worse, that it will incur losses in the future. Thus, market participants deduct the respective discounted amounts expected to be lost (i.e., the negative franchise value) from the liquidation value to calculate a bank's fair equity value. The characteristic of TBTF will only affect the franchise value. TBTF benefits, in particular funding benefits, and TBTF drawbacks, in particular TBTF regulation, can only affect banks on a going concern basis that envisage maintaining their banking license. Mathematically, the *P/TCE* discount of G-SIBs means that the market expects a narrowing spread between profitability (*RoTCE*) and opportunity costs

[27]Dermine (2014).

(*CoE*). It is unclear, however, whether profitability is expected to decrease or opportunity costs to increase, or both.

The design of this regression analysis makes it possible to exclude all kinds of conceivable factors—other than the G-SIB designation—for such a valuation discount. In other words, the discovered discount cannot be explained by differences in profitability, business model, size, efficiency, risk, asset quality, profit distribution, or growth, which are represented by the various regressors and prevailed in the analysed period. However, valuation is always driven by future characteristics of a bank, in particular profitability expectations (see Sect. 9.3.3). Therefore, it can be concluded with conviction that the market expects a significant change in G-SIBs' characteristics in the future which are negative for shareholder wealth. In other words, the analysis has revealed that there is large and significant discrepancy of forward-looking market views versus backward-looking fundamentals of G-SIBs.

Conversion to an Absolute Discount

The relative discount of P/TCE can be converted into absolute or monetary terms for the purpose of vividness. Table 12.4 illustrates the conversion as of the latest analysed point in time (end of Q3 2015). Here, investors attribute on average a negative premium of 0.75x P/TCE to G-SIBs. Moreover, all G-SIBs taken together trade at 0.98x P/TCE as of Q3 2015. However, without the G-SIB designation they would theoretically trade at 1.73x P/TCE, which would translate to a € 1.6 trillion higher market capitalisation (MarketCap), which would in turn equal an absolute discount of 43 percent.[28] The broader discount range of between 0.5x–1.0x P/TCE translates to a market capitalisation discount of 24–58 percent.[29]

Assumed Reasons for a G-SIB Discount

The effects weighing on the valuations of G-SIBs have been grouped into four categories (see Sect. 9.1.4): the TFBT designation effect, the TBTF effect, the reverse TBTF effect, and the regulatory TBTF burden effect. The negative G-SIB coefficients lead to the unambiguous conclusion that the negative effects outbalance the positive effect of TBTF with regard to shareholder wealth. While this analysis does not indicate anything about the individual impact strength of the four effects, share-price event studies (see Sect. 9.1.4.5) prove that the TBTF designation effect and the TBTF regulatory burden effect exist in relation to the FSB regulation (see Sect. 7.4). However, these studies have been unable to track which effect dominates. The TBTF effects on G-SIBs are coined as follows:

---

[28]MarketCap is the total market value of all outstanding common shares.

[29]There are certain caveats with regard to this illustrative calculation. First, the same average relative discount has been applied to all G-SIBs, although they might be impacted differently by the G-SIB status with different associated G-SIB discounts. Second, due to the relative nature of the discount, banks with a lower relative valuation are more impacted on an absolute basis.

Table 12.4 Absolute G-SIB Discounts (as of Q3 2015)

(€ in billions)	Actual		Projection		Discount
	MarketCap	*P/TCE*	*P/TCE*	MarketCap	Proj. vs act.
Agricultural Bank of China	110.0	0.75x	1.50x	219.7	-50 %
BBVA	47.7	1.15x	1.90x	78.7	-39 %
Santander	67.8	1.14x	1.89x	112.3	-40 %
Bank of America	145.6	1.04x	1.78x	250.5	-42 %
Bank of China	113.3	0.71x	1.45x	233.0	-51 %
Bank of New York Mellon	38.3	3.07x	3.81x	47.7	-20 %
Barclays	55.6	0.84x	1.59x	104.9	-47 %
BNP Paribas	65.3	0.91x	1.66x	118.8	-45 %
Citigroup	132.4	0.82x	1.57x	253.0	-48 %
Crédit Agricole	27.0	0.83x	1.57x	51.4	-47 %
Credit Suisse	36.1	1.10x	1.85x	60.6	-40 %
Deutsche Bank	33.2	0.60x	1.35x	74.3	-55 %
Goldman Sachs	66.6	1.03x	1.77x	115.2	-42 %
HSBC	132.3	0.97x	1.71x	234.5	-44 %
ICBC	183.8	0.82x	1.57x	350.2	-48 %
ING	48.9	1.08x	1.83x	82.7	-41 %
JPMorgan Chase	201.1	1.33x	2.08x	313.7	-36 %
Mitsubishi UFJ FG	74.0	0.73x	1.48x	150.0	-51 %
Mizuho FG	41.2	0.73x	1.47x	83.5	-51 %
Morgan Stanley	54.7	1.06x	1.80x	93.4	-41 %
Nordea	40.1	1.50x	2.25x	60.1	-33 %
Royal Bank of Scotland	49.3	0.80x	1.54x	95.7	-48 %
Société Générale	31.7	0.79x	1.54x	61.8	-49 %
Standard Chartered	20.5	0.54x	1.29x	48.7	-58 %
State Street	24.3	2.42x	3.16x	31.8	-24 %
Sumitomo Mitsui FG	45.8	0.74x	1.49x	91.9	-50 %
UBS	62.0	1.47x	2.21x	93.5	-34 %
UniCredit	33.3	0.78x	1.53x	65.1	-49 %
Wells Fargo	235.0	1.88x	2.62x	328.7	-28 %
Total G-SIBs	2,217.2	0.98x	1.73x	3,905.4	-43 %

- G-SIB designation effect: The positive effect of being designated as a G-SIB can already be derived from the descriptive statistics (see Sect. 11.5). G-SIBs' lower bankruptcy risk is mirrored by lower funding costs, while all analysed (bank-internal) risk metrics suggest otherwise. Again, the share-price reaction studies also prove the positive effect on stock prices (see Sect. 9.1.4.5). On the other hand, bail-in legislations and resolution regimes will inevitably diminish the funding benefits associated with the G-SIB designation. More recent studies show that G-SIB funding benefits have decreased (see Sect. 4.2.3).
- G-SIB effect: Since the implementation of the FSB, no G-SIBs have been bailed out or publicly supported. Therefore, this positive effect on valuation cannot yet be observed.

- Reverse G-SIB effect: Since the implementation of the FSB, no G-SIBs have been close to failing or even were allowed by the regulator to declare bankruptcy. Therefore, this negative effect on valuation cannot yet be observed.
- Regulatory G-SIB burden effect: The FSB regulation negatively impacts the equity values of G-SIBs as proven by share-price reaction studies (see Sect. 9.1.4.5). However, the question remains which regulatory measures have the largest impacts on valuation. The following impacts on expected G-SIB fundamentals could conceivably drag down profitability or growth, or increase opportunity costs:
  - Lower leverage (D/TCE): The impact of higher capital requirements on shareholder wealth is complex and controversial (see Sect. 6.1.4), in particular because capital is deeply connected with risk-taking and funding costs. Capital surcharges for G-SIBs seem to be the preeminent factor impacting G-SIBs' profitability through lower possible leverage. Figure 12.3 illustrates the significant impact of changing equity ratios (E/A) on bank profitability (*RoE*). For the sake of simplicity, funding costs (*CoD*) and cost efficiency (*CIR*) are held stable at two percent and 65 percent, respectively. Hence, four percent *RoA* while maintaining an eight percent E/A will result in 9.5 percent *RoE*. A G-SIB capital surcharge of three percent will lift the capital ratio to 11 percent and drags down the *RoE* to 7.1 percent.[30]

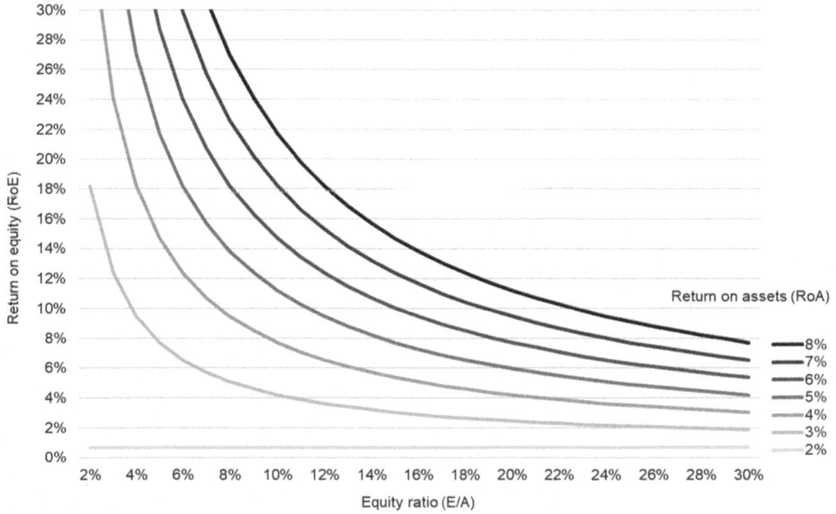

Fig. 12.3 Development of Profitability (*RoE*) at Various Equity Ratios (E/A). (Note: Cost of debt (*CoD*) is fixed at 2 % and cost-income ratio (*CIR*) is fixed at 65 %)

[30]Dagher et al. (2016) present a literature overview with regard to estimates of the transitional and steady-state impact of higher capital requirements on the cost and volume of bank credit.

- Worsening cost efficiency (*CIR*): Bank regulation is responsible for a significant part of a bank's cost base.[31] These regulatory costs are further inflated by the comprehensive supervision and additional obligations required by the FSB.
- Higher cost of debt (*CoD*): The cost of debt is increased by the requirements for G-SIBs to hold a substantial portion of liabilities that qualify as TLAC. These instruments are relatively more expensive than most other forms of bank funding.
- Higher opportunity costs (*CoE*): At least temporarily, the design of the G-SIB regulation was unclear to the financial markets. For instance, some FSB members inspired a discussion on even more radical regulation, such as the break-up of G-SIBs. This regulatory uncertainty likely boosted the capital costs of G-SIBs.

Interpretation of G-SIB Discount Development

The negative coefficients of between 0.6x–0.8x are relatively stable from Q3 2011 onwards with highly robust significance. In earlier quarters, the coefficients are less stable, and the statistical significance is less confirmative in some quarters (significance of 0.002–0.739). Discount developed in a certain direction can be interpreted in connection with existing share-price reaction studies (see Sect. 9.1.4). Five time periods are categorised to connect the main events leading to the G-SIB regulation (Table 7.2) and the development of the G-SIB valuation discounts:

1. Q2 2008–Q3 2008: TBTF discount already exists in pre-FSB era: The data suggests that even in the time before the announcement of the FSB regulation, the valuation of banks that would later be designated G-SIBs was depressed. As the statistical significance is only mediocre (0.005 and 0.113, respectively), the valuation discount of 0.3x–0.6x P/TCE should only be viewed as an indication.
2. Q4 2008: Highest discount after the G-20 call for TBTF regulation: On 17 November 2008, the G-20 countries agreed on concerted actions to tackle the problem of G-SIBs. The G-SIB discount achieved a peak of 1.1x P/TCE (significance 0.000) at the end of the quarter following this announcement. This is in line with the results of Moenninghoff, Ongena, and Wieandt (2015), who measure negative abnormal stock returns of G-SIBs of 2.79 percent with a one-day event window.
3. Q1 2009–Q3 2010: Uncertainty of G-SIB regulation and valuation: There is a high fluctuation of G-SIB discounts (between 0.1x and 1.1x P/TCE) while statistical significance is weak in some quarters. The uncertainty surrounding the ultimate G-SIB regulation can be considered as one reason for this, because concrete recommendations were not made until 1 November 2010. Moreover, positive G-SIB designation effects played a role in this period. The designation of the G-SIBs, which was leaked

[31] Cf. Demirgüç-Kunt, Laeven, and Levine (2004).

for the first time on 20 November 2009, causes a positive abnormal share-price reactions event of G-SIBs.[32]

4. Q4 2010–Q3 2012: G-SIB discount builds up as FSB regulation is agreed upon: During this time period, the core elements of the G-SIB regulation were endorsed, in particular the capital surcharges, which acted as the most decisive turning point in TBTF regulation. At the same time, further designation events no longer acted as such a catalyst for G-SIB share prices.[33] This resulted in gradually increasing discounts of 0.4x to 0.9x *P/TCE*.
5. Q4 2012–Q3 2015: G-SIB discount stabilises as uncertainty disappears: In this time period, there was little surprise for investors (abnormal share-price reactions) with regard to incremental G-SIB regulation,[34] while G-SIBs worked on meeting the requirements. The valuation discounts settle at 0.6x–0.7x *P/TCE*, while statistical significance remains strong.

12.2.4 Limitation of the Study

The conclusions of this study are consistent with substantial evidence provided by prior studies. However, conclusive proof that the findings are incontestable does not yet exist, as evidenced by the following limitations of the study.

No Causal Relationship

It can be ruled out that the results are an aberration related to the regression data because event studies have already proven the direct relationship of the G-SIB designation and abnormal share-price returns (see Sect. 9.1.4.5). Moreover, by controlling for many exogenous factors, this analysis has clear benefits compared to pure share-price reaction studies. Nevertheless, due to the long period analysed, it is not possible to attribute certain events directly to valuation developments. Thus, qualitative conclusions made based on quantitative results (also in connection with findings of other empirical studies) should be viewed cautiously. Moreover, the data availability for G-SIBs is insufficient for the earlier quarters (before Q4 2010) of the analysed period. This prohibits the drawing of any conclusion for these quarters, in particular for Q3 2009.

Unknown Impact Factors

In this study, extensive efforts have been made to include as many explanatory factors as possible and to exclude potential distortions. While the regression results are statistically highly significant, a substantial part of the cross-section of *P/TCE* is still not explained

---

[32]Moenninghoff, Ongena, and Wieandt (2015).

[33]Cf. Moenninghoff, Ongena, and Wieandt (2015).

[34]Cf. Moenninghoff, Ongena, and Wieandt (2015).

by all the regressors. In other words, other unobserved effects could be explained in the model through the G-SIB dummy which also affect non-G-SIBs. The robustness of the regression suffers in particular from the strong bias of the sub-sample G-SIBs towards the largest banks of the full sample. The following lists the main potential impact factors that generally only apply to the largest banks, but not necessarily only to G-SIBs, and have not been or could not be controlled for explicitly.

- Capital forbearance: It has been evidenced that during the GFC, the value of distressed assets, such as mortgage-backed securities, and regulatory capital were overstated and bank losses were understated in the financial accounts.[35] This is true, above all, for very large banks with complex and illiquid financial assets. The reasons for this are not only flawed accounting rules and management discretion, but also regulators' attempts to preserve book capital through forbearance. Research indicates that this is not an inherent procyclical bias in fair-value accounting, but an extraordinary feature of the GFC.[36] The fact that valuation levels remained depressed for several years after the GFC, i.e. long after the potential delay of loss recognition, suggests that this might be not the main impact factor.[37] However, it reinforces several researchers' view that the bold decline of banks' P/BV during the GFC largely comes from distortion. Other prominent academics locate the main source of the decline of banks' P/BV in the value appreciation of bank intangibles (see Sect. 9.3.4), which was accounted for in the regression analysis.
- Litigation and restructuring costs: Following the GFC, predominantly major players in the US and Europe were hit by large fines (imposed by courts and regulators) and settlements (arranged with prosecutors) in misconduct cases due to their adverse business models. In the US, the majority of fines were related to mortgage activities, and in the EU, to mis-selling of investment products and market manipulation. Between the years 2010 and 2014, the respective fines reached a cumulative total of around € 200 billion for all banks, and around 85 percent of these litigation costs were incurred against 10 G-SIBs. Without these costs and provisioning for future litigation costs, the total accumulated net profits of G-SIBs in the EU would have been roughly 30 percent higher. Moreover, in a broad sense, misconduct costs are not restricted to direct penalties: they also involve further redress costs, costs of expanded legal departments and external consultants, lower future sales and funding conditions from reputational damage, and restructuring costs to amend the business model.[38]

[35]Huizinga and Laeven (2012).

[36]Laux and Leuz (2010).

[37]Calomiris and Nissim (2014).

[38]European Systemic Risk Board (ESRB) (June 2015, 12–16).

- Holding discount: There is limited evidence on economies of scope and positive diversification effects of large banks' non-interest income streams from an efficiency point of view (see Sect. 5.1). When shifting to an equity valuation perspective, the evidence is equally unclear. Some researchers argue that bank equity investors dislike financial conglomerates.[39] Lending and non-lending financial services are valued higher if kept separate, since investors place higher opportunity costs on these bank holdings; this is why it is referred to as holding discount. In relation to the TBTF doctrine, a holding discount can also be considered as a 'too-big-to-manage' problem. The main theory behind this is intensified agency problems in financial conglomerates,[40] such as inefficient cross-subsidisation, operational complexity, opacity of the hybrid conglomerate model, and value shifting between shareholders and debtholders.[41] Many academics, however, reject the idea of a general holding discount of banks,[42] and some even find substantial premiums for the very largest banks.[43] However, the most recent study on the effect of diversification on bank valuation reconciles previous studies: Guerry and Wallmeier (2017) find a significant diversification discount at the end of the 1990s which decreases over time and practically disappears after the GFC. They also show that the pre-GFC discount is considerably smaller in a robust regression that accounts for the share of non-interest income.

12.2.5 Areas of Future Research

The GFC triggered an enormous amount of research connected to the TBTF problem in banking (see Part I). On the empirical side, the vast majority of studies are devoted to the impact of TBTF on debt-like instruments, while much fewer focus on the impact on equity (see Sect. 9.1). The present study is the first research into relative valuation differences of G-SIBs. There are several ways in which future studies could extend the scope to strengthen the present findings. For instance, they could extend the time period or exclude more exogenous factors. Furthermore, future research should overcome or address the limitations of this study described above. A further way of assessing the

[39]E.g., DeLong (2001, 221) and Laeven and Levine (2007).

[40]Laeven and Levine (2007, 331).

[41]van Lelyveld and Knot (2009, 2319)

[42]E.g., van Lelyveld and Knot (2009) and Elsas, Hackethal, and Holzhäuser (2010, 1274).

[43]E.g., Schmid and Walter (2009).

relationship between valuation and TBTF designation could be the combination of an event study and a multivariate regression model[44] to test how sensitive P/TCE is to certain regressors around certain event dates.[45] More research is also needed to further address the gap in quantifying the shareholder moral hazard and the appropriate regulatory responses to the TBTF doctrine. In addition, future research should explore the factors influencing the degree to which various stakeholders benefit from shareholder wealth transfer. It might take another financial crisis triggered by the TBTF doctrine for those areas to be investigated.

---

[44]In accordance with Binder (1985).

[45]Ricci (2015) conducted this kind of analysis with respect to the impact of the ECB's monetary policy announcements on large European banks.

Conclusion 13

This final chapter summarises the previous chapter of Pt. II (see Sect. 13.1) and makes forward-looking recommendations for bank management and policymakers based on the research findings (see Sect. 13.2).

13.1 Summary

Recapitulation

The GFC triggered the production of an enormous amount of research connected to the TBTF problem in banking (see Pt. I). Most of the empirical research on TBTF is dedicated to measuring funding benefits of G-SIBs coming from implicit government guarantees (IGG) that lead to creditor moral hazards. However, there are also effects on equity prices of G-SIBs, as previously evidenced by share-price reaction studies (see Chap. 9). The present study divides these effects into four categories:

1. The TBTF designation effect describes the designation of certain banks as TBTF by an official body and causes positive abnormal share-price reactions.
2. The TBTF effect describes the situation in which the TBTF doctrine is strengthened, such as by the bailout of a G-SIB, and causes positive abnormal share-price reactions.
3. The reverse TBTF effect describes a situation in which the TBTF doctrine is weakened, such as the failure of a bank perceived to be TBTF, and causes negative abnormal share-price reactions.
4. The regulatory TBTF burden effect describes the announcement of additional regulatory measures that target G-SIBs and causes negative abnormal share-price reactions.

T. F. Lesche, *Too-Big-to-Fail in Banking*, Finanzwirtschaft, Banken und Bankmanagement I Finance, Banks and Bank Management, https://doi.org/10.1007/978-3-658-34182-4_13

The question remains how these effects in total impact the relative equity valuation of G-SIBs versus other banks. This is the why this first research piece on the matter sets a non-directional hypothesis (see Chap. 10).

G-SIBs in this study were identified as the global-systemically important banks (G-SIBs) designated by the Financial Stability Board (FSB). The analysis was conducted on a quarterly basis for more than 750 global banks for the period of Q2 2008 until Q3 2015. It appears that G-SIBs have different financial characteristics than non-G-SIBs. They are not only significantly larger, but also conduct investment banking activities that are per se riskier and more profitable. Nonetheless, G-SIBs can fund themselves more cheaply, which once again proves the hypothesis of TBTF funding benefits. This study developed an innovative two-way fixed-effect regression model to take into account these structural differences of the G-SIB sub-sample and to track the relative valuation development of G-SIBs over time (Chap. 11). Relative bank valuation was measured in terms of price-to-tangible common equity (P/TCE): a refined version of price-to-book value, the most common relative bank valuation measure. Bank characteristics are measured with historical financial data based on the decomposition of return on equity (RoE), cost of equity (CoE), and growth (g) based on the Gordon growth model. This captured banks' profitability, business model, size, efficiency, risk, asset quality, profit distribution, and growth.

Main Findings

On average, G-SIBs are confronted with a substantial valuation discount. The market expects a significant change in the financial profile of G-SIBs in the future which negatively impacts shareholder wealth. From the end of 2011 until the end of 2015, a stable discount of 0.6x–0.8x P/TCE is highly statistically significant. Without this discount, the market capitalisation of all 29 G-SIBs would be € 1.6 trillion higher, in absolute terms and as of Q3 2015, which equals an absolute G-SIB discount of 43 percent (see Chap. 12).

This study concludes that the negative effect of being a G-SIB outweighs the positive effect and in total leads to a relative valuation discount. In other words, the *G-SIB designation effect*, which positively impacts G-SIBs' share prices because of funding benefits from IGG, is dominated by the *regulatory G-SIB burden effect*, which negatively impacts G-SIBs' share prices because of lower profitability from capital surcharges and other regulatory requirements for G-SIBs. It can be inferred that there is a wealth transfer from G-SIB shareholders to other bank stakeholders. Benefiters could be the public, in the form of internalised deadweight losses and lower systemic risk; debt holders, in the form of higher risk-adjusted yields; and bank employees, in the form of higher salaries. The findings re-open the debate about whether a break-up would unlock shareholder value and whether G-SIBs are regulated efficiently.

13.2 Recommendations

For Bank Managements

In general, G-SIBs have a serious corporate governance problem. In theory, bank management should primarily represent shareholders' interests. Based on this study's findings, however, this is not the case because G-SIBs' equity valuations are substantially depressed. Size is now a regulatory negative and G-SIBs are only large for the benefit of their creditors and employees. It is not surprising that no G-SIB is privately run by its owners. However, these bank management moral hazards are concealed from shareholders, because as of now the profitability of G-SIBs is still higher because their business models are different than those of non-G-SIBs. Only when controlling for structural differences—particularly risk and opportunity costs, as done in this study—the significant G-SIB valuation discount becomes apparent. Hence, G-SIB management can lift substantial value for shareholders by shrinking banks' balance sheets or by divesting divisions into parts to lose their TBTF status.[1] First, a G-SIB break-up would lead to possible capital distribution to shareholders from lower capital requirements for each stand-alone business. Second, lower regulatory costs and a lower capital base increase capital returns (*RoE*) for shareholders, which should ultimately lead to a disappearance of the G-SIB discount and to a multiple re-rating of the individual bank parts in line with non-G-SIBs peers. Nevertheless, the execution risk of such a comprehensive restructuring needs to be considered.[2]

The valuation situation of G-SIBs during and after the GFC is not dissimilar to the situation of the largest US banks during and some years after the Great Depression. At the time, market capitalisations of those banks dropped below their book values (P/BV of below one). This discount encouraged bank investors to pressure bank managements to increase shareholder wealth by disposing of bank assets separately. In response, a number of the largest banks sold off their equity brokerage business, which in turn paved the way for the regulatory response of restrictions, the passage of the *Glass-Steagall Act* in 1933. In other words, the market was leading where regulators had feared treading.[3] Nowadays, it seems that G-SIBs' managements justify the bank size rather than making it a virtue of necessity. G-SIBs' managements often claim scope economies or megabank economies in capital market activities. However, there is very little academic evidence to support these arguments (see Sect. 5.1). Some bankers even argue that megabanks perform 'missioncritical services [...] that regional and community banks simply cannot

[1]Demirgüç-Kunt and Huizinga (2013) come to a similar conclusion but from a different reasoning. They find that a bank's P/BV 'is negatively related to the size of its liabilities-to-GDP ratio'. They infer that 'some systemically important banks can increase their value by downsizing or splitting up'.

[2]Cf. Goldman Sachs (5 January 2015, 1).

[3]A. G. Haldane and Madouros (31 August 2012).

do'. This could be interpreted as bank managers simply dodging their responsibility towards shareholders with regard to rightsizing.

The disruptive power of financial-technology start-ups (fintechs) can possibly be considered a self-healing process in this context. On the one hand, traditional banks need to rethink their business model since technology—like in other businesses—is leading to a disaggregation of banking into its fundamental components: intermediation and services.[4] On the other hand, fintechs have developed independently from G-SIBs and are bringing back modularity into the banking systems. Modularity deployed in organisational structure has enhanced systemic resilience ever since.

For Policymakers

This study analysed banks concerned by the FSB regulation. This G-20 initiative is the first to tackle the TBTF problem with uniform measures for G-SIBs on a global reach (see Sect. 7.4). The objective of the FSB regulation announced in 2009 was to create a less procyclical financial system that would not allow leverage of peak levels during the GFC. Various measures, in particular substantially higher capital requirements, ensure that risks are only be taken where not only profits but also potential losses are borne by banks themselves.[5]

An analysis based on market views, such as *P/TCE*, is important for policymakers because market values remove errors in accounting for the book values of tangible assets, such as unrecognised losses, and anticipate the impact of announced regulatory measures.[6] Bank valuation mirrors market expectations and certainty of future profit- and loss-streams to the bank owners. G-SIBs' lower valuations imply either lower overall profitability (from lower risk-taking or weaker government guarantees) or higher opportunity costs of investors, or both. The reduction of relative G-SIB valuation represents a reduction in IGGs at shareholders' expense. This is why a positive conclusion can be drawn with regard to the FSB's initial objectives from this perspective. Moreover, an important finding is that the unintended consequences of the G-SIB designation effect of the FSB regulation (by publicly extending IGGs to G-SIBs) is more than offset by the regulatory burden associated with it. The FSB regulation clearly drags down equity valuations through different channels, probably mainly through capital surcharges and credible resolution regimes. Hence, G-SIBs internalise at least some of the social costs of their systemic importance.

While some of the costs of the banking reforms for market participants may be measurable in the short term, the existence of overall social benefits, particularly in terms of avoiding crises, is far more doubtful and difficult to measure. The assumption that capital surcharges are an effective threat and enough to increase overall safety and soundness

[4]Huertas (2014, 142–43).

[5]Financial Stability Board (FSB) (25 September 2009, 1).

[6]Cf. Calomiris and Nissim (2014, 434).

of the financial system may be overestimated. On the one hand and at least in the short term, the FSB regulation has made G-SIBs weaker in terms of profitability and valuation. Ideally, G-SIBs should have strong charter and franchise values to resist contagion effects in economic distress. On the other hand and in the long term, the FSB measures may create new incentives for G-SIBs to conduct undesirable business activities that increase risk in the financial system.

References

Abrams, Jay B. 2012. "Regression Analysis in the Market Approach: Using the Gordon Model as a Guide to Selecting Independent Variables." *Value Examiner* March/April: 8–21.

Abreu, José Filipe, and Mohamed Azzim Gulamhussen. 2013. "The Stock Market Reaction to the Public Announcement of a Supranational List of Too-Big-to-Fail Banks During the Financial Crisis." *Journal of International Financial Markets, Institutions & Money* 25: 49–72.

Acharya, Viral V. 2009. "A Theory of Systemic Risk and Design of Prudential Bank Regulation." *Journal of Financial Stability* 5 (3): 224–55.

Acharya, Viral V., and Hassan Naqvi. 2012. "The Seeds of a Crisis: A Theory of Bank Liquidity and Risk Taking over the Business Cycle." *Journal of Financial Economics* 106 (2): 349–66.

Acharya, Viral V., Lasse Heje Pedersen, Thomas Philippon, and Matthew Richardson. 2017. "Measuring Systemic Risk." *The Review of Financial Studies* 30 (1): 2–47.

Acharya, Viral V., and Matthew Richardson. 2009. *Restoring Financial Stability: How to Repair a Failed System.* Wiley Finance Series. Hoboken, N.J.: John Wiley & Sons.

Acharya, Viral V., and Tanju Yorulmazer. 2007. "Too Many to Fail—an Analysis of Time-Inconsistency in Bank Closure Policies." *Journal of Financial Intermediation* 16: 1–31.

Adams, Michael, and Markus Rudolf. 24 November 2006. "A New Approach to the Valuation of Banks." https://www.ibrarian.net/navon/paper/A_new_approach_to_the_valuation_of_banks.pdf?paperid=9046180.

Admati, Anat R., Peter M. DeMarzo, Martin F. Hellwig, and Paul Pfleiderer. 2013. "Fallacies, Irrelevant Facts, and Myths in the Discussion of Capital Regulation: Why Bank Equity Is Not Socially Expensive." *Rock Center for Corporate Governance at Stanford University Working Paper* 161. https://ssrn.com/abstract=2349739.

Admati, Anat R., and Martin F. Hellwig. 2013. *The Bankers' New Clothes: What's Wrong with Banking and What to Do About It.* Princeton; Oxford: Princeton University Press.

Adrian, Tobias, and Markus K. Brunnermeier. 2016. "CoVaR." *American Economic Review* 106 (7): 1705–41.

Akerlof, George A. 1970. "The Market for 'Lemons': Quality Uncertainty and the Market Mechanism." *The Quarterly Journal of Economics* 84 (3): 488–500.

Akhigbe, Aigbe, and Ann Marie Whyte. 2001. "The Impact of FDICIA on Bank Returns and Risk: Evidence from the Capital Markets." *Journal of Banking & Finance* 25: 393–417.

Alam, Pervaiz, and Charles A. Brown. 2006. "Disaggregated Earnings and the Prediction of ROE and Stock Prices: A Case of the Banking Industry." *Review of Accounting and Finance* 5: 443–63.

T. F. Lesche, *Too-Big-to-Fail in Banking,* Finanzwirtschaft, Banken und Bankmanagement I Finance, Banks and Bank Management, https://doi.org/10.1007/978-3-658-34182-4

Alessandri, Piergiorgio, Sergio Masciantonio, and Andrea Zaghini. 2015. "Tracking Banks' Systemic Importance Before and After the Crisis." *International Finance* 18 (2): 157–86.

Allegret, Jean-Pierre, Hélène Raymond, and Houda Rharrabti. 2017. "The Impact of the European Sovereign Debt Crisis on Banks Stocks. Some Evidence of Shift Contagion in Europe." *Journal of Banking & Finance* 74: 24–37.

Allen, Franklin, Elena Carletti, and Xian Gu. 2015. "The Roles of Banks in Financial Systems." In *The Oxford Handbook of Banking*, edited by Allen N. Berger, Philip Molyneux, and John O. S. Wilson, 27–46. New York.

Allen, Franklin, and Douglas Gale. 1998. "Optimal Financial Crises." *The Journal of Finance* 53 (4): 1245–84.

Allen, Franklin, and Douglas Gale. 2000. "Financial Contagion." *Journal of Political Economy* 108 (1): 1–33.

Allen, Franklin, and Douglas Gale. 2004. "Financial Fragility, Liquidity, and Asset Prices." *Journal of the European Economic Association* 2 (6): 1015–48.

Amel, Dean, Colleen Barnes, Fabio Panetta, and Carmelo Salleo. 2004. "Consolidation and Efficiency in the Financial Sector: A Review of the International Evidence." *Journal of Banking & Finance* 28: 2493–2519.

Andrews, Donald W. K. 1991. "Heteroskedasticity and Autocorrelation Consistent Covariance Matrix Estimation." *Econometrica* 59 (3): 817–58.

Angbazo, Lazarus, and Anthony Saunders. 1996. "The Effect of TBTF Deregulation on Bank Cost of Funds." *Financial Institutions Center at the Wharton School - Working Papers* 97 (25).

Anginer, Deniz, Asli Demirgüç-Kunt, and Min Zhu. 2014a. "How Does Competition Affect Bank Systemic Risk?" *Journal of Financial Intermediation* 23: 1–26.

Anginer, Deniz, Asli Demirgüç-Kunt, and Min Zhu. 2014b. "How Does Deposit Insurance Affect Bank Risk? Evidence from the Recent Crisis." *Journal of Banking & Finance* 48: 312–21.

Anglo Irish Bank. 2009. "Annual Report and Accounts 2008." https://www.ibrc.ie/About_us/Financial_information/Archived_reports/Annual_Report_2008.pdf.

Araten, Michel. 2014. "Credit Ratings as Indicators of Implicit Government Support for Global Systemically Important Banks." *Journal of Risk Management in Financial Institutions* 7 (4): 345–52.

Araten, Michel, and Christopher Turner. 2013. "Understanding the Funding Cost Differences Between Global Systemically Important Banks (G-SIBs) and non-G-SIBs in the USA." *Journal of Risk Management in Financial Institutions* 6 (4): 387–410.

Arping, Stefan. 2017. "Deposit Competition and Loan Markets." *Journal of Banking & Finance* 80: 108–18.

Athanasoglou, Panayiotis P., Sophocles N. Brissimis, and Matthaios D. Delis. 2008. "Bank-Specific, Industry-Specific and Macroeconomic Determinants of Bank Profitability." *Journal of International Financial Markets, Institutions and Money* 18: 121–36.

Autor, David. 2004. "Externalities, the Coase Theorem and Market Remedies." https://ocw.mit.edu/courses/economics/14-03-microeconomic-theory-and-public-policy-fall-2010/lecture-notes/.

Avgouleas, Emilios, Charles Goodhart, and Dirk Schoenmaker. 2013. "Bank Resolution Plans as a Catalyst for Global Financial Reform." *Journal of Financial Stability* 9: 210–18.

Baele, Lieven, Olivier De Jonghe, and Rudi Vander Vennet. 2007. "Does the Stock Market Value Bank Diversification?" *Journal of Banking & Finance* 31: 1999–2023.

Bagehot, Walter. 1873. *Lombard Street: A Description of the Money Market*. London: Henry S. King & Co.

Baily, Martin N., John Y. Campbell, John H. Cochrane, Douglas W. Diamond, Darrell Duffie, Kenneth R. French, Anil K. Kashyap, et al. 2013. "Aligning Incentives at Systemically

Important Financial Institutions: A Proposal by the Squam Lake Group." *Journal of Applied Corporate Finance* 25 (4): 37–40.
Balasubramnian, Bhanu, and Ken B. Cyree. 2011. "Market Discipline of Banks: Why Are Yield Spreads on Bank-Issued Subordinated Notes and Debentures Not Sensitive to Bank Risks?" *Journal of Banking & Finance* 35: 21–35.
Ball, Ray, and Philip Brown. 1968. "An Empirical Evaluation of Accounting Income Numbers." *Journal of Accounting Research* 6 (2): 159–78.
Banz, Rolf W. 1991. "The Relationship Between Return and Market Value of Common Stocks." *Journal of Financial Economics* 9 (1): 3–18.
Barba, Robert. 2015. "In Deals, Emphasis Is Back on Earnings." *American Banker Magazine* 125 (3): 12.
Barber, Brad M., and John D. Lyon. 1997. "Firm Size, Book-to-Market Ratios, and Security Returns: A Holdout Sample of Financial Firms." *The Journal of Finance* 52 (2): 875–83.
Barros, Carlos Pestana, Candida Ferreira, and Jonathan Williams. 2007. "Analysing the Determinants of Performance of Best and Worst European Banks: A Mixed Logit Approach." *Journal of Banking & Finance* 31: 2189–2203.
Barth, James R., Gerard Caprio, and Ross Levine. 2004. "Bank Regulation and Supervision: What Works Best?" *Journal of Financial Intermediation* 13: 205–48.
Barth, James R., Apanard Prabha, and Phillip Swagel. 2012. "Just How Big Is the Too-Big-to-Fail Problem?" *Journal of Banking Regulation* 13 (4): 265–99.
Barth, Mary E. 1994. "Fair Value Accounting: Evidence from Investment Securities and the Market Valuation from Banks." *The Accounting Review* 69 (1): 1–25.
Basel Committee on Banking Supervision (BCBS). June 1999. "A New Capital Adequacy Framework: Consultative Paper." https://www.bis.org/publ/bcbs50.pdf.
Basel Committee on Banking Supervision (BCBS). July 2013. "Global Systemically Important Banks: Updated Assessment Methodology and the Higher Loss Absorbency Requirement." https://www.bis.org/publ/bcbs255.pdf.
Basel Committee on Banking Supervision (BCBS). November 2014. "The G-SIB Assessment Methodology – Score Calculation." https://www.bis.org/bcbs/publ/d296.pdf.
Basel Committee on Banking Supervision (BCBS). October 2015. "A Brief History of the Basel Committee." https://www.bis.org/bcbs/history.pdf.
Basel Committee on Banking Supervision (BCBS). December 2017. "Basel Iii: Finalising Post-Crisis Reforms." https://www.bis.org/bcbs/publ/d424.pdf.
Bassett, William F., and Thomas F. Brady. 2001. "The Economic Performance of Small Banks, 1985–2000." *Federal Reserve Bulletin* November: 719–28.
Basu, S. 1977. "Investment Performance of Common Stocks in Relation to Their Price-Earnings Ratios: A Test of the Efficient Market Hypothesis." *The Journal of Finance* 32 (3): 663–82.
Beaver, William H., Roger Clarke, and William F. Wright. 1979. "The Association Between Unsystematic Security Returns and the Magnitude of Earnings Forecast Errors." *Journal of Accounting Research* 17 (2): 316–40.
Beaver, William H., Carol Eger, Stephen Ryan, and Mark Wolfson. 1989. "Financial Reporting, Supplemental Disclosures, and Bank Share Prices." *Journal of Accounting Research* 27 (2): 157–78.
Beccalli, Elena, Mario Anolli, and Giuliana Borello. 2015. "Are European Banks Too Big? Evidence on Economies of Scale." *Journal of Banking & Finance* 58: 232–46.
Beccalli, Elena, Barbara Casu, and Claudia Girardone. 2006. "Efficiency and Stock Performance in European Banking." *Journal of Business Finance & Accounting* 33 (1/2): 245–62.
Beccalli, Elena, and Pascal Frantz. 2009. "M&A Operations and Performance in Banking." *Journal of Financial Services Research* 36 (2/3): 203–26.

Beltratti, Andrea, and Giovanna Paladino. 2015. "Bank Leverage and Profitability: Evidence from a Sample of International Banks." *Review of Financial Economics* 27: 46–57.

Benston, George J., William C. Hunter, and Larry D. Wall. 1995. "Motivations for Bank Mergers and Acquisitions: Enhancing the Deposit Insurance Put Option Versus Earnings Diversification." *Journal of Money, Credit and Banking* 27 (3): 777–88.

Benston, George J., and Georg G. Kaufman. 1997. "FDICIA After Five Years." *Journal of Economic Perspectives* 11 (3): 139–58.

Berger, Allen N. 1995. "The Relationship Between Capital and Earnings in Banking." *Journal of Money, Credit and Banking* 27 (2): 432–56.

Berger, Allen N., and Emilia Bonaccorsi di Patti. 2006. "Capital Structure and Firm Performance: A New Approach to Testing Agency Theory and an Application to the Banking Industry." *Journal of Banking & Finance* 30: 1065–1102.

Berger, Allen N., and Christa H. S. Bouwman. 2013. "How Does Capital Affect Bank Performance During Financial Crises?" *Journal of Financial Economics* 109: 146–76.

Berger, Allen N., Rebecca S. Demsetz, and Philip E. Strahan. 1999. "The Consolidation of the Financial Services Industry: Causes, Consequences, and Implications for the Future." *Journal of Banking & Finance* 23: 135–94.

Berger, Allen N., and David B. Humphrey. 1994. "Bank Scale Economies, Mergers, Concentration, and Efficiency: The U.S. Experience." *Financial Institutions Center at the Wharton School – Working Papers* 94 (25).

Berger, Allen N., and David B. Humphrey. 1997. "Efficiency of Financial Institutions: International Survey and Directions for Future Research." *European Journal of Operational Research* 98: 175–212.

Berger, Allen N., and Loretta J. Mester. 1997. "Inside the Black Box: What Explains Differences in the Efficiencies of Financial Institutions?" *Journal of Banking & Finance* 21 (7): 895–947.

Bernanke, Ben S. 1983. "Nonmonetary Effects of the Financial Crisis in the Propagation of the Great Depression." *American Economic Review* 73 (3): 257–76.

Bernanke, Ben S. 2 September 2010. "Causes of the Recent Financial and Economic Crisis." *Statement Before the Financial Crisis Inquiry Commission, Washington, D.C.* https://www.federalreserve.gov/newsevents/testimony/bernanke20100902a.pdf.

Bernanke, Ben S., and James Harold. 1991. "The Gold Standard, Deflation, and Financial Crisis in the Great Depression: An International Comparison." In *Financial Markets and Financial Crises*, edited by R. Glenn Hubbard, 33–68. A National Bureau of Economic Research Project Report. Chicago; London: University of Chicago Press.

Bernstein Research. 2003. "Valuation: Looking at Valuation One More Time, Now Based on Tangible Book Values." *Brokerage Industry: Capital Markets Quarterly Summary & Valuation Analysis*, 53–59.

Bertsatos, Georgios, and Plutarchos Sakellaris. 2016. "A Dynamic Model of Bank Valuation." *Economics Letters* 145: 15–18.

Besanko, David, and George Kanatas. 1996. "The Regulation of Bank Capital: Do Capital Standards Promote Bank Safety?" *Journal of Financial Intermediation* 5: 160–83.

Bhagat, Sanjai, Brian Bolton, and Jun Lu. 2015. "Size, Leverage, and Risk-Taking of Financial Institutions." *Journal of Banking & Finance* 59: 520–37.

Bhandari, Laxmi Chand. 1988. "Debt/Equity Ratio and Expected Common Stock Returns: Empirical Evidence." *The Journal of Finance* 43 (2): 507–28.

Billio, Monica, Mila Getmansky, Andrew W. Lo, and Loriana Pelizzon. 2012. "Econometric Measures of Connectedness and Systemic Risk in the Finance and Insurance Sectors." *Journal of Financial Economics* 104: 535–59.

Binder, John J. 1985. "On the Use of the Multivariate Regression Model in Event Studies." *Journal of Accounting Research* 23 (1): 370–83.

Binham, Caroline. 25 April 2017. "Basel Puts New Banking Policy Initiatives on Hold Until 2019 Pending Review." *Financial Times.*

Bisias, Dimitrios, Mark Flood, Andrew W. Lo, and Stavros Valavanis. 2012. "A Survey of Systemic Risk Analytics." *Annual Review of Financial Economics* 4: 255–96.

Black, Fischer, Michael C. Jensen, and Myron Scholes. 1972. "The Capital Asset Pricing Model: Some Empirical Tests." In *Studies in the Theory of Capital Markets*, edited by Michael C. Jensen. New York: Praeger.

Black, Harold A., M. Cary Collins, and Breck L. Robinson. 2000. "The Impact of the Failure of Continental Illinois and the Too-Big-to-Fail Doctrine on Changes in Operating Efficiency." *Managerial Finance* 26 (2): 42–56.

Black, Harold A., M. Cary Collins, Breck L. Robinson, and Robert L. Schweitzer. 1997. "Changes in Market Perception of Riskiness: The Case of Too-Big-to-Fail." *Journal of Financial Research* 20 (3): 389–406.

Blankespoor, Elizabeth, Thomas J. Linsmeier, Kathy R. Petroni, and Catherine Shakespeare. 2013. "Fair Value Accounting for Financial Instruments: Does It Improve the Association Between Bank Leverage and Credit Risk?" *The Accounting Review* 88 (4): 1143–77.

Blinder, Alan S. 2010. "The Squam Lake Report: Fifteen Economists in Search of Financial Reform." *Journal of Monetary Economics* 57: 892–902.

Bliss, Robert R. 2001. "Market Discipline and Subordinated Debt: A Review of Some Salient Issues." *Economic Perspectives* 25 (1): 24–45.

Blum, Jürg. 1999. "Do Capital Adequacy Requirements Reduce Risks in Banking?" *Journal of Banking & Finance* 23: 755–71.

Blum, Jürg, and Martin Hellwig. 1995. "The Macroeconomic Implications of Capital Adequacy Requirements for Banks" 39 (739–749).

Blundell-Wignall, Adrian, and Paul E. Atkinson. 2010. "Thinking Beyond Basel III: Necessary Solutions for Capital and Liquidity." *OECD Journal: Financial Market Trends* 2010 (1): 1–23.

Blundell-Wignall, Adrian, and Paul E. Atkinson. 2012. "Deleveraging, Traditional Versus Capital Markets Banking and the Urgent Need to Separate and Recapitalise G-SIFI Banks." *OECD Journal: Financial Market Trends* 2012 (1): 1–44.

Bongini, Paola, and Laura Nieri. 2014. "Identifying and Regulating Systemically Important Financial Institutions." *Economic Notes by Banca Monte Dei Paschi Di Siena SpA* 43 (1): 39–62.

Bongini, Paola, Laura Nieri, and Matteo Pelagatti. 2015. "The Importance of Being Systemically Important Financial Institutions." *Journal of Banking & Finance* 50: 562–74.

Boot, Arnold W. A., and Anjan V. Thakor. 1997. "Financial System Architecture." *The Review of Financial Studies* 10 (3): 693–733.

Bordo, Michael D. 2003. "MARKET Discipline and Financial Crisis Policy: A Historical Perspective." *Research in Financial Services* 15: 157–82.

Bordo, Michael D., and John Landon-Lane. 2010. "The Banking Panics in the United States in the 1930s: Some Lessons for Today." *Oxford Review of Economic Policy* 26 (3): 486–509.

Bougheas, Spiros. 1999. "Contagious Bank Runs." *International Review of Economics and Finance* 8 (2): 131–46.

Bourke, Philip. 1989. "Concentration and Other Determinants of Bank Profitability in Europe, North America and Australia." *Journal of Banking & Finance* 13: 65–79.

Boyd, John H., and Mark Gertler. 1993. "U.S. Commercial Banking: Trends, Cycles, and Policy." *NBER Macroeconomics Annual* 8: 319–77.

Boyd, John H., Stanley L. Graham, and R. Shawn Hewitt. 1993. "Bank Holding Company Mergers with Nonbank Financial Firms: Effects on the Risk of Failure." *Journal of Banking & Finance* 17: 43–63.

Boyd, John H., and Amanda Heitz. 2016. "The Social Costs and Benefits of Too-Big-to-Fail Banks: A 'Bounding' Exercise." *Journal of Banking & Finance* 68: 251–65.

Boyd, John H., Kwak Sungkyu, and Bruce Smith. 2005. "The Real Output Losses Associated with Modern Banking Crises." *Journal of Money, Credit and Banking* 37 (6): 977–99.

Branch, Ben, Anurag Sharma, Chetan Chawla, and Feng Tu. 2014. "An Updated Model of Price-to-Book." *Journal of Applied Finance* 24 (1): 73–93.

Brealey, Richard A., and Stewart C. Myers. 2003. *Principles of Corporate Finance*. 7th ed. The Mcgraw-Hill/Irwin Series in Finance, Insurance, and Real Estate. Boston, Mass.; London: McGraw-Hill/Irwin.

Brewer III, Elijah, and Julapa Jagtiani. 2013. "How Much Did Banks Pay to Become Too-Big-to-Fail and to Become Systemically Important?" *Journal of Financial Services Research* 43: 1–35.

Brewer III, Elijah, and Ann Marie Klingenhagen. 2010. "Be Careful What You Wish for: The Stock Market Reactions to Bailing Out Large Financial Institutions: Evidence from the USA." *Journal of Financial Regulation and Compliance* 18 (1): 56–69.

Brief, Richard P., and Raef A. Lawson. 1992. "The Role of the Accounting Rate of Return in Financial Statement Analysis." *The Accounting Review* 67 (2): 411–26.

Brock, Philip L. 2000. "Financial Safety Nets: Lessons from Chile." *The World Bank Research Observer* 15 (1): 69–84.

Brown, Craig O., and I. Serdar Dinç. 2011. "Too Many to Fail? Evidence of Regulatory Forbearance When the Banking Sector Is Weak." *Review of Financial Studies* 24 (4): 1378–1405.

Brown, Lawrence D., and Michael S. Rozeff. 1978. "The Superiority of Analyst Forecasts as Measures of Expectations: Evidence from Earnings." *The Journal of Finance* 33 (1): 1–16.

Brown, Martin, Stefan T. Trautmann, and Razvan Vlahu. 2012. "Contagious Bank Runs: Experimental Evidence." *DNB Working Paper* 363.

Brownlees, Christian, and Robert F. Engle. 2017. "SRISK: A Conditional Capital Shortfall Measure of Systemic Risk." *The Review of Financial Studies* 30 (1): 48–79.

Brunnermeier, Markus K., and Lasse Heje Pedersen. 2009. "Market Liquidity and Funding Liquidity." *Review of Financial Studies* 22 (6): 2201–38.

Bugeja, Martin, and Natalie Gallery. 2006. "Is Older Goodwill Value Relevant?" *Accounting & Finance* 46 (4): 519–35.

Bulkley, George, Richard D. F. Harris, and Renata Herrerias. 2004. "Why Does Book-to-Market Value of Equity Forecast Cross-Section Stock Returns?" *International Review of Financial Analysis* 13: 153–60.

Calem, Paul, and Rafael Rob. 1999. "The Impact of Capital-Based Regulation on Bank Risk-Taking." *Journal of Financial Intermediation* 8: 317–52.

Calomiris, Charles W. 2013. "Reforming Banks Without Destroying Their Productivity and Value." *Journal of Applied Corporate Finance* 25 (4): 14–20.

Calomiris, Charles W., and Richard J. Herring. 2013. "How to Design a Contingent Convertible Debt Requirement That Helps Solve Our Too-Big-to-Fail Problem." *Journal of Applied Corporate Finance* 25 (2): 39–62.

Calomiris, Charles W., R. Glenn James, and Hubbard Stock. 1986. "The Farm Debt Crisis and Public Policy." *Brookings Papers on Economic Activity* 2: 441–85.

Calomiris, Charles W., and Doron Nissim. 2007. "Activity-Based Valuation of Bank Holding Companies." *NBER Working Paper* 12918.

Calomiris, Charles W., and Doron Nissim. 2014. "Crisis-Related Shifts in the Market Valuation of Banking Activities." *Journal of Financial Intermediation* 23: 400–435.

Calvo, Guillermo A. 1978. "ON the Time Consistency of Optimal Policy in a Monetary Economy." *Econometrica* 46 (6): 1411–28.

Caprio, Gerard, Luc Laeven, and Ross Levine. 2007. "Governance and Bank Valuation." *Journal of Financial Intermediation* 16: 584–617.

Carmassi, Jacopo, and Richard J. Herring. 2013. "Living Wills and Cross-Border Resolution of Systemically Important Banks." *Journal of Financial Economic Policy* 5 (4): 361–87.

Carmassi, Jacopo, and Richard J. Herring. 2014. "Corporate Structures, Transparency and Resolvability of Global Systemically Important Banks." *Financial Institutions Center at the Wharton School - Working Papers* 15 (10).

Carrington, Tim. 20 September 1984. "U.S. Won't Let 11 Biggest Banks in Nation Fall." *Wall Street Journal*, 1.

Chakrabort, Shankha, and Tridip Ray. 2006. "Bank-Based Versus Market-Based Financial Systems: A Growth-Theoretic Analysis." *Journal of Monetary Economics* 53: 329–50.

Chan, Louis K. C., Yasushi Hamao, and Josef Lakonishok. 1991. "Fundamentals and Stock Returns in Japan." *The Journal of Finance* 46 (5): 1739–64.

Chari, V. V., and Ravi Jagannathan. 1988. "Banking Panics, Information, and Rational Expectations Equilibrium." *The Journal of Finance* 43 (3): 749–61.

Chauvin, Keith W., and Mark Hirschey. 1994. "Goodwill, Profitability, and the Market Value of the Firm." *Journal of Accounting and Public Policy* 13 (2): 159–80.

Cheng, Ing-Haw, Harrison Hong, and José A. Scheinkman. 2015. "Yesterday's Heroes: Compensation and Risk at Financial Firms." *The Journal of Finance* 70 (2): 839–79.

Choi, Won W., Sung S. Kwon, and Gerald J. Lobo. 2000. "Market Valuation of Intangible Assets." *Journal of Business Research* 49: 35–45.

Chow, Julian T. S., and Jay Surti. 2011. "Making Banks Safer: Can Volcker and Vickers Do It?" *IMF Working Papers* 11 (236).

Christiansen, Hans. 2001. "Moral Hazard and International Financial Crises in the 1990s." *OECD Journal: Financial Market Trends* 78: 115–40.

Churyk, Natalie Tatiana. 2005. "Reporting Goodwill: Are the New Accounting Standards Consistent with Market Valuations?" *Journal of Business Research* 58: 1353–61.

Cifuentes, Rodrigo, Gianluigi Ferrucci, and Hyun Song Shin. 2005. "Liquidity Risk and Contagion." *Journal of the European Economic Association* 3 (2/3): 556–66.

Clarkson, Peter, J. Douglas Hanna, Gordon D. Richardson, and Rex Thompson. 2011. "The Impact of IFRS Adoption on the Value Relevance of Book Value and Earnings." *Journal of Contemporary Accounting & Economics* 7: 1–17.

Coase, Ronald H. 1937. "The Nature of the Firm." *Economica* 4 (16): 386–405.

Coase, Ronald H. 1960. "The Problem of Social Cost." *Journal of Law and Economics* 3: 1–44.

Cobbs, John. 27 January 1975. "When Companies Get Too Big to Fail." *Business Week*, 16.

Cohen, Jacob. 1988. *Statistical Power Analysis for the Behavioral Sciences*. 2nd ed. Hillsdale, N.J.: Lawrence Erlbaum Associates.

Cohen, Jacob. 1990. "Things I Have Learned (so Far)." *American Psychologist* 45 (12): 1304–12.

Cohen, Jacob, and Patricia Cohen. 1983. *Applied Multiple Regression Correlation Analysis for the Behavioral Sciences*. 2nd ed. Hillsdale, N.J.: Lawrence Erlbaum Associates.

Collins, Daniel W., and S. P. Kothari. 1989. "AN Analysis of Intertemporal and Cross-Sectional Determinants of Earnings Response Coefficients." *Journal of Accounting and Economics* 11: 143–81.

Committee on Banking, Finance and Urban Affairs. 18–19 September and 4 October 1984. "Inquiry into Continental Illinois Corp. and Continental Illinois National Bank." https://fraser.stlouisfed.org/docs/historical/house/house_cinb1984.pdf.

Cooper, Michael J., William E. Jackson III, and Gary A. Patterson. 2003. "Evidence of Predictability in the Cross-Section of Bank Stock Returns." *Journal of Banking & Finance* 27: 817–50.

Cooper, Russell, and Thomas W. Ross. 2002. "Bank Runs: Deposit Insurance and Capital Requirements." *International Economic Review* 43 (1): 55–72.

Cordella, Tito, and Eduardo Levy Yeyati. 2003. "Bank Bailouts: Moral Hazard Vs. Value Effect." *Journal of Financial Intermediation* 12: 300–330.

Creswell, John W. 2014. *Research Design: Qualitative, Quantitative, and Mixed Methods Approaches*. 4th ed. Los Angeles, Calif.: SAGE.

Cubillas, Elena, Ana I. Fernández, and Francisco González. 2016. "How Credible Is a Too-Big-to-Fail Policy? International Evidence from Market Discipline." *Journal of Financial Intermediation* 29: 46–67.

Çelik, Şaban. 2012. "Theoretical and Empirical Review of Asset Pricing Models: A Structural Synthesis." *International Journal of Economics and Financial Issues* 2 (2): 141–78.

Dagher, Jihad, Giovanni Dell'Ariccia, Luc Laeven, Lev Ratnovski, and Hui Tong. 2016. "Benefits and Costs of Bank Capital." *IMF Staff Discussion Note* 16 (4).

Damodaran, Aswath. 2012. *Investment Valuation: Tools and Techniques for Determining the Value of Any Asset*. 3rd ed. Wiley Finance. Hoboken, N.J.: John Wiley & Sons.

Davies, Richard, and Belinda Tracey. 2014. "Too Big to Be Efficient? The Impact of Implicit Subsidies on Estimates of Scale Economies for Banks." *Journal of Money, Credit and Banking* Supplement to Vol. 46 (1): 219–53.

De Bandt, Olivier, and Philipp Hartmann. 2000. "Systemic Risk: A Survey." *European Central Bank – Working Paper Series* 35.

De Bondt, Werner. 2010. "The Crisis of 2008 and Financial Reform." *Qualitative Research in Financial Markets* 2 (3): 137–56.

DeFerrari, Lisa M., and David E. Palmer. 2001. "Supervision of Large Complex Banking Organizations." *Federal Reserve Bulletin* February: 47–57.

Degryse, Hans, Moshe Kim, and Steven Ongena. 2009. *Microeconometrics of Banking: Methods, Applications, and Results*. Oxford: Oxford University Press.

de Haan, Jakob, Sander Oosterloo, and Dirk Schoenmaker. 2015. *Financial Markets and Institutions: A European Perspective*. 3rd ed. Cambridge: Cambridge University Press.

Deli, Yota D., and Iftekhar Hasan. 2017. "Real Effects of Bank Capital Regulations: Global Evidence." *Journal of Banking & Finance* 82: 217–28.

DeLong, Gayle L. 2001. "Stockholder Gains from Focusing Versus Diversifying Bank Mergers." *Journal of Financial Economics* 59: 221–52.

Demirgüç-Kunt, Asli, and Enrica Detragiache. 2002. "Does Deposit Insurance Increase Banking System Stability? An Empirical Investigation." *Journal of Monetary Economics* 49: 1373–1406.

Demirgüç-Kunt, Asli, Enrica Detragiache, and Ouarda Merrouche. 2013. "Bank Capital: Lessons from the Financial Crisis." *Journal of Money, Credit and Banking* 45 (6): 1147–64.

Demirgüç-Kunt, Asli, and Harry Huizinga. 2013. "Are Banks Too Big to Fail or Too Big to Save? International Evidence from Equity Prices and CDS Spreads." *Journal of Banking & Finance* 37: 875–94.

Demirgüç-Kunt, Asli, Edward Kane, and Harry Huizinga. 1999. "Determinants of Commercial Bank Interest Margins and Profitability: Some International Evidence." *The World Bank Economic Review* 13 (2): 379–408.

Demirgüç-Kunt, Asli, and Edward J. Kane. 2002. "Deposit Insurance Around the Globe: Where Does It Work?" *Journal of Economic Perspectives* 16 (2): 175–95.

Demirgüç-Kunt, Asli, Edward J. Kane, and Luc Laeven. 2008. "Determinants of Deposit-Insurance Adoption and Design." *Journal of Financial Intermediation* 17: 407–38.

Demirgüç-Kunt, Asli, Edward Kane, and Luc Laeven. 2014. "Deposit Insurance Database." *IMF Working Papers* 14 (118).

Demirgüç-Kunt, Asli, Luc Laeven, and Ross Levine. 2004. "Regulations, Market Structure, Institutions, and the Cost of Financial Intermediation." *Journal of Money, Credit and Banking* 36 (3): 593–622.

Demsetz, Harold. 1967. "Toward a Theory of Property Rights." *The American Economic Review* 57 (2): 347–59.

Demsetz, Rebecca S., Marc R. Saidenberg, and Philip E. Strahan. 1996. "Banks with Something to Lose: The Disciplinary Role of Franchise Value." *Economic Policy Review* 2 (2): 1–14.

Demsetz, Rebecca S., and Philip E. Strahan. 1997. "Diversification, Size, and Risk at Bank Holding Companies." *Journal of Money, Credit and Banking* 29 (3): 300–313.

Denk, Oliver, Sebastian Schich, and Boris Cournède. 2014. "Why Implicit Bank Debt Guarantees Matter: Some Empirical Evidence." *OECD Journal: Financial Market Trends* 2014 (2).

Dermine, Jean. 2014. *Bank Valuation and Value-Based Management: Deposit and Loan Pricing, Performance Evaluation, and Risk*. 2nd ed. McGraw-Hill Education.

Deutsche Bank. 4 April 2016. "A Short European Banks Primer." *Markets Research.*

De Vincentiis, Paola. 2013. "Does the Status of G-SIB Make Any Difference for International Investors?" *Annual International Conference on Qualitative & Quantitative Economics Research*, 114–21.

De Vries, C. G. 2005. "The Simple Economics of Bank Fragility." *Journal of Banking & Finance* 29 (4): 803–25.

Dewatripont, M., and Jean Tirole. 1994. *The Prudential Regulation of Banks*. Cambridge, Mass.; London: MIT Press.

Dewenter, Kathryn L., and Alan C. Hess. October 2013. "The Financial Stability Board and Global Systemically Important Banks: Unintended Consequences?" https://ssrn.com/abstract=2338665.

DeYoung, Robert. 1993. "Determinants of Cost Efficiencies in Bank Mergers." *Office of the Comptroller of the Currency, E&PA Working Paper* 93 (1).

DeYoung, Robert. 2010. "Scale Economies Are a Distraction." *The Region* 24 (3): 14–16.

DeYoung, Robert, Douglas D. Evanoff, and Philip Molyneux. 2009. "Mergers and Acquisitions of Financial Institutions: A Review of the Post-2000 Literature." *Journal of Financial Services Research* 36 (2/3): 87–110.

Diamond, Douglas W. 1984. "Financial Intermediation and Delegated Monitoring." *The Review of Economic Studies* 51 (3): 393–414.

Diamond, Douglas W., and Philip H. Dybvig. 1983. "Bank Runs, Deposit Insurance, and Liquidity." *Journal of Political Economy* 91 (3): 401–19.

Diamond, Douglas W., and Raghuram G. Rajan. 2000. "A Theory of Bank Capital." *The Journal of Finance* 55 (6): 2431–65.

Dietrich, Andreas, and Gabrielle Wanzenried. 2011. "Determinants of Bank Profitability Before and During the Crisis: Evidence from Switzerland." *Journal of International Financial Markets, Institutions & Money* 21: 307–27.

Dimson, Elroy, and Massoud Mussavian. 1999. "Three Centuries of Asset Pricing." *Journal of Banking & Finance* 23: 1745–69.

Duffie, Darrell. 2010. "The Failure Mechanics of Dealer Banks." *Journal of Economic Perspectives* 24 (1): 51–72.

Edmonds, Timothy. 30 December 2013. "The Independent Commission on Banking: The Vickers Report." https://researchbriefings.files.parliament.uk/documents/SN06171/SN06171.pdf.

Eisenhardt, Kathleen M. 1989. "Agency Theory: An Assessment and Review." *Academy of Management Review* 14 (1): 57–74.

Elliott, John A., and Hanna J. Douglas. 1991. "The Evaluation by the Financial Markets of Changes in Bank Loan Loss Reserve Levels." *Accounting Review* 66 (4): 847–61.

Ellis, Luci, Andy Haldane, and Fariborz Moshirian. 2014. "Systemic Risk, Governance and Global Financial Stability." *Journal of Banking & Finance* 45: 175–81.

Elsas, Ralf, Andreas Hackethal, and Markus Holzhäuser. 2010. "The Anatomy of Bank Diversification." *Journal of Banking & Finance* 34: 1274–87.

Ely, Kirsten, and Gregory Waymire. 1999. "Intangible Assets and Stock Prices in the Pre-SEC Era." *Journal of Accounting Research* 37 (3): 17–44.

Engle, Robert, Eric Jondeau, and Michael Rockinger. 2015. "Systemic Risk in Europe." *Review of Finance* 19 (1): 145–90.

Ennis, Huberto M., and H. S. Malek. 2005. "Bank Risk of Failure and the Too-Big-to-Fail Policy." *Economic Quarterly* 91 (2): 21–44.

Enrich, David, and Monica Langley. 23 February 2009. "U.S. Eyes Large Stake in Citi." *The Wall Street Journal.* https://www.wsj.com/articles/SB123535148618845005.

European Banking Authority (EBA). 25 April 2016. "EBA Discloses First List of O-SIIs in the EU." https://www.eba.europa.eu/-/eba-discloses-first-list-of-o-siis-in-the--1.

European Central Bank. "Banking Union." https://www.bankingsupervision.europa.eu/about/bankingunion/html/index.en.html.

European Systemic Risk Board (ESRB). June 2015. "Report on Misconduct Risk in the Banking Sector." https://www.esrb.europa.eu/pub/pdf/other/150625_report_misconduct_risk.en.pdf.

Fairfield, Patricia M. 1994. "P/E, P/B and the Present Value of Future Dividends." *Financial Analysts Journal* 50 (4): 23–31.

Fairfield, Patricia M., Richard J. Sweeney, and Teri Lombardi Yohn. 1996. "Accounting Classification and the Predictive Content of Earnings." *The Accounting Review* 71 (3): 337–55.

Fama, Eugene F., Lawrence Fisher, Michael C. Jensen, and Richard Roll. 1969. "The Adjustment of Stock Prices to New Information." *International Economic Review* 10 (1): 1–21.

Fama, Eugene F., and Kenneth R. French. 1992. "The Cross-Section of Expected Stock Returns." *The Journal of Finance* 47 (2): 427–65.

Fama, Eugene F., and Kenneth R. French. 1993. "Common Risk Factors in the Returns on Stocks and Bonds." *Journal of Financial Economics* 33: 3–56.

Fama, Eugene F., and Kenneth R. French. 1995. "Size and Book-to-Market Factors in Earnings and Returns." *The Journal of Finance* 50 (1): 131–55.

Fama, Eugene F., and James D. MacBeth. 1973. "Risk, Return, and Equilibrium: Empirical Tests." *Journal of Political Economy* 81 (3): 607–36.

Fecht, Falko, and Wolf Wagner. 2009. "The Marketability of Bank Assets, Managerial Rents and Banking Stability." *Journal of Financial Stability* 5 (3): 272–82.

Federal Deposit Insurance Corporation (FDIC). 1984. "The First Fifty Years: A History of the FDIC 1933–1983." Washington, D.C.: Federal Deposit Insurance Corporation. https://www.fdic.gov/bank/analytical/firstfifty/.

Federal Deposit Insurance Corporation (FDIC). 1997. "History of the Eighties – Lessons for the Future." Edited by George Hanc. Federal Deposit Insurance Corporation. https://www.fdic.gov/bank/historical/history/vol1.html.

Federal Deposit Insurance Corporation (FDIC). 1998. *Managing the Crisis: The FDIC and RTC Experience 1980–1994.*

Federal Deposit Insurance Corporation (FDIC). August 2014. "TBTF Subsidy for Large Banks–Literature Review." https://www.fdic.gov/news/news/speeches/literature-review.pdf.

Federal Deposit Insurance Corporation (FDIC). 23 December 2014. "Resolutions Handbook." https://www.fdic.gov/about/freedom/drr_handbook.pdf.

Federal Deposit Insurance Corporation (FDIC) & Bank of England (BoE). 10 December 2012. "Resolving Globally Active, Systemically Important, Financial Institutions." https://www.bankofengland.co.uk/publications/Documents/news/2012/nr156.pdf.

Federal Reserve Bank of Minneapolis. 16 November 2016. "The Minneapolis Plan to End Too Big to Fail." https://www.minneapolisfed.org/~/media/files/publications/studies/endingtbtf/the-minneapolis-plan/the-minneapolis-plan-to-end-too-big-to-fail-2016.pdf.

Federal Reserve Committee on Branch, Group, and Chain Banking. 1930. "Branch Banking in the United States." https://fraser.stlouisfed.org/docs/historical/federal%20reserve%20history/frcom_br_gp_ch_banking/branch_banking_us.pdf.

Feldstein, Martin S., ed. 1991. *The Risk of Economic Crisis*. A National Bureau of Economic Research Conference Report. Chicago; London: University of Chicago Press.

Fender, Ingo, and Patrick McGuire. 2010. "Bank Structure, Funding Risk and the Transmission of Shocks Across Countries: Concepts and Measurement." *BIS Quarterly Review* September: 63–79.

Feng, Guohua, and Apostolos Serletis. 2010. "Efficiency, Technical Change, and Returns to Scale in Large US Banks: Panel Data Evidence from an Output Distance Function Satisfying Theoretical Regularity." *Journal of Banking & Finance* 34 (1): 127–38.

Fieberg, Christian, Finn Marten Körner, Jörg Prokop, and Armin Varmaz. 2015. "Big Is Beautiful: The Information Content of Bank Rating Changes." *The Journal of Risk Finance* 16 (3): 233–52.

Field, Andy P. 2009. *Discovering Statistics Using SPSS*. 3rd ed. Introducing Statistical Methods. Los Angeles i.e. Thousand Oaks, Calif.; London: SAGE Publications.

Financial Services Authority (FSA). March 2009. "The Turner Review: A Regulatory Response to the Global Banking Crisis." https://www.fsa.gov.uk/pubs/other/turner_review.pdf.

Financial Stability Board (FSB). 25 September 2009. "Improving Financial Regulation: Report of the Financial Stability Board to G20 Leaders."

Financial Stability Board (FSB).2 November 2010. "Intensity and Effectiveness of SIFI Supervision: Recommendations for Enhanced Supervision." https://www.fsb.org/wp-content/uploads/r_101101.pdf.

Financial Stability Board (FSB). 4 November 2011. "Policy Measures to Address Systemically Important Financial Institutions." https://www.fsb.org/wp-content/uploads/Policy-Measures-to-Address-Systemically-Important-Financial-Institutions.pdf.

Financial Stability Board (FSB). 1 November 2012. "Update of Group of Global Systemically Important Banks (G-SIBs)." https://www.fsb.org/wp-content/uploads/r_121031ac.pdf.

Financial Stability Board (FSB). 2 September 2013. "Progress and Next Steps Towards Ending 'Too-Big-to-Fail' (TBTF): Report of the Financial Stability Board to the G-20." https://www.fsb.org/wp-content/uploads/r_130902.pdf.

Financial Stability Board (FSB). 11 November 2013. "2013 Update of Group of Global Systemically Important Banks (G-SIBs)." https://www.fsb.org/wp-content/uploads/r_131111.pdf.

Financial Stability Board (FSB). 6 November 2014. "2014 Update of List of Global Systemically Important Banks (G-SIBs)." https://www.fsb.org/wp-content/uploads/r_141106b.pdf.

Financial Stability Board (FSB). 10 November 2014. "Adequacy of Loss-Absorbing Capacity of Global Systemically Important Banks in Resolution: Consultative Document." https://www.fsb.org/wp-content/uploads/TLAC-Condoc-6-Nov-2014-FINAL.pdf.

Financial Stability Board (FSB). 3 November 2015. "2015 Update of List of Global Systemically Important Banks (G-SIBs)." https://www.fsb.org/wp-content/uploads/2015-update-of-list-of-global-systemically-important-banks-G-SIBs.pdf.

Financial Stability Board (FSB). 9 November 2015. "FSB Issues Final Total Loss-Absorbing Capacity Standard for Global Systemically Important Banks." https://www.financialstability-board.org/wp-content/uploads/20151106-TLAC-Press-Release.pdf.

Financial Stability Board (FSB). 21 November 2016. "2016 List of Global Systemically Important Banks (G-Sibs)." https://www.fsb.org/wp-content/uploads/2016-list-of-global-systemically-important-banks-G-SIBs.pdf.

Flannery, Mark J. 2001. "The Faces of 'Market Discipline'." *Journal of Financial Services Research* 20 (107): 107–19.

Flannery, Mark J., and Sorin M. Sorescu. 1996. "Evidence of Bank Market Discipline in Subordinated Debenture Yields: 1983-1991." *The Journal of Finance* 51 (4): 1347–77.

Ford, Jonathan. 17 April 2016. "Why Megabanks Do Not Want to Think About Death." *Financial Times*. https://www.ft.com/content/fa8bd3a2-0476-11e6-a70d-4e39ac32c284.

Fratianni, Michele, and Francesco Marchionne. 2013. "The Banking Bailout of the Subprime Crisis: Was the Bang Worth the Buck?" *Journal of International Financial Markets, Institutions & Money* 23: 240–64.

Freixas, Xavier. 23 June 1999. "Optimal Bail Out Policy, Conditionality and Constructive Ambiguity." https://papers.ssrn.com/sol3/papers.cfm?abstract_id=199054.

Freixas, Xavier. 2010. "Post-Crisis Challenges to Bank Regulation." *Economic Policy* 25 (62): 375–99.

Freixas, Xavier, Curzio Giannini, Glenn Hoggarth, and Farouk Soussa. 2000. "Lender of Last Resort: What Have We Learned Since Bagehot?" *Journal of Financial Services Research* 18 (1): 63–84.

Freixas, Xavier, and Jean-Charles Rochet. 2008. *Microeconomics of Banking*. 2nd ed. Cambridge, Mass.; London: MIT Press.

French, Kenneth R., Martin N. Baily, John Y. Campbell, John H. Cochrane, Douglas W. Diamond, Darrell Duffie, Anil K. Kashyap, et al. 2010a. *The Squam Lake Report: Fixing the Financial System*. Princeton, N.J.; Woodstock: Princeton University Press.

French, Kenneth R., Martin N. Baily, John Y. Campbell, John H. Cochrane, Douglas W. Diamond, Darrell Duffie, Anil K. Kashyap, et al. 2010b. "The Squam Lake Report: Fixing the Financial System." *Journal of Applied Corporate Finance* 22 (3): 8–21.

Friedman, Milton, and Anna Jacobson Schwartz. 1963. *A Monetary History of the United States 1867-1960*. Princeton: Princeton University Press.

Frost, Stephen M. 2004. *The Bank Analyst's Handbook: Money, Risk, and Conjuring Tricks*. Chichester: John Wiley & Sons.

Furfine, Craig. 2006. "The Costs and Benefits of Moral Suasion: Evidence from the Rescue of Long-Term Capital Management." *Journal of Business* 79 (2): 593–622.

Furlong, Frederick T., and Michael C. Keeley. 1989. "Capital Regulation and Rank Risk-Taking: A Note." *Journal of Banking & Finance* 13: 883–91.

Furlong, Frederick T., and Simon Kwan. April 2005. "Market-to-Book, Charter Value, and Bank Risk-Taking – a Recent Perspective." https://www.bis.org/bcbs/events/rtf05Kwan.pdf.

Gambacorta, Leonardo, and Paolo Emilio Mistrulli. 2004. "Does Bank Capital Affect Lending Behavior?" *Journal of Financial Intermediation* 13: 436–57.

Gandhi, Priyank, and Hanno Lustig. 2015. "Size Anomalies in U.S. Bank Stock Returns." *The Journal of Finance* 70 (2): 733–68.

Gao, Yu, Scott Liao, and Xue Wang. 2017. "Capital Markets' Assessment of the Economic Impact of the Dodd–Frank Act on Systemically Important Financial Firms." *Journal of Banking & Finance* In press.

Garcia, Gillian G. H. 1999. "Deposit Insurance: A Survey of Actual and Best Practices." *IMF Working Papers* 99 (54): 1–49.

Garel, Alexandre, and Arthur Petit-Romec. 2017. "Bank Capital in the Crisis: It's Not Just How Much You Have but Who Provides It." *Journal of Banking & Finance* 75: 152–66.

Gennotte, Gerard, and David Pyle. 1991. "Capital Controls and Bank Risk." *Journal of Banking & Finance* 15: 805–324.

Gilbert, R. Alton, and Levis A. Kochin. 1989. "Local Economic Effects of Bank Failures." *Journal of Financial Services Research* 3 (4): 333–45.

Goddard, John, Philip Molyneux, and John O. S. Wilson. 2004. "The Profitability of European Banks: A Cross-Sectional and Dynamic Panel Analysis." *The Manchester School* 72 (3): 363–81.

Goetzmann, William N., and Philippe Jorion. 1993. "Testing the Predictive Power of Dividend Yield." *The Journal of Finance* 48 (2): 663–79.

Goldman Sachs. 5 January 2015. "New Capital Rules Reignite the JPM Breakup Debate." *Equity Research.*

Goodhart, C. A. E., and H. Huang. 2000. "A Simple Model of an International Lender of Last Resort." *Economic Notes by Banca Monte Dei Paschi Di Siena SpA* 29 (1): 1–11.

Goodhart, Charles A. E., and Haizhou Huang. 2005. "The Lender of Last Resort." *Journal of Banking & Finance* 29 (5): 1059–82.

Gordon, Myron J., and Eli Shapiro. 1956. "CAPITAL Equipment Analysis: THE Required Rate of Profit." *Management Science* 3 (1): 102–10.

Gorton, Gary, and Anthony M. Santomero. 1990. "Market Discipline and Bank Subordinated Debt: Note." *Journal of Money, Credit and Banking* 22 (1): 119–28.

Górnicka, Lucyna A., and Marius A. Zoican. 2016. "Too-International-to-Fail? Supranational Bank Resolution and Market Discipline." *Journal of Banking & Finance* 65: 41–58.

Greene, William H. 2002. *Econometric Analysis*. 5th ed. Upper Saddle River, NJ: Prentice Hall.

Grochulski, Borys. 2011. "Financial Firm Resolution Policy as a Time-Consistency Problem." *Economic Quarterly* 97 (2): 133–52.

Gropp, Reint, Christian Gruendl, and Andre Guettler. 2014. "The Impact of Public Guarantees on Bank Risk-Taking: Evidence from a Natural Experiment." *Review of Finance* 18 (2): 457–88.

Gropp, Reint, Hendrik Hakenes, and Isabel Schnabel. 2010. "Competition, Risk-Shifting, and Public Bail-Out Policies." *Max Planck Institute for Research on Collective Goods* 5.

Gropp, Reint, and Jukka Vesala. 2004. "Deposit Insurance, Moral Hazard and Market Monitoring." *Review of Finance* 8 (4): 571–602.

Gross, Stephanie. 2006. *Banks and Shareholder Value: An Overview of Bank Valuation and Empirical Evidence on Shareholder Value for Banks*. Gabler Ed. Wissenschaft. Wiesbaden: Deutscher Universitäts-Verlag.

Grossman, Sanford J., and Oliver D. Hart. 1986. "The Costs and Benefits of Ownership: A Theory of Vertical and Lateral Integration." *Journal of Political Economy* 94 (4): 691–719.

Guerry, Nicolas, and Martin Wallmeier. 2017. "Valuation of Diversified Banks: New Evidence." *Journal of Banking & Finance* 80: 203–14.

Gup, Benton E. 2004. "What Does Too Big to Fail Mean?" In *Too Big to Fail: Policies and Practices in Government Bailouts*, edited by Benton E. Gup. Westport, Conn.; London: Praeger.

Haldane, Andrew G. 30 March 2010. "The $100 Billion Question." Institute of Regulation; Risk, Hong Kong. https://www.bis.org/review/r100406d.pdf.

Haldane, Andrew G. 2012. "Control Rights (and Wrongs)." *Economic Affairs* 32 (2): 47–58.

Haldane, Andrew G., and Vasileios Madouros, eds. 31 August 2012. *The Dog and the Frisbee*.

Hale, Thomas. 30 March 2016. "European Banks: New Rules, Old Problems: The Wiping of Billions of Novo Banco Debt May Mark a New Era in Which Bank Bondholders Are No Longer King." *Financial Times*.

Hale, Thomas, Caroline Binham, and Laura Noonan. 9 November 2015. "Global Banks Must Raise EUR1.1tn in Special Debt by 2022." *Financial Times*. https://www.ft.com/content/10ec3f08-863f-11e5-90de-f44762bf9896.

Hammami, Yacine, and Anna Lindahl. 2014. "An Intertemporal Capital Asset Pricing Model with Bank Credit Growth as a State Variable." *Journal of Banking & Finance* 39: 14–28.

Hansen, Lars Peter. 2014. "Challenges in Identifying and Measuring Systemic Risk." In *Risk Topography*, edited by Markus Konrad Brunnermeier and Arvind Krishnamurthy, 15–30. National Bureau of Economic Research Conference Report. Chicago; London: University of Chicago Press.

Hanson, Samuel G., Anil K. Kashyap, and Jeremy C. Stein. 2011. "A Macroprudential Approach to Financial Regulation." *Journal of Economic Perspectives* 25 (1): 3–28.

Harasim, Janina. 2008. "THE Role of Intangible Assets in Banks Competitiveness and Effectiveness." *Journal of Economics & Management* 4: 42–57.

Harris, Robert S., and Felicia C. Marston. 1994. "Value Versus Growth Stocks: Book-to-Market, Growth, and Beta." *Financial Analysts Journal* 50 (5): 18–24.

Hellwig, Martin F. 1998. "Systemische Risiken Im Finanzsektor." *Sonderforschungsbereich 504, University of Mannheim* 30: 1–31.

Hetzel, Robert L. 1991. "Too Big to Fail: Origins, Consequences, and Outlook." *Federal Reserve Bank of Richmond – Economic Review*, 1–15.

Hilscher, Jens, and Alon Raviv. 2014. "Bank Stability and Market Discipline: The Effect of Contingent Capital on Risk Taking and Default Probability." *Journal of Corporate Finance* 29: 542–60.

Hirschey, Mark, and Vernon J. Richardson. 2002. "Information Content of Accounting Goodwill Numbers." *Journal of Accounting and Public Policy* 21: 173–91.

Hodrick, Robert J. 1992. "Dividend Yields and Expected Stock Returns: Alternative Procedures for Inference and Measurement." *Review of Financial Studies* 5 (2): 357–86.

Hoggarth, Glenn, Patricia Jackson, and Erlend Nier. 2005. "Banking Crises and the Design of Safety Nets." *Journal of Banking & Finance* 29: 143–59.

Hoggarth, Glenn, Ricardo Reis, and Victoria Saporta. 2002. "Costs of Banking System Instability: Some Empirical Evidence." *Journal of Banking & Finance* 26: 825–55.

Homma, Tetsushi, Yoshiro Tsutsui, and Hirofumi Uchida. 2014. "Firm Growth and Efficiency in the Banking Industry: A New Test of the Efficient Structure Hypothesis." *Journal of Banking & Finance* 40: 143–53.

Honohan, Patrick, and Daniela Klingebiel. 2003. "The Fiscal Cost Implications of an Accommodating Approach to Banking Crises." *Journal of Banking & Finance* 27: 1539–60.

Hoover, Herbert. 1952. *The Great Depression: 1929–1941*. New York: The Macmillan Company.

Huang, Xin, Hao Zhou, and Haibin Zhu. 2009. "A Framework for Assessing the Systemic Risk of Major Financial Institutions." *Journal of Banking & Finance* 33: 2036–49.

Huertas, Thomas F. 2 October 2009. "Too Big to Fail, Too Complex to Contemplate: What to Do About Systemically Important Firms." https://www.lse.ac.uk/fmg/documents/events/conferences/2009/tooBig/Huertas.pdf.

Huertas, Thomas F. 2014. *Safe to Fail: How Resolution Will Revolutionise Banking*. Hampshire; New York: Palgrave Macmillan.

Hughes, Joseph P., and Loretta J. Mester. 1993. "A Quality and Risk-Adjusted Cost Function for Banks: Evidence on the 'Too-Big-to-Fail' Doctrine." *Journal of Productivity Analysis* 4 (3): 293–315.

Hughes, Joseph P., and Loretta J. Mester. 2013. "Who Said Large Banks Don't Experience Scale Economies? Evidence from a Risk-Return-Driven Cost Function." *Journal of Financial Intermediation* 22: 559–85.

Hughes, Joseph P., Loretta J. Mester, and Choon-Geol Moon. 2001. "Are Scale Economies in Banking Elusive or Illusive? Evidence Obtained by Incorporating Capital Structure and Risk-Taking into Models of Bank Production." *Journal of Banking & Finance* 25 (12): 2169–2208.

Huizinga, Harry, and Luc Laeven. 2012. "Bank Valuation and Accounting Discretion During a Financial Crisis." *Journal of Financial Economics* 106: 614–34.

Ignatowski, Magdalena, and Josef Korte. 2015. "Wishful Thinking or Effective Threat? Tightening Bank Resolution Regimes and Bank Risk-Taking." *Journal of Financial Stability* 14: 264–81.

Imam, Shahed, Richard Barker, and Colin Clubb. 2008. "The Use of Valuation Models by UK Investment Analysts." *European Accounting Review* 17 (3): 503–35.

Imbierowicz, Björn, and Christian Rauch. 2014. "The Relationship Between Liquidity Risk and Credit Risk in Banks." *Journal of Banking & Finance* 40: 242–56.

Independent Commission on Banking. September 2011. "Final Report: Recommendations." https://www.ecgi.org/documents/icb_final_report_12sep2011.pdf.

International Monetary Fund (IMF). June 2010. "A Fair and Substantial Contribution by the Financial Sector: Final Report for the G-20." https://www.imf.org/external/np/g20/pdf/062710b.pdf.

International Monetary Fund (IMF). April 2014. "Global Financial Stability Report: Moving from Liquidity- to Growth-Driven Markets." https://www.imf.org/External/Pubs/FT/GFSR/2014/01/pdf/text.pdf.

Iwanicz-Drozdowska, Małgorzata. 2014. "Global Systemically Important Banks – How to Identify and Regulate Them?" *Journal of Economics & Management* 18: 145–58.

Jablecki, Juliusz. 2009. "The Impact of Basel I Capital Requirements on Bank Behavior and the Efficacy of Monetary Policy." *International Journal of Economic Sciences & Applied Research* 2 (1): 16–35.

Jacklin, Charles J., and Sudipto Bhattacharya. 1988. "Distinguishing Panics and Information-Based Bank Runs: Welfare and Policy Implications." *Journal of Political Economy* 96 (3): 568–92.

Jagtiani, Julapa, Georg G. Kaufman, and Catharine Lemieux. 2002. "The Effect of Credit Risk on Bank and Bank Holding Company Bond Yields: Evidence from the Post-FDICIA Period." *Journal of Financial Research* 25 (4): 559–75.

Jarque, Arantxa, and David A. Price. 2015. "Living Wills: A Tool for Curbing Too Big to Fail." *Economic Quarterly* 101 (1): 77–94.

Jayaratine, Jith, and Donald P. Morgan. 2000. "Capital Market Frictions and Deposit Constraints at Banks." *Journal of Money, Credit and Banking* 32 (1): 74–92.

Jenkins, Patrick. 1 November 2010. "Regulators Outline Banking Blueprint." *Financial Times*. https://www.ft.com/cms/s/0/f658affc-e5f1-11df-af15-00144feabdc0.html.

Jenkins, Patrick. 18 April 2016. "Bank Bondholders Need Rights Like Shareholders." *Financial Times*.

Jenkins, Patrick. 31 August 2017. "A Decade on from the Financial Crisis, What Have We Learnt?" *Financial Times*.

Jenkins, Patrick, and Paul J. Davies. 30 November 2009. "Thirty Groups on Systemic Risk List." *Financial Times*. https://www.ft.com/cms/s/0/c680e0da-dd4e-11de-ad60-00144feabdc0.html.

Jennings, Ross, John Robinson, Thompson II B. Thompson II, and Linda Duvall. 1996. "The Relation Between Accounting Goodwill Numbers and Equity Values." *Journal of Business Finance & Accounting* 23 (4): 513–33.

Jensen, Michael C., and William H. Meckling. 1976. "Theory of the Firm: Managerial Behavior, Agency Costs and Ownership Structure." *Journal of Financial Economics* 3 (4): 305–60.

Johnson, Mark A., and Abdullah Mamun. 2012. "The Failure of Lehman Brothers and Its Impact on Other Financial Institutions." *Applied Financial Economics* 22 (5): 375–85.

Johnston, R. Barry, Effie Psalida, Phil de Imus, Jeanne Gobat, Mangal Goswami, Christian Mulder, and Francisco Vazquez. 2009. "Addressing Information Gaps." *IMF Staff Position Note* 9 (6).

Jones, Jeffrey S., Scott A. Miller, and Timothy J. Yeager. 2011. "Charter Value, Tobin's Q and Bank Risk During the Subprime Financial Crisis." *Journal of Economics and Business* 63: 372–91.

Jopson, Barney, and Lauren Leatherby. 13 March 2017. "FT Explainer: Dodd-Frank picked to pieces: Wholesale Abolition Is Unlikely but Parts of the Act Are More Vulnerable Than Others." *Financial Times*.

Jopson, Barney, Courtney Weaver, and Ben McLannahan. 8 April 2016. "Explaining Bernie Sanders' 'Too Big to Fail' Plan." *Financial Times*. https://www.ft.com/content/8a176bc0-fda2-11e5-a31a-7930bacb3f5f.

Jorda, Oscar, Bjorn Richter, Moritz Schularick, and Alan M. Taylor. 2017. "Bank Capital Redux: Solvency, Liquidity, and Crisis." *Federal Reserve Bank of San Francisco Working Paper Series* 6.

Jordan, Dan J., Rice Douglas, Jacques Sanchez, and Donald H. Wort. 2011. "Explaining Bank Market-to-Book Ratios: Evidence from 2006 to 2009." *Journal of Banking & Finance* 35: 2047–55.

Jordan, Linda. 2014. "The Inadequacy of Regulation F in Effectively Reducing Systemic Risk Post FDICIA." *Fordham Journal of Corporate & Financial Law* 19 (2): 425–54.

Kacperczyk, Marcin, and Philipp Schnabl. 2010. "When Safe Proved Risky: Commercial Paper During the Financial Crisis of 2007–2009." *Journal of Economic Perspectives* 24 (1): 29–50.

Kane, Edward J. 1986. "Appearance and Reality in Deposit Insurance." *Journal of Banking & Finance* 10 (2/3): 175–88.

Kane, Edward J. 1987. "Dangers of Capital Forbearance: The Case of the FSLIC and 'Zombie' S&Ls." *Contemporary Economic Policy* 5 (1): 77–83.

Kane, Edward J. 1996. "Opportunity Cost of Capital Forbearance During the Final Years of the FSLIC Mess." *The Quarterly Review of Economics and Finance* 36 (3): 271–90.

Kane, Edward J. 2000. "Incentives for Banking Megamergers: What Motives Might Regulators Infer from Event-Study Evidence?" *Journal of Money, Credit & Banking* 32 (3): 671–701.

Kane, Edward J. 2001. "Dynamic Inconsistency of Capital Forbearance: Long-Run Vs. Short-Run Effects of Too-Big-to-Fail Policymaking." *Pacific-Basin Finance Journal* 9 (4): 281–99.

Kane, Edward J. 2015. "Perspectives on Banking and Banking Crises." *Banking & Financial Services Policy Report* 34 (5): 10–16.

Kareken, John H., and Neil Wallace. 1978. "Deposit Insurance and Bank Regulation: A Partial-Equilibrium Exposition." *Journal of Business* 51 (3): 413–38.

Kashkari, Neel. 16 February 2016. "Lessons from the Crisis: Ending Too Big to Fail: Remarks at the Brookings Institution, Washington, D.C." Washington, D.C.

Kashyap, Anil K., and Jeremy C. Stein. 2000. "What Do a Million Observations on Banks Say About the Transmission of Monetary Policy?" *American Economic Review* 90 (3): 407–28.

Kaufman, George G., ed. 1994. *Reforming Financial Institutions and Markets in the United States: Towards Rebuilding a Safe and More Efficient System*. Boston; London: Kluwer Academic.

Kaufman, Georg G. 1995. "FDICIA and Bank Capital." *Journal of Banking & Finance* 19: 721–22.

Kaufman, Georg G. 2000. "Banking and Currency Crises and Systemic Risk: Lessons from Recent Events." *Federal Reserve Bank of Chicago Economic Perspectives* 25 (3): 9–28.

Kaufman, Georg G. 2002. "Too Big to Fail in Banking: What Remains?" *The Quarterly Review of Economics and Finance* 42: 423–36.

Kaufman, Georg G. 2014. "Too Big to Fail in Banking: What Does It Mean?" *Journal of Financial Stability* 13: 214–23.

Kaufman, Georg G. 2015. "Banking and Public Policy: Too Big to Fail." *Economic Inquiry* 53 (1): 1–8.

Kauko, Karlo. 2014. "Do Bailouts Cause Moral Hazards or Franchise Value in Banking?" *Kyklos* 67 (1): 82–92.

Keeley, Michael C. 1990. "Deposit Insurance, Risk, and Market Power in Banking." *American Economic Review* 80 (5): 1183–1200.

Kindleberger, Charles Poor, and Robert Z. Aliber. 2005. *Manias, Panics, and Crashes: A History of Financial Crises*. 5th ed. Wiley Investment Classics. Hoboken, N.J.: John Wiley & Sons.

King, Michael R. 2009a. "The Cost of Equity for Global Banks: A CAPM Perspective from 1990 to 2009." *BIS Quarterly Review* September: 59–73.

King, Michael R. 2009b. "Time to Buy or Just Buying Time? The Market Reaction to Bank Rescue Packages." *BIS Working Papers* 288.

Kleinow, Jacob. 2014. "The Value of Being Systemically Important: Event Study on Regulatory Announcements for Banks." *Applied Financial Economics* 24 (24): 1585–1604.

Kleinow, Jacob. 2016. *Systemrelevante Finanzinstitute: Systemrisiko Und Regulierung Im Europäischen Kontext*. 1st ed. Wiesbaden: Springer Fachmedien Wiesbaden GmbH; Springer Gabler.

Kohlbeck, Mark. 2004. "Investor Valuations and Measuring Bank Intangible Assets." *Journal of Accounting, Auditing & Finance* 19 (1): 29–60.

Koller, Tim, Marc H. Goedhart, and David Wessels. 2015. *Valuation: Measuring and Managing the Value of Companies*. 6th ed. The Wiley Finance Series. Hoboken, N.J.: McKinsey and Company; John Wiley & Sons.

Korte, Josef. 2015. "Catharsis—the Real Effects of Bank Insolvency and Resolution." *Journal of Financial Stability* 16: 213–31.

Kovner, Anna, James Vickery, and Lily Zhou. 2014. "Do Big Banks Have Lower Operating Costs?" *Economic Policy Review* Special Issue (2): 1–27.

KPMG. June 2011. "Illustrative Financial Statements: Banks."

Kydland, Finn E., and Edward C. Prescott. 1977. "Rules Rather Than Discretion: The Inconsistency of Optimal Plans." *Journal of Political Economy* 85 (3): 473–91.

Kyle, Albert S., and Wei Xiong. 2001. "Contagion as a Wealth Effect." *The Journal of Finance* 56 (4): 1401–40.

Labonte, Marc. 30 June 2015. "Systemically Important or 'Too Big to Fail' Financial Institutions." https://www.fas.org/sgp/crs/misc/R42150.pdf.

Laeven, Luc. 2002. "International Evidence on the Value of Deposit Insurance." *The Quarterly Review of Economics and Finance* 42: 721–32.

Laeven, Luc. 2004. "The Political Economy of Deposit Insurance." *Journal of Financial Services Research* 26 (3): 201–24.

Laeven, Luc, and Ross Levine. 2007. "Is There a Diversification Discount in Financial Conglomerates?" *Journal of Financial Economics* 85: 331–67.

Laeven, Luc, Lev Ratnovski, and Hui Tong. 2016. "Bank Size, Capital, and Systemic Risk: Some International Evidence." *Journal of Banking & Finance* 69: S25–S34.

Laeven, Luc, and Fabián Valencia. 2013a. "Resolution of Banking Crises." In *Handbook of Safeguarding Global Financial Stability*, edited by Gerard Caprio, Philippe Bacchetta, James R. Barth, Takeo Hoshi, Philip R. Lane, David G. Mayes, Atif Mian, and Michael Taylor, 231–58. London; Waltham, MA: Academic Press.

Laeven, Luc, and Fabián Valencia. 2013b. "Systemic Banking Crises Database." *IMF Economic Review* 61 (2): 225–70.

Lagunoff, Roger, and Stacey L. Schreft. 2001. "A Model of Financial Fragility." *Journal of Economic Theory* 99 (1–2): 220–64.

Lakonishok, Josef, Andrei Shleifer, and Robert W. Vishny. 1994. "Contrarian Investment, Extrapolation, and Risk." *The Journal of Finance* 49 (5): 1541–78.

Landier, Augustin, and David Thesmar. 2014. "Regulating Systemic Risk Through Transparency: Trade-Offs in Making Data Public." In *Risk Topography*, edited by Markus Konrad Brunnermeier and Arvind Krishnamurthy, 31–44. National Bureau of Economic Research Conference Report. Chicago; London: University of Chicago Press.

Laux, Christian, and Christian Leuz. 2010. "Did Fair-Value Accounting Contribute to the Financial Crisis?" *Journal of Economic Perspectives* 24 (1): 93–118.

Leathers, Charles G., and J. Patrick Raines. 2004. "Some Historical Perspectives on Too Big to Fail Policies." In *Too Big to Fail: Policies and Practices in Government Bailouts*, edited by Benton E. Gup, 3–27. Westport, Conn.; London: Praeger.

Lepetit, Laetitia, Emmanuelle Nys, Philippe Rous, and Amine Tarazi. 2008a. "Bank Income Structure and Risk: An Empirical Analysis of European Banks." *Journal of Banking & Finance* 32 (8): 1452–67.

Lepetit, Laetitia, Emmanuelle Nys, Philippe Rous, and Amine Tarazi. 2008b. "The Expansion of Services in European Banking: Implications for Loan Pricing and Interest Margins." *Journal of Banking & Finance* 32 (11): 2325–35.

Levine, Ross. 2002. "Bank-Based or Market-Based Financial Systems: Which Is Better?" *Journal of Financial Intermediation* 11: 398–428.

Liang, Kung-Yee, and Scott L. Zeger. 1986. "Longitudinal Data Analysis Using Generalized Linear Models." *Biometrika* 73 (1): 13–22.

Liikanen, Erkki. 2 October 2012. "High-Level Expert Group on Reforming the Structure of the EU Banking Sector." https://ec.europa.eu/internal_market/bank/docs/high-level_expert_group/report_en.pdf.

Lintner, John. 1956. "Distribution of Incomes of Corporations Among Dividends, Retained Earnings, and Taxes." *American Economic Review* 46 (2): 97–113.

Lintner, John. 1965. "The Valuation of Risk Assets and the Selection of Risky Investments in Stock Portfolios and Capital Budgets." *The Review of Economics and Statistics* 47 (1): 13–37.

Lipe, Robert C. 1986. "The Information Contained in the Components of Earnings." *Journal of Accounting Research* 24 (3): 37–64.

Lorz, Stephan. 22 December 2016. "Bail-in stirbt Maastricht-Tod." *Börsen-Zeitung* 247: 6.

Loudis, Bert, and Meraj Allahrakha. 2016. "Systemic Importance Data Shed Light on Banking Risks." *OFR Brief Series* 3.

MacKinlay, A. Craig. 1997. "Event Studies in Economics and Finance." *Journal of Economic Literature* 35 (1): 13–39.

Maes, Stan, and Schoutens Schoutens. 2012. "Contingent Capital: An in-Depth Discussion." *Economic Notes by Banca Monte Dei Paschi Di Siena SpA* 41 (1/2): 59–79.

Mankiw, N. Gregory. 2015. *Principles of Microeconomics*. 7th ed. Australia; Stamford CT: Cengage Learning.

Marcus, Alan J. 1984. "Deregulation and Bank Financial Policy." *Journal of Banking & Finance* 8 (4): 557–65.

Markowitz, Harry M. 1959. *Portfolio Selection: Efficient Diversification of Investments*. Cowles Foundation Monograph No. 16. New York: John Wiley & Sons.
McCarthy, Mark G., and Douglas K. Schneider. 1995. "Market Perception of Goodwill: Some Empirical Evidence." *Accounting & Business Research* 26 (1): 69–81.
McGuire, Patrick, and Goetz von Peter. 2009. "The Us Dollar Shortage in Global Banking." *BIS Quarterly Review* March: 47–63.
Merton, Robert C. 1973. "Theory of Rational Option Pricing." *The Bell Journal of Economics and Management Science* 4 (1): 141–83.
Merton, Robert C. 1974. "On the Pricing of Corporate Debt: The Risk Structure of Interest Rates." *The Journal of Finance* 29 (2): 449–70.
Merton, Robert C. 1977. "An Analytic Derivation of the Cost of Deposit Insurance and Loan Guarantees an Application of Modern Option Pricing Theory." *Journal of Banking & Finance* 1 (1): 3–11.
Mester, Loretta J. 2010. "Scale Economies in Banking and Financial Regulatory Reform." *The Region* 24 (3): 10–13.
Meyer, Laurence H. 14 June 1999. "Market Discipline as a Complement to Bank Supervision and Regulation: Remarks Before the Conference on Reforming Bank Capital Standards." New York. https://www.federalreserve.gov/boarddocs/speeches/1999/19990614.htm.
Miles, David, Jing Yang, and Gilberto Marcheggiano. 2011. "Optimal Bank Capital." *Bank of England External MPC Unit Discussion Papers* 31.
Ming-Li, Yao, and Chiung-Ju Liang. 2005. "An Investigation into the Differences Between the Book Value and Market Value of Commercial Banks: An Empirical Study." *International Journal of Management* 22 (1): 89–100.
Mishkin, Frederic S. 1996. "Understanding Financial Crises: A Developing Country Perspective." *NBER Working Paper* 5600.
Mishkin, Frederic S. 2004. *The Economics of Money, Banking, and Financial Markets*. 7th ed. The Addison-Wesley Series in Economics. Boston: Pearson.
Mishkin, Frederic S. 2006. "How Big a Problem Is Too Big to Fail? A Review of Gary Stern and Ron Feldman's Too Big to Fail: The Hazards of Bank Bailouts." *Journal of Economic Literature* 44 (4): 988–1004.
Mishkin, Frederic S., and Niklas J. Westelius. 2008. "Inflation Band Targeting and Optimal Inflation Contracts." *Journal of Money, Credit and Banking* 40 (4): 557–82.
Modigliani, Franco, and Merton H. Miller. 1958. "The Cost of Capital, Corporation Finance and the Theory of Investment." *The American Economic Review* 48 (3): 261–97.
Moenninghoff, Sebastian C., Steven Ongena, and Axel Wieandt. 2015. "The Perennial Challenge to Counter Too-Big-to-Fail in Banking: Empirical Evidence from the New International Regulation Dealing with Global Systemically Important Banks." *Journal of Banking & Finance* 61: 221–36.
Molyneux, Philip, and Franco Fiordelisi. 2010. "The Determinants of Shareholder Value in European Banking." *Journal of Banking & Finance* 34: 1189–1200.
Molyneux, Philip, Klaus Schaeck, and Tim Mi Zhou. 2014. "'Too Systemically Important to Fail' in Banking – Evidence from Bank Mergers and Acquisitions." *Journal of International Money & Finance* 49: 258–82.
Molyneux, Philip, and John Thornton. 1992. "Determinants of European Bank Profitability: A Note." *Journal of Banking & Finance* 16: 1173–8.
Monopolkommission. 9 July 2014. "XXth Biennial Report (2012/2013): Chapter VI Competition in the Financial Markets." https://www.monopolkommission.de/images/PDF/HG/HG20/HGXX_Chapter_VI_Financial_Markets.pdf.
Moosa, Imad. 2010. "The Myth of Too Big to Fail." *Journal of Banking Regulation* 11 (4): 319–33.

Morgan, Donald P., and Kevin J. Stiroh. 2005. "'Too Big to Fail After All These Years." *Federal Reserve Bank of New York - Staff Reports* 220.

Morrison, Alan D. 2011. "Systemic Risks and the 'Too-Big-to-Fail' Problem'." *Oxford Review of Economic Policy* 27 (3): 498–516.

Mossin, Jan. 1966. "Equilibrium in a Capital Asset Market." *Econometrica* 34 (4): 768–83.

Moulton, Brent R. 1990. "An Illustration of a Pitfall in Estimating the Effects of Aggregate Variables on Micro Units." *Review of Economics & Statistics* 72 (2): 334–38.

Moyer, R. Charles, and Robert E. Lamy. 1992. "'Too Big to Fail': Rationale, Consequences, and Alternatives." *Business Economics* 27 (3): 19–24.

Mukherjee, Tarun K., and William P. Dukes. 1989. "A Multivariate Analysis of Small Bank Stock Valuation." *Quarterly Journal of Business & Economics* 28 (2): 3–18.

Musgrave, Richard A., and Peggy B. Musgrave. 1989. *Public Finance in Theory and Practice*. 5th ed. New York; London: McGraw-Hill.

Naqvi, Hassan. 2015. "Banking Crises and the Lender of Last Resort: How Crucial Is the Role of Information?" *Journal of Banking & Finance* 54: 20–29.

Newey, Whitney K., and Kenneth D. West. 1987. "A Simple, Positive Semi-Definite, Heteroskedasticity and Autocorrelation Consistent Covariance Matrix." *Econometrica* 55 (3): 703–8.

Nguyen, James. 2012. "The Relationship Between Net Interest Margin and Noninterest Income Using a System Estimation Approach." *Journal of Banking & Finance* 36 (9): 2429–37.

Niskanen, William A. 1994. *Bureaucracy and Public Economics*. Aldershot: Elgar.

Niu, Jijun. 2016. "Loan Growth and Bank Valuations." *Quarterly Review of Economics & Finance* 61: 185–91.

Noss, Joseph, and Rhiannon Sowerbutts. 2012. "The Implicit Subsidy of Banks." *Bank of England – Financial Stability Paper* 15.

Noss, Joseph, and Priscilla Toffano. 2016. "Estimating the Impact of Changes in Aggregate Bank Capital Requirements on Lending and Growth During an Upswing." *Journal of Banking & Finance* 62: 15–27.

O'Driscoll, Jr., Gerald P. 1988. "Bank Failures: The Deposit Insurance Connection." *Contemporary Policy Issues* 6 (2): 1–12.

O'Hara, Maureen, and Wayne Shaw. 1990. "Deposit Insurance and Wealth Effects: The Value of Being Too Big to Fail." *The Journal of Finance* 45 (5): 1587–1600.

Ohlson, James A. 1995. "Earnings, Book Values, and Dividends in Equity Valuation." *Contemporary Accounting Research* 11 (2): 661–87.

Ohlson, James A., and Stephen H. Penman. 1992. "Disaggregated Accounting Data as Explanatory Variables for Returns." *Journal of Accounting, Auditing & Finance* 7 (4): 553–73.

Oliveira, Raquel de F., Rafael F. Schiozer, and Lucas A. B. de C. Barros. 2015. "Depositors' Perception of 'Too-Big-to-Fail'." *Review of Finance* 19 (1): 191–227.

Ötker-Robe, İnci, Aditya Narain, Anna Ilyina, and Jay Surti. 2011. "The Too-Important-to-Fail Conundrum: Impossible to Ignore and Difficult to Resolve." *IMF Discussion Note* 11 (12).

Palia, Darius, and Robert Porter. 2004. "The Impact of Capital Requirements and Managerial Compensation on Bank Charter Value." *Review of Quantitative Finance & Accounting* 23 (3): 191–206.

Panageas, Stavros. 2010. "Bailouts, the Incentive to Manage Risk, and Financial Crises." *Journal of Financial Economics* 95: 296–311.

Panetta, Fabio, Thomas Faeh, Giuseppe Grande, Corrinne Ho, Michael King, Aviram Levy, Federico M. Signoretti, Marco Taboga, and Andrea Zaghini. 2009. "An Assessment of Financial Sector Rescue Programmes." *BIS Papers* 48.

Park, Sangkyun. 1997. "Risk-Taking Behavior of Banks Under Regulation." *Journal of Banking & Finance* 21 (4): 491–507.

Park, Sangkyun, and Stavros Peristiani. 2007. "Are Bank Shareholders Enemies of Regulators or a Potential Source of Market Discipline?" *Journal of Banking & Finance* 31 (8): 2493–2515.

Park, Young S., and Jung-Jin Lee. 2003. "An Empirical Study on the Relevance of Applying Relative Valuation Models to Investment Strategies in the Japanese Stock Market." *Japan and the World Economy* 15: 331–39.

Pasiouras, Fotios, and Kyriaki Kosmidou. 2007. "Factors Influencing the Profitability of Domestic and Foreign Commercial Banks in the European Union." *Research in International Business and Finance* 21: 222–37.

Pazarbasioglu, Ceyla, Jianping Zhou, Vanessa Le Leslé, and Michael Moore. 2011. "Contingent Capital: Economic Rationale and Design Features." *IMF Staff Position Note* 11 (1).

Peek, Joe, and Eric S. Rosengren. 2005. "Unnatural Selection: Perverse Incentives and the Misallocation of Credit in Japan." *American Economic Review* 95 (4): 1144–66.

Penas, Maria Fabiana, and Haluk Unal. 2004. "Gains in Bank Mergers: Evidence from the Bond Markets." *Journal of Financial Economics* 74: 149–79.

Penati, Alessandro, and Aris Protopapadakis. 1988. "The Effect of Implicit Deposit Insurance on Banks' Portfolio Choices with an Application to International 'Overexposure'." *Journal of Monetary Economics* 21: 107–26.

Perotti, Enrico, Lev Ratnovski, and Razvan Vlahu. 2011. "Capital Regulation and Tail Risk." *International Journal of Central Banking* 7 (4): 123–63.

Petersen, Mitchell A. 2009. "Estimating Standard Errors in Finance Panel Data Sets: Comparing Approaches." *Review of Financial Studies* 22 (1): 435–80.

Petria, Nicolae, Bogdan Capraru, and Iulian Ihnatov. 2015. "Determinants of Banks' Profitability: Evidence from EU 27 Banking Systems." *Procedia Economics and Finance* 20: 518–24.

Pigou, Arthur Cecil. 1920. *The Economics of Welfare*. London: Macmillan and Co.

Pituch, Keenan A., and James Stevens. 2016. *Applied Multivariate Statistics for the Social Sciences: Analyses with Sas and Ibm's Spss*. 6th ed. New York: Routledge/Taylor & Francis Group.

Plantin, Guillaume. 2015. "Shadow Banking and Bank Capital Regulation." *Review of Financial Studies* 28 (1): 146–75.

Pop, Adrian, and Diana Pop. 2009. "Requiem for Market Discipline and the Specter of TBTF in Japanese Banking." *The Quarterly Review of Economics and Finance* 49: 1429–59.

PricewaterhouseCoopers. September 2015. "IFRS and US GAAP: Similarities and Differences." https://www.pwc.com/us/en/cfodirect/assets/pdf/accounting-guides/pwc-ifrs-us-gaap-similarities-and-differences-2015.pdf.

Qayyum, Abdul, Sajawal Khan, and Ejaz Ghani. 2006. "X-Efficiency, Scale Economies, Technological Progress, and Competition: The Banking Sector in Pakistan." *The Pakistan Development Review* 45 (4): 733–48.

Ramirez, Carlos D., and Philip A. Shively. 2012. "The Effect of Bank Failures on Economic Activity: Evidence from U.S. States in the Early 20th Century." *Journal of Money, Credit and Banking* 44 (2/3): 433–55.

Reinhart, Carmen M., and Kenneth S. Rogoff. 2011. *This Time Is Different: Eight Centuries of Financial Folly*. Princeton, N.J.; Oxford: Princeton University Press.

Ricci, Ornella. 2015. "The Impact of Monetary Policy Announcements on the Stock Price of Large European Banks During the Financial Crisis." *Journal of Banking & Finance* 52: 245–55.

Rime, Bertrand. 9 May 2005. "Do 'Too Big to Fail' Expectations Boost Large Banks Issuer Ratings?" https://www.bis.org/bcbs/events/rtf05Rime.pdf.

Ritchken, Peter, James B. Thomson, Ramon P. DeGennaro, and Anlong Li. 1993. "On Flexibility, Capital Structure and Investment Decisions for the Insured Bank." *Journal of Banking & Finance* 17 (6): 1133–46.

Rogoff, Kenneth. 1985. "The Optimal Degree of Commitment to an Intermediate Monetary Target." *Quarterly Journal of Economics* 100 (4): 1169–89.

Rolnick, Arthur J, and Warren E. Weber. 1982. "Free Banking, Wildcat Banking, and Shinplasters." *Federal Reserve Bank of Minneapolis Quarterly Review* 6 (3): 10–19.

Rose, Andrew K., and Tomasz Wieladek. 2012. "Too Big to Fail: Some Empirical Evidence on the Causes and Consequences of Public Banking Interventions in the UK." *Journal of International Money* 31: 2038–51.

Ross, Stephen A. 1976. "The Arbitrage Theory of Capital Asset Pricing." *Journal of Economic Theory* 13 (3): 341–60.

Royal Swedish Academy of Sciences. 14 October 2013. "Understanding Asset Prices." https://www.nobelprize.org/nobel_prizes/economic-sciences/laureates/2013/advanced-economic-sciences2013.pdf.

Rozeff, Michael S. 1984. "Dividend Yields Are Equity Risk Premiums." *Journal of Portfolio Management* 11 (1): 68–75.

Rubens, Jack H., and Jeffrey J. Corrigan. 1990. "Commercial Bank Capital Ratios as Predictors of Investor Risk Perception." *American Business Review*, 25–30.

Samartin, Margarita. 2003. "Should Bank Runs Be Prevented?" *Journal of Banking & Finance* 27: 977–1000.

Sandbu, Martin. 25 August 2017. "Banking Union Will Transform Europe's Politics." *Financial Times*.

Saunders, Anthony, and Marcia Millon Cornett. 2008. *Financial Institutions Management: A Risk Management Approach*. 6th ed. The Mcgraw-Hill/Irwin Series in Finance, Insurance, and Real Estate. Boston: McGraw-Hill Irwin.

Saunders, Anthony, Elizabeth Strock, and Nickolaos G. Travlos. 1990. "Ownership Structure, Deregulation, and Bank Risk Taking." *The Journal of Finance* 45 (2): 643–54.

Saunders, Anthony, and Berry Wilson. 2001. "An Analysis of Bank Charter Value and Its Risk-Constraining Incentives." *Journal of Financial Services Research* 19 (2/3): 185–95.

Sawada, Michiru. 2013. "How Does the Stock Market Value Bank Diversification? Empirical Evidence from Japanese Banks." *Pacific-Basin Finance Journal* 25: 40–61.

Schäfer, Alexander, Isabel Schnabel, and Beatrice Weder di Mauro. 2016. "Financial Sector Reform After the Subprime Crisis: Has Anything Happened?" *Review of Finance* 20 (1): 77–125.

Schich, Sebastian, and Byoung-Hwan Kim. 2010. "Systemic Financial Crises: How to Fund Resolution." *OECD Journal: Financial Market Trends* 2010 (2).

Schich, Sebastian, and Sofia Lindh. 2012. "Implicit Guarantees for Bank Debt: Where Do We Stand?" *OECD Journal: Financial Market Trends* 2012 (1).

Schildbach, Jan. 2017. "Large or Small? How to Measure Bank Size." *Deutsche Bank Research*.

Schmid, Markus M., and Ingo Walter. 2009. "Do Financial Conglomerates Create or Destroy Economic Value?" *Journal of Financial Intermediation* 18: 193–216.

Schoenmaker, Dirk. 2011. "The Financial Trilemma." *Economics Letters* 111: 57–59.

Schweikhard, Frederic A., and Zoe Tsesmelidakis. 1 November 2012. "The Impact of Government Interventions on CDS and Equity Markets." https://ssrn.com/abstract=1573377.

Sennholz, Hans F., ed. 1992. *Bankers and Regulators*. New York: Irvington-on-Hudson.

Shachmurove, Yochanan. 2011. "A Historical Overview of Financial Crises in the United States." *Global Finance Journal* 22: 217–31.

Shaffer, Sherrill. 1993. "Can Megamergers Improve Bank Efficiency?" *Journal of Banking & Finance* 17: 423–36.

Sharma, Anurag, Ben Branch, Chetan Chgawla, and Liping Qiu. 2013. "Explaining Market-to-Book: The Relative Impact of Firm Performance, Growth, and Risk." *B>Quest*, 1–32.

Sharma, Nishi. 2012. "Intangible Assets: A Study of Valuation Methods." *BVIMR Management Edge* 5 (1): 61–69.

Sharpe, William F. 1964. "Capital Asset Prices: A Theory of Market Equilibrium Under Conditions of Risk." *The Journal of Finance* 19 (3): 425–42.

Shih, Yi-Cheng, Sheng-Syan Chen, Cheng-Few Lee, and Po-Jung Chen. 2014. "The Evolution of Capital Asset Pricing Models." *Review of Quantitative Finance & Accounting* 42 (3): 415–48.

Shleifer, Andrei, and Robert W. Vishny. 1992. "Liquidation Values and Debt Capacity: A Market Equilibrium Approach." *The Journal of Finance* 47 (4): 1343–66.

Shleifer, Andrei, and Robert W. Vishny. 2010. "Unstable Banking." *Journal of Financial Economics* 97 (3): 306–18.

Slovin, Myron B., Marie E. Sushka, and John A. Polonchek. 1993. "The Value of Bank Durability: Borrowers as Bank Stakeholders." *The Journal of Finance* 48 (1): 247–66.

SNL Financial. 28 September 2015. "SNL Office User Guide."

Song, Fenghua, and Anjan V. Thakor. 2010. "Financial System Architecture and the Co-Evolution of Banks and Capital Markets." *Economic Journal* 120 (547): 1021–55.

Soussa, Farouk. 2000. *Too Big to Fail: Moral Hazard and Unfair Competition?* Financial Stability and Central Banks. London: Bank of England. Centre for Central Banking Studies; Centre for Central Banking Studies, Bank of England.

Sprague, Irvine H. 1988. *Bailout: An Insider's Account of Bank Failures & Rescues*. New York: Perseus Books.

Squam Lake Working Group on Financial Regulation. 2009. "Improving Resolution Options for Systemically Relevant Financial Institutions." *Council on Foreign Relations – Working Paper*.

Stan, Mitchell, and Michael L. McIntyre. 2012. "Too Big to Fail? Size and Risk in Banking." *Academy of Banking Studies Journal* 11 (2): 11–21.

Stern, Gary H., and Ron Feldman. 2009a. "Addressing TBTF by Shrinking Financial Institutions: An Initial Assessment." *The Region* 23 (2): 8–13.

Stern, Gary H., and Ron J. Feldman. 2009b. *Too Big to Fail: The Hazards of Bank Bailouts*. 2nd ed. Washington, D.C.: Brookings Institution Press.

Stiroh, Kevin J. 2000. "How Did Bank Holding Companies Prosper in the 1990s?" *Journal of Banking & Finance* 24: 1703–45.

Stiroh, Kevin J. 2006. "A Portfolio View of Banking with Interest and Noninterest Activities." *Journal of Money, Credit and Banking* 38 (5): 1351–61.

Stiroh, Kevin J., and Adrienne Rumble. 2006. "The Dark Side of Diversification: The Case of US Financial Holding Companies." *Journal of Banking & Finance* 30: 2131–61.

Stock, James H., and Mark W. Watson. 2012. *Introduction to Econometrics*. 3rd ed. The Pearson Series in Economics. Boston, Mass.; London: Pearson Education.

Strahan, Philip E. 2013. "Too Big to Fail: Causes, Consequences, and Policy Responses." *Annual Review of Financial Economics* 5: 43–61.

Strahan, Philip E., and Başak Tanyeri. 2015. "Once Burned, Twice Shy: Money Market Fund Responses to a Systemic Liquidity Shock." *Journal of Financial & Quantitative Analysis* 50 (1/2): 119–44.

Sundaresan, Suresh, and Zhenyu Wang. 2015. "On the Design of Contingent Capital with a Market Trigger." *The Journal of Finance* 70 (2): 881–920.

Swary, Itzhak. 1986. "Stock Market Reaction to Regulatory Action in the Continental Illinois Crisis." *Journal of Business* 59 (3): 451–73.

Tabachnick, Barbara G., and Linda S. Fidell. 2007. *Using Multivariate Statistics*. 5th ed. Boston Mass.; London: Pearson/A&B.

Tabak, Benjamin M., Dimas M. Fazio, and Daniel O. Cajueiro. 2013. "Systemically Important Banks and Financial Stability: The Case of Latin America." *Journal of Banking & Finance* 37: 3855–66.

Tadesse, Solomon. 2002. "Financial Architecture and Economic Performance: International Evidence." *Journal of Financial Intermediation* 11 (4): 429–55.

Tasca, Paolo, Pavlin Mavrodiev, and Frank Schweitzer. 2014. "Quantifying the Impact of Leveraging and Diversification on Systemic Risk." *Journal of Financial Stability* 15: 43–52.

Temzelides, Ted. 1997. "Are Bank Runs Contagious?" *Business Review (Federal Reserve Bank of Philadelphia)*, 3–14.

Thomas, Alban. 2003. "Advanced Econometrics: Panel Data Econometrics and GMM Estimation." https://www2.toulouse.inra.fr/lerna/chercheurs/thomas/panel%20DEEQA.pdf.

Toader, Oana. 2015. "Estimating the Impact of Higher Capital Requirements on the Cost of Equity: An Empirical Study of European Banks." *International Economics and Economic Policy* 12: 411–36.

Tobin, James. 1958. "Liquidity Preference as Behavior Towards Risk." *The Review of Economic Studies* 25 (2): 65–86.

Tobin, James. 1969. "A General Equilibrium Approach to Monetary Theory." *Journal of Money, Credit and Banking* 1 (1): 15–29.

Tobin, James, and William C. Brainard. 1977. "Asset Market and the Cost of Capital." *Private Values and Public Policy*, 235–62.

Todd, Walker F. 1992. "History of and Rationales for the Reconstruction Finance Corporation." *Economic Review* 28 (4): 22–35.

Todd, Walker F., and James B. Thomson. 1990. "An Insider's View of the Political Economy of the Too Big to Fail Doctrine." *Federal Reserve Bank of Cleveland - Working Paper* 9017.

Tomuleasda, Ioana-Iuliana, and Vasile Cocris. 2014. "Measuring the Financial Performance of the European Systemically Important Banks." *Financial Studies* 18 (4): 31–51.

Trescott, Paul B. 1992. "The Failure of the Bank of United States, 1930." *Journal of Money, Credit and Banking* 24 (3): 384–99.

Tsesmelidakis, Zoe, and Robert C. Merton. July 2013. "The Value of Implicit Guarantees." https://ssrn.com/abstract=2231317.

Tucker, Paul. 27–28 May 2009. "The Repertoire of Official Sector Interventions in the Financial System – Last Resort Lending, Market-Making, and Capital: Speech Delivered to the Bank of Japan 2009 International Conference 'Financial System and Monetary Policy: Implementation'." Bank of Japan, Tokyo.

Udell, Gregory F. 2010. "Are Bank Bailouts Un-American?" *Business Horizons* 53: 463–67.

Ueda, Kenichi, and Beatrice Weder di Mauro. 2013. "Quantifying Structural Subsidy Values for Systemically Important Financial Institutions." *Journal of Banking & Finance* 37 (10): 3830–42.

UK Asset Resolution. 1 February 2016a. "FAQs." https://www.n-ram.co.uk/corporate/share-information/faqs.

UK Asset Resolution. 1 February 2016b. "Nationalisation FAQs." https://www.bbg.co.uk/corporate/nationalisation/nationalisation-faqs.

U.S. Congressional Budget Office. January 1992. "The Economic Effects of the Savings & Loan Crisis." https://www.cbo.gov/sites/default/files/102nd-congress-1991-1992/reports/1992_01_theeconeffectsofthesavings.pdf.

US Department of the Treasury. 2011. "Office of the Comptroller of the Currency: A Short History."

U.S. Government Accountability Office (GAO). 16 January 2013. "Financial Regulatory Reform: Financial Crisis Losses and Potential Impacts of the Dodd-Frank Act." https://www.gao.gov/products/GAO-13-180.

van Bekkum, Sjoerd. 2016. "Ireland's 2010 EU/IMF Intervention: Costs and Benefits." *Journal of Banking & Finance* 72: 175–83.

Vander Vennet, Rudi. 2002. "Cost and Profit Efficiency of Financial Conglomerates and Universal Banks in Europe." *Journal of Money, Credit and Banking* 34 (1): 254–82.

VanHoose, David. 2007. "Theories of Bank Behavior Under Capital Regulation." *Journal of Banking & Finance* 31: 3680–97.

van Lelyveld, Iman, and Klaas Knot. 2009. "Do Financial Conglomerates Create or Destroy Value? Evidence for the EU." *Journal of Banking & Finance* 33: 2312–21.

van Rixtel, Adrian, and Gabriele Gasperini. 2013. "Financial Crises and Bank Funding: Recent Experience in the Euro Area." *BIS Working Papers* 406.

Varaiya, Nikhil, Roger A. Kerin, and David Weeks. 1987. "The Relationship Between Growth, Profitability, and Firm Value." *Strategic Management Journal* 8 (5): 487–97.

Varmaz, Armin, Christian Fieberg, and Jörg Prokop. 2015. "The Value Relevance of 'Too-Big-to-Fail' Guarantees." *The Journal of Risk Finance* 16 (5): 498–518.

Veronesi, Pietro, and Luigi Zingales. 2010. "Paulson's Gift." *Journal of Financial Economics* 97: 339–68.

Viñals, Jose, and Jonathan Fiechter. 2010. "The Making of Good Supervision: Learning to Say 'No'." *IMF Staff Position Note* 10 (8).

Viñals, Jose, Ceyla Pazarbasioglu, Jay Surti, Aditya Narain, Michaela Erbenova, and Julian T. S. Chow. 2013. "Creating a Safer Financial System: Will the Volcker, Vickers, and Liikanen Structural Measures Help?" *IMF Staff Discussion Note* 13 (4).

Völz, Manja, and Michael Wedow. 2011. "Does Banks' Size Distort Market Prices? Evidence for Too-Big-to-Fail in the CDS Market." *Journal of Empirical Finance* 18: 195–210.

Wall, Larry D. 2010. "Too Big to Fail After FDICIA." *Federal Reserve Bank of Atlanta - Economic Review* 1: 1–16.

Wasserstein, Ronald L., and Nicole A. Lazar. 2016. "The ASA's Statement on P-Values: Context, Process, and Purpose." *The American Statistician* 70 (2): 129–33.

Weitzman, Martin L. 1974. "Prices Vs. Quantities." *Review of Economic Studies* 41 (4): 477–91.

Weiß, Gregor N. F., Denefa Bostandzic, and Sascha Neumann. 2014. "What Factors Drive Systemic Risk During International Financial Crises?" *Journal of Banking & Finance* 41: 78–96.

Weiß, Gregor N. F., Sascha Neumann, and Denefa Bostandzic. 2014. "Systemic Risk and Bank Consolidation: International Evidence." *Journal of Banking & Finance* 40: 165–81.

Wheelock, David C., and Subal C. Kumbhakar. 1995. "Which Banks Choose Deposit Insurance? Evidence of Adverse Selection and Moral Hazard in a Voluntary Insurance System." *Journal of Money, Credit and Banking* 27 (1): 186–201.

Wheelock, David C., and David Lopez. 2012. "Too Big to Fail: The Pros and Cons of Breaking up Big Banks." *Regional Economist* 20 (4): 10–11.

Wheelock, David C., and Paul W. Wilson. 1995. "Explaning Bank Failures: Deposit Insurance, Regulation, and Efficiency." *Review of Economics & Statistics* 77 (4): 689–700.

Wheelock, David C., and Paul W. Wilson. 2012. "Do Large Banks Have Lower Costs? New Estimates of Returns to Scale for U.S. Banks." *Journal of Money, Credit and Banking* 44 (1): 171–99.

White, Halbert. 1980. "A Heteroskedasticity-Consistent Covariance Matrix Estimator and a Direct Test for Heteroskedasticity." *Econometrica* 48 (4): 817–38.

Wilcox, Jarrod W. 1984. "The P/B-ROE Valuation Model." *Financial Analysts Journal* 40 (1): 58–66.

Wilcox, Jarrod W., and Thomas K. Philips. 2005. "The PB-ROE Valuation Model Revisited." *Journal of Portfolio Management* 31 (4): 56–66.

Willett, T. D., and C. Wihlborg. 2013. "Varieties of European Crises." In *Handbook of Safeguarding Global Financial Stability*, edited by Gerard Caprio, Philippe Bacchetta, James R. Barth, Takeo Hoshi, Philip R. Lane, David G. Mayes, Atif Mian, and Michael Taylor, 309–22. London; Waltham, MA: Academic Press.

Williams, Barry, and Laurie Prather. 2010. "Bank Risk and Return: The Impact of Bank Non-Interest Income." *International Journal of Managerial Finance* 6 (3): 220–44.

Williams, John Burr. 1938. *The Theory of Investment Value*. Burlington: Fraser.

Williamson, Oliver E. 1979. "Transaction-Cost Economics: The Governance of Contractual Relations." *Journal of Law and Economics* 22 (2): 233–61.

Wittkowski, Bernd. 9 March 2016. "Fiktion und Fakten." *Börsen-Zeitung*, no. 47: 1.

Wolgast, Michael. 2001. "'Too Big to Fail': Effects on Competition and Implications for Banking Supervision." *Journal of Financial Regulation and Compliance* 9 (4): 361–72.

Wooldridge, Jeffrey M. 2001. *Econometric Analysis of Cross Section and Panel Data*. Cambridge, Mass.: MIT Press.

Zhou, Jianping, Virginia Rutledge, Wouter Bossu, Marc Dobler, Nadege Jassaud, and Michael Moore. 2012. "From Bail-Out to Bail-in: Mandatory Debt Restructuring of Systemic Financial Institutions." *IMF Staff Discussion Note* 12 (3).

Zimmer, Daniel, Thomas Weck, and Nils-Peter Schepp. 2015. "Wiederherstellung Des Wettbewerbs Als Ordnungsprinzip Auf Den Finanzmärkten: Ist Die Bankenunion Ein Taugliches Mittel Hierzu?" In *Wettbewerbsbeschränkungen Auf Staatlich Gelenkten Märkten*, edited by Torsten Körber, 11:73–102. Kartell- Und Regulierungsrecht. Baden-Baden: Nomos.

Zulauf, Daniel. 2 April 2016. "Schweiz Spürt Enge Der Märkte: Nationalbank Hortet Ausländische Aktien Im Wert von Rund 100 Mrd. Sfr – Strenge Kriterien Für Die Anlage." *Börsen-Zeitung* 63: 4.

The manufacturer's authorised representative in the EU is Springer Nature Customer Service Centre GmbH, Europaplatz 3, 69115 Heidelberg, Germany. If you have any concerns regarding our products, please contact ProductSafety@springernature.com

Printed and bound by CPI Group (UK) Ltd, Croydon, CR0 4YY
30/09/2026
02225688-0011